Lost Years

Lost Years
My 1,632 Days in
Vietnamese Reeducation Camps

TRAN TRI VU

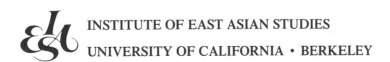

INSTITUTE OF EAST ASIAN STUDIES

UNIVERSITY OF CALIFORNIA • BERKELEY

A publication of the Institute of East Asian Studies, University of California, Berkeley. Although the Institute is responsible for the selection and acceptance of manuscripts in this series, responsibility for the opinions expressed and for the accuracy of statements rests with their authors.

The Indochina Research Monograph series is one of several publications series sponsored by the Institute of East Asian Studies in conjunction with its constituent units. The others include the China Research Monograph series, the Japan Research Monograph series, the Korea Research Monograph series, and the Research Papers and Policy Studies series. A list of recent publications appears at the back of the book.

Correspondence may be sent to:
Ms. Joanne Sandstrom, Managing Editor
Institute of East Asian Studies
University of California
Berkeley, CA 94720

For my only treasures on earth, my dear wife and my daughter
And for those who will truly understand, my camp compatriots of the lost years

Contents

Foreword

Human beings, sad to say, become fully aware of the true value of freedom only when they are deprived of it. For someone who is gifted with a writer's instinct, such an experience often produces a passion to chronicle in detail the intense mental agony that inevitably follows. In *Lost Years* the inspirational passion is restrained and controlled by its author in an unexpected and wholly admirable way. The result is a very illuminating account of the suffering of one southern Vietnamese among perhaps hundreds of thousands who were confined to "reeducation" camps by the country's communist authorities after the fall of Saigon in 1975. This restraint and subtlety, combined with a uniquely Vietnamese quality that embraces both courage and gentleness, make the narrative exceptionally moving. A strident, shriller tone would not have been as effective.

So this is not a relentless recital of physical torture and horror or an anticommunist diatribe, which one might have expected. It is above all else honest and often understated. The writing indeed is invested with such humanity that it is possible to feel as much sympathy at times for the *bodoi* supervising the camps as for their inmates. It throws equally fascinating light on the relationships among the detainees themsleves. At times the very ordinariness of the experience impresses itself deeply in the mind of the reader. It was neither the harshest nor the easiest of reeducation camp experiences. Some former prisoners have described how they were beaten and tortured and shackled in "tiger cages" or dark cement cells; other stories tell of deaths from substandard diets, labor accidents in the jungle, lack of medical care, and executions for escape attempts. While recording some such instances but without focusing on extremes, this account conveys the experience of many unfortunate noncommunist Vietnamese who were ensnared by the process because of "suspect" past affiliations. Unlike other reporters about reeducation camps, Tran Tri Vu's skill and sensitivity make him an extraordinary observer, enabling the reader to sense each numbing day with tangible intensity.

My own connection with this book has two separate strands. The first is one of chance. While working as a British correspondent in Peking during the late 1960s, I became an innocent "political" prisoner of the Cultural Revolution. I was held in solitary confinement in a house close to the walls of the Forbidden City for two years and two months in retaliation for the imprisonment of Chinese communist journalists who rioted in Hong Kong. On emerging in late 1969 after the last Hong Kong detainee had been freed, I wrote a book entitled *Hostage in Peking*, so I know personally how important it can be for a prisoner, on regaining his freedom, to set down for publication the details of what he feels was an unjust persecution. For this reason alone, when the translator of Tran Tri Vu's manuscript approached me with the first chapter or two, I immediately offered encouragement and undertook to assist as much as I could in finding a publisher.

The second strand is related directly to Vietnam. The translator came to me in late 1984 chiefly because I had spent four years form 1978 to 1982 researching and writing a novel entitled *Saigon*, which deals comprehensively with Vietnam's often tragic history over a fifty-year period, from 1925 to 1975. In the course of working on the book, I developed a lasting admiration for the courage, resilience, and elusive charm of a remarkable people. In the novel I eschewed black-and-white judgments, and in writing it, I became aware that Vietnamese of all persuasions had endured more than their fair share of tragedy and suffering during the twentieth century. Unfortunately, I was never able to visit Vietnam while writing the novel; no visa was ever granted to me, but I made friends among the Vietnamese communities in Paris and Washington, where I pursued research during lengthy visits. But in January 1988 I visited Vietnam for the first time, and then by chance, on the eve of Tet, I found myself standing on the platform of Saigon's main railway station while a grimy train rumbled in from the North carrying a large number of prisoners who had been released after thirteen years of "reeducation." Among them were former South Vietnamese generals, a one-time minister of defense, and other high-ranking army officers and government officials.

It was the largest-ever release of long-term detainees; over 3,000 were granted amnesty for Tet, and the atmosphere at the station was extremely emotional. Fretful, tearful crowds of relatives and friends clamored outside the closed gates leading to the platforms. Vietnamese television cameras were present to record the event, and I waited among a small group of foreign journalists who had been formally invited to witness the event from a privileged place on the platform. For those returning home, thirteen shadowy years were ending in a blaze of publicity.

In the melee I was able to tape-record brief interviews in English with two former generals; like most of the released prisoners who crowded the open windows of the train as it rolled in, they were lean-faced. But smiles wreathed their features as they swung threadbare bundles of belongings down from the carriage. When I asked one general what he had missed most, he grinned and said he had climbed out of the train at every station on the long journey to try different kinds of soups—noodles, vegetable, meat. Voices broke a little when I asked different individuals if they hoped to leave Vietnam and go abroad to join their wives and families. It was too early to say, they murmured. Remembering my own difficulties when I faced crowds of reporters at Heathrow airport in

London, I found it difficult to frame questions. But one wiry senior officer admitted that "praying to ancestors" had helped him survive.

In Hanoi some days earlier I had been told in advance by government officials about the impending release. About another 2,000 detainees remained in the camps, they said, but it would not be long before these people too were released. On the platform at Saigon it was impossible not to be moved by the reunions. Many people wept. I spoke to a Vietnamese who had originally fought the French with the Viet Minh, had gone North in 1954, and had then taken part in the final communist assault on Saigon in 1975. When I asked him how he had reacted to the emotional scenes, he said simply that he agreed heartily with the decision to release the prisoners, and on seeing their tears flowing freely, he had felt like crying himself.

That remark reminded me afresh of the great complexities that have beset Vietnam during this century. Spurred on by growing poverty and dislocation, the government in Hanoi has been accelerating economic reforms since the end of 1986; foreign investment was being avidly sought, and the reeducation process, which had been the subject of much international criticism, was seemingly being wound up in a related series of policy changes. Another page was being turned in Vietnam's history. Since 1975 the country had existed politically in a near-vacuum, but thirteen years later it was trying, Chinese-style, to "open to the outside world" in order to boost its stagnant economy.

Although "reeducation" on a mass scale in Vietnam had almost run its course by early 1988, this moving story of what it all meant to one individual over four and a half years ought, in an ideal world, to reduce the chances of such things ever happening again. Experience, unfortunately, in a world that is far from ideal, tends to teach us otherwise. But we must at least hope it will have that effect. In any event, Tran Tri Vu's book makes a valuable contribution to an important corner of twentieth-century history. For that reason among many others, it deserves to be widely read.

Anthony Grey
London, Spring 1988

Preface

I finished this memoir in London at the end of the winter of 1982. I then showed it to friends, who suggested that I condense it if I hoped to have it published. My reluctant abridgement was completed in June of 1984.

Reading over this abridged version, I feel that unfortunately it lacks cohesion in some places. My greatest regret, however, is that I have been able to write only briefly about so many of the people I have known. Their names, even if I used their true names, would mean nothing to most readers, for they were people who neither had the money to bribe their way out of the camps nor were well-known figures of the former regime whose plight might draw the attention of international organizations. I have mentioned only a few names here, among the ones I liked and did not like. How can I forget ex-pilot Tuong, suffering badly from asthma brought on by the damp jungle weather, who forever sang, "What's New in Paris, My Darling." How can I forget the Khmer who had such muscular fingers that, before the disbelieving eyes of camp doctors and dentists, he could extract teeth using only his thumb and finger. How can I forget cruel, conceited Dr. Cung, deputy group leader, assigning heavy work to members of his group whose bodies were racked with hunger and their hearts torn by desperation. How can I forget the expression on ex-pilot Ut's face as he forced us to work on and on cutting bamboo when we had not filled our norm. How can I describe it all, the hunger, the sickness, the despair, the desperation, when I am not a trained writer. I wanted to set down an account that would cause readers to feel sympathy for those in the reeducation camps, but I was not really up to the task. I hope my former companions in suffering and misfortune will forgive my shortcomings.

As I was working in London on the last pages of the abridged version, some people were staging a huge demonstration in the street outside my room. They were protesting the installation in Britain of American rockets that were to be aimed at the Russian missiles pointed at them, and at me too. While aware that these demonstrators meant well, it broke my heart to think that probably they were ignorant of the suffering in Kampuchea, Lebanon, Iraq, Iran, Afghanistan, Laos, Vietnam, El Salvador, Nicaragua, and other countries caused by weapons supplied by big countries. Oh God! Have mercy on us! We fear our own deaths while cruel and unjust death comes to others like an irresistible force. In Europe milk is poured on the ground as a protest against agricultural policy while

xiv   *Preface*

thousands of African children starve for lack of milk. Can any philosophy or ideology justify such death and hunger? Can people organize a demonstration to safeguard their own peace and ignore the collapse in other parts of the world? Against such a backdrop, can a modest book, written by an unknown person, achieve anything?

Yet I want to sound a note of optimism and faith. Despite everything, there remain in this world havens of hope, people moved by humanitarian feelings. To them I want to express my gratitude in these opening lines.

I was able to survive it all, the sickness and the accidents, because of my wife. She waited determinedly despite advice from others not to do so, despite the fact that she had the papers to allow her and our daughter to go to France. Instead, she came deep into the jungle to visit and comfort me.

I must mention the humanitarian intervention of Mr. P.T.L. who interceded on my behalf with Hanoi's Ministry of Foreign Affairs and gained my release; I have yet to meet and thank him.

I wish also to express my gratitude to the people and government of France, as well as other peoples and governments, for the assistance they have given to Vietnamese. I do not know what I can do to be worthy of this generosity and kindness, except to devote the remainder of my life to those acts that are inspired by the spirit of international brotherhood, love of mankind, and a just peace.

Finally, I would be remiss if I did not express my profound gratitude to the many people—Vietnamese, French, English, American—without whose help, advice, and encouragement I would not have been able to write and publish this book. Especially, I wish to thank Ton That Uan, Nguyen Van Canh, Vu Quang, Chu Ba Anh, Mrs. Phan Thong Khanh Minh, Vu Van Thiet, R. Brother Tran Van Nghiem, Paul Louis Tate, Robert Scalapino and Douglas Pike of the Institute of East Asian Studies at the University of California at Berkeley, William Philips of Little, Brown & Co., Laura Fillmore, Al Santoli, Anthony Grey, and, particularly, my editor, Myrna Pike.

Translator's Note

This book is the result of more than a year of hard work. Done by a person whose mother tongue is not English, the translation must sometimes seem "un-English to readers, for which the translator humbly offers his sincere apology. However, the "un-Englishness" of the style is intentional on a number of occasions—whenever some *couleur locale* is felt to be required, especially when rendering the peculiar way the Vietnamese communists express themselves. A number of footnotes have been added to help the readers to understand certain details, facts, and situations. If there is any error, the fault is mine and mine only.

Nguyen Phuc

The names of the author and the translator are pseudonyms.

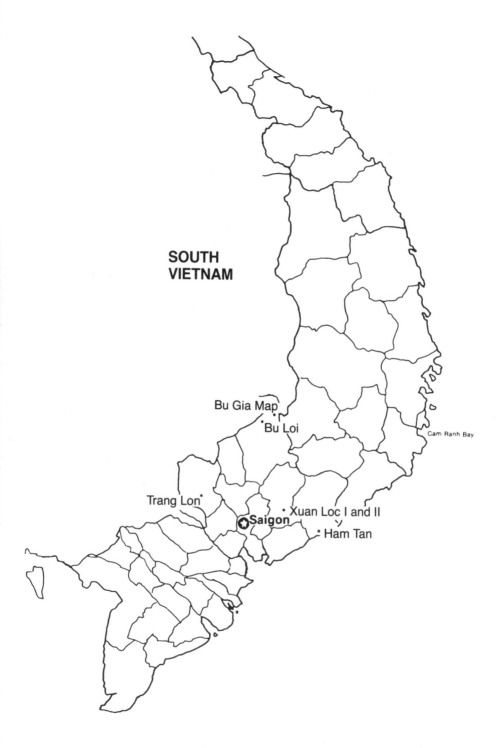

SOUTH VIETNAM

Bu Gia Map
Bu Loi

Cam Ranh Bay

Trang Lon

Xuan Loc I and II

Saigon

Ham Tan

Chapter 1

Camp One: Trang Lon

Into a rucksack I put those things needed for a seven-day stay[1] at the camp: two pairs of trousers, shirts, a mosquito net, a blanket, a piece of canvas to be used for a sleeping mat, toothpaste, soap, medicines (for colds or dysentery), and money. The money I tucked away very carefully.

When taking leave of my wife and little daughter, I tried to put on a calm appearance. But both my wife and I had the premonition that this departure would be an ill-fated one. Seeing my child babbling away happily, my heart ached at the thought of their uncertain future.

Earlier, before I was due to present myself to the authorities for "reeducation," a *bodoi*[2] had come twice to my house and urged me in a soft voice to report in good time.

Before I decided to take the risk, I made careful inquiries into this business of "reporting for reeducation." The information I had gathered was full of contradictions. Some said all servicemen attending previous seven-day reeducation sessions had returned safely home, but that smacked too much of communist propaganda. Still, that was what I told my wife to reassure her. One person whose accounts I felt I could trust was Duong Cong Hien—a tricky chap though—who had connections with communist officials in Hanoi. After the fall of South Vietnam, he announced that his family had been awarded a first-class medal posthumously for his father, who had fought and died in the war of resistance against the French. Hien's uncles were all high-ranking cadres in the North. However, he was sincere enough to reveal that reeducation would take quite a few years. "No less than that, I'm afraid." he said.

On the eve of the deadline to report, a communist cadre, followed by a bunch of kids, came to stand in front of my house. With his loudspeaker pointed in our direction, he read the official order. Then he and the kids shouted slogans

---

[1] The official communiqué stipulated that the period of "reeducation" for junior officers and civil servants was seven days. For many of them, it was seven years.

[2] North Vietnamese appellation for soldiers. Throughout the book, *bộdội* will be used for the politicized soldier of Communist Vietnam.

praising the "clement" policy of the "Revolution" and condemning the stub-bornness of those who refused to report for reeducation. For people like me, it was very clear that if we did not report, we would not be left alone.

I was to report to Nguyen Lam school near Cholon.[3] When I arrived, I stopped to read the notices that covered the gatepost, then someone shouted shrilly in a voice that sounded like a child's: "Why don't you go in to report? What are you waiting for?"

Then came a more affable voice; "Come in! We are about to call it a day." This was the voice of a cadre sitting at a table in the center of the schoolyard. Behind him was a group of people sitting on their heels. I approached the cadre. "Name?"

"Tran Tri Vu."

"Rank?"

"Reserve lieutenant."

"'Lieutenant' is enough. Why complicate things with 'reserve'?"

Giggles came from the group of squatting persons followed by a shout from the *bodoi* with a child's voice, "What are you fellows laughing at?"

The old cadre, more calmly: "Order, please!" Then, to me, "Branch?"

"Officer seconded to the Education Department."

"Another of those fellows! Don't you know which branch you belong to when you have not been taught to pilot a plane or drive a tank? You are infantry, understand? You're like the others who declared they have been 'seconded' in an attempt to conceal their actual branch. Isn't that so?"

"Oh no! I—"

"Enough! Go and sit there, behind the others."

I joined the squatting group of men who looked at me with mocking smiles. Later on, this "seconded" business caused me to be reprimanded time and again.

We remained squatting until our legs grew numb and until the group grew large enough that the *bodoi* decided to move us. The new place was a classroom.

"This is where you stay for the time being," the *bodoi* said. "If anybody wants to go out, he has to ask the guard in the corridor; you cannot go out unless you've got his permission. Two persons at the most will be allowed to leave the room at one time. Got it?" Somebody answered yes in a low voice, but the *bodoi*, as if vexed, repeated angrily. "Have you understood?" Seeing that he meant business, everybody replied yes in a loud voice. The *bodoi* then ordered the group leader, who had been appointed before I arrived, to sit at the door facing the group, as if to watch over us. The *bodoi* returned to the schoolyard.

The leader of our group was Pham Van Tuong, a dentist and medical corps

---

[3]*Cholón,* meaning "big market," is the Chinese section of Saigon.

lieutenant. We introduced ourselves all around. The man who arrived minutes before me was Nguyen Van Long, a lieutenant in the Rangers. He introduced himself by saying, "I've a lot of 'blood debts' to pay, I'm afraid."

It was then 6 P.M., June 26, 1975. The people in the room responded to the situation as their ages and natures dictated. Middle-aged persons remained silent, their hearts heavy with worry; the younger ones seemed not too worried and tried to make fun of the discipline that had just been imposed on them. But the jokes did not make many of us laugh. Long said, "Those child-soldiers have been particularly harsh today."

"You're right," I concurred. "They are very short-tempered."

We were talking in low voices when a *bodoi* appeared and spoke through the door before proceeding to another room to repeat his order: "Be ready for dinner. Put your belongings in order. When going out, remain in line and obey the order of the guard."

A van with the words Ai Hue Restaurant painted on its sides was parked in the yard. Someone clapped his hands, and a shout came in reproof: "Don't you fellows know how to keep discipline?"

Someone complained, "How can they joke under the circumstances?"

Long said teasingly, "Oh, come on! Let them have a little fun!"

Later, I was told that the person who had complained was Mr. Cuc, the oldest member of our group. "We have to avoid being insulted," he explained; "that would be a great humiliation for us."

"We have already suffered humiliation," Long countered. "Is there any greater humiliation than losing the war?"

Everybody in the room intervened noisily. "Now, come off it." "Leave him alone."

Long looked at me with a smile, but I shook my head, uneasy at what had happened. As fate would have it, Long, old Mr. Cuc, Tuong, and I were destined to be together for a long time.

Dinner that evening was characteristic of the irony of our situation. The restaurateur was one of the most famous in Cholon. Food was served on expensive china. The waitresses wore the usual shiny black trousers and white Chinese coats embroidered with the name of the restaurant. But the rice was brown rice, and the food consisted of fried pickled cabbage, fat meat cooked with brine, and thin cabbage soup. The only things reminiscent of the restaurant's normal cuisine were the tiny saucers of soy sauce and pickled red pepper. The waitresses told us that the *bodoi* had come to their restaurant and asked that meals be prepared for people reporting for reeducation. The *bodoi* provided the rice and some money, but the restaurateur still suffered a great loss. Said one of the waitresses with a laugh, "Our boss had to comply for fear of the consequences. After all, we have to support the Revolution, don't we!"

We ate our meal standing around the school tables. As we picked out the husks left in the rice, some tried to joke about the restaurant buying brown rice by mistake.

After the meal, we were brought back to the classroom, and two by two we were allowed to go outside to relieve outselves. At 8 o'clock we were ordered to keep silent and go to sleep, but we continued with our muffled conversation. Those who had come the day before told me to lie down on the floor wherever I liked. Most of us had brought along a large piece of cloth to serve as a blanket. Half of it was now used as a mat, the other half as a blanket and a protection against mosquitoes. A few had managed to hang their mosquito nets. By midnight, the whole room was quiet except for some snoring. I could not sleep; hundreds of questions kept turning around in my head. I felt an unusual need to urinate. I asked to go out and was led outside by a *bodoi*. The scene there was extraordinary. The place was crawling with *bodoi*; every five meters two of them were standing guard. When I got back to the room, I still could not sleep. It appeared that old Mr. Cuc and I were the only persons still awake in the room. Mr. Cuc was counting beads on his rosary and silently saying his prayers.

Suddenly, hurried footsteps were heard in the corridor. I looked at my watch: 1 A.M. A *bodoi* came into each room in turn; his voice was not too loud, but it was enough to cause everybody to awaken in alarm, "Everybody get up and prepare for maneuvers."

Long, still not quite awake, shot back, "The war is over. What do we need maneuvers for?"

Nobody paid any attention to him. All were busy putting things into their bags. The corridor outside was full of *bodoi*. One of them, paper in hand, entered the room, "Are you people team no. 6? Where's Pham Van Tuong? Get your people out and have them stay in line in the yard. Stand at the position assigned to your team. Hurry up with your preparations!"

In the yard we found some of the other teams already there waiting behind numbered tables. Careful preparations seemed to have been made. Additional electric bulbs illuminated the courtyard, and a cadre in a brand-new uniform stood on a platform in front of the teams, which drew up in perfectly straight lines.

"Listen to me! Keep silent and listen carefully," the *bodoi* said. "I don't want to use a loudspeaker and disturb our fellow citizens' sleep. You will be brought to a reeducation school. You will travel in trucks, and you'll be a little crowded. You will observe strict discipline when on the road and obey the orders of the guards. To avoid accidents, you will part for the time being with breakable or pointed objects; the guards will collect them and return them to you on arrival. I repeat, all knives, razor blades, glass bottles, and breakable utensils should be handed to the guards. You will be given back your belongings when we arrive at the school. Now, let the guards execute the order."

Everyone hurried to comply; all breakables, knives, and scissors were taken out of individual bags and put into sacks bearing the number of each team. Glass bottles outnumbered the other things. A *bodoi* growled, "Why the hell are you bringing so many bottles?"

Most of us had brought along steamed salted fish or ground sesame mixed with salt to last us for one week, the officially stated reeducation period, so somebody answered, "It's our provision for the week." Many *bodoi* burst into laughter.

We were then marched to the street, where an endless convoy of army trucks was waiting. These vehicles were smaller than the U.S. 2½-ton General Motors trucks but bigger than the Dodge 4 × 4s. We piled in, thirty-four to each; our team numbered forty, so six of us packed into another truck. My name was in the middle of the list, so I was able to travel with most of my new friends. Although our friendship was only two days old, we had the impression that we were already very close to one another.

It was very crowded in the truck, which was covered from top to bottom with a tarpaulin, yet one place had to be reserved in a front corner and another in the rear for the guards. People sat on each other's legs and on our canvas bags. The sound of quarreling and swearing voices filled the air. The guard at the rear shouted, "If anybody among you commits a breach of discipline, I shall deal with him on the spot."

The term *xu ly,*[4] used angrily by the *bodoi* and heard by us Southerners for the first time in our lives, sounded threatening enough to reduce us to silence. Shifting frequently in our crammed positions, Long and I sat against one side of the truck and were able to look out through some small holes in the tarpaulin. We caught sight of people standing at the doors of their homes looking out. They did not switch on any lights.

Although outwardly calm, we were besieged with worries. Long whispered in my ear, "It is highly probable that we shall be brought to North Vietnam. The field officers who reported two days ago were rumored to have been sent to the North." The words "sent to the North," which I had come across many times already, had been haunting all of us long before we presented ourselves for reeducation.

Outside the *bodoi* shouted to one another; then we heard a long whistle and the noise of motors starting up. The convoy began to move slowly. Deep inside me, I felt that a momentous event was happening. As the wheels of the trucks began to turn, it was clear to me that I was at that moment being separated from something very intimate, very precious, and that the separation would be eternal. I felt the hopelessness of a person faced with a fait accompli, regretting

---

[4]A term invented in the North meaning "to decide," "to judge," and, sometimes, "to deal with." It was misused by the illiterate *bodoi* and cadres as "to punish."

that it ever happened, and remorseful for having let it happen. It was a painful and bitter feeling.

I kept listening to noises and mentally taking note of every bend in the road in order to guess which direction we were taking. At first, when it seemed that we were driving along the road running parallel to the Phu Tho racetrack, I thought to myself, "Perhaps we're going to take the Bien Hoa highway! If so, will it be the Central Highlands? the North?" But the trucks kept going straight ahead, bumped slightly for a while, then turned left, decidedly not toward the highway. I tried to look through the holes in the tarpaulin, but the vehicles bumped so much that I could not catch sight of anything.

Now the trucks slowed down, but there was more rolling; I guessed that we had left the city. I was sure of it when echoes from both sides of the street suddenly changed in tempo and the convoy speeded up. For which camp were we bound? For a long time, the convoy moved along the seemingly deserted road. The two guards stuck their heads outside because of the stifling atmosphere in the truck, but they took care to block our view.

Old Mr. Cuc beside me was saying his prayers in a low voice, as he had been doing since the convoy started to move. I could hear only the beginning of the sentence, "Hail Mary . . ."; then the voice died down, then began again with "Holy Mary." The voice kept rising and falling like a wave, muffled by the noise of the motor. At times, the truck slowed down, then turned right or left. Despite my attempts to estimate distances and directions, I couldn't keep track of the route we were following, and I gave up. The only thing I was sure of, based on the creaking noise of the vehicle, was that we were not running on the new highway. Everybody in the vehicle was asleep except Mr. Cuc and me. Long must have been the first to fall asleep; it had been some time since he first leaned his full weight on my shoulder.

The truck was running on a very straight road when it suddenly slowed down and stopped. The guard at the back directed his flashlight at us and said, "Keep quiet, all of you! I'll fire if anybody moves."

Nobody answered, for most were not quite awake, but a moment later, somebody said, "Let us down, please. We need to urinate very badly."

The guard shouted, "Quiet!"

The guard at the front raised the tarpaulin and spoke to somebody outside, "Let them get down for a piss."

A voice answered, "Wait until we have deployed our guards."

Moments later a *bodoi* approached, saying, "The comrade guard at the rear will come down to stand guard. Each of you in turn will be permitted to get down to relieve himself, then will return to the truck and another will take his place. You in the truck, do you hear me clearly?"

Everybody joyfully answered in unison, "Loud and clear!"

So we took our turns. How cool and fresh the air outside was! The roadside was covered with grass. I tried to observe our surroundings, but they were shrouded in complete darkness. In the flickering of the guard's flashlight, I recognized a tree that grew at the side of the road; with its small trunk and big leaves, it was indeed the *dieu* tree, characteristic of the southern Vietnam landscape.

Back in the truck, there was much shifting about and sounds of dispute as more comfortable positions were sought, and again, shouts from the guards; then all was quiet. We sat this way for a long time waiting for the convoy to restart. Outside, our driver was heard discussing food and drinks with someone who suddenly called out, "One of you two comrades get down to have a snack; then it will be the other's turn."

The guard at the rear told the one in front to go ahead with his meal. The latter jumped down. "What is there to eat?" he asked.

"Rice gruel," the man said.

"Oh God! You travel by night in a crowded truck and all you have to eat is just gruel! You'll probably end up with a hell of a need to piss! Did Logistics run so low on rice that we have only gruel to eat?"

"I guess you don't like rice gruel much, but I suggest you smell it before you turn it down. It's chicken gruel, see! If this had been supplied to us in B2,[5] a lot of fellows' lives could have been saved."

"Oh! Is it true, comrade, that you have spent some time in B2?"

"You talk of B2, but do you have any idea of what it was? I was there only a few months, yet I nearly died of malaria and B-52 bombs."

"Just the thought of life in B2 is enough to give me the creeps! It's a great merit for you to have been in B2."

"Eat your food now; there are others waiting. The gruel is still hot. Don't eat it all, though. You'll be soundly beaten if you do!" Then there was laughter.

The two guards finished eating and returned to the truck, but there was no sign of the convoy resuming its journey. It was a long hour before the vehicles restarted their motors. I made a quick calculation. We started at 1 A.M.; when we stopped to relieve ourselves, it was 4 A.M. The *dieu* tree we saw a moment ago was proof that we were still in the Mekong Delta region. If the convoy had gone toward the north, there would have been no sign of such trees.

After an hour's travel, we saw a faint light in the sky behind us. Clearly, we were going westward. I shook Long's arm; he stretched his shoulders and asked, "Can't you sleep? For me, sleep comes very easily."

I bent down close to his ear. "It seems we are going in the Tay Ninh direction," I said.

---

[5]B2 was a North Vietnamese base in the central highlands, near the junction of the frontier between Vietnam, Kampuchea, and Laos where the Ho Chi Minh Trail emerges. This was an area of intensive

"Really?" he answered. "As long as we do not have to go to the North, I am content." Having said that he went back to sleep.

Dawn came. Old Mr. Cuc, who had managed to get a little sleep, awoke. Others were beginning to wake up, and the truck now buzzed with the sound of murmured conversation. Suddenly Old Cuc said close to my ear, "Somebody remarked that we are going in the direction of Tay Ninh, not northward." I looked at Long; he was asleep. Barely an hour and the news had gone the rounds of the truck!

The day grew lighter and lighter. Suddenly, voices, the noise of motorbikes, and the creaking of ox carts were all around us. Our vehicle slowed down. Long peered through the holes in the tarpaulin; then it was my turn. A great number of people on bicycles, most of them men, crowded the road.

Long said, "So it's true! Those people are rubber plantation workers. We are indeed near Tay Ninh. I know this place like the back of my hand. I was stationed here for a long time and took part in lots of operations in this area."

Our convoy turned right and seemed to be caught in a bottleneck. The *bodoi* called out shrilly to one another.

"Which 'D' is that?"[6]

"Is this Gia Long school?"

"Comrades, listen to me! This is the new instruction. You don't have to observe the prearranged order. Wherever there is an open space, just drive in; return to base after you have turned your people over to the camp management. Remember to take down the name of the person responsible for their reception; note how many you have turned over. Now go! You there, drive on. Don't delay."

The guard at the back jumped down and walked behind the truck. The going was very slow in the jam of vehicles. We stopped and were ordered to get down and line up. We were in an open yard with a jumble of barbed wire lying all over. Long said with a smile, "This is the place I liked most. The club was over there!"

We soon found out that this was the former artillery base of Trang Lon. Except for the observation tower, still intact, the barracks were crumbling. Here and there on the ground lay an assortment of wooden containers, shell cases, and booster powder in the shape of sticks with five cylindrical perforations on the inside. It was then 7 o'clock in the morning. After traveling all night, we expected to arrive at a place far away from Saigon. We did not expect the convoy to cover a bare hundred kilometers. Only much later did we learn that the North Vietnamese military traveled very slowly, averaging around 40 km per hour.

---

bombings by B-52s and systematic defoliation. Also, this is where malaria took its heaviest toll of *bodoi*.

[6]North Vietnamese code name for battalion.

We had been told we would be brought to a school to be "reeducated," but looking around, we saw only ruins and no place to live. Now, it was line up, roll call, head count, then waiting. Very long waiting. The trucks that brought us had long been gone. Tired of waiting, we squatted on the ground; some, too exhausted, used their bags as cushions. Only one *bodoi* stood guard. At long last, the guard himself was fed up; he called out, "What about this group? Why hasn't anybody come out to take them in charge?"

Finally, a man who appeared to be an officer[7] appeared and led us to a corner of the yard near a little wooden shed about 4 meters by 5, which seemed to have served as some sort of office. Another group was already there, busy cleaning up the place. The officer instructed us to help out, adding, "Make preparations to stay here. All of you will be grouped into a B.[8] Pham Van Tuong will be your leader. Now, clean the place, then rest."

Having given his order, he left as if in a great hurry. A look at the shed showed that those who came before us had taken over the space under the portion of the roof that was still intact, leaving us the corner with a crumbling roof, perhaps damaged by heavy artillery. A number of young fellows, Long among them, rushed in to protest. "The instruction was that this place is for all of us, so you have no right to reserve the best space for yourselves and leave us without a roof. We must divide equally between us. Without a roof over our heads, it will be the end of us when it rains!" They took the bags that preempted the space under the intact roof and stacked them in a corner; then they said to the rest of us, "Come on, put your belongings in this corner for the time being. We'll wait for the *bodoi* to settle our differences."

Some of their men were no less aggressive than ours; they rushed forward, some grasping long pieces of wood, obviously intending to fight it out. The middle-aged among us hurriedly intervened. "Stop it! How can you think of fighting at this point? Where's Tuong? It's his duty to settle this. It's not proper to call in the *bodoi*."

At last, Tuong came in; he seemed embarrassed to have been called upon to arbitrate. After much convincing, he agreed to settle the difference and suggested that, since everybody wanted a good place but nobody was willing to yield, we draw lots. Voices rose in angry protest. That solution pleased no one. After some discussion, the two groups agreed to divide the room into two sections, each with a good portion of roof overhead to cover people's belongings. In the end, however, everybody decided to put their things where they were going to sleep instead of leaving them in the roofed corner for fear of theft.

It was nearly noon when we were asked to go and fetch our ration of rice for the midday meal. Again there was a dispute, this time over who would be given

---

[7]Until 1978, North Vietnamese officers seldom wore military badges, except on formal occasions.
[8]North Vietnamese code name for platoon.

the task of cooking rice. Finally, some of the younger ones volunteered. A roofed but open-sided garage had been temporarily converted into a kitchen. The scene there was simply chaotic! Rice was being cooked in coverless Chinese woks placed on a few bricks arranged around the fire. A couple of the woks overturned, but the "cooks" hurriedly scooped up the rice, added some water, adjusted the position of the bricks, and continued with the cooking. When the water began to boil, the woks were covered with rice sacks, the steam seeping through the jute like white smoke. A sample showed the rice was not done; there was not enough steam. More wood was added to the fire. The result was three layers of rice in the woks, the bottom one burned black and inedible, the middle one well cooked but too dry, and the top layer undercooked. When the rice was served out, each of us was given some of the burned rice, which had to be thrown away, a little of the cooked rice, and a little of the uncooked. The distribution couldn't have been more impartial. When the *bodoi* came to check and supervise the rationing, we were given the first lesson in "revolutionary" ethics. "Uncle Ho said, 'Do not fear shortage; what should be feared is unequal distribution!'" We commented on the teaching while eating our first meal at the "school."

Worried about possible ill effects on our health if the present way of cooking rice went on, I called Long aside and explained the proper way of cooking rice in Chinese woks. I had been a boy scout in my early youth and had some experience cooking rice for many people when we went camping. The canvas should be soaked in water before being placed on the wok; if possible, a board of suitable size should be placed on top of the canvas to prevent the steam from escaping. Long then called out, "Hey, Tuong! This Mr. Vu is an expert on cooking rice in Chinese woks!"

Because of this lesson in the art of rice cooking, I was called upon to join the kitchen team. The next day we requested permission to go and pick up the scrap wood that was lying around (most of it from artillery shell containers) to make covers for woks. We made makeshift hammers and tools to extract nails. The woks were round and more than a meter in diameter, but we could only make square covers because we had no saw. (Some time later, I was promoted to leader of the team of carpenters, as the kitchen team became overmanned and the work almost routine. I joined the carpentry team by chance, almost against my will, but from then on I was put down as chief carpenter in my records, wherever I was transferred.)

The advantage of working in teams was that information could be gathered. In the first few days, we were all anxious to get through with reeducation and return home as soon as possible. But seven days dragged by and nothing happened. Every day we were led away by the *bodoi* to work at such tasks as clearing the camp, digging latrines, and carrying water for bathing and washing. Sometimes we were ordered to help the *bodoi* by sweeping the yard, chopping wood, and carrying rice and foodstuffs for Logistics. Back in our shed in the evening, we recounted all information gathered during the day. First, we learned that this Trang Lon base was crowded with officers, from second lieutenants to captains. Although the *bodoi* repeatedly and threateningly reminded us not to talk to men from other units—"not to communicate indiscriminately," as they put it—nevertheless, whenever we came across each other, we spoke in low voices, asking for information. The latrine area was jokingly named "radio station." The latrines were dug side by side in a small space in an attempt to confine the foul smell. When a person went there, he would call out to the other side of the wattle[9] to see if anybody else was present. Long took every occasion to go to the latrines to hunt for information, and he never failed to come back with some news for us. This was how we knew, for instance, that the shed we saw standing behind the earthen wall to our left was assigned to B7 (Battalion 7), composed mostly of civil servants. Le Quang Uyen, the former governor of the National Bank, was among its inmates.

A word here about the terminology used by the *bodoi* regarding the organization of the camp inmates into units. A small number was grouped into an "A" (a squad), three As constituted a "B" (a platoon), three Bs made up a "C" (a company), and four Cs formed a "D" (a battalion). My first unit was A1 B3 C1 D4; in other words, I belonged to squad 1, platoon 3, company 1, battalion 4.

The concentration of so many people in one place, inmates and *bodoi*, gave rise to many problems. The stock of wood used for cooking was soon used up as were the wooden shell containers. We resorted to the poles and beams of the fortifications and later tore down derelict constructions, even small wooden buildings. Whole blocks of pinewood, donated by the United States for construction of buildings were used to cook our meals. The sheds we lived in were overcrowded. The rainy season had just begun. Many of us became ill from sleeping on the dirt floors. Seven days passed without any reeducation being given to us or any date for our release mentioned. Morale plummeted, resulting in more sickness; some were not able to find any sleep at night. Secret thoughts now began to be expressed openly, in loud voices. "We have been duped! That is quite clear since we have not been released after seven days!" Others could not help giving physical vent to their anger and frustration. The situation became unbearable.

The *bodoi* also showed signs of a change in attitude. At first, when they led us to work at clearing the camp, they conversed with us as if with ordinary acquaintances. Now they dropped a few paces behind us, walking in stubborn silence, no longer willing to talk. Later, when some *bodoi* came to our carpentry shop to order furniture made for them, one young man revealed that they had been ordered not to "communicate" with people who were to be reeducated.

In the first few days, the young *bodoi* especially were easily accessible. They

---

[9]A wattle is made of flexible wood strips woven through bamboo.

told us about the situation in the North, and we told them about the South. At times they agreed to take our little money and buy food for us at the local market; in this way, we were able to improve our daily diet of rice and salt with some fish sauce, sugar, or instant noodles. (The containers of food and medicine that we brought with us and had to turn in at the start of our journey had disappeared without trace. We asked for them many times but were told they had all been broken during the move and had to be thrown away.) Now, with the order forbidding communication between us and the *bodoi*, we were virtually cut off from this source of supply.

The rice rationed out was nearly rotten. The rice sacks, bearing the words People's Republic of China, were probably stockpiled in hideouts in damp forest areas, and as a result the rice was mildewed. When washing it, we had to take infinite precautions to keep it from breaking into minute pieces. After three weeks of a diet of rotten rice and salt, almost all of us developed stomach troubles, from constipation to dysentery. We looked for any kind of edible, or thought-to-be-edible, greens that grew on grassy patches or on fences; these we used as vegetables or potions to help alleviate our pains.

Then one afternoon we were ordered to get ready to assemble in the yard, giving rise to conjecture and speculation. Some said that a great number of vehicles had arrived at noon; were they to take us back to Saigon? Others told us a *bodoi* had revealed that we would be scattered to various places because there were too many here at Trang Lon. A few worried about money that, in violation of the rules, they had managed to give the *bodoi* for the purchase of food; if we had to go now, the money would be irretrievably lost. We had to wait until late in the evening before the *bodoi* arrived and ordered us to assemble for roll call. To the naïve question of whether we should bring our luggage with us, a childish-looking *bodoi* shouted, "What for? Are you mad?"

After we assembled, we had to wait for the other units to arrive. This was the first time the whole D4 was gathered together. At last a *bodoi* gave the order. "Everybody prepare to greet the camp leader!"

Only then did we realize that the camp leader was the short fellow who often came to our shed to chat with us. He said his name was Ha. As he was the only fat *bodoi,* we nicknamed him Fatty Ha. We sat down on the ground at his instruction; after looking us over, he declared, "I have been too busy organizing things concerning your life here and have not had the opportunity to participate in your activities. Now, my superiors judge that it is time I told you a number of things you ought to know. First, I shall inform you of the regulations governing reeducation; second, I'll be giving you explanations on some of the issues that may be raised; finally, we shall all participate in a constructive working session." He then called out to another *bodoi* to ask him to read the regulations; they began "Democratic Republic of Vietnam—Independence, Freedom, Happiness . . ."

As the *bodoi* read on, the sound of whispered comments increased. Some observed that the appellation Provisional Government of South Vietnam was not used in the official document. Others drew attention to the presence of more and more *bodoi* around us. Suddenly, there was a shout. "Stop! No more reading, please! There's too much disorder!"

Fatty Ha stepped forward and said, "I want to draw your attention to the fact that the regiment's commander will be coming to observe our meeting. Therefore, you must listen attentively, in complete silence. This is very important. Now, comrade, go on with your reading!"

The more we heard, the more silent we became; everything we heard was appalling. Following rules on "clean eating, neat living" came regulations permitting us to write home once a month to "boost the morale of our families," to watch movies (North Vietnamese propaganda films, of course) once every quarter, to have visits by relatives. And if we showed good will and progress in reeducation, we would be allowed to go home soon. We were transfixed with fear. When the *bodoi* had finished reading, tumultuous protests and queries rose from our ranks.

"Why did you say that reeducation would last only seven days?"

"You don't wait long to cheat us, do you?"

"Remember! The communiqué [on reeducation] is still there! The ink hasn't dried yet!"

There were shouts from the *bodoi*'s side, too. At the same time, they moved to surround us, their rifles pointed in our direction. Two orders followed. "Everybody stand up! Now, sit down, everybody!"

Having given us the order to sit in lines, Fatty Ha again stepped forward to say, "You should learn to keep order at every meeting. From now on, any disorderly conduct shall be severely dealt with!" Then he spoke about the clement policy of the "Revolution" and kept repeating, "Your crimes deserve the death penalty. But the Revolution, out of clemency, has permitted you to be reeducated; after completion of your reeducation you will be sent back to your families."

What we had feared had become reality. The communiqué had been worded in ambiguous terms to lure as many of us as possible into reporting for reeducation. The speech ended with explanatory replies to our queries, for example, no one had said that our reeducation would take only seven days, the communiqué had urged us to bring a seven-day supply of food for the travel, just in case, and so on.

At this point, Fatty Ha burst into laughter. The *bodoi* standing behind him guffawed. Within our ranks, somebody swore loudly, and a voice rose, "How clever the Revolution is!"

A *bodoi* shouted, "You don't know how to keep quiet, do you?"

As an introduction to the meeting proper, Fatty Ha said, "As you are not yet familiar with the 'revolutionary' way of life, some of you, even after some time in this place, are still careless in your speech and actions, which denotes a real resistance to progress. You are here to be reeducated in order to become progressive socialists, and as such you will be returned to your families, we hope soon."

With these words, which seemed to come right out of a manual, he began a detailed enumeration of the offenses committed by us since our arrival at the camp. Each unit was mentioned in turn in the indictment. When our turn came, we were quite amazed because all the details were true. They included words we had used to make fun of the Revolution and such acts as asking the *bodoi* to buy things in town for us and using more water than necessary when cooking rice in order to obtain a thin soup in addition to the cooked rice. Although no names were mentioned, we all knew perfectly well which offense applied to which person among us. In particular, the charge related to some words considered "offensive" applied to the very words I had said to Long only and no one else "Although the *bodoi* are 'revolutionaries,' money has the same effect on them as it has on us." I had told him this when he hesitated to ask the *bodoi* to make a purchase for him; I knew they vied with each other to oblige us in order to make some profits out of the dealings.

As he went on, Fatty Ha became more and more violent to the point of uttering threats. "Remember this: The Revolution is clement, but it does not mean the Revolution does not know how to punish as they deserve those of you who are obstinate enough to resort to psychological warfare here. Don't be surprised if later on severe and pitiless measures are taken against the culprits."

Then, in more conciliatory tones, he promised to overlook past offenses if the culprits showed sincere repentance. Concluding this "constructive" session, he told team leaders to look among their members for musical people who would be taught revolutionary songs, which they in turn would teach their companions to sing. "From now on," he said, "when beginning and ending a working session, we shall sing those songs to create an enthusiastic atmosphere that will no doubt bring good results."

The session ended late at night. Although the weather was fine, our hair and shirts were wet from dew. On the way back to our shed, nobody felt like talking; we were all upset, frustrated, and worried to the point of fear. It was now quite certain that our reeducation would take a long time, not seven days, not one month . . . We were all the more worried because we had proof that the "eyes and ears" of the Revolution were among us. Most of us were exposed for offenses we had committed. As for me, I was convinced that Long was the "mole"; no doubt about it!

It had been our habit to gather every night for some talk, but that night, without a word being exchanged, everybody spread his mat and got into his mosquito net. The silence was heavy. I could not sleep. Hundreds of questions, hundreds of thoughts went through my head. Around me, nobody seemed able to sleep. From time to time, someone turned over and sighed deeply. Someone swore angrily; another moaned as if in high fever. I did not expect such reactions after the first session. As far as I was concerned, I had learned an important lesson. From now on, I would constantly be on my guard vis-à-vis my companions; I would not confide my thoughts or joke with anybody. I had not expected Long to be so evil-minded. I thought he was a straightforward young fellow, as youth must be. Who would have suspected he was such a scoundrel! He had introduced himself as someone owing a debt of blood to the Revolution. He insulted the communists and was abusive about communism and very often made fun of the *bodoi*. All this had been meant to trap us into revealing ourselves.

The next day I got up early as usual, washed, then had a cigarette while waiting for daylight. But many of my companions arose late. Tuong, our team leader, had to urge them many times to roll down their mosquito nets, put things in order, and clean the place. Some had fever and could not get up. As usual, the *bodoi* came to call the roll. Those who were in good health had to stand in line in the courtyard and wait for the *bodoi* to finish counting the sick who remained in the shed. It was a day unlike the other days. Everyone looked sullen and worn out; everyone kept a stubborn silence and avoided talking to one another. The atmosphere was heavy. When time came to cook our meal, the kitchen team members called out to each other to go and fetch the daily ration of rice. My companions on the carpentry team and I went to the *bodoi's* shack to repair some tables and chairs. Coming across Long, I behaved as if I had not seen him. Mealtime was at 10 A.M. Each of us was given his share, which we ate in silence, each absorbed in his own thoughts. Only the young ones, who seemed not to care much, were chatting away in their corner.

Each day, food was supposed to be distributed twice, at 10 A.M. and 4 P.M., but usually there would be some delay. The camp medical orderly used to make his rounds of the sheds daily to take down the names of the sick and distribute medicine. On this day, he found more people reporting sick than usual, and he revealed that the number of sick people in the other units also had increased considerably. As usual, he gave his patients tablets bearing Chinese characters. A pharmacist among us tasted them and declared the drug was some sort of quinine.

The day dragged on at a snail's pace. Food was distributed later than usual because the work parties came back late. In the evening a *bodoi* came for roll call, after which he declared, "You have to have faith in the Revolution. After a period of reeducation you will be sent home. Reeducation cannot begin yet because we still have no suitable place for it. We have to wait until a meeting room is available."

After roll call, each went silently about preparing for bed. As I was not in the habit of going to bed early, I sat fanning myself with a piece of thick paper, hoping for a fresh breeze. Long came to sit beside me. Neither of us spoke. At long last, he said, "Why is everybody so silent tonight? You, who usually are so calm, also seem worried."

"I am not worried. Since coming to this place, we have been taken good care of by the Revolution. So why should I have to worry? By the way, when making your report to the Revolution to acquire merit, don't forget to report truthfully what I am now telling you."

"God! So, you suspect me of having reported on you, don't you? I swear—"

"Don't swear! I sincerely hope the Revolution will release you sooner than the rest of us. But, please, do not be so wicked as to harm other people. The words 'The revolutionaries are as greedy as we are' were those I said to you and only to you. Yet you had the heart to report fully my words."

"Good Lord! You suspect me to be the informer, and I suspect somebody else. I used that phrase when talking to Chiem Van Trung, Ong Tran Thinh, and Vo Tai. When Fatty Ha mentioned it, I knew I had been reported on."

I looked at Long, trying to read his thoughts. I didn't expect him to be that clever. Indeed, he was quick to come to his own defense. It seemed best that I not make an enemy of him. I said, "Fine, if you didn't report on me. Let's drop the subject. However, from now on, don't ever disclose anything to anyone because the 'eyes and ears' of the *bodoi* are everywhere. The proof is they know everything."

"Yes, I am really worried. Everybody in the kitchen team suspects everybody else of being a mole. The rice soup affair was first suggested by others; I had nothing to do with it."

Feeling that a long talk with him wouldn't do me any good, I pretended to be sleepy and retreated to my bed. Beside me, old Mr. Cuc was saying his prayers, his voice lower than usual.

A few more days had passed when one morning a *bodoi* brought me a table to repair. While I was working on it, the *bodoi* asked about my native place and family. Sensing kindness in him, I risked a question. "How much longer do you think we have to be here before we can hope for release? I am asking in all sincerity, otherwise I'll be worrying myself to death."

The *bodoi* shook his head and looked around, then replied in a low voice, "I am telling you because you appear to be a nice fellow. You must absolutely not tell anybody. You should know that at the moment my superiors are setting up 'connections' among the camp inmates in order to get daily reports on your activities. If they know you are 'communicating' with me, both you and I will be punished.

"All of you are so naïve! Now that you are here, what good do you think your protests can do you? They will serve no purpose. In a few days, you will have to write an account of your past history and you will be classified into categories. Then you'll begin your political education and do lots of other things. You won't be home soon. I don't know how long you'll have to stay, but it will be some time before the question of who's going to be released, who's going to stay on, can be raised. In the North, there are still people who have been held in reeducation camps since the signing of the Geneva Accord.

"How soon you are released depends on how serious our superiors assess your offenses. As far as you are concerned, I would think that your offenses are not too serious since all of you here are junior officers. You must keep up your morale. Even we ourselves sometimes write home to complain about our hardships and are subject to harsh criticism going on for several nights on end, so much so that our heads ache. You get used to it.

"What you have to remember is this: Speak with restraint; avoid making impulsive remarks. On your way to work, most of you fellows have been speaking thoughtlessly; the comrade guards have reported on you lots of times. That will be very harmful to you. Your offenses may be minor, but by being reported on, you'll end up being classified as 'bad elements'!"

After this enlightening talk, I became much more cautious. The revelation by the *bodoi* that some were still in camps from the time of the 1954 Accord came as a shock. I could not imagine people undergoing reeducation for twenty years. A terrifying prospect!

A month passed, and our tension began to wear off. Meanwhile, we discovered there were at least two moles among us. Men on the lookout at the latrines saw two inmates, one short, one tall, talking to the *bodoi* much longer than it took to make a deal for purchases. We had quite a few tall ones, but only two short ones: Thinh and Tai.

Since there might be even more than two moles, it would be dangerous to say much about whom we suspected. No one said anything that smacked of politics either. Even when making jokes, we had to think of some indirect way of speaking, and we had to keep from laughing out loud.

Long kept engaging me in conversation, but I did not say anything special; I just listened. One evening before bedtime, he said to me, "I wonder if you know that we met many newly arrived *bodoi* this afternoon. Earlier, we heard the guys from Logistics talk about going to buy things at the market for the new security fellows. The new ones wore proper, clean clothes and had brand new bikes. Some of them passed us as we were busy carrying rice and shouted, 'Don't you know how to make way?' "

Long added that rumors held that this security team had come to begin investigating us. This tallied with the carpentry team's orders to make repairs in a number of rooms and make bunks to accommodate several persons. Some thought was evident in the preparations, which denoted the importance of the incoming team.

The next day, many trucks arrived and parked alongside the warehouses. In the afternoon, we were ordered to stop work and wait for instructions. Comments and speculation now were more subdued. The kitchen team was told to begin cooking earlier than usual because we had to meet right after the meal. When we had finished eating, we were told to assemble in the main courtyard. Since this second gathering of the whole battalion took place during daylight, we had an opportunity to look for acquaintances, and there was some cheerfulness in the air.

After roll call, Fatty Ha made a quick check, then made his introduction. "Today we have a special guest from General Headquarters coming here to meet and work with you."

A man who appeared to be a high-ranking officer stepped forward; he said, "In execution of my superiors' order, I came here today to work with you. I would think that you have been quite anxious to begin your reeducation. Is that right?"

From the crowd the answer came as an explosion, "Right! Correct!"

Using good mob psychology, he asked another question, extremely mischievous this time. "You're anxious to begin reeducation so you can return soon to your wives and children, aren't you?"

"True! Very true! O Revolution, have pity!"

As usual, our assembly took every opportunity to have fun; the men laughed and spoke loudly while answering the question. From the *bodoi* came a shout. "Order! Don't you know how to observe discipline?"

The cadre from General Headquarters put on a severe air and said, "Right! Everyone wants to go home. But do you deserve the favor? As you have not begun your reeducation, you cannot yet realize the extent of your offenses. I firmly believe—I am sure—that is so. When reeducation begins in earnest, you will realize by yourselves that you cannot be sent home yet because you do not yet deserve to be."

Listening to those words, we became silent, expecting more threats. The cadre now came to the point: "Today, the team responsible for your reeducation and I came here to give you the chance to go back soon to your families. That means we shall give you the opportunity to prove your sincere repentance for your guilt and your sincere belief in the tolerant and magnanimous policy of the Revolution. Do you want to take that opportunity?"

There were some reluctant answers, but most of us were vaguely aware of a trap being set and were quiet. The cadre reiterated his question in expectation of a more unanimous response. "Do you want to take that opportunity we are offering you?"

"Yes, we do!"

"Then I solemnly inform you that you will have that opportunity tomorrow. Tomorrow you will begin writing an account of your past actions up until the day you were liberated by the Revolution. What you are going to declare, what you are going to put down on paper, will be used to assess the degree of your repentance, not as information nor as grounds for indictment. As you know, when your General Staff took to their heels, they left behind all the files on all of you. If we want to assess your crimes, all we have to do is go through them. The account you will write tomorrow will provide you with the opportunity to prove your faith in the Revolution, your sincerity in repenting your offenses, and to decide for yourselves which social class you belonged to in the previous regime. If you are 'progressive,' you will have the chance to acquire merit in the eyes of the Revolution. So tomorrow you will work toward a basis for the Revolution to show its leniency to you."

When he had finished, Fatty Ha stepped out to make another introduction. "Now, the regiment commander is going to have a word with you."

A man in neater attire than the other *bodoi* stepped forward. "You are here to be reeducated and acquire a new personality. Once you leave the camp to return home, you will indeed have a new personality. If you do not cooperate in this, you will have to stay on and continue your reeducation until you have made real progress; only then will you be sent home. In undertaking your reeducation, the Revolution has unlimited patience. Whether you get sent home sooner or later depends entirely upon you. The sooner the better for you and for us. Remember, the Revolution always provides you with the conditions necessary for you to be able to return home. The account you're going to write tomorrow will be extremely important. It will offer you the chance for an early return to your families if you are sincere in your declarations.

"You can hide anything you want. But we are going to review your statements and shall surely know what you have tried to hide. The means are not lacking. We can cross-check your individual records in the former military files with reports from local authorities of the hamlets, villages, or wards where you lived or where you worked; we can compare your statements with those of your parents, wives, children, brothers, and sisters. There's no way for you to hide anything. The People know everything, the Revolution knows everything. Therefore, I sincerely advise you to be honest and accurate and, in particular, to be complete in your declarations. Another point I want to make concerns your diet. Although the Revolution is short of supplies, it always takes good care of you. Lately, we have been too busy to organize Logistics adequately; therefore we have not been able to purchase food for you. Now, we have instructions for supplying food, so from tomorrow we shall distribute food together with your daily ration of rice. This is proof of the Revolution's thoughtfulness, and you have to prove yourselves worthy of the clemency and generosity of the Revolution."

After the speech, we were ordered to break ranks and return to our barracks. If it had not been for the business of writing accounts, the announcement of food distribution would have been good news because most of us had had only salt to eat with rice all this month. But the urging, the threats related to making accurate and complete declarations, had everybody so worried that no one had the heart to think of food. From that day on, as a rule, whenever our diet improved, we expected something unpleasant to happen.

The next morning we were ordered to assemble in front of our shed. The place was crowded with *bodoi*. Each squad was assigned a *bodoi* wearing a leather satchel on his hip. (Leather satchels or K54s [pistols a bit smaller than a Colt 45] were signs that the persons wearing them were officers. We seldom saw *bodoi* wearing military badges, so it was difficult to distinguish ranks.)

The *bodoi* responsible for guiding us in writing our accounts told us to copy down the form we were to follow, which he explained in minute detail. The more we wrote, the more amazed we became. In addition to name, rank, service number, unit, and army branch, we had to make declarations concerning wives and children, parents, brothers and sisters, wife's parents and brothers and sisters, and immediate superiors. After the preliminaries, we had to detail our histories. What had been our occupations and addresses before 1945? after 1945? We had to answer hundreds of questions, all numbered. We were not permitted to leave any unanswered. If we could not give an answer, we had to explain why.

We had to specify our relatives' previous and present occupations and addresses. If they were deceased, we had to state precisely the circumstances of their deaths, whether illness or some other cause, and the place where they died. Questions requiring detailed answers—which could be used as grounds for indictment—were those concerned with promotions and/or awards of military decorations. We had to tell why we had been promoted, what feats of arms led to a military decoration, and when and where. "Special declarations" included the drawing of organization charts of units we had been assigned to, revealing hiding places of documents, caches of arms and other military equipment, and identifying agents planted by the Americans or the *nguy*.[10]

Just reading the questionnaire made it hard for those who had performed feats of valor or had held important posts to sleep or eat. But the physical act of writing the account was even more frightening. Paper and pens were distributed; each squad of twelve persons was placed under the control of three or four *bodoi*, who kept going round and round, watching, reading the answers, and making such comments as "That's not enough," "That's still too vague," or "That shows your intention to hide some part of your past."

Long drew the most criticism from the *bodoi*. Just to answer the question

---

[10]The word used by the North Vietnamese when speaking of their Southern opponents. As an adjective, *nguy* means "false, deceptive." *Nguy* also means "traitor" or "puppet," depending on the context.

about his military career took him more than one day. He was told to give a detailed account of the "search-and-destroy" operations he had ordered when in command of each of his various stations, of how many prisoners he had taken, and who had been the highest ranking officer among them. When Long said he had taken no prisoners, the *bodoi* told him to put down the words, "There was an order to kill all prisoners of war, so none was kept." To this Long retorted there had been no such order, but the *bodoi* countered, "Even now, you still persist in defending your superiors!"

Finally, the *bodoi* told Long to take a break, think about the matter, weigh seriously his answers, and either tell the truth and return home early or hide it and take the consequences. Later, Long told me that he had to take his chance by answering that he had indeed taken prisoners whom he had turned over to command headquarters for interrogation. Regarding military decorations, Long declared that he had been awarded six crosses for gallantry. The *bodoi* instructed him to give details of the battles in which he had won the awards, such as how many *bodoi* had he killed and how many civilian houses had he burned.

The *bodoi* said that if our accounts did not list details of our offenses, they would be considered proof of guilty reticence. In my case, when I answered that I had been seconded for service to the Ministry of Education right after my graduation from Thu Duc Military Academy, the *bodoi* responsible for my supervision showed disbelief. Finally, I had to say that secondment for teaching had been a political assignment. Only then was the answer accepted.

A fellow from my squad named Nguyen Van Que had been a paymaster; not knowing how to aggravate his own offenses, he declared he had increased bonuses as an incentive to his men to kill more communist soldiers. Even medical officers had to invent something to show their "sincerity." When the *bodoi* read in their statements that they had given medical care to Viet Cong prisoners, they took it as an attempt to minimize their offenses. Finally, for lack of "crimes," they resorted to saying they had speeded the recovery of wounded soldiers and quickly pushed them back to the battlefront to kill communists. Dr. Nguyen Khiem, unable to find any serious offense he could charge himself with, was obliged to plead guilty to the "crime" of having successfully operated on General Phu, then commander of the Second Army Corps, for an eye ailment; he wrote that he had missed the opportunity of making himself worthy of the Revolution by speeding General Phu's blindness. He had cured him and rendered him all the more capable of leading his soldiers to kill more Viet Cong.

The account that was read aloud in public as an exemplary one was that written by an artillery lieutenant, Phan The Thé, who noted that he had been decorated at the Quang Tri battle when, in a period of three days, his battery fired 44,000 rounds of 105mm artillery shells at Viet Cong units, killing and wounding at least 27,000 Viet Cong soldiers. The *bodoi* who read the statement, declared after the reading, "There, you see! When you sincerely confess to a crime, you give all the details. To plead guilty to the killing and wounding of 27,000 revolutionary fighters has been indeed a bold gesture; but the more serious the offense, the more sincere such a confession proves to be. I urge you to follow Thé's example."

We applauded. Thé stood up, bowed as people used to do in a theater, his face bearing a mocking smile. Later, Thé told me that an artillery expert, reading the statement, would laugh himself to death. He said a battery was incapable of firing 44,000 shells in three days. Besides, a 105mm artillery shell was not a tiny thing. It would have been an achievement just to transport that many shells to the battlefront within three days, let alone fire them. When asked by the *bodoi* how he knew 27,000 enemy soldiers had been killed, Thé answered that he based his estimates on the theoretical number of casualties inflicted by one 105mm shell, which he multiplied by 44,000, then reduced the total by the ratio of misses and duds; the result was 27,000 enemies put out of action. Thé concluded his story with a peal of laughter, saying, "I am not sure whether there could have been as many as 10,000 VC taking part in that entire action. And my sole battery killed 27,000 of them!"

The writing of accounts was expected to take seven days. In fact, it took ten. During those ten days, we went through the most tense hours of our lives. We also came across some of the most ludicrous instances of black comedy that we could ever have imagined. The longest account written, breaking all records, was that of Lieutenant Nguyen Van Thuong, a recruiting officer at the Long An military subsector. The reason was not that he had committed so many crimes; it was because he had two wives, both living under the same roof. Besides having to account for many brothers and sisters, he had to give particulars concerning his two wives' relatives who happened to have grandparents—I forgot whether it was on the paternal or maternal side—who had concubines. Each night after we had gone to bed, Thuong would still be working away by the light of a candle with special permission of the *bodoi*. Each of us had to produce three copies of the account; Thuong's was as thick as a book. I could easily imagine the enormous amount of time he spent producing the three copies.

During this period our diet improved markedly; besides the usual ration of rice, we had soup made with water convolvulus and on every other day fish cooked with salt. But the anguish, mental exertion and lack of sleep involved in writing our accounts took its toll. By the time we had finished, we felt we had lost weight.

Those who had distinguished themselves in the fight against the communists or had relatives of distinction began to worry after the "account" business was completed. Clearly, this obligation to write accounts of past history was the first act of mental terrorism inflicted on us by the Northern victors. When making our declarations, we had to try to show sincerity and repentance for our "offenses";

Time passed slowly. Every day we worked at clearing the camp. Trang Lon had been a very big military base. The team responsible for receiving the daily ration of rice, counting the number of similar teams from other units, arrived at a figure of more than 22,000 junior officers now living in this camp. We had begun by clearing the space around our shed; after a few weeks, the area to be cleared widened to reach beyond the barbed-wire fence where a great number of artillery shells lay around. One morning while working in the carpentry shop, I suddenly heard a loud explosion; half an hour later I saw someone being carried into the infirmary. It was revealed that while working in the assigned area, he accidentally touched an M-79 bullet; M-79 bullets rarely failed to explode after being fired, but if that was the case, they would then explode at the slightest touch. This explosion tore off the man's arm and sent a shell fragment into his forehead; he died instantly, our first casualty. This was also the first opportunity for me to see how the *bodoi* treated the dead. They waited for their officer to come and examine the deceased. The officer instructed us to wrap the body in a rubberized piece of canvas and bury it immediately. It was all over by the midday meal, but we could not help talking for some time about that cold and unceremonious way of burying the dead.

The next day, as I was again working to repair some furniture salvaged from somewhere by the *bodoi*, I heard voices calling out, then the noise of people running. I rushed out to encounter a horrible scene. A corpse burned black was lying on the ground. Smoke still poured from the body, and the air was filled with the fishy smell of burned human fat. A teammate of the dead man said he was Bi, the pharmacist. He had seemed somewhat crazed since he finished writing his account, and that day, while sweeping the area, he collected all the gunpowder lying around and made it into a pile. Then he called out to his companions who were busy sweeping the ground, "Farewell, buddies! I am going now!" Everybody thought he was joking. Nobody knew he had a lighted butt in his hand until he set fire to the pile of powder he was sitting on. The powder went up instantly; the others rushed forward, but he was already a charred corpse when they reached him. The scene was ghastly.

The *bodoi* in charge ran forward, dispersed us, and sent us back to work with shouts. Then they fired three volleys into the air, and a moment later a squad arrived at the scene. This time they themselves wrapped the body in a poncho and carried it to the infirmary. Soon after, a number of my companions were instructed to bury the dead man. At lunch, everyone was discussing the pharmacist's death. Our morale, already low after writing the accounts, dropped still more because of the two deaths. The young fellows who usually joked on every occasion now became sullen and much less talkative.

One evening, as Long sat silently beside me, I said, "You seem thoughtful tonight, like a philosopher."

"Thinking about all this makes me very angry! I tell you if I had met with these *bodoi* before, they would not have lived to see these days." Then, without any urging from me, he began to relate the battles he had fought in the highlands and in Kampuchea. He spoke passionately of the counterattacks that had routed the *bodoi*. Finally, he said in a complaining voice, "My star destined me to be a soldier. I have taken part in many battles; a lot of my companions-in-arms have died or been wounded, but I went through the war without a scratch. In particular, when a battle was about to start, I was so calm, so clear-headed. And the decisions I took were always the right ones. Anyway, had I died then, I would have been spared this misery. Frankly speaking, I have not so far found myself inferior to them on any account, and yet, here I am, at their beck and call. If I could get hold of those generals who fled like rabbits, I would surely tear them to pieces!"

Thinking that a long conversation would attract attention, I sighed and left him to go to bed. In that crowded and derelict shed we slept so close to one another that we could easily hear the murmurs of someone lying on the far side. That night, Long was heard alternately sighing and cursing. Whom he cursed was not clear.

There were few real combat officers among us. They included Long, Thé, and Tien, a paratroop intelligence officer whose main job had been to request B-52 bombers when required (his declaration describing this job infuriated the *bodoi*). The rest of us were either medical or desk officers, or had been seconded, like me, to other government departments.

Each day spent in the camp led to a new discovery. Perhaps our situation had sharpened our senses. The sight of a new arrival or the noise of a vehicle coming to camp was sufficient to give rise to guesses about what would happen next. For some inexplicable reason, we had all begun to keep our belongings packed, ready for departure. Usually, we hung our quickly washed clothes on the barbed-wire fence, but now, without anyone actually saying so, we were all afraid of being transferred suddenly to another camp, so no one washed his clothes anymore for fear of having to carry them wet in his bag.

One day around noon we were ordered to return to our shed and prepare to assemble. Everybody hurried back to the shed to pack his belongings, the main worry being how to hide money where it wouldn't be pinched by one's companions. Some of the men had already been robbed. At around 3 P.M., the order came to carry all our baggage outside. It was absolutely forbidden to leave anything behind in the shed. There was no longer any doubt; we were going to be transferred. Where to?

After we had formed into lines, the *bodoi* arrived in force. They repeated the instruction on bringing everything out of the shed; then they went in and searched it thoroughly. Finally, Fatty Ha told us the reason for the assembly. "We have received instructions to give you permission to register all valuables you have brought with you in order to prevent theft. This is proof that the Revolution cares for your well-being. You will register rings, watches, money, and other valuables in your possession. Receipts will be issued. There will be a special team responsible for the receipt of monies. When you want some cash for your expenses, ask the team for it. We shall keep your watches, rings, and other jewelry for you; they will be returned to you when you are allowed to go home."

A *bodoi* was detailed to show us how to register personal jewelry. Pieces were to be wrapped in moisture-proof plastic together with a piece of paper with each individual's name and unit written on it. We had to queue to register our money in exchange for a receipt. The only valuables I had were my watch and ring, which I registered; as for money, I told myself that if I left it in the custody of the *bodoi*, I would not be able to spend it as I liked; therefore, I registered only a token amount. I hid the rest and intended to throw it away if I could no longer hide it. The registration of jewelry and money lasted until dusk.

In spite of all the hullabaloo, there was still no news of a transfer. The next day, when a *bodoi* came to my shop with a wooden case to be repaired, I asked him why he would want to repair such a heavy case.

"It's because it's heavy that I chose it. Cases have to be solid to avoid breakages. If your case is light and thin, it will break into pieces when your vehicle goes down a steep slope." I decided to try to stock some supplies for a possible move.

Soon after our arrival at the camp, the area around the fence close to the latrines had become a marketplace. At first, money had to be advanced before goods were received; later, the *bodoi* displayed all kinds of merchandise for sale, and money was exchanged for goods on the spot. That evening I asked Chiem Van Tuong, the navy intelligence lieutenant, to get me ten packets of instant noodles. Tuong was a very resourceful chap and was particularly skillful in making connections with the *bodoi*. Tuong told me to follow him. At the "market" I discovered that all of us had registered only part of our money and kept the rest.

I carefully hid the packets of instant noodles in my rucksack; this was the first time I had bought that much. I assumed that the camp management knew only too well about these transactions, in principle forbidden; if it really wanted to, it could have stamped out this practice simply by paying a surprise visit to the "market." A lot of us would have been caught red-handed. People in the other sectors were also engaged in trading with the *bodoi*, and some had even asked them to transmit letters to relatives living in Tay Ninh and had received replies, brought back by the *bodoi*. In reality, the majority of the *bodoi* had no hatred for us; on the contrary, some even showed real compassion toward us. However, they were very reserved; they, too, seemed not very happy with their situation.

From the very begining, we had had to learn how to deal not only with the *bodoi* but also with our campmates. We were a heterogeneous group. In a situation like ours, where one was subject to confusion and hopelessness, a morally unstable person could easily indulge in irrational or bad behavior. Given the opportunity, many would cheat in the distribution of food or steal from their companions. Others would try to acquire merit vis-à-vis the *bodoi*—at the expense of their campmates—in the hope of early release. We lived in a situation, therefore, where we felt ourselves threatened from all sides, not knowing when and from where the next blow would come and feeling helpless to defend ourselves.

In the account form, one question on family background had to do with relatives who had worked for the Revolution. We had to make a precise statement, and quite a few of us had answered the question in detail; but we were very secretive about it with our companions. Somehow, we knew that Vo Tai, a navy lieutenant, had a certificate issued to him by a district commissar praising him for having successfully negotiated the surrender to the Revolution of a South Vietnamese paratroop squad. One of our men happened to know the real story, which was completely different from the version cited in the certificate. On the day of the surrender, the incumbent South Vietnamese president, Duong Van Minh, ordered his troops to put down their arms and wait for the arrival of the North Vietnamese soldiers. The paratroop squad, stationed near the Gia Dinh Cancer Institute, threw down its arms at a spot close to Tai's brother-in-law's house. Tai lost no time in reporting that fact to the commissar who he knew had lived in the neighborhood for a long time and worked clandestinely for the Revolution. As a result, Tai was given that valuable certificate.

Two other fellows were also in possession of certificates issued by the Revolution. One was Nguyen Van Quang, known in civilian life as Tanker Quang from the fact that he had been the owner of two tanker trucks, which used to carry petrol for the Shell Oil Company. In the army, he had been the officer in charge of the Bien Hoa P.O.L. Depot.[11] In his account, he declared he had supplied petrol to the Revolution. But his main hope for an early release lay with his father-in-law, who was said to have died in the North. Only after the occupation of the South by the Northern army had his mother-in-law been informed that her husband not only was alive but appeared to occupy an important govenment post in Hanoi. After inquiry, it was revealed that he was in fact the vice minister for light industries. Tanker Quang reported for reeducation on his father-in-law's pledge that he would be sent home in a matter of days. He could not help being impatient waiting for his release, but after a month had passed without any news from his father-in-law, he began to use abusive language about him, such as, "You really cannot trust the Viet Cong to keep their word!" and "God help those who rely on them for help!" The other man with connections was Hoang Xuan Hai, a lieutenant in the artillery corps; his

---

[11]Petroleum, oil, and lubricants warehouse. South Vietnamese military adopted the U.S. Army nomenclature for the sake of convenience and to avoid misunderstanding.

uncle was a "propaganda and indoctrination" commissar of the Lao Dong (Labor) Party (renamed Communist Party after 1976). We paid particular attention to these men because they could be used by the *bodoi* to spy on us.

We came into contact with the *bodoi* responsible for supervising our team only at the evening roll call. It was then that offenses we had committed during the day were recited to us. Clearly, the informers had made very detailed reports. All of this was very disheartening. To think that among compatriots in misfortune there were still those who had the heart to harm others solely in the hope of personal favor from the *bodoi*!

After only one month—more or less—at the camp, we discovered we had changed a great deal. We were more reserved with each other, but at the same time we tried to get information. The most valuable source was the *bodoi* themselves, who were usually very secretive. We watched them closely, trying to divine what was going to happen. These last few days, they were busy making preparations as if for an imminent move. They asked the carpentry shop to make small wooden boxes for them; they washed, folded, and put away their new clothes. They bustled about selling merchandise in the hope of more profit. Coming across each other, they exchanged information and addresses. Preparations were the most obvious in Logistics. Things such as jute sacks and the aluminum basins for fish sauce and salt that were loaned to us when we came for the rations were ordered returned.

One morning, the *bodoi* woke each other up while it was still dark; soon their area was alive with bustle and animation. Hearing this, we got up at once, folded mats and mosquito nets, had a quick bite of what was left that was still edible, packed our belongings, and got ready for departure. When the time came to go to work and no *bodoi* came to fetch us, we were certain that something unusual was going to happen. At 10 A.M., the *bodoi* swarmed into our place, ordering us to go out and form into lines, taking all our baggage. The *bodoi* throroughly searched the shed, then went through our baggage. Knives, scissors, glass bottles, and all metal articles were confiscated. They were overjoyed on coming across some shiny nail clippers. These they immediately pocketed; some even showed them to comrades as if they were prizes they had won. The search lasted for two whole hours. Talking to each other while eating our noon meal, we discovered that many of us had had razor blades, a lighter, nail clippers, or money confiscated.

After we had eaten, we were instructed to cook the evening meal, distribute it immediately, and prepare to move. Soon after food distribution, we were brought to an open space where we fell in line and waited for our transport. We waited until late afternoon with no sign of any vehicles. Then at dusk, convoy after convoy drove into the camp. We had the impression that the whole camp was to be on the move.

Long and I and some other healthy fellows were detailed to help Logistics move equipment and materials. They took down all the corrugated iron roofs, barbed-wire fences, and telephone lines, stacking the coils of barbed wire and telephone wire in the trucks together with plywood in various stages of construction and sacks of rice, salt, dried fish, and kitchen utensils. When we finished, all that remained of the camp were the shed skeletons. The *bodoi* dismantled everything that was usable. We told ourselves they might be planning to return to the North.

When it was dark enough, we were ordered to eat then go to the latrine before getting in the trucks. We went through the same misery as before—crowding into a completely covered vehicle and submerging ourselves in the stifling heat and stale air inside. We were very anxious about our destination. Long said, "This time, I am certain we are going to the North."

Meanwhile I was thinking hard. We had piled sack after sack of fresh water convolvulus, crates containing pots of hot pepper plants, and bushes of lemon grass onto the trucks reserved for the Logistics team. I surmised that we were not being transferred to a camp in North Vietnam because those things would spoil or die on such a journey. Therefore, we were not going that far. After half an hour, the truck became unbearably hot, and the *bodoi* sitting at the back agreed to let us roll up the tarpaulin to let in some fresh air. We were now able to get a look around us.

The convoy was not rolling very fast, the trucks keeping an interval of about five meters between them. Strikingly, every truck had only one headlight, the right one. That was a characteristic of a North Vietnamese army convoy. Regardless of whether the vehicle was brand new or not, the headlight on the left side was always removed. Was it to avoid detection by enemy planes? Or was it to economize on batteries and bulbs? Whatever the reason, we always saw a single line of lights whenever the convoy negotiated a bend in the road.

Bodoi were stationed on both sides of the road we followed, which meant that our journey had been carefully planned. The darkness was slightly pierced by flickers of oil lamps lighting the few thatched huts along the road. The homes of the poor peasants of the South are open to the winds, as open and simple as the hearts of their owners! We caught glimpses of people silhouetted inside the huts looking on as the convoy rumbled by.

After quite a long time we began to realize that we were heading in the direction of Saigon. The news was passed on to everybody in the truck. Then, we saw in the distance flashes of blue mercury light. So it was true! Before us was the city of Saigon. Suddenly, we were trembling with excitement; it was as if we were going to join a person whom we loved dearly. We had been deprived of the sight of this light—a token of civilization—for more than a month; now that it appeared suddenly before us, we could not help being moved almost to tears.

When we had reported for reeducation, we had thought we would be given the opportunity to learn about the new regime and maybe to live with it. But now we clearly realized that the men sitting in this truck were all prisoners. We did not know our destination or how we were going to be treatd by the *bodoi* from now on. Our collective impression was that harsh treatment was to be expected. After more than a month of a life not unlike that of prisoners, subject to constant surveillance and privation, and, especially, forced to write an account of our past lives designed to make us guilty of offenses we never had any idea of, we realized that all the ideas and beliefs that had constituted the moral and spiritual foundation of our lives had been thrown into utter confusion. Until recently, we had firmly believed in the usefulness and intrinsic value of such occupations as teachers, engineers, doctors, nurses—and of soldiers whose duty had been to protect the country, freedom, and democracy. But now we were turned into criminals about to pay for having engaged in those very occupations!

It was blatantly unjust and cruel! Our generation in the South was suddenly charged with wrongdoing because we had not lived in the North, had not been used to the way of reasoning of the Northern people, had not accepted their ideology. Our skin was the same color, we spoke the same language, our ethnic origin and geographic location were the same, and yet we were completely different from them. When Northern soldiers poured into the South, they had appeared to our eyes as country folks who had strayed into a big town. Despite the fact that they had weapons and we had none, that they were the victors and we the vanquished, our first impression was that they had many things in common with us. Therefore, some exchanges of views had been attempted in the hope of a mutual understanding.

It had been useless. Living in their company, observing their way of life and thinking, and especially experiencing our treatment in the camp, we had come to realize that between us and them was a barrier that could never be overcome. The position they had adopted for themselves and for us, which they forced us to accept, was that they were the People and we were not, even in this southern part of the country, where they were the minority and we the majority.

Later, we discovered that those first impressions only touched the outward appearance of things. Reality, deep down, was far different.

Chapter 2

Camp Two: Xuan Loc I

As we approached the outskirts of Saigon, the convoy changed direction and headed northeast, passing Thu Duc and, finally, Bien Hoa. Reaching a straight and deserted section of the road, the convoy slowed to a stop. The *bodoi* deployed along the road, and we were permitted to get down one by one to relieve ourselves. Back in our vehicles, we sat waiting for a long time; it was still dark. Finally, the trucks restarted their engines and resumed the journey, the dull and continuous rumbling of the motors lulling us to a fitful sleep.

With a start, I opened my eyes; it was dawn in its rosy loveliness. Looking behind us, we saw orchard after orchard of Javanese rambutans, a famous product of this northeastern part of the Delta. The convoy was heading toward Xuan Loc—the capital of Long Khanh Province—which lay on the road to the North. Is that where we were headed? Suddenly, the convoy turned left and entered Long Khanh. The houses on both sides of the streets still had their doors and windows closed for the night. One of the men said softly, "This is the area around the municipal stadium. We are now entering what used to be the regional military subsector headquarters and the Eighteenth Division headquarters."

The convoy drove along a road bordered by barbed-wire fences. Beyond were a few scattered barracks, so we expected to find better accommodation than at Trang Lon. It had rained here during the night, and the truck slid and lurched on the muddy road. When we came to a stop, a voice ordered "Everybody out!" We climbed down and passed our bags from hand to hand. Standing on the wet grass, we looked around for the buildings we hoped would be there, but all we saw were desolate barracks with most of the corrugated iron roofs and walls removed; only a few of them looked fit to be lived in.

It was now full daylight; people began to move about on the road outside the camp, looking at us with curiosity. We still had our bags on our shoulders because there was no dry spot around.

At last, a group of *bodoi* came to lead us to a building, which had probably been used as a vehicle repair shop, judging by the patches of oil on the cement floor. It had a steel frame and only a few corrugated iron sheets left on its roof. Guided by our Trang Lon camp experience, we immediately went off in search of building materials.

By the end of the day we had patched up our "house," which looked rather strange with its roof and walls made of assorted discarded materials—pieces of cardboard, jute sacks, rubber mudguards from M-113 personnel carriers, and such. (The camp had previously housed an ARVN [Army of the Republic of Vietnam] armored unit.) Each of us was allotted a 70-cm-wide space to lie on, our belongings placed at the head of the space. Only when night came did we realize that, as a sleeping place, a cement floor is extremely cold and damp. (At Trang Lon, the floor of our shed was rammed-down soil and I hardly felt cold.) The next day, when detailed to clear the place of trash, we tried to find something we could use to cover the floor. I had the good luck to come across two M-113 mudguards, which I used as a mattress. I was more fortunate than those of my companions who had to sleep on a piece of cardboard or even a thin sheet of plastic. The first week at Long Khanh camp was spent in making improvements to our dwelling place; afterwards, we worked at clearing the area around the *bodoi*'s quarters. We still had to eat the moldy rice supplied by Chinese aid.

One day, when tidying a place littered with sheets from a copybook, I managed to conceal the clean ones to use as toilet paper. That evening, after the meal, I occupied myself by tearing up the paper and dividing it into small bundles for later use. That was how I came across the copies of lessons that had served for political indoctrination of the *bodoi*. On one page, scrawled in a poor hand, were the words "the situation in Saigon." I read that the city had a population of 3 million, including 400,000 workers, 300,000 prostitutes, and 100,000 hoodlums. These figures were underlined in red. The lesson ended with advice to "exercise the utmost vigilance because this is the den of the reactionary military power and puppet government; we must avoid any contact whatsoever with the local people."

Later on, I learned that many of my companions had also picked up sheets of paper lying about that dealt with the same subject. This helped us understand why it was more difficult to strike up a conversation with the *bodoi* at this camp than with those at Trang Lon. The camp was surrounded by a double fence, and the *bodoi* always made their rounds or stood guard outside the outer fence, so there was no way to make contact with them, let alone ask them to buy things for us. Each day, a *bodoi*—one of a group of "study monitors," each responsible for one company—came for the morning and evening roll calls. A special amenity was provided us: an infirmary for the sick.

Before we had left Trang Lon camp, many of the men had begun to get scabies, perhaps due to the dirty well water. The soil around the well was sandy, and dirty water on the ground seeped into it. The small quantity of soap and toothpaste we had brought with us had been used up after the first few weeks, and sanitary conditions became worse and worse. Scabies soon became an insoluble problem. Because we were sleeping so close together, it gradually spread from person to person. Each day, I watched anxiously as the disease got closer to where I slept.

We asked the *bodoi* for help, but instead of giving us medicine, they advised us to look for guava or cassia leaves to rub ourselves with before bathing. Some of the *bodoi* were kind enough to get the leaves for us, but this treatment had no effect. Our bodies had lost their resistance, and the number of sick increased every day.

A fellow in my squad named Phuoc, a native of Hau Giang Province, had a talent for catching live snakes with his bare hands and a strange way of eating them. Whenever he caught a snake, he instantly opened its belly with his fingernails at the exact position of the gall bladder, which he took out and swallowed uncooked. This habit of his earned him the nickname Phuoc Ran (literally, Phuoc Snake). He liked to chat with me, and one day he told me that the best preventive measure against scabies was to swallow a few raw snake gall bladders each week. Since the Long Khanh area swarmed with snakes of every kind and description, Phuoc managed to catch one or two almost every day; after swallowing the gall bladder, he would choose the best portion of the reptile to grill for his meal. This diet was perhaps the reason for his healthy complexion and freedom from scabies. I was panicky enough to ask Phuoc to provide me with some gall bladders. I felt some disgust at first, but I soon found out that swallowing a raw snake gall bladder was not so terrible as I had thought. Just plucked out of the belly of the snake it would still be warm, its outer skin intact; it was like swallowing raw chicken meat. There were no aftereffects.

Each day while we worked at clearing the camp, a few of us would be detailed to look for metal sheets to be used in erecting a hall where reeducation sessions would take place. Preparations for reeducation made everybody glad because they renewed our hope of being allowed to return home at the completion of the "course."

As we waited impatiently for reeducation to begin, life became harsher, especially where our daily fare was concerned. We had only salt to eat with rice; fish was distributed on rare occasions and in negligible quantities. After a short time at the Long Khanh camp, everybody had become all skin and bones. One day I came across Chiem Van Tuong as he was sawing the end off an ampule of "calcium corbiere" solution. Only after much urging on my part did he disclose that he had asked the male nurse at the infirmary to buy tonic for him. The next day, I got permission to go to the infirmary with Tuong; the result was very satisfactory. I gave the nurse some money for which I could obtain any tonic I wanted. In addition, I asked him to buy some sugar for me, if that was possible. I stressed that it did not matter if the price was high, provided he could get the sugar.

The following day, I put on a loose shirt to go to the infirmary. The nurse said, as he handed me a small parcel, "I have used up the money you gave me. Take care when taking this back; we'll be in big trouble if you don't!" I went back to our shed, bending my body as if I was suffering from stomach pains and clutching the package hidden inside my shirt. I thrust the parcel deep inside my rucksack and only opened it when nobody was around. It contained a box of calcium solution and twenty-seven tablets of brown sugar, weighing approximately one kilogram.

The sugar looked dirty but when I put it in my mouth, it tasted oh, so delicious! I had never suspected that sugar could be so succulent, so refreshing! From that day on, at each meal, I surreptitiously took out a half-tablet of sugar, which I ate with rice. My body became much stronger. From time to time, my diet was enriched with a chunk of roasted snake. So, I had sugar and I had meat! Consequently, I was able to keep my spirits up better than most of my companions. In particular, I was one of only six detainees not infected with scabies out of a total of sixty-two. In the whole camp, over 90 percent of the inmates were estimated to be infected.

The scabies situation became worse and worse. There were moments when I thought that some of my companions had contracted leprosy because they had sores all over their bodies, oozing smelly pus that caused their clothes to stick to their skin. Whenever they took their clothes off, blood and bits of skin came off in various places, and it was very painful. We had to ask some men to take care of the most serious cases and do such chores as draw water from the well and boil salted water for them to wash their bodies. They could not do these things themselves, for their hands were covered with suppurating sores. Besides, we did not want them to use the well or wash themselves near it for fear of contaminating the water, which, among other things, was used for cooking.

Things got even worse when the nurse's purchasing of medicine and other goods in the local market was discovered. At first, the number of people involved was small, and the transaction was limited to the purchase of medicine. Perhaps the experience some of the *bodoi* had gained at Trang Lon caused discipline at this camp to be much more stringent. Each time we tried to enter into conversation with a *bodoi*, we got answers that smacked of propaganda, one identical to another. The case of the nurse was an exception, and it constituted our only way to communicate with the outside world. But gradually, both we and the nurse became careless and the transactions too conspicuous. Finally, he was transferred to another unit and was said to have been subjected to disciplinary measures.

Actually, the action taken against the nurse originated from a rivalry between factions of the *bodoi* themselves. Our battalion—coded D4—had three individuals addressed as commanders. At first, we were amazed at the command structure of the *bodoi*'s armed forces and were unable to understand why there should be that many commanders in one unit. Later, it was explained that this was due to the fixed division of duties among the three. The political commander, with the rank of commissar, represented the Party; the military and administrative head was called the executive commander; and the supply and distribution of food and other necessities fell under the reponsibility of the logistics commander. The military commander of D4 was a Southerner named Hung; the political commissar, Sau, was also from the South; the logistics commander, who was also in charge of our reeducation, was a Northerner.

While at work clearing the camp or doing various chores, we usually witnessed instances of rivalry between the Northerners and Southerners. For instance, the Northern commander would change orders that the other two had given us. When Commander Sau instructed us to clear an area to widen a pathway, the Northerner told us to hoe up the place to plant sweet potatoes instead; sometimes, while we were working under Commander Hung's order, we would suddenly be told by the Northern commander to stop work and follow him to do something else. If we ventured to remind him of Hung's order, the reply would be, "Forget it! Just follow me!" Hung, on hearing our explanation for not doing our assigned work, would shake his head but show no other reaction.

One day, when the nurse—a Northerner—was in the midst of selling medicines and other goods to us, one of the Southern commanders, as if just passing by, entered the infirmary and caught him in the act. The next day, the nurse did not show up and an instruction was issued for those of us who had given money to him to inform the camp administration and get a refund. Quite a few men who had given money to the nurse, and even letters for him to stamp and post in town, became so fearful of being discovered that they lost sleep and appetite.

From then on, we were deprived of almost everything. From time to time, some vegetables or sea fish were distributed, but the distribution was irregular and the quantities minimal. Besides, those with scabies were afraid of eating sea fish. As for me, I still had a few packets of instant noodles left; these I ground into powder, using an empty bottle, and ate as a substitute for salted ground sesame. My provision of sugar, though used sparingly, was finally exhausted, and I chided myself for not having saved some in anticipation of sickness. Some of the men craved sugar so much that they plucked the stems of dried maize and chewed them because their sweet taste was vaguely similar to sugar cane.

Each day, I was detailed to search for usable metal sheets to cover the roof of a big building, probably a former meeting hall. But metal sheets were hard to find, and the work dragged on endlessly. The 1975 rainy season had arrived, and only a quarter of the roof was covered. The majority of the inmates worked at hoeing a plot of land to plant peanuts, but their progress was slow. Most of them had never used a hoe before, and with their bodies weakened by scabies and malnutrition and their morale low, they very easily succumbed to fatigue. Some developed fevers after only a few days of this work. I had played tennis in my early youth and I seemed to have more bodily strength than most of my companions. Besides, roofing the meeting hall required less physical effort than hoeing the ground.

A fellow in my team named Binh was a mechanical wizard; he first tried his hand at turning metal sheets into water pails. Later the *bodoi* asked him to make suitcases for them. The suitcases he turned out were very solid and pretty, but quite heavy; an empty one would weight as much as seven or eight kilos. Binh suggested using aluminum sheets instead, and, as a result, I was instructed by the study monitors to search for aluminum sheets, which were even harder to find than metal ones.

Despite the strict discipline at the camp, which forbade transactions between the *bodoi* and the detainees, we suspected that some of the *bodoi* were not averse to making some profit by buying things for us. A number of them also managed to make extra money by other means. One day, I saw a *bodoi* steal into the area where we lived, pull down some still usable metal sheets, carry them over to the fence, and put them down on the ground. He then attached to each sheet a long cord and slid the end of the cord under the fence. I did not grasp the purpose of this maneuver until the next day, when I got up on the roof of the building to do my usual work and saw two *bodoi* drive a three-wheel Lambretta scooter up to the fence. They simply tugged at the rope and the metal sheets slid slowly and smoothly over the grass onto the road. In an instant the scooter, loaded with the sheets, was gone. Only then did I understand why whole metal sheets were so hard to find and why so many roofs and walls were devoid of them. Because aluminum sheets were light, of a good size, easy to move, and, especially, could be sold at a very high price, almost none could be found. Still, we had to hunt for them now to make suitcases for the study monitors! From time to time, we came across one; if it was part of the roof of a shed detainees lived in, we had to wait until they were out at work to remove it and replace it with a much heavier corrugated iron sheet, all under the supervision of a monitor.

At Trang Lon we thought we had reached the bottom of human misery, but here we were under tighter control and more deprived; our life was more miserable, and the diseases we suffered from were more serious. The *bodoi* had only one kind of medicine against all forms of disease: antimalaria tablets produced in China! Each time after examining a patient, the nurse would either prescribe the use of leaves or herbs or would give him some pills; in the latter case, whether the illness was headache, cold, flu, diarrhea, or something more serious with suspicion of bacterial contamination, the treatment would invariably be antimalaria tablets. There were more than thirty medical doctors of various ages in my unit. Whenever we were sick, we asked the doctors to examine us and diagnose the illness; then we would go to the infirmary to request sick leave.

One day a fellow named Xuong, working at clearing rubbish from a patch of land, came across a detonator; he tried to take it apart, intending to use the case to hold cigarettes, when it suddenly exploded in his hand and ripped open his thumb and index finger. Taken to the infirmary, he was brought to the regiment's dispensary for emergency treatment. Before that, he was examined by our doctors and his wound hurriedly dressed. The doctors thought the injury was not too serious and predicted at most the probable amputation of the injured fingertips. More than a month later, Xuong returned to the camp and showed us his wound. To our shock—especially our doctors'—his entire right hand had been amputated from the wrist! Xuong told us that the regimental surgeon had opened the wound with a scalpel, but because of the lack of antibiotics, gangrene developed. Finally, the surgeon decided to amputate. Xuong then was given several injections and some antibiotic medication, and the wound healed relatively rapidly. He became fed up with life and attempted to commit suicide, but we managed to dissuade him. From time to time he sat in a corner, holding his head and crying his heart out. His misfortune bacame a subject of discussion among the inmates, and this was reported to the *bodoi* by the informers. A number of surgeons among us were heavily reprimanded and threatened with the entry of the "offense" into their personal records.

Hardship and privation naturally led to complaints, but the informers, in order to acquire merit in the eyes of the *bodoi*, distorted reports and made false accusations concerning such complaints. Many an evening at roll call, we were obliged to remain in line for an entire hour to listen to the study monitor make "constructive comments" or, in plain Vietnamese, severely reprimand offend-ers. The *bodoi* particularly disliked jokes. They seemed to suffer from inferiority complexes and to laugh openly in front of them was an offense that was sometimes severely dealt with. Once a *bodoi*, leading us out to work at clearing the camp, startled us by shouting, "Stop, all of you!" When everybody had stopped, the *bodoi*, who was older than many of the others—the average age was twenty—began to rebuke us severely. "You want to make fun of the Revolution, don't you? Do you know that your lives are in our hands? What are you laughing at? You're in a very merry mood, I suppose!"

We learned that on the way to our work site some of our young fellows had been playfully joking with each other, but the *bodoi* thought they had been making fun of him. Despite the reprimands, threats of longer detention, and reports of informers, our young men kept on telling jokes and stories, some newly invented, just to make fun of the stupid *bodoi*.

It was evident that the jokers were reported on, but so were those who did not say anything. It seemed the informers had to make one or two reports each day to show their zeal, so they sometimes had to concoct something. One evening when the study monitor came for roll call, he singled some of us out and addressed us in these threatening words. "Some of you like Vu, Tuong, and Cuc have so far kept silent, but we know what's in your minds and what you're attempting to do. You have yet to 'reeducate' yourselves. If you still oppose the Revolution, the Revolution will go on keeping you in order to reeducate you. And we will reeducate you until you are really improved. We'd rather keep you here until you're dead and buried than release you when you have not yet completed your reeducation, lest you should engage in antirevolutionary activities."

Listening to his words, we stood transfixed with fear; we wondered what it was that that the informers had told the *bodoi* that could lead to such an outburst. Afterward, Long teased old Mr. Cuc again. "Really, my dear Mr. Cuc, God has abandoned you! The more you pray, the more 'tainted' your personal records have become! When will you be able to return home?"

That evening at roll call, Long became the target for reprimand and threat. We began to search for the informer to punish him as he deserved; to our surprise, we found that there were at least three or four informers among the sixty detainees in our platoon. Among the three or four suspects, a fellow named Vo Tai seemed the most obvious. He was a native of Thua Thien Province and a former navy lieutenant. His parents had died when he was still a child, so he went to live with his brother-in-law in the married military quarters behind the Gia Dinh Cancer Institute. His brother-in-law, a former intelligence officer, had been arrested shortly after the fall of Saigon, and his family had had no news of him since; perhaps his "crime" had been too serious for reeducation. In spite of all that, Vo Tai seemed to be set on acquiring merit in the eyes of the *bodoi* in the hope of early release. Besides, he firmly believed in the value of the certificate that had been issued to him by the Binh Thanh district commissar attesting to his good service to the Revolution.

The young fellows in my team discussed the possibility of getting rid of Vo Tai, but the older members felt the moment had not yet arrived for us to resort to this drastic measure. In particular, our team leader, Phan Van Tuong, argued against it; he begged and insisted and even spread the rumor that release was imminent. "I've heard the study monitor say that when we have completed our political education, most of us will be sent home with the exception of those who have comitted serious offenses; they will stay a little while longer." This immediately placated many of us, and we swallowed our anger. At every moment and in every camp there was a rumor going about that a great number of detainees were soon to be released. I believed the rumor to be spread by the *bodoi* in an effort to prevent trouble that could arise from despair. But then sometimes I thought that it was invented by the detainees in an attempt to deceive those around them and even themselves. In that context, the so-called information given by Phan Van Tuong went the rounds of the camp very rapidly. Shortly thereafter, on my way out to work at roofing a building reserved for the *bodoi*, I met some men from another platoon who stopped me to ask whether it was true that the study monitor had told us we would be released soon after completing our political education.

It could be said that our life in the camp consisted solely of trying to realize three main objectives: first, to look for anything that was edible; second, to hunt for information among members of other teams; and, third, to observe the *bodoi*, how they lived, what they said and did.

We had only salt or dried fish to eat now and then with rice and hardly any vegetables at all. Whenever we came across wild greens thought to be edible, we picked them to take back and cook in a tin can when evening came. Our usual joke was, "Just take it! It's refreshing. If it does not help your height, it must help your width" (i.e., it can't hurt). Snake catching had become common practice, and now rats and lizards, even, were caught, grilled, and eaten. Within a few months, nothing edible remained around the place where we lived. Snakes, rats, lizards, wild cress, amaranth, purslane—all had disappeared.

As for bits of information or, rather, rumors, they had become wilder and wilder. Once, someone spread the "news" that the Revolution was having talks with the Americans regarding war reparations that the latter were supposed to pay; if satisfaction was obtained, all *nguy* would be released!

Pursuing our third objective—to observe the *bodoi*'s way of life—we began to realize that they were trying to imitate us more each day. Soon after arriving at this camp I found a chair with broken legs, which, using improvised tools, I nailed down at the foot of a big tree. After each distribution of rice, I went to sit in the chair to eat my meal more comfortably. Most men sat on the verandah outside the shed or walked back and forth in the shade of a tree while eating. The *bodoi* had rather uncouth eating habits. Rice, vegetables, and dried fish were portioned out into aluminum washbasins; at mealtime they sat in groups of six around the basins, each armed with an aluminum bowl and a pair of chopsticks. If the basin contained soup, they just tilted it to pour the soup into their bowls but slopping most of it all over the ground. After they had finished eating, they drank their tea from the same bowl. They washed their own bowls and chopsticks, so the kitchen hands only had to wash the woks, pans, and basins.

After a few weeks at the camp, we had managed to turn discarded rifle racks into "dining" tables, and each of us had his own chair. As a result, we were reported by the informers to be still clinging to a life of comfort. Some were even accused of having stolen rice sacks and stuffing them with dried grass to use as mattresses. The study monitor reprimanded us several times for having petty bourgeois habits and warned us that he would subject us to an indefinite period of reeducation if we did not change our ways.

One day Commander Hung came to the building where I was working on the roof and called up to me. "Do you know anything about carpentry?"

"Yes," I answered. "I have done some carpentry work." The next day I was detailed to repair tables and chairs that had been salvaged by the *bodoi*. I wondered where all the tables and chairs that had furnished the former base had gone, compelling the *bodoi* to collect pieces fit only for the junk yard. I gathered a few volunteers to do the work. Nobody had any experience with joinery, and we worked by trial and error. Fortunately, the *bodoi* declared themselves satisfied with the results, and we began repairing office furniture. Each of the camp commanders was very happy to get his own desk and chair. After this we were ordered to repair beds, using bed frames the *bodoi* had salvaged from somewhere. Up to now they had been sleeping on planks placed on piles of bricks, with two or three bricks to a pile. The result of our first week's work was that every commander had a room of his own, complete with desk, chair, and bed.

I was reluctant to go back to my exhausting work on the roofs, especially because the weather now was so changeable, from intense heat to rain to wind. I therefore requested permission to make tables and chairs for the mess. I suggested, "Seeing that you have to squat uncomfortably on the ground to have your meals, we propose to make some tables and benches for the mess so that you will feel more at ease when eating."

The chief monitor, a Northerner named Hau, cut me short. "Don't talk nonsense! There's nothing uncomfortable in the way the *bodoi* are having their meals. Now that you are here to be reeducated, you still think of comfort! That's a completely wrong way of thinking! You have to learn to endure hardship. That'll be for your own good." Seeing that the matter had turned to my disadvantage, I pretended to be busy, noisily hammering in a nail.

There must have been a discussion of my suggestion because the next day, while I was busy repairing a chair, Commander Sau came to speak to me. "I have been informed of the proposal you made yesterday about making tables and benches for the mess. I agree with the suggestion. I give you the permission to select a few more men and commence work immediately. You can dismantle the little wooden house at the other end of the yard and use the wood."

That evening, I asked among my companions for volunteers, saying, "We're going to work under a roof, out of the sun and rain, and besides, the *bodoi* will let us have some tea and smoke a pipe or two." The men vied with one another to volunteer, and I selected five healthy-looking ones for the work. The doctors and teachers who had not been selected because of their frailty protested angrily with a hint of retaliation. "Damn! Do you want to set up your own faction? All right, go ahead—" I hastened to explain that dismantling the wooden house would be very hard work, especially when we had to do much sawing.

A few days later, we carried to the mess a number of roughly made tables and benches; there was even a stand for the tea container. Hearing about this, regimental headquarters sent in an officer to "observe and assess," and as a result, all the other battalions were instructed to set up their own carpentry teams to produce tables and chairs. From then on, the *bodoi* always used the tables and benches when having their meals; sometimes they held their indoctrination and singing sessions in the mess instead of on the grassy patch outside, where they had previously met in the evenings. The *bodoi*'s living quarters had electricity, but ours did not.

After the tables and benches for the mess were finished, we were instructed to repair tables, chairs, beds, and even wardrobes for the lower ranking *bodoi*. We did not know where they had come across those pieces of furniture, which grew in number every day and were in various stages of disrepair. Many of the *bodoi* asked me in private to pay special attention to their items and repair them as soon as possible. I agreed, and we were paid with either a few cigarettes or a pinch of tobacco, the kind used for water pipes. We asked them to buy goods for us, but they refused on the pretext that they had been forbidden to do this by their superior officers. However, from time to time, a *bodoi* would approach us, intent on selling the cigarettes they had been issued but had not smoked. These were a brand called Chien Si Cong Hoa (Fighters of the Republic) produced for the former Army of the Republic of Vietnam. Still visible on the outer cover were the words "To eliminate Communism is to love one's Country."

In contrast to the less than perfect *bodoi* at Trang Lon who surreptitiously sold us instant noodles at night, the ones at this camp appeared to have been thoroughly indoctrinated. They put on airs, quite impressed with their own importance. Each time they opened their mouths, it was to boast that people in the North were much better off than people in the South. When asked what life in the North was like, they would answer, "Oh, we have plenty of everything. For example, if you want to eat chicken, it's always available." We pretended to complain. "Life is very hard here in the South. If we want chicken, we have to save up for an entire month to buy one."

One *bodoi*, eighteen or nineteen years old, saw an opportunity to propagandize. "Truth to tell, the South is also wealthy; but you have been heavily exploited by the Americans and *nguy*, and that's what has made your life so difficult. From now on, the Revolution will devote itself to rebuilding the South. You will see, the people will soon be able to enjoy life as much as they please."

It was hard to keep from laughing out loud; I had heard those words repeated again and again. Probably the argument and assertion had been part of his indoctrination. We felt much pity for him.

Conversation with the childlike *bodoi* never failed to provide us with a new subject for discussion. Their proselytizing efforts failed to make converts of us, but they shed light on their way of thinking and their conception of the South, which was very remote from reality. After only a few months' living in the South, however, the *bodoi* began to show signs of the influence the Southern way of life was having on them. We began to see them wearing wristwatches, and a few of them carried small radios, which they played at maximum volume. They also began to smoke cigarettes. In our presence, they would ostentatiously produce a cigarette, light it, and take short puffs, then blow the smoke out very quickly, the way new smokers do.

Among the study monitors was a simple and candid fellow named Dong, a native of Quang Binh Province. He often talked to us, assuring us that as our "offenses" were not too serious, that we should be treated with leniency and not harshly like other "culprits." Sometimes, seeing that we badly needed tobacco, he bought some for us, taking no profit for himself.

After three months at the camp, everybody took to smoking water pipes because the tobacco was easier to find. We competed with each other to see who could make the most resonant sound. Little by little we became real addicts; each evening we challenged each other to see who could draw on the pipe the longest, leaving some giddy and faint. One of the beginners was Dr. Bui Tran Anh, who went earnestly about his smoking and soon became one of the best performers. When short of tobacco we would look for Monitor Dong and asked him to buy some for us. Sometimes, in the midst of work, we would yawn loudly and blame the shortage of tobacco for our lack of energy. Dong became quite attached to us. One day we induced him to speak about the North by asking, "We've heard that our fellow citizens in the North can now afford to mix less sweet potato, manioc, or maize in their rice. Is that true?"

Dong replied candidly, "No, there's still not much improvement because we have not yet produced enough rice to meet the needs of the population. Recently, I've been home on leave in the province of Thanh Hoa, and people there still have to mix about 40 percent potatoes or cassava roots in their rice. Anyway, that can be considered an improvement; during the war, vegetables or grains other than rice in the mixture were often more than 60 percent. Many families had rice only once a day; at other meals they either had maize, sweet potato, or manioc. Between harvests, all they had to eat for months was manioc or sweet potato." Dong also said that the roads in the South were excellent, much better than in the North. Beyond Quang Tri Province, when vehicles going North entered Vinh Linh district in the northern sector of the demilitarized zone, the road became bumpy and very dusty. "We have to recognize that the South has a more modern economic structure than the North," he concluded. He was the only *bodoi* I came across during the whole reeducation period who frankly conceded that the North suffered from shortage and underdevelopment.

Since our arrival at Long Khanh camp, we had been ordered to assemble from time to time to listen to readings from newspapers. Only propaganda articles claiming, for example, that "the whole nation is now enthusiastically preparing itself to take the road toward socialism" were read. Except for this, we were almost completely cut off from news of the outside world. After a reading, the senior study monitor, Hau, would say somthing like, "Can you see that? People outside have made tremendous progress; meanwhile, you have as yet to be reeducated. In other words, you're still behind the times. You cannot be released now because the People will not leave you alone."

Listening to him, one would think that there was much activity outside the camp devoted to learning about the new regime and its ideology, that the whole population had now been converted to communism. However, we were able to get some information about the situation outside because we had a few occasions to go out to places where the local inhabitants were going about their daily business.

When we first came to Long Khanh camp, we cooked our meals with kindling wood supplied by contractors. Later on, it appeared that the prices had been raised, so the camp command decided to have the inmates go to the nearby rubber plantation to cut wood for the kitchen. They said that "money could be saved that way and used for additional food for the inmates." For us, cutting wood on the plantation would be a welcome opportunity to see the outside world.

The first day we were to go out, everybody volunteered. Even the weaklings among us asked to go. There were then about 1,200 inmates, but only 100 at a time were allowed to go out to cut wood. The business of selecting people gave rise to discussion, even harsh exchanges. But after the first day of work, there was no more dispute. The *bodoi* had set a definite route for us to follow, bypassing the town; security was very strict. At the worksite, near Xuan Loc village, men from the local self-defense forces were deployed all around the area. The wood we were to get was from the dead rubber trees. If a tree had already fallen, our work was fairly easy; otherwise, we had to fell the tree with chopping knives, then saw the trunk into lengths that one man could carry on his shoulders. The sawing proved difficult with our rudimentary saws, so we eventually cut the trunks into lengths for two persons to carry. Our limbs shook from the exertion required to fell the trees; carrying the logs all the way back to camp was even harder. We paused to rest several times, but still we were fagged out at the end of the day's work.

Our strength had greatly diminished since we had reported for reeducation some six months before. Even with our two meager meals a day—two bowls of rice eaten with salt and cooked bindweed and, from time to time, a piece of dried fish—we would not have felt particularly hungry if it had not been for this hard labor. Still, the main cause of our weakness was our flagging morale. From the moment we began to realize that we could not find out a date for our release, everybody felt morally spent. Sickness increased, as did arguments and fighting among ourselves. We did not realize that we hadn't the strength for hard work until we began wood cutting and log carrying. After we got back to camp on the first day, several of the men fell sick and did not recover until two or three days later. We also saw our hopes of going out and meeting people on the outside dashed, because of both the close watch and our exhaustion. From then on, nobody argued about his "right" to go out to work.

Those of us who were strong enough continued with the work and had some luck; as I was in relatively better health than most of my companions, I was always in the work party. The surveillance of the first days became less strict as time went on. At the beginning, controls were strict because the work was considered experimental, and officers from regimental headquarters came to observe how it was organized. When the work became routine, the *bodoi* themselves decided that for a change we would go through the market area on our way to and from the plantation. This decision was of great benefit to us.

At first, the local folks just stood watching us with pity in their eyes. Then one day, an elderly woman ran toward us from the roadside, a bunch of bananas in her hand. Giving each of us one banana, she said to the *bodoi*, "I guess the good sirs won't have the heart to forbid me giving some bananas to these poor fellows!"

The nearest *bodoi*, taken by surprise, did not know how to react other than to rush forward and pull the old lady away, shouting, "All of you must give the bananas back; you cannot accept the gift if you are not permitted to."

We put the bananas down on the side of the road for fear of being punished later.

The old woman was furious. She said loudly, "What kind of *bodoi* are you, who are so wicked? Did Uncle Ho teach you to behave that way? You treat your countrymen worse than the colonialists did!"

The *bodoi* in charge forced the whole team to run out of the market area. On our return from the worksite, although heavily burdened with logs, we had to follow a longer route along the edge of town. Later, it seemed that some sort of report had been made, and the next time we went out for wood the *bodoi*'s sudden change of attitude took us by surprise. When we were about 500 meters away from camp, they told us to stop, and one of them asked, "Do any of you have money?" Perplexed and worried, we thought we would be searched and our money confiscated. But the *bodoi* added, "I ask because I am going to give you permission to appoint a representative to go to the market and buy some things for you. If you behave yourselves, your representative will be allowed to go to the market; if you don't, not only will you not be allowed to buy things, you will not be permitted to go through the market area on the way back to camp. Are you willing to behave?"

We answered unanimously, "Yes, we are."

How could we not be willing! We immediately began to discuss the choice of a representative and to collect money. We were not prepared for this favor, so very few of us had brought along any money. I always tucked some away in my clothes in the belief that there would somehow be an opportunity to spend it, and for that reason, I was chosen to do the shopping.

The faded khaki battledress I wore was a clear indication of my status; added to that was the AK-toting *bodoi* following on my heels. The effect was that everybody in the marketplace smiled at me. A woman exclaimed, "My! My! Are you shopping today? What a blessing!" I just smiled. I had given my word not to speak to or, in the *bodoi*'s parlance, "communicate" with my fellow citizens. How long since I had last walked among so many people? I looked around before making up my mind what to buy; I hesitated between meat and sugar. I had in my pocket only 700 *dong*, 500 belonging to me and 200 to two other fellows. I asked the *bodoi* who followed me, "Can you allow me to buy some meat and some sugar?"

He said, "It's up to you to buy what you like, but don't buy anything bulky; if someone from the regiment sees you, I myself cannot escape being blamed for this."

I went to a shop and asked for some sugar. The woman owner did not answer me when I inquired about the price; instead she asked, "Are you a reeducation camp prisoner?"[1]

I nodded without replying. I produced 200 *dong* and said, "Please give me 200 *dong* worth of the cheapest sugar."

The woman gave me two parcels of sugar wrapped beforehand, saying, "This is a real bargain, see. By the way, haven't you anything to carry it with?" Then she went into the back of the shop and returned with a used plastic bag. She placed the two parcels in the bag, then turned to speak to the *bodoi*. "Thank you for allowing them to do some shopping. We are all Vietnamese, aren't we? Now that peace has come, we should love one another like brothers and sisters. There's no point in treating one another harshly!"

The embarrassed *bodoi* replied, "These fellows are undergoing reeducation; they will be sent home after they have completed it. Nobody has any intention of treating them harshly."

I took the bag and said, "Thank you very much, madam." I nodded my head several times to signal that I would have liked to say more but couldn't under the circumstances. Then I asked the *bodoi* to show me where meat was sold.

Before he could answer, a boy who had followed us since we had entered the market pointed the way, saying, "Uncle,[2] follow this row; at the end, turn left; that's where the meat stalls are." I smiled and thanked him. But the boy, who was a little over ten, said, "Are you a reeducation prisoner? Do you happen to know my father? His name is Tuan. He's also in a reeducation camp, but we don't know where!"

I looked at him and shook my head. The *bodoi* shouted at the boy, "What are you asking for? Get lost, brat!" Terrified, the boy ran away, then stopped to look after us.

When I reached the spot, I saw only two meat counters. An old woman sat

---

[1]People in South Vietnam soon had no illusions about "reeducation" and spoke of inmates as "prisoners."

[2]The word for "you" in Vietnamese varies according to the speaker's relationship to the person addressed. *Chú* (lit. "uncle") is used to address an older male, about the same age as the speaker's father or uncle.

behind one and a plump young girl with rosy cheeks behind the other. For good manners, I addressed the old lady first. "Please give me 500 *dong* worth of meat, the kind with plenty of fat. Also, see to it that it's not the expensive kind."

The woman picked up her knife and chose a piece of meat apparently tainted because it had turned slightly brownish. She put the meat on the scale, then cut off a small slice, probably because the piece was overweight. At that moment, the girl at the other counter remarked, "He's a reeducation camp prisoner, don't you know? Treat him as you think right, Ma!"

The old lady raised her eyes to look at me, then burst out laughing. "Good God! Blast my eyes! I thought you were somebody from the plantation. Reeducation camp prisoner, are you? Then, Heaven forbid, there's no question of buying or selling!" With that, she grasped a small jute bag, the kind used to hold sand for construction, and put the piece of meat on the scale and all the meat displayed on the counter into it. Her daughter helped tie the bag with a piece of string. I looked at her and told myself how good-looking she was. She was perhaps not very beautiful, but to my eyes she was so charming, so graceful! Never before had I felt so much pleasure while out shopping!

Bag of meat on my shoulder and parcels of sugar in my hand, I returned to the bus station where my companions were waiting. Everybody was surprised when they saw the size of the bag on my shoulder. The leader of the *bodoi* was also surprised. Reading his thoughts, I approached him to make my report. "I beg to report that I have completed my purchase. The meat vendor has given me plenty of meat." I then turned to the men. "The old lady had the kindness to give us all the meat on her counter. I suggest that we distribute it equally among us; everybody will have his share."

My companions answered noisily, "Agreed! This guy has proved to be a good buyer indeed. Next time, you will go to the market again, understand?"

On arriving at the plantation, I asked for permission to distribute the meat. As for the sugar, I gave the parcels to the two fellows who had contributed money for the purchase; but infected by the general generous attitude, they volunteered to distribute the sugar to everyone. Each was given a half tablet of sugar which he instantly put into his mouth. As the work party was divided into teams, each responsible both for cutting and sawing trees and carrying the logs, I divided the meat into as many portions as there were teams. Someone suggested that I should be paid for my efforts, but I declined, saying this had been a piece of luck for all of us.

That afternoon, before returning to camp, the *bodoi* advised us to be particularly cautious: "Remember, keep silent! Don't tell other people about this; otherwise, they will make noise about the whole thing and you'll get into big trouble." On our way back, we felt much stronger than before; we were not sure whether this was due to the half tablet of sugar we had eaten or to the share of meat we carried with us.

From then on, each time we went out to cut wood, we were able to buy some goods. Moreover, when we reached the rubber plantation, the women selling cakes or rice gruel would already be there waiting for us. Even the ice cream boy came. Many of us had no money, so they offered their goods free of charge as a sign of support. On these occasions, some men had managed to send word to their families. And some wives came from Saigon and waited for a whole week to meet their husbands.

This was how a fellow named Qui, formerly employed at the Finance and Accounting Directorate, came face to face with his wife, who was dressed as a vendor carrying a basket of cooked bananas. At first, he did not recognize her. Only when she called him softly by name did recognition dawn. He could only utter a few incoherent words before he suddenly fainted!

We surrounded him; the *bodoi* also ran forward. We said, "This fellow has fainted because of the draft."

The *bodoi* asked, "Is there anybody here who knows about first aid?"

Before anybody could answer, his wife said, "Let me 'scrape off the draft' for him.[3] I have some medicated balm with me, as you can see."

The *bodoi* stood watching. They were amazed to see the woman cry while "scraping off the draft" from the reeducation prisoner. A moment later, Qui regained consciousness, and, seeing his wife at his side, he broke into tears. His companions tried to signal him. "Why are you crying? You are very lucky to meet this lady who happens to have medicine with her and is kind enough to 'scrape off the draft' for you; otherwise, you'll have no chance to meet your wife and children again."

Only then did Qui realize the situation; yet he kept crying and saying, "Oh God! Oh God!"

His wife, seeing a *bodoi* approach, said hurriedly, "Do sit still! I have to 'pinch away the draft' from your temples to make you quite awake." While pinching at his temples, she said, "Please don't cry! Try to keep yourself in good health so you can finish reeducation and return to us. Don't you love your wife and children?"

She too was crying softly while saying this; the *bodoi* watching the scene laughed, "How strange you are! What are you crying for? Don't you hear what this young woman tells you to boost your spirits?"

Whereupon, Qui burst out crying louder than before and hiccoughing like a child. Fearing discovery, we surrounded him, making believe we were laughing at him and chiding him. "Stop it! What does all this crying mean?" His wife, choked with emotion, wiped her husband's tears with her shirt sleeves. The *bodoi,* still uncomprehending, laughed out loud. We pretended to follow suit, but looking at one another, we found that everybody's eyes were filled with tears.

---

[3]Literal translation from Vietnamese. This is a popular method of curing flu and cold or of treating fainting spells (those believed to be caused by drafts), which consists of spreading medicated oil or ointment on the skin of the patient (particularly on the back) and rubbing vigorously with a dull metal

Finally, Qui's wife stood up, took some cakes from her basket, and handed them to him. "Now, take these back to the camp, and eat them when you feel like it!" She seemed to have realized the danger of discovery by the *bodoi*, so she added impatiently, "Try to keep yourself in good health and get good results in reeducation so you can go home soon. I'm sure your wife and children love you and are waiting for you."

Qui, still not completely in control, made signs with his hand to decline the offer of the cakes. Our younger fellows pretended to jeer at him. "Come on! It's a personal gift from the lady, you have to take it. She'll be insulted if you keep on crying."

Fearing the situation was getting out of hand, I approached Qui and whispered threateningly, "For God's sake, take it! We'll be in big trouble if they know; besides, we won't be allowed to come here any more." I then turned to his wife and said in a low voice, "Please go now. He's in good shape, I assure you. If you stay too long you will betray yourselves, both you and your husband, and the consequences will be very serious."

She stood up, put the cakes beside him, and walked away. Everybody watched her go, particularly Qui, with the pain showing on his face. She stopped some distance away and sat down at the foot of a tree, looking in our direction. Qui sat with his head in his hands, from time to time raising his head to look at her. She lingered for a long time before she finally walked away. When we were allowed to pause for a drink of water, we approached the place where she had been sitting and discovered that she had furtively placed by the tree a pile of cooked bananas together with a packet of sesame mixed with salt and sugar—a kind of food that frequently appeared on the tables of the poor. We crowded around and began to eat. As for the *bodoi*, they stood at a distance watching us, as they did every time we gathered together.

If the business of wood cutting remains vivid in my memory it's because of the deep impressions made on me by the generosity of the meat vendor and Qui's moving encounter with his wife. After this, bad luck befell me.

Usually, after the morning roll call we were detailed to attend to various chores in the camp. Food was distributed at noon, and after an hour's rest we resumed work until late afternoon. After the evening meal we spent some time waiting for roll call, and this was when the study monitor made his comments about the day's work: This team had done well, that team had not been active enough, and so on, ending with a few remarks on a number of individuals. Most of the time, when nothing had happened, he went through the routine mechanically; he spoke vaguely and stuck to generalities, sometimes with a hint of

---

object (e.g., a coin or a spoon). Medically speaking, the rubbing helps activate circulation, and the medicated oil also helps.

threat. But if there had been a fight among us or some report by informers, he would spend a whole hour throwing insults and threats at us while we stood at attention, tired, uncomfortable, and mosquito-bitten.

For my part, as I had been extremely cautious in my words and deeds, I felt I had succeeded in not attracting the attention of informers because I had not been alluded to in the monitor's remarks. Unfortunately, my sense of security was false. One evening after roll call, I was summoned to a barrack occupied by the *bodoi*. I was ordered to wait in a room whose only furniture was a table I had helped repair and a chair. Soon a man I recognized as Commander Sau, the political commissar from the South, entered the room. A small bulb suspended from the ceiling shed a feeble light on the scene. Commander Sau sat down; he looked very imposing, sitting there behind the table. He began to speak. "Well, Mr. Vu! Do you know why I've asked you to come for a 'working session' with me?"

I replied, "No, I really don't."

"According to reports from the comrades 'down there,' it seems that lately you've been trying to influence people to serve your own aims. Do you plan to recruit followers to organize your own faction? If so, what for? Is it to sabotage the Revolution? How can a man in your position still think of scheming?"

I waited until he had finished speaking to venture a cautious request. "Could the commander allow me to explain myself?"

"Why not? If you have anything to say, say it." The tone of his voice was not particularly menacing, compared to the study monitors', especially Chief Monitor Hau's.

I began, "Since I presented myself for reeducation, my companions have often falsely reported on me, I don't know why. I reported for reeducation simply to learn about the policy of the Revolution in order to abide by the law after completion of my reeducation period. When I found out I had been reported on, I became cautious and tried not to hurt anybody's feelings or do anything wrong—"

"What about the report concerning your attempt to influence people and organize your own clique to do your bidding?"

"Certainly not true!"

"Then why did you pay for the meat with your own money and distribute it to your companions without asking them to repay you?"

"May I give the commander a full account of the story?"

"Certainly. Didn't I tell you that I wanted to know all about it?"

Clearly, this political commissar intended to show his kindness by being obliging. I proceeded to describe the meat purchase, the vendor's gift, and the distribution. I stressed that it all came about thanks to the kindness of the comrade *bodoi* and that he had permitted me to accept the gift of meat and distribute it to my friends. "I have no intention to form a clique."

"Then why did you draw water from the well for others to clean themselves?"

Obviously, the informers had paid close attention to me! Again, I said cautiously, "Could the commissar allow me to explain this?"

"Certainly! Go ahead!"

"If I often draw water for some of the men, it is because they are infected with scabies; their hands have festered to the point that it is hard for them to draw water from the well. I am particularly fearful that if they handle the bucket, the well water may become polluted because I think that scabies is extremely contagious. I first suggested that we take turns drawing water for those infected with scabies; however, my companions challenged me to set an example, so I had to draw water for Tri, who was the most affected one in our team. Since then, whenever those with scabies want to have a bath or wash some clothes, they approach me and ask me to go to the well and draw water for them. That is the truth. I don't understand why people can be so bad as to report falsely on others, instead of helping them as they should—"

"You have no right to pass judgment on other people and say so-and-so is bad. Everybody has the duty to report to the Revolution any suspicious act committed by other persons. Do you understand?"

"Yes, I do."

"That's enough for the moment. I shall collate your statement with the reports to get a better idea of the situation. But I warn you: Whatever you want to do, you first have to ask for the permission of the study monitors. You must absolutely not take the liberty of doing anything with regard to other persons. Including giving them help. Is that clear?"

"Yes."

"Good! You may go now." As I was about to leave the room, the commander called out, "Just a minute! Wait here for somebody to take you back to your place. Where is the comrade on duty? Take him back 'down there.'"

On the way back I told myself what a close shave this was. I was glad that I had had the wit to make the *bodoi* responsible for the free distribution of meat. Only much later did I realize how important and valuable a piece of meat was.

Nearly three months had elapsed since we had come to Xuan Loc. Every day one team would be detailed to work on the meeting hall, another would work at various chores in the camp, and a third would hoe the ground to plant vegetables and sweet potatoes. But what we were all waiting for, namely, reeducation, had not as yet materialized, although it was mentioned often enough. The meeting hall was still unfinished because not enough metal sheets could be found to cover its roof.

One day, while working on the roof, using corrugated iron sheets taken from a dismantled watchtower, I suddenly heard snatches of singing and hand clapping. It was then 9 A.M. I listened attentively and heard a voice, amplified by a loudspeaker and carried by the wind, speaking about reeducation and some sort of policy. At about noon, songs and clapping were heard again. I guessed they came from another camp or barrack close by. Probably, reeducation had already begun in some of the other units.

The next day, ordered to go out and fetch more iron sheets for the meeting hall, we were led along a narrow path toward the back of the camp. It was then that we discovered that not too far away were a number of other camps, and at the sight of us the inmates rushed forward waving. The *bodoi* standing guard fired warning shots in the air. But the men kept laughing and yelling.

We crossed a shallow spring, probably filled with water only recently from the look of the banks, and after an hour of walking we came to a hill on the top of which stood rows of nearly completed houses, originally built to serve as married quarters for the ARVN. Each house had two rooms, separated from the kitchen by a narrow open space; behind the kitchen were the bathroom and water closet. The only things missing to make the houses livable were doors and windows. The roofs were made of new, shiny corrugated iron sheets, and we were ordered to dismantle them. We were very surprised because, to our eyes, these houses had great value. They were new, and the bathrooms and lavatories were fitted with new and relatively expensive porcelain equipment. But our order was precise: "Dismantle the roofs to get the sheets!" One of the men observed, "If one of these houses was allocated to my family, we would consider ourselves very lucky. Besides, from up here we have a fine view over the valley. We could not ask for better than this."

Within two hours, with nearly 1,000 inmates working on the project, almost all eighty houses had lost their roofs. While the dismantling was completed quickly and without much difficulty, carrying the sheets back to camp was exhausting work. The sheets were of a good size and quite heavy, and each person was able to carry two at the most. Some men could carry only one, and even then they had to stop several times before reaching camp.

After the evening meal, instead of being allowed to rest, we had to return twice to the worksite. Only those who were sick or plagued with scabies were allowed to turn in. It was late in the evening when we finished. The following day extra men were detailed to roof the meeting hall, and two days later the work was completed.

Our carpentry team then was ordered to make benches and construct a platform. We thought the benches were for us to sit on during the lessons, so we asked the monitor where to find enough wood to make that many. He pointed to a pile of three or four planks lying in the kitchen, and we understood then that the benches were only for the instructors responsible for our reeducation.

The pace of activity continued as the date for reeducation to begin drew nearer. More *bodoi* arrived at the camp; they came on brand-new bicycles and were full of self-importance. One day, while I was busy arranging tables and chairs on the platform, some *bodoi* came by to watch. The study monitor spoke to them with deference and some solemnity. One of the newly arrived cadres pointed at me and asked, "Who is this fellow?"

"I beg to report to the comrade that his name is Vu; he is a former secondary school teacher. He was drafted into the *nguy* army where he reached the rank of first lieutenant."

The cadre then turned to me. "So, you are a university graduate, are you? As a lieutenant, you were able to do only as you were bidden. Your offenses cannot be very serious." Not knowing what to reply, I just answered with a "yes." The cadre said, as if giving an order before walking away, "Good! Now, carry on with your work. In a few days, you will begin your reeducation. Only then will you be able to assess the nature and extent of your offenses."

That night, his words haunted me so that I couldn't sleep. Reeducation indeed! I had believed that reeducation would help us to learn about the new regime; I had not expected that it could serve to indict us. This business seemed to contain a good many traps; I'd better be on my guard.

As for my companions, the majority appeared visibly pleased that reeducation would begin soon because they thought they would be allowed to go home at the end of it. Many times we had been chided by the monitors for being unreasonably impatient, so now that we really were going to begin, it was only logical that we would be sent home soon. Things could not go otherwise!

On the eve of the day the "course" was due to begin, the team leaders were summoned to a meeting to discuss preparations. The communist cadres called the business of going to the classroom to study "*len lop*."[4] When the great day arrived, we were told to put on clean clothes. In the lecture hall we had to stand in perfectly straight lines. The platform was full of *bodoi*, most dressed about the same but a few of them wearing red military badges. We stood facing the stage, waiting. When a man who appeared to be a high-ranking cadre entered the hall, an order was shouted, "Everybody! Get ready to greet the commandant!"

We watched as he took his seat in the middle of the platform. He must have commanded a unit higher than a battalion as we knew by sight every cadre in the battalion responsible for our camp. Nobody gave military salutes, which was surprising among soldiers; they simply stood at attention. (Only much later did we see them drill in marching and saluting.) A monitor shouted an order, "Let the team leaders present their teams!"

One after the other, the team leaders stepped forward and reported the number of persons in their teams, the number present, the number of absentees, and the reason for the absences.

---

[4]Literally, "go up to the class." The Vietnamese language does not lack words to express the simple fact of attending classes. But if the communists intentionally coined this new expression, it may

This first session already promised to be thorny. The commandant, seeing that more than one hundred were listed as absent angrily demanded, "Who gave them permission to remain in their barracks? Reeducation, for them, is a matter of life and death. How can they be absent from the class?" He turned to the *bodoi* sitting beside him and ordered him to go to the barracks, check on those who had reported sick, and see that all except those who were seriously ill came to the meeting hall. Half an hour later the presentation of teams resumed. The number of absentees was now reduced to a little more than forty, the latecomers being those seriously infected with scabies. They were unable to sit down, so they had to stand at the far end of the hall when the teams were given permission to sit.

The commandant waited until then to make his introductory speech. He spoke through a loudspeaker that would have been much more effective in a smaller room. He stressed that in reeducating us, the Revolution aimed at equipping us with a stock of knowledge and the proper logic to serve as a basis for us to determine our position vis-à-vis the People. He concluded, "I would like to emphasize advice that will be repeated over and over again, and that advice is from now on, you will speak and act exactly the way the Revolution teaches you to do. You must absolutely not think, speak, or act in any other way. Decidedly, you have to speak and act according to the teachings of the Revolution only."

He then introduced the cadre who would give us the first lesson, saying, "Let me introduce to you the comrade instructor who will give you the first lesson: 'U.S. imperialism has ultimately and permanently failed in its war of aggression against Vietnam.'"

The instructor was a young cadre who read the lesson from a small book, pausing from time to time to amplify his text with examples. These often contradicted what he had just read and were grossly exaggerated to the point of being simply farcical. But as the study monitors were constantly circulating among us, no one dared give vent to his feelings. The lesson made little mention of the efforts involved in the conduct of the war against the United States. Instead, figures were used to demonstrate that the Americans had resorted to every possible means to win but finally had to withdraw. Figures quoted included assertions that more than 3 million GIs had been involved in the war, that the American presence reached its peak when 600,000 troops, including those of "satellite states," fought alongside 1 million *nguy* soldiers, that at one time, 90 percent of the American war industry had been put at the service of the war in Vietnam, and 80 percent of American scientists had been given the task of devising plans and finding means to conquer Vietnam. In the end, the lesson only succeeded in painting the absurd picture of the whole of the United

---

carry a connotation reflecting their belief that political studies or, more precisely, the study of Marxism-Leninism, elevated their ideological standing.

States devoting itself entirely to the war in Vietnam. This lesson was expounded in class for three days running, the second day being reserved for discussion and the third for the task of writing what was called an "account of results obtained."

During the lesson, we had to squat or sit on the ground, and we had to appear to pay close attention to the instructor. The slightest inattention would immediately be noticed by the monitors, one of whom would approach the "culprit," saying, "Hey, you there! What are you doing? You don't want to listen to the lesson, do you?" He then would go to the team leader and ask him to take down the name of the man who had just been admonished. Everyone, therefore, had to appear to be very attentive, all the time furiously taking notes. Paper and pens were distributed. We were allowed a five-minute break after each hour of "lecture," four hours in the morning and three in the afternoon. After the first day, we ached all over as if we had been sick for a long time. We all agreed that we would rather work and sweat at labor than go through this kind of course. The *bodoi* were similarly affected. On the first day many came to watch, but by the second day, only the study monitors and the instructor remained in the hall. At the end of the course, a lone monitor sat dozing in a corner, heedless of the droning of the tired instructor. However, when somebody from regimental headquarters was present, the *bodoi* appeared in force.

A discussion session followed the three-day lecture. Groups of fifteen sat in circles on the ground; and to prevent us from drifting into small talk, the *bodoi* and study monitors sat down near us. But as there were many more of us than them, they had to move from one group to another about every half hour. Therefore, the "discussions" actually took place only when the *bodoi* were near, and the informers, fortunately, did not report on this cheating. When we did "discuss," we took turns to speak in support of the instructor's assertion that the Americans had lost the war. But we had no conviction in what we said, and several times we were forced by the monitors or instructor to speak out with more enthusiasm.

I soon realized that I had been singled out for special attention. The instructor remained with our group for a long time, and when my turn came to speak, I concurred in saying that the Americans had used all the means at their disposal but had not won the war. At this, the instructor addressed me by name, which showed that I had been reported on by the monitors. "Mr. Vu, come over here! I want to have a word with you in private." Everybody looked at me; one thing was clear, I was a marked man! "You are an academic, aren't you?"

"Yes. Like most of my companions here, I've been through higher education. The doctors have been the longest in higher education—"

"But they've all studied technical subjects; you're the only one who's read bourgeois literature!"

"Well, I intended to seek admission to a polytechnic, but I was unsuccessful, so I had to go to a training college to become a teacher."

"I've heard that because you're a man of intellect your companions have a high regard for you. Is that true?"

"Oh, that's not true at all! On the contrary, I think that because of my poor intellectual capacity, I've been the scorn of the team. My companions think they are better educated than I am—"

"There's nothing wrong with being an academic, so there's no point denying it. I wanted to have a discussion with you just for the sake of discussion, that's all; I have no intention to harm you. Remember, the more sincere you prove to be, the more appreciative the Revolution will be of your attitude. The Revolution particularly appreciates complete sincerity.

"I am aware that you must have had some doubt or disagreement; but you, like all your companions, prefer to remain silent and let it pass by. If that's the way you study politics, then how can you hope to make progress? The study of politics demands great efforts, much brain searching, and clashes of opinion. If all you can think of is flattery, then you will have failed completely. Therefore, I want you to mention to me some point in the lesson you disagree with or think questionable. I assure you that I'm not going to give you bad marks; on the contrary, you will be highly rated. Now, bring up some point, any point."

I was petrified! Clearly a trap was being set for me, and I was in for big trouble. I searched for a reply, but everything I could think of seemed equally risky. At long last, I said lamely, "The lesson was so consistent and convincing that I cannot think of anything to question. Give me some time to think about it; I am sure I shall come up with something. Could I discuss the matter with my companions, comrade cadre?"

"It's clear that you're not being entirely sincere. This is proof that you do not yet know how to reeducate yourself. Anyway, that will do for the moment. Think the matter over; you may as well discuss it with your coampanions. In any case, you must come up with something you really think questionable or are in disagreement with."

He stood up, shook his head, then left to join another group. I returned to my own group and said, "Obviously, the gods and my ancestors haven't favored me with their protection! The instructor ordered me to raise a point I find to be controversial or disagree with. I tried to find one but couldn't come up with anything. So he has agreed that I discuss the matter with all of you."

"Discuss indeed! Vu! Do you really mean to drag us into your misfortune? You'll get us in trouble."

"No way, old man! I have no suggestions to make. Just listening to what you said is enough to give me the creeps! I agree entirely with the instructor. So, leave me alone and let me return safely to my wife and kids. To ask me to raise a question is to drive me into a corner!" Everyone snickered.

But old Mr. Cuc said earnestly, "Stop joking, please! We're being drawn into a dangerous situation, and this is no time for fun. We have to find some mild criticism to end the matter."

A *bodoi*, hearing our raised voices, came near us. We quieted down so he went to another group. Someone said, "Suppose we say that the Americans had not done their utmost, otherwise Hanoi would not have been left unscathed as it is now."

"That won't do. That means that we do not believe in what the Revolution has been claiming. We'll be 'kaput' if we raise that point!"

"Or suppose we question that the Americans lost the war. We all know the United States withdrew its troops a couple of years before the *bodoi* launched their attack against the South. It should be said that the Republic of Vietnam lost the war instead of the United States."

"No, that's worse! They've said that it was the Americans who were beaten; we cannot contradict them. Besides, we are *nguy*, and there's no such thing as the Republic of Vietnam; if we use that, we'll be done for!"

"Wait, I've thought of something. I suggest we ask why, being in possession of atomic bombs, the Americans did not resort to that means in order to win the war."

"Quite right! Hurrah for Mr. Cuc! There's no political implication in the question. Besides, we don't run the risk of contradicting them."

The question was a trifle simplistic, but it was something we could safely bring up; that was in itself a sort of reassurance. In the afternoon, about half an hour after we had resumed our discussion, the instructor called me aside. As I came up, he squatted on the ground and laughed conceitedly. "Well? Do you have any question? Any disagreement? Speak up!"

"Requesting the comrade cadre's permission, my companions and I have the following question. We've been told that the Americans used every means available but to no avail. Then why didn't they resort to atomic bombs of which they had plenty?"

"Is that the only question?"

"Yes, comrade cadre. That's the only one."

The instructor looked long and severely at me, and my heart raced. Finally, he said, "Obviously, you're not being sincere. You still try to hide many things from me. Your companions questioned our statement that the Americans had done their utmost and used all the means in their possession; your companions also said that the Republic of Vietnam lost the war, not the United States. But you mention only the question of atomic bombs. That's bad, very bad."

I was appalled. Clearly, the informers had done their work well! I tried to argue. "The other points were not agreed upon by all of us. That's why I didn't bring them up—"

"All right! I'll give you a last chance to prove your sincerity; just raise a question, an instance of disagreement of your own so that I can judge whether or not you have shown repentance. You're free to comply or not."

Having said this, he stared at me with a frightfully menacing look in his eyes. I tried to concentrate, convinced that I had better raise a strong question if I wanted to get out of this fix. "Frankly, if the comrade cadre wants me to raise queries about this lesson, I have none. The fact that the United States lost the war was due to reasons obvious to everybody. Nobody has any doubt about that. If I wonder about something it's my failure to understand how the Americans could be so stupid!"

"It's the only point, is it?"

Aware of the danger of raising a single question, I hurriedly continued. "No, I haven't finished. I have many questions, but they have more depth; they are related to ideas and politics. For example, I don't understand why, after having won back our independence, we have to embrace communism. I want to know the policy of the Revolution for bringing prosperity to our country. And I want to know how people like us should live and behave in the new Vietnam. My questions are many. I want especially to have a better understanding of Marxist-Leninist ideology, of which I have only superficial knowledge. Right now, I would like to know how I can purchase a volume of Lenin's selected works to read while I am in this camp.

"As to whether the Americans lost or won the war, it's irrelevant to what is in my mind, and I have no question on the lesson given by the comrade cadre. I speak in all sincerity. I should think that if I am asked to have faith in the Revolution, I should be given the opportunity to study the Revolution."

"I'd say that there's some sincerity in what you've said. However, your questions demand a higher level of study. As yet you're not in a position to enter deeply into the subject. The 'road to socialism'—which you wrongly called the 'road to communism,' since it takes a long, long time to build communism—is a subject which only Party members, after many long years of study under the guidance of the Party, can understand; and yet, nobody can claim to have a thorough knowledge of the matter. Even people like myself don't know more than what we have been taught by the Party. You have to be very patient before you reach the state where you can effectively tackle the subject. As for your desire to purchase books about the Revolution, it's a laudable idea. I shall refer it to higher authorities for consideration and approval. Now, go back to your group to continue the discussion."

He left without any further reprimands. I felt as if a heavy weight had been lifted from my shoulders, but the respite was only temporary because obviously the camp command was keeping an eye on me.

After two days of discussion, we were ordered back to the lecture hall to be given the answers to our questions, especially those of our group, which was considered to have performed the best. The instructor praised the sincerity shown by our group. We had raised questions, despite the risk of punishment by the Revolution, thus showing that we had faith in the Revolution. As we listened, we were more and more surprised by the change in his attitude.

Answering our queries, he said that under five successive presidents, the United States had concentrated all its efforts toward winning the war, but to no avail. Finally, the Americans had had to resort to the last "devilish scheme," namely, the Vietnamization of the war; that, too, had failed. He added, "Ambassador Bunker himself has said, 'The Vietnamization of the war only changes the color of the skin of the dead,'" upon which he laughed in self-satisfaction. I wasn't sure whether Ambassador Bunker had expressed such an opinion, but this was the first time I had ever heard of it. The Americans were known to be in the habit of making blunt statements, but I didn't think Ambassador Bunker had been callous enough to ever use those words!

The instructor then repeated our question, "Why didn't the Americans use their atomic bombs to raze Hanoi?" He laughed and said loudly, very satisfied with himself, "Why? Why couldn't they use their atomic bombs? Ha! Ha! Ha! Because the Party had means with which to lock their arms as well as close 'their eyes and mouth' on many occasions. The superior skill of the Party consists in its knowledge of how to fight and defeat a much stronger, richer enemy equipped with much more modern weapons. The Party used the American people to fight the American government, the American press to indict the American leaders, and the U.S. Congress to discourage the U.S. administration. The White House and the Pentagon have been beaten on American soil. We beat the Americans in America itself. Therefore, the Americans lost before they were able to make use of all their strength. Ha! Ha!"

He spoke passionately and opinionatedly, then burst out laughing, just as actors do on the stage. It was so funny that we could not help laughing out loud. The instructor, taking our response for acclaim, was so pleased that he didn't hesitate to praise us. "You're quite right to laugh and show your joy that way. It's very true that our Party is above par! There's no doubt about the infallibility of our Party! No wonder it triumphs over its enemies!"

His attitude was so ludicrous that we clapped our hands and laughed even louder; and we applauded more when we saw the instructor himself clap his hands. It was much later that we came to understand the custom among communists to clap their hands in response to applause from the audience. To me, this was all painfully comical! We despised the conceited attitude of the instructor, but we were unable to do anything but clap our hands in jest, which he inferred as an expression of allegiance to the Party. However, it should be conceded that at that moment many of us naïvely believed that the communists were actually as clever as they claimed to be.

At long last, sensing the ridicule of our prolonged handclapping, the instructor shouted into the loudspeaker, "That's enough! After all, when in class, we must keep some measure of discipline."

The study monitors and *bodoi*, more aware of the true significance of our response, followed suit with a vengeance. "Silence! And make sure to sit in straight lines! What are you laughing at? Are you shutting out the instructor's argument?''

The atmosphere in the room became as heavy as before, although amused smiles still lingered on the lips of many of us. The instructor, his good humor apparently unabated, resumed his explanations. "As to saying that the Americans have not been beaten, that we have won and you have lost, this is truly a gross error. To make this clear, I'm telling you that in this war, there were only two sides: The Americans are the losing side and the Vietnamese people are the winning side. You haven't lost because you too are part of the Vietnamese people. But because you have not completed your reeducation, you cannot yet be regarded as belonging to the People. Don't you agree?"

Again, the audience clapped noisily, and voices were heard rising above the general din. "We have not lost, but it's a shame to have us sitting down here!" "We have not lost, we have simply been defeated!" "We're all of the People, but *we* of the People are detained by *you* of the People! How strange!"

The instructor signaled for everybody to be silent. The monitors shouted for order. It took several minutes for the tumult to die down. The instructor went on. "There are many points you cannot understand for the moment, but later when you have been reeducated by the Party and the government to become really advanced politically, you will agree entirely with our Party and government. You will then take your places among the People. But not yet. Some of you even want to study Marxist-Leninist philosophy or socialist ideology, but it's too early. It will be a long time before this can be done. If you want to study here, I'm afraid you will have to stay for a few more decades. And it's not sure you would then be able to exhaust the subject."

Everyone burst out laughing. Somebody was heard to say, "Let's put it off until later then! For the moment, a brief study will do." The confusion was such that the monitors had to shout in anger to restore order.

Finally, the instructor gave us a subject for the "results obtained" paper we were required to write. The subject was on why we can say that the Americans have failed in Vietnam for good. He reminded us that we should make good use of the data given in class. The writing of the paper took the whole of that Saturday and for some of the men, even part of Sunday. Some, wanting to show their application and enthusiasm, went so far as to give, besides the facts and figures supplied in class, their own ideas to support the instructor's assertions. As for me, conscious of the fact that I had been under close surveillance, I limited myself to writing a short paper reflecting entirely what had been explained to us in class.

On Monday we were allowed to have a break and time to take a bath and wash our clothes. During the whole study period, our diet was improved by the addition of green vegetables, either Dalat cabbage or chowchow. It had been a long time since we last had eaten vegetables, which made the ones we ate now so extraordinarily delicious. What was lacking in quantity was more than made up by what we, long deprived, considered quality. We soon found that whenever something was to be gained by propaganda, there would be some improvement in our diet. Eating and drinking would always play an important role when they could be used to promote the aims of the Revolution.

On Tuesday we were summoned to the lecture hall to attend a critique session on our papers. The instructor started by severely chiding us for sloppy writing: "It's not clear whether, by scribbling on your papers, you intended to test our literacy or just do away with a bothersome task. In any case, I would venture a general remark. The habit of scrawling instead of writing properly is a bourgeois characteristic and a bad one at that! The bourgeoisie don't pay any attention to the true significance of writing. Script was invented for people to communicate with one another, not to complicate things. Many of you have contracted the bourgeois bad habit of writing sloppily, without proper respect for the reader. You must get rid of that habit; otherwise, we will have to take appropriate measures against it."

For us who sat on the floor listening, those words gave us a sickening feeling as we realized that anything whatsoever could be used as grounds for indictment. Scribbling was a crime of the bourgeoisie?

Commenting on the content of the papers, the instructor was severely critical of those who wrote lengthy accounts. "Why did you put down more than what had been explained to you? Was it because you thought that we of the Revolution were not articulate enough and you had to make additions to be more clear and complete? Or was it because you thought yourselves to be more clever than the Revolution, that you have a better understanding of things than we have? That's a bad habit which must be got rid of. The Revolution wants you to think and speak exactly as you are told. What is asked of you is very easy but, at the same time, very difficult to do. What you hear, you must repeat exactly, no more, no less. That's the first step in learning to speak and act according to the way of the Revolution."

The young fellows among us were glad that those who had written lengthy papers in the hope of being highly rated were reprimanded. They whispered, "It serves you right! You wanted to write a long paper and now you are accused of contempt of the Revolution! So much for you!"

But the instructor did not mention any names, speaking only in general terms. I knew I was out of danger, that nothing in my paper had attracted attention. Replying to a question as to why the lesson had not made much mention of the heroic achievements of the People in the fight against the Americans, he said, "The whole People knew about that because it was mentioned daily by the media. If you have not heard of that, it was because your eyes were covered and your ears plugged by the *nguy* and the Americans."

To illustrate, he cited many "instances" of heroic deeds performed by the People, most of which were too absurd to be credible. For example, he told about a guerrilla fighter who single-handedly had routed a whole U.S. company; about a young woman who lured the pilot of a combat aircraft—"the one with flappable wings, you know"—to "fly low in order to have a good look at her nudity" as she was bathing in the river, and when he was within range, grasped her rifle and shot him in the head. He told us many more stories, each more incredible than the last.

The only thing he said that made some sense concerned the weapons used in the war by the two sides. "Our weapons were far superior to the enemy's. Our fighters, when shown the M-1 rifles or Sten submachine gun, were certain that victory would be ours because they were armed with AK-47s. By the time their troops were equipped with M-16 rifles, ours had already had AK-50s long before. Our T-54 tanks were unbeatable. When these were replaced by more modern and powerful ones, they had just begun to bring M-48 tanks into the battle. When their B-52 bombers invaded Hanoi air space, we had already completed the installation of high-altitude SAMs [surface-to-air-missiles]. When their B-52s were shot down, the Americans were completely taken by surprise. Their intelligence service had no idea of the supply of high-altitude missiles to our army by the USSR. They did not expect that we already possessed SAMs. As far as weaponry was concerned, we always were a step ahead of the Americans."

During the lecture, the discussion period, the writing of the "results obtained" paper, and the critique session when the instructor made comments, answered our queries, and dealt with "pending matters" (i.e., bad habits we had not yet got rid of), we were forced to listen to innumerable boastful, conceited, and incredible statements. None among us cared to bring up those wild allegations for discussion; we just shook our heads and smiled.

The day we were allowed to rest, take a bath and wash our clothes, and prepare for the second lesson, an unexpected event occurred. A little after noon, two *bodoi* and a monitor came to the shack next door and told a man to pack and follow them to battalion headquarters. Within minutes, the news was hawked around the camp. The man was later identified as Tuong, the pharmacist, who was known to have relatives in the Politburo; they probably speeded up his release. Tuong himself had confided to his friends that he was going to be released soon. At the evening roll call, the monitor imparted the news skillfully. "Don't be surprised when you see that some people are released while others are not. Of course, you all will be released, sooner or later. However, those who deserve it are entitled to an early release, compared to other people."

By the following day, those words had gone the rounds of the camp. To all appearances, no one talked to anyone else about this or anything of the sort, but whatever news or story came up would spread at the speed of sound. Sometimes, the same piece of news was whispered to me by two or three different people; often it was merely the product of imagination.

From the moment it was known that one of us had been released, a number of men in my squad became restless: Tanker Quang, whose father-in-law was minister for light industries in Hanoi; next came Hoang Xuan Hai, who had an uncle who was a "propaganda and indoctrination" commissar in the Lao Dong Party; then there was Vo Tai, who had a certificate acknowledging his service to the Revolution. If we had to look for informers, we could in all probability find them among these three and perhaps several others. It was feared that the more impatient they were, the more eager they would be to report on us. As for the rest of us, it was very difficult to tell who was a mole. We were all in the same humiliating situation, we shared the same suffering; it would be a sin to claim that a certain one among us was an informer. What if we were wrong! When we talked to each other, we found we all had the same thoughts, that we all felt the same sadness and shame.

That evening Long came to tell me that out of a total of 1,200 inmates, three had been released. This quickly became the only topic of discussion in the whole camp.

A criticism, evidently aimed at the *bodoi*, pointed out the inconsistency between the assertion that reeducation was a matter of life and death and the fact of the early release of a number of people who had not yet completed their reeducation. Some of the men raised their voices as if to challenge the informers. "Nothing ever is a matter of life and death. What's always true is that when you have relatives in high places, you have more chances than people who don't. That's a definite advantage some have over the rest of us!"

Criticism of the early releases was dismissed as groundless when the second lesson began. After the class had been presented to him and he had requested all the sick to report for the lecture, the instructor—a new arrival—immediately warned of unpleasant consequences for those "who wanted to sow confusion and distract people from the rightful duty of reeducation." He asked, "Who told you that the persons who left had been released? I tell you now that nobody can be released without having completed reeducation. Those people have simply been transferred to another camp for special reasons."

The instructor stammered when he spoke and appeared to be short-tempered; when he was angry, his stammering became more pronounced. The topic of the second lesson was that all *nguy*—both servicemen and civil servants—are equally guilty of offenses against the People and the fatherland. Just listening to the title of the lesson was enough for us to realize that we had come to a thorny period in our reeducation. Similarly, the selection of this particular instructor was clearly intentional. The man spoke with the Quang Nam accent; he was thin and had the sickly pale complexion of chronic malaria sufferers.

Right from the beginning, he denounced us. "Until this very minute, you still stubbornly think that you are not guilty of anything or, at the most, only minor offenses. To say or think so is a proof of extreme obstinancy on your part. You yourselves have been the mainstay of the Americans and the *nguy*; without you, the Americans and their valets would have been incapable of doing anything. If the war lasted long, it was because of your opposition to the Revolution and the People. The strength of a nation comes from its working people; in the same way, the antirevolutionary war draws its vitality from the likes of you. If you had not sided with the enemy, our country would have been reunified long ago. The Americans and *nguy* were able to cause havoc only with your support. Now you claim to be innocent. Can anybody accept that?"

His diatribe, amplified by the loudspeaker, sent cold shivers down our spines. The whole room was silent as if everyone was holding his breath. We took down notes automatically on the lesson so passively and dejectedly that the *bodoi* themselves commented that we had lost heart because the condemnation was so severe. From time to time, the instructor interrupted his lecture to ask, in a tone he wanted to sound friendly, "Don't you agree?" But the class did not respond. In unspoken agreement, we all kept silent. At last, the instructor pointed to the person sitting nearest to him and asked him to stand up and "give his personal opinion" of the lesson.

The man stood up and said, "Thanks to the Revolution's guidance, I now clearly realize that all of us deserve death because of our opposition to the Revolution. We accept the verdict."

The instructor insisted, "If you know that you deserve death, what do you plan to do? What is your wish? What do you want to say to the Revolution?" He obviously was urging the man to appeal to the Revolution for clemency, which was what the majority of the class also expected to hear.

The man just stood there, facing the instructor, and replied calmly, "I want exactly what the Revolution wants. That is, whatever intention the Revolution has concerning us, we are perfectly willing to abide by it. This is because we have been told to think, speak, and act according to the teaching of the Revolution. As far as I am concerned, I expect the Revolution to treat me exactly as it intends to. And I shall entirely agree."

The instructor, angered by the man's firm reply, said, "Your attitude is as negative as it is stubborn! You will see later where that attitude leads you to."

During the whole second lecture, the atmosphere was so heavy as to be almost unbearable. Intuitively, I felt the presence of a current of opposition or, at least, noncooperation between the instructor-cadre and the inmates sitting on the floor. The lesson emphasized three points: (1) The former administration was the political tool of American imperialism; (2) the *nguy* army was the war machine of American imperialism; and (3) the political parties and those who chose to live under and work for the former regime were reactionaries and, in an indirect way, the servants of American imperialism. This continued to be the argument used to indict any person accused of antirevolutionary activities. Some *bodoi* put it in a nutshell: Any antirevolutionary activity is, without the shadow of a doubt, planned or instigated by the Americans.

The discussion session was desperately dull. Nobody volunteered any remarks of his own. Each time we were ordered to speak, it was only to "plead guilty as accused." Except for that, we ventured no idea, no question, no hostile remark. The monitors and *bodoi* tried to make us bring up ideas to make the session more lively, but we kept on acknowledging our crimes and refused to say more. The instructor was very annoyed. He threatened to prolong the discussion until "the required objective is achieved."

The next day, he came to watch our group discuss the lesson, we who had been praised for our "sincere and progressive attitude." I tried to stay in the background, but the instructor looked directly at me with a wicked smile on his face. With his pale complexion and skinny appearance, he might have given a vague impression of kindness had he not smiled. At that moment, his sarcastic smirk upset every one of us. He looked at Long and asked, "Suppose you tell me what you think of your offenses."

Long turned pale; he stammered, "Er! Er! I owe the Revolution a debt of blood; my crime, er—deserves death."

"Is that all? All of you really are extremely obstinate elements! If you cannot give the reason for your crimes, your acknowledgment of the crimes is not sincere at all! And you, Mr. Vu, you too will no doubt merely acknowledge having committed crimes punishable by death, will you not?"

I realized I had to give a specific answer, so I ventured a few cautious words. "If the comrade cadre allows me to speak and promises not to take offense, I shall give my opinion."

"It has not been my intention to forbid you to say what's on your mind. Instead, I want you to speak up and say everything you have doubts about."

I plunged ahead. "I've noticed that from the very beginning you have been particularly short-tempered, and we have taken great care not to add more fuel to your anger. Some of us have even remarked that you seem to be filled with hate for us. I myself, after listening to your lecture, believe that you really hate us. You are the first person who we feel has a strong hatred for us. So we have no choice but to acknowledge every crime we are accused of."

"Nonsense! That's complete nonsense! I have been given the task of making you realize your guilt, but at this moment I have no hate whatsoever for you. If we had met during the war, I would undoubtedly have looked upon you as enemies. But now, it's different—"

His stammering got worse and worse as he spoke, and he seemed to get more agitated. Finally, he stood up and said, "If that's the way you think I am, I give you permission to write down your questions, collect them, and show them to me for reply. That way, you don't have to fear my short temper. Continue with your discussion, open your minds to one another; completely! Write your questions on paper; no need to mention who has made which query. That way, there will be no need to worry."

He left to go to the other discussion groups where he repeated the instruction he had given us. In my group we began to "open our minds" with such innocuous queries as "Many cadres have admitted that, as junior officers or civil servants all we did was to obey orders, so why are we now accused of having committed crimes punishable by death?" or "What would be the punishment for a serious crime?"

Finally, a man raised the question, "Regarding our crime of having committed hostile acts against the North Vietnamese Revolution, mightn't it be said that the responsibility for it vis-à-vis history should also be shared by the Revolution? This is because the Revolution itself signed the 1954 Geneva Accord agreeing to the partition of Vietnam, even if the partition was temporary. This was the origin of our being drawn into the ranks of opponents of the Revolution. If, after the battle of Dien Bien Phu, the Revolution had decided to make the most of the situation and push forward to final victory, we ourselves would now have become authentic *bodoi* and not criminals as we are looked upon at present."

Long, the ranger lieutenant, expressed the opinion that "our offenses must have been minor ones because we took it upon ourselves to lay down our arms and let the *bodoi* advance without difficulty into South Vietnam, thus avoiding destruction and losses to our country. If we had decided to fight to the last man, things would probably have been much different from what they are now." Seeing that the comments were becoming bolder and bolder, some of us wavered, but the majority decided to go on. We thought the informers would make a report on our discussion in any case, and besides, all of us had shown more firmness and courage and none of the fear we had displayed in the first lesson.

We were surprised when we went back to the lecture hall to be given answers to our questions to find that the instructor showed more gentleness toward us and, especially, did not make any mention of the questions raised by our group.

The subject for our "results obtained" paper required each of us to go into his personal history: "Depending on the social category you belong to, state the reason why that category [*nguy* army or civil service] was guilty of offenses against the Revolution and the People. Give an account of your own offenses. Highlight the most prominent." This time, we wrote short, concise papers. I mentioned as an offense of mine having been a teacher whose task was "to inculcate in young people the concept of freedom and democracy to serve as an instrument to fight against the Revolution." I also wrote that I judged myself as not having done anything particularly remarkable in the past.

At the following session, the instructor answered our questions and commented on our papers in a tone that, albeit critical, was much less severe than it had been when he first spoke to us. Still, the atmosphere was heavy and uncomfortable. As someone said afterwards: "If they force us to plead guilty to a maximum of crimes, it is probably to justify putting all of us in prisons like this one."

Long became utterly discouraged, desperate even. He told me he had in his possession some poison with which to put an end to his life whenever he felt "too humiliated." I did not know whether he was sincere or not, so I said, "You'll be wasting your life if you die now. There are many things we don't know yet or haven't experienced. It would be a pity if we died now!"

Long said, "I am filled with frustration and anger. To think that these *bodoi*, so weak, so stupid, have beaten us is more than I can bear—"

Angry tears choked his words. I was deeply moved, and to try to boost his morale, I told him that I had noticed that many people had managed to keep up unyielding spirits, as if they had never known defeat despite their confinement in the camps. I told him what for me was the most memorable story of the day when the *bodoi* swarmed into Saigon.

"I can never forget that Southern army soldier I came across in the afternoon of that fateful day, April 29, 1975. The picture is still vivid in my mind, like the symbol of a tragedy, a betrayal, and a painful and sorrowful loss. After Duong Van Minh gave the order to the last remaining units—who were then quite prepared to defend Saigon to the last—to lay down their arms, the *bodoi* immediately swarmed into the city like a river overflowing its banks. ARVN units of paratroopers, marines, and rangers, their discipline and fighting spirit still intact in the face of the most desperate situation when the generals and colonels had run away like rabbits, found encouragement and solace in their pride and determination to fight to the last man and then die an honorable death. They had lived as fighters, and they wanted to die as fighters. But they had been ordered to lay down their arms; more, they had been abandoned by their superiors, who had not told them what to do in the face of events to come. So, when the *bodoi* flooded Saigon, they wandered aimlessly through the city.

"At nightfall, there were still men stripped to the waist, walking briskly toward the suburbs, some of them wearing only their underwear. They moved silently, their muscular torsos in sharp contrast to the thin bodies of the childlike *bodoi*, so strange-looking in their too ample uniforms. I did not know where they were going, so I asked one of them, a man whose skin the sun and lack of sleep had grayed and darkened, 'Where are you going? Don't you feel cold without your shirt?'

"The man stopped and looked at me for quite some time; then, apparently satisfied he could trust me, he finally asked, 'Do you have an extra pair of trousers you think you could give me?'

" 'Just a minute.' " I ran into the house and brought out a shirt and a pair of trousers and handed them to him. He hurriedly put them on. I asked, " 'Are you an ARVN soldier? What's your rank and where do you plan to go?'

" 'I am a paratroop sergeant; my unit has been disbanded as ordered; each of us is free to go and look for his relatives. I have no relatives in this area, so I will go to Phu Lam and find a place to spend the night. Tomorrow, I shall see—'

" 'Where is your commanding officer?'

" 'The lieutenant commanding my unit cried when we separated. He told us to take off our uniforms to avoid being humiliated. I don't know where he has gone. His native place is far north, in the highlands. Are you also army?'

"I was embarrassed, but I hurriedly denied it, for fear he should ask to be accommodated for the night. 'Er, no. But all my friends have been drafted into the army.'

" 'That was lucky for you! If you were army like us you would be unable to control your fury! I guess I cannot close my eyes if I die now.[5] Good-bye. And thank you very much.' He walked away, his open palm making a downward movement as if to say 'Let's forget all about it.'

"I looked after the man who recently had been a fighter as he walked into the dusk, and my heart was heavy with sorrow and pity. Tears of shame streamed down my cheeks. Like a supernatural being, he had illuminated my own conscience. I saw myself as a vile coward because I had failed him. The war was lost because of people like me, but he would not be defeated, not now or ever! In my eyes, he was a fighter who could never be vanquished, even though he had known failure. If the war was lost, it was not because of his doing or of people like him; his humiliation was due to other people's mistakes. He was like you, Long. I sincerely believe you have not lost the war because you had no part in bringing about this shameful debacle."

As he listened, Long wiped away his tears with his arm, like a child. He said in a voice choking with emotion, "I too can never forget the moment of separation between me and my men. When I told them to find ways to return to their families, they cried and said to me, 'What's the use? The bastards have

---

[5]Vietnamese expression, based on the popular belief that if a person's cherished wish, strong desire for vengeance, etc., is not yet fulfilled at the moment of his death, his eyes will not close.

occupied the whole of Central Vietnam; there's no place for us to go back to.'

"You know, they had followed me to many a battlefront. We had been through thick and thin together, sometimes coming within a hair's breadth of death. Yet then, I had to leave them to their fates because I myself did not know where to go! In the end, four of them who came from the same place got into a 'Conex' [a metal container used to pack weapons or other military equipment for transport] and blew themselves to bits with a grenade. From then on, I have constantly been plagued with guilt. You are the first person I've told the story to."

Long's story left me all the sadder. I regretted suspecting him of being an informer.

"How can people think that we have been fighting for the Americans?" Long asked. "What kind of money can buy hundreds of thousands of men and women who gave their lives as a sacrifice for this country? Don't they see that we have accepted sacrifices and hardships only to protect this free land of ours?"

"Yes," I said, "we have been hurt in the propaganda battle. Our sacrifices can only be appreciated by us alone. The enemy's propaganda activities abroad were much more efficient than ours. They used every means to convince people that we were nothing but mercenaries in the pay of the Americans."

"Rubbish! No mercenaries would fight in conditions where hardship and death were the only outcome. On the other hand, I don't think the Americans had the intention to exploit our country, did they?"

"Well, things were very complex and very ugly; they were not as simple as you might think. While we were enduring the hardships of war and accepting sacrifices to preserve this piece of land, countless organizations abroad condemned the Americans for their involvement in the Vietnam War and claimed that we were mere creatures of the Americans! If we must go to the root of the problem, it is our leaders who are to blame for having brought this on the whole nation. They all were people who lacked the necessary knowledge, experience, and authority to uphold our sovereignty and national prestige, and the result was this national humiliation. At the Geneva Conference, our delegation was forced to sit behind the French, and we did not protest! In Paris, our delegation put their signature to an agreement that had been negotiated behind our back by Washington and Hanoi! Our leaders were imbeciles and our allies tricky bastards; because of that, we are now subjected to this shameful treatment."

"Only now am I aware of the problem as you have explained it. During the war, I was too busy fighting the enemy in my own area of responsibility to pay much attention to the whole picture. It is really unfair! The world should have understood that we only wanted to live in freedom. If they thought it was so much better for us to submit to the communists, why didn't they themselves adopt communism in the first place?"

"I think we have said enough! The more we talk about it, the more angry we get. The sad reality is, at the present moment all of us in the South are guilty of 'opposition to the Revolution and the People'!"

I stood up to end the conversation; Long remained seated, his sad look reflecting utter despair.

The lesson involving self-assessment of guilt and self-indictment brought about much bitter reflection. The atmosphere in the camp was heavy and fraught with menace. In forcing us to acknowledge our many offenses, was it not their intention to cast us into a future they had already decided on? No one among us felt there was any prospect of comfort and security in the days to come.

Usually at the start of a study session, the monitors would ask us to sing in unison, while clapping to a beat, such revolutionary songs as "Solidarity" or "As if Uncle Ho Was Present in the Great Victory Celebration." But now, we clapped and hummed through the songs as a matter of form, and threats by the *bodoi* did not produce more enthusiasm. The cadres seemed to realize what was behind our reluctance, which was probably why the third lesson took place in a much more relaxed atmosphere. This time the instructor, younger than the other two, from time to time enlivened his lecture with a joke. The lesson began with a statement that became unbearably tedious as it was repeated over and over: "Vietnam is a country endowed with a fertile land and 'forests of gold and seas of silver.'" The lesson listed Vietnam's potential in terms of land, sea, and, especially, mineral resources. The instructor gave a few examples that made us clap our hands and laugh out loud because they were so idiotic and ludicrous. For instance, he said, "Residue from Hongay coal, which we spread over the surface of roads, is in great demand by the Japanese, who plan to convert this material into as many as 117 articles of merchandise! You see, only one item that we discard as waste material is sufficient to arouse the lust of the Japanese imperialists. But in order to safeguard our sovereignty, instead of selling it, we prefer to wait until we have the capability of manufacturing the goods ourselves!" Speaking about the Vietnamese language, he told a story of a Cuban specialist, a member of a construction support team, who was filled with admiration when he went through the Quang Tri area and heard a woman scold her child with "You naughty boy, you're such a vandal!" because he thought that even when showering abuse, the Vietnamese language still sounded like music. Hearing this, we all clapped our hands in derision. Somebody swore in exasperation, wondering why he did not choose a quotation from our treasure of famous poems if he wished to discuss the language.

The more we listened to the various instructors who came to give lectures, the more doubtful we became of the intellectual level of people from the North; someone remarked with irony that perhaps we were so ignorant that such instructors had to be sent to see to our education! Bay, a former physics teacher and native of the South, complained, "In the past, the expression 'talk like a

Vem'[6] was often used to praise a person for eloquence. Now that we've heard authentic Vems talk, it stinks!"

During the entire discussion period that followed, we picked out the most ludicrous, the most stupid examples given by the instructor to discuss. Some of the men feared reports by the informers, but we kept on because we felt the informers would be reluctant to report what we said about the idiocy of the cadres.

The subject of the next lesson was "The Vietnamese Labor Party is the Party that has led the Vietnamese people from one victory to another and to final victory." Roughly speaking, it recalled that in the course of our history there had been a great number of struggles aimed at either winning back or defending national independence, including resistance movements against the French; but these were all short-lived. The Vietnamese people had to wait until the formation of the Party in 1930 to be able to secure continuous and permanent victory. In discussing this propaganda, all we had to do was praise the Party, and everything went smoothly for us.

The final lesson dealt with the topic "To love one's country is to love socialism." It served to coerce people into admitting that socialism—and only socialism—could truly protect the fatherland. When discussing the lesson, many of us raised the question of why many nonsocialist countries were independent and their nationals living in comfort and happiness. This was rejected at once by the instructor, who said there was no country that was truly independent and no people living in happiness unless socialism had been adopted. He noted that in nonsocialist countries there were still strikes and fights for pay raises, which proved that their nationals were not yet living in happiness. Only in socialist countries were there no strikes. He pointed to the USSR as an example of a socialist country where people lived in complete happiness and said that as a consequence, it had been noted that the USSR had achieved the most success of any country in the world. The discussion ended with everybody expressing the hope that Vietnam could catch up fairly quickly with the Soviet Union. Having enumerated outstanding Soviet achievements and affirming that the Soviet Union was first in everything, the instructor said, "I've noticed that many of you, though outwardly accepting what I've told you, inwardly still have doubts. It's because you are so fearful of the Americans and admire them so much that you can't see anybody more capable than the Americans."

We applauded. The instructor, thinking we were showing appreciation for his remark, also clapped his hands and said, "That's true! When you admire the

---

[6]Popular and derogatory pronunciation of V.M. (Vei + Em = Vem), the abbreviation for Viet Minh, itself a short form of Việt Nam Độc Lập Đồng Minh Hội (League for the Independence of Vietnam). The Viet Minh was dominated by the communists, so by the 1950s for the man in the street, "Viet Minh" most of the time was equivalent to "communist."

Americans so much that you worship them, you tend to be blinded by your feelings—"

A ripple of applause and laughter went through the audience. The irony was that from the very beginning of the reeducation period, the *bodoi* had spoken with awe about the Soviet Union out of all proportion to reason so that listeners were either amazed or irritated. Some *bodoi* even stated that "when the Americans brought their B-52s into the war, they had no inkling that the Soviet Union had already deployed sophisticated weapons 'in the clouds,' and when the bombers arrived, they were immediately shot down."

The Soviet Union was set up as a perfect model of socialist achievement. Still, the instructor did not bring much enthusiasm into his argument in support of the idea that "to love one's country is to love socialism," nor did he seem to mind much our lukewarm attitude during the discussion.

After more than a month of this kind of political education, we felt completely drained. Sitting all day in the lecture hall or staying around our shed to participate in the discussions or write the "results obtained" papers, we had little time for physical exercise. Although our diet had been improved by a relatively regular supply of food, every one of us had become obviously thinner. Then we were informed that we would have to rewrite our personal histories, taking into account recent developments and the fact that we have been "equipped with new concepts and logic."

We all felt we were in for an unpleasant surprise and we were right. The instructor explained that this time, besides the necessary account of past history, we also had to assess, politically, each member of our families as well as the things we had done in the past. Finally, the account was to be brought before the group for "constructive criticism," which meant that members of the group would "help" by making accusations so that "each could see more clearly his own offenses."

In making declarations about relatives, we had to mention their guilt as well. For example, when I stated that my grandfather had been a district civil servant, I had to add that he belonged to the feudalistic social category; my father, who had been a teacher in the days of French colonization, had to be considered a member of the intelligentsia, therefore, a lackey of the French imperialists. If a man's father had been a farmer, he had to specify whether he belonged to the "landlord" category (if he owned his own ricefields) or was a "poor farmhand" (if he worked the land for the owner). Similar social categories were applied to all occupations. The cadres who supervised the writing kept impressing us with the implications of each of us having to make three copies of the account, one to be sent to our place of birth, one to our present address or former employer, and the last copy to the central government. The officials at these places would evaluate the account for accuracy and note untrue or incomplete statements. This caused many of us to write and rewrite, over and over, for fear of being accused of insincerity. The whole business was a headache, and then came the reading of the account before one's group, followed by a critique and assessment of the writer's sincerity and willingness to acknowledge his guilt. Whole mornings had to be devoted to reading and criticizing the accounts; at the most, three papers could be got through at each session. At the end of the session, every remark about or criticism of an account had to be written down on a piece of paper and attached to it.

In the hope of acquiring merit in the eyes of the Revolution, some people became very cooperative. They went so far as to accuse others in their group of downgrading their previous ranks to minimize their guilt. One could never have imagined that reeducation could lead to such degradation!

On the evening of the day that we finished criticizing the accounts, Long sat down to talk with me. He confided his fear that when his account was sent to his native place, it would be discovered that his father was not a poor farmhand, as he had declared, but was in fact a landlord. I relieved his worries somewhat by expressing my doubts about the feasibility of sending such an enormous number of documents to various destinations for checking.

"According to my estimates," I told him, "the number of civil servants on reeducation amounts to tens of thousands; the number of officers must be in excess of 100,000; 'capitalists,' members of political parties, and religious groups also would total more than 100,000. The sum total of all the accounts would amount to more than a million. They wouldn't have enough personnel and cadres to deal with this business of checking up on each and every one of us."

Long told me later that many men believed the Revolution eventually would do the checks because they would not have to tackle the whole task at once but could take their time about it; they also might examine only the accounts of people they were ordered to pay special attention to.

During private talks with one another, we discovered that the majority of inmates, in their desire to be left alone for the time being, had accused themselves of the most serious offenses they could think of. A number of men who had not occupied any important position or who came from poor families and, consequently, had no grounds for self-indictment had, as a last resort, invented such offenses as "opposition to communism" or "hatred of communism" as a result of watching pictures of the great massacre of the civilian population by the communists during the Tet Mau Than (1968) offensive in the ancient capital of Hue. Much against our will, we accused ourselves in very strong terms to avoid having such harmful remarks as "attempt to hide past offenses" or "unwillingness to show repentance" entered into our records.

Like all things, the study period too came at last to an end. To me, it had been like a nightmare, assessing my own parents and grandparents, representing them as members of certain social categories, and accusing myself of offenses I had had no idea of. And yet, after doing this, we were still not free of anxiety or the fear of being accused of something. I wanted to forget about the whole affair, if only to give relief to my mind, but many were so obsessed by this business of writing their past histories and judging their offenses that they behaved like dotards. Some would complain to anyone willing to listen: "My guilt was such that it will be difficult for me to be pardoned by the Revolution!" Depending on his nature, each person had a different attitude in the face of a given situation. There were those who seemed not to care what happened; at night, they would lie down and sleep soundly as usual. Others, when faced with a problem, would worry incessantly, their faces haggard from sleeplessness and despair.

A week after we had completed our political studies, we were ordered to assemble in the yard. A *bodoi* called out the name of Tanker Quang, told him to return to his shed, pack, and get ready for "transfer to another camp." The rest of us were told to stay where we were, lined up in the sun, thus preventing us from getting news to our families through him. Nobody was fooled by this "transfer" business; everybody knew that Quang was being released because of his father-in-law's intervention.

The fact that only one person was released at the end of the political studies worried all of us. Up to now, if few had been allowed to return home, it was because we had not yet been reeducated; things should be different now that we had been through political indoctrination, yet nothing had changed. Some of the men tried to elicit a clue from the monitors but only got noncommittal answers to questions. "Don't worry!" they told us. "Rest assured; you'll be released in due course. Surely, some will be released earlier, some later than the others. You cannot go home all at the same time because the offenses committed by one person are different from those of another." Worries grew as the days passed without further releases; many risked putting direct questions to high-ranking cadres they chanced to meet. Meanwhile, it was rumored that a great number of inmates at other camps had been released, but I believed the rumor had been spread by the cadres themselves to try to alleviate our worries and impatience, maybe to prevent a possible mutiny.

One day the *bodoi* summoned us to the meeting hall where a cadre from regimental headquarters attempted to explain that our reeducation was not yet completed; we had just finished the first stage; his superiors were making preparations for the second stage. When we raised questions, we got only vague answers. We made it clear that we were not satisfied. Finally the cadre said, "I have been instructed by my superiors to come here to give you the necessary explanations. I have told you everything my superiors wanted me to convey to you, but you are not satisfied. Well, I'll personally tell you this, as a friend. You cannot return home at this moment. Outside, a campaign for the building of our new society is being launched; the People will not leave you alone if you return among them now! It's better to bide your time. Stay here, continue with your reeducation, wait until you get good results, and return home at the opportune moment. You want me to specify how long it will take. I don't really know, so I cannot tell you. However, I can tell you this much, on my honor as a communist: although your reeducation cannot be completed in a short time, it will not take a very long time either. So, be patient and apply yourselves to your studies."

Hearing these tortuous tautological explanations, most of us realized that we had no hope of being released after reeducation. Our confinement no doubt was indefinite! Our spirits had never been lower than at this moment.

The political study period had ended. The camp had been cleared of rubbish. Every cultivatable piece of land had been hoed up to grow greens and sweet potatoes, and we had not much left to do. Each day small groups were detailed to do some weeding at various spots. The end of the year was drawing near.

The scabies plague was reaching tragic proportions. In my platoon of sixty men, only six, including myself, were still unaffected by the disease. The *bodoi* finally realized the seriousness of the situation. One day the chief monitor, making his inspection rounds, saw people lying on the floor inside their mosquito nets. Returning to his office, he assembled his teams of monitors to reprimand them. Their voices were easily overheard where I was weeding outside the office.

"Why did you let them sleep until this hour without telling them to take down their mosquito nets?"

A monitor answered back, "Go and see for yourself! They have scabies. With pus and blood oozing all over their bodies, they cannot put on their clothes. And this attracts flies. If we do not allow them to take cover inside their mosquito nets, the flies will spread scabies everywhere. You have to make a report to higher authorities and request medicine to be supplied to us. Otherwise, we ourselves will be infected!"

Commander Sau intervened. "The fact is we have made several reports on the situation, but there has been no response as yet!"

A few days later a *bodoi* came to our barrack and gáve us a big bunch of leaves—guava, cassia, origanum—with the recommendation that we boil the leaves and have those infected with scabies bathe with the water. Some fellows after such bathing felt itchy all over; their moaning was frightful to listen to. The doctors among us said that a few injections of an antibiotic would be all that was necessary to cure the condition. The monitors took note of this information and decided to send a messenger to regimental headquarters. But when he returned, he said only that the "regiment is running out of medicines and is waiting for supplies from higher echelon. Only emergency cases are allowed to be transferred to the regimental infirmary." Three people were suggested as fitting this description, but the chief monitor did not agree, claiming that three were too many. Finally he gave permission for Tri, a man in my platoon, to go. For some reason he was still waiting several days later for the order to depart, although he was packed and ready to leave at a moment's notice.

Christmas was approaching, and from a Catholic church nearby, the music of Christmas carols was beginning to reach us through a loudspeaker pointed in our direction. On the afternoon of Christmas Eve, we sat listening to the music from the church, our hearts filled with sadness. Nobody said anything to anybody; only an occasional groan and moan were heard. We were overcome with homesickness and grief. Suddenly, a *bodoi* appeared and told us to get ready to bring Tri to the regimental infirmary and appoint somebody to accompany him. I hastened to volunteer. It was then five o'clock; a moment later, the *bodoi* returned and gave the order to depart. Tri found it impossible to put his clothes back on; his body was covered with pus and his feet with sores. Unable to put his sandals on, he borrowed a pair of makeshift sabots made from a piece of wood with narrow strips of rubber for straps. He could only walk with short steps, the straps of the sabots rubbing against his insteps, which soon were running with blood. I walked beside him with his bag of clothes in my hand. The *bodoi*, his AK slung on his shoulder, followed a few paces behind. We took a long time to get out of the camp, and some distance farther on the *bodoi* came up to me and said, "We have to walk faster; otherwise, it will be dark before we arrive."

Tri moaned, "I can't; my blood spurts out at each step and it's very painful. I would like very much to walk faster, but I can't."

The *bodoi* said encouragingly, "Try harder, will you! Once there, you will have medicine and be cured. I think you're lucky to be allowed to go to the infirmary. If you stayed back at the camp, you would never be cured of this disease."

He seemed to be a kind sort of fellow, so I started up a conversation with him. "Do you know that in Saigon people are now celebrating Christmas? This Xuan Loc district itself has a big Catholic population. There must be much merrymaking in the streets."

The *bodoi* drew near and spoke in a low voice. "I've noticed that people in this town are having a big Christmas celebration. There's a Catholic fellow in our battalion, you know."

"Have you visited Saigon yet?"

"Not yet. I have a relative living in Saigon, but I haven't been bold enough to look for him. I wouldn't dare disclose that I have a relative who worked for the *nguy* government. My cousin migrated to the South in 1954; he has sent me a number of postcards from his new place. I still keep his address, but I haven't had a chance to write to him; I'm afraid of discovery if his letters are sent to the camp."

"Why don't you ask somebody in town—anybody for that matter—to let you use his address? The people in this town are kindhearted and willing to help. If you ask them, they won't hesitate to oblige you."

"Yes, that's a good idea. But don't tell anybody. If my superiors knew that I was in contact with you, I'd be disciplined."

"Don't worry! I don't talk much. By the way, I'd like to ask you something. Why do you think we have not been released since we completed reeducation?"

"How naïve of you! Reeducation is not the main purpose! The intention is to keep you in custody while they carry out their plan to abolish the old regime. Besides, it will take time to build the new society; it seems that the People are already beginning to show their opposition to the reform. In the North, after the return of the Party to Hanoi in 1954, a great number of people were arrested and put in prison for a long time. There are people who, even now, are being kept in detention! I believe you will have to wait for quite a long time yet. In the meantime, I would advise you to be very cautious when speaking to people; don't say anything rash; otherwise you'll be reported on and that's very dangerous. Living under the new regime demands that you know how to behave. Even I cannot disclose my relationship with people in the South. If that is known, I will have to forego my hope of being admitted to a communist youth organization and to the Party; and if you are not a member of a Party organization, you cannot be nominated to attend proficiency courses, which lead to promotion to higher ranks. Ah! We are approaching regimental head-quarters now. Please walk in front of me."

The *bodoi* stopped and waited until Tri and I got about two meters ahead of him; then he followed with his rifle pointed at our backs.

No one was on duty when we arrived at the infirmary. The place was full of camp internees lying around, most of them wrapped up in blankets and moaning audibly. Obviously, these were serious malaria cases. The *bodoi* went to look for the duty officer. Finally, someone who looked more presentable than the other *bodoi* appeared. He took Tri's name, entered it into a register, then asked, "Why did you come so late? It's nearly seven o'clock. I am not authorized to admit him to the infirmary until the doctor has examined him and made his decision."

We waited a long time before the doctor arrived. He was definitely an important person, and he asked coldly, "What's your illness? I see that you can walk; then it's not serious."

The *bodoi* who came with us answered, "Begging the comrade's permission, I'd like to report that this man is seriously infected with scabies. He has lost a lot of blood, so we have asked Regiment's permission to bring him here for treatment."

"What does Regiment know about it? The decision is mine alone after proper examination of the patient. You there, come here!" Tri dragged himself forward toward the light of the lamp. The doctor looked at him and shook his head. "This is not scabies! This is V.D.! We do not accept such cases here. Probably this is a consequence of your overindulgence in sexual pleasures in the past, is it not?"

The *bodoi* looked at me with apprehension; if we had to bring Tri back to camp, we would have a very hard time, indeed. He hastened to reply, "Begging leave to report to the comrade, there are at least 100 men suffering from the same disease at our camp. This one is the most serious. They have among them many doctors, and they also diagnosed the illness as scabies, not V.D."

"Pooh! What do they know about making diagnoses?"

In desperation, Tri took the risk of insisting on the real nature of his illness. "I request to be given a careful examination. I warrant you that I am not affected by V.D. If it's V.D., feel free to have me shot on the spot."

The doctor hesitated, not knowing what to do. Finally he reached for the register, jotted down a few words, then said, "Well, I'll admit him for the time being, for observation. If necessary, I'll contact the battalion and tell them to take him back."

"Thank you, comrade," the *bodoi* answered promptly.

The doctor did not reply. I put the bag of clothes at Tri's side and bade him good luck. I got out of the room, the *bodoi* hard on my heels with his rifle leveled. Only after we were outside the headquarters area did he move forward to walk beside me, his rifle now slung on his shoulder. "It's our bad luck to have met this doctor," he said. "He's the most difficult one there. If he's on duty when any of us report sick, we just leave. If he did examine us, we would be dismissed with a few quinine tablets and no sick leave."

We were walking on a public road now declared out of bounds because it was situated within the military zone. About 300 meters away was one of the streets of the town with a few meagerly lighted shops on each side of the street. As we approached, I saw among the vendors a couple of girls selling sweets and cigarettes. I asked, "Could you allow me to stop and buy some cigarettes?"

"Yes, you can do some buying but don't be too long. If someone from the camp saw us, we'd be in for big trouble!"

"Don't worry! It won't take me more than a few minutes."

I quickly took one of the 500-*dong* notes hidden carefully in the lapel of my jacket and went toward the half-lit area with the *bodoi* at my heels. Sweets, bananas, and cigarettes were displayed on the counter. I first asked for some cigarettes. After paying for them, I told the vendor I wanted to buy sweets. She looked at me and said, "For a *bodoi,* you're strangely dressed."

Before I could reply, the *bodoi* answered quickly, "He's a fellow on reeducation. My superiors decided to send him out to buy cigarettes and sweets. Do you or do you not want to sell?"

The young vendor said teasingly in her Southern accent, "Ah! How unkind this young *bodoi* is! Can't I ask when I see something strange?" She took the change from the cigarette sale and turned to me. "These are sweets made in the West; they cost as much as 500 *dong*. But this is a bargain sale, in support of the ones who are in there." She handed me the pack of sweets, then added another one. I nodded my thanks.

"Let's go back now," the *bodoi* urged me on.

I had not expected such luck when I volunteered to accompany Tri to the infirmary. On the way back to the camp, the *bodoi* moved a few paces behind me for fear of meeting his comrades from the battalion; many people were now seen walking toward the center of the town. I held my two packs of sweets under my armpits to look as if I carried nothing on me. Anyway, the street lamps were too dim for anybody to notice me. Reaching the camp, I said to the *bodoi*, "Thank you. You have been most kind to us. We shall always be grateful."

He answered, "There's nothing to thank me for. I have no enmity for you. Be patient and try to endure your hardship." With that, he dragged the "concertina" of barbed wire across the entrance to our area.

We celebrated Christmas night by eating sweets and listening to the music coming from the church. We savored each piece of sweetmeat, for it had been a long time since we last had the chance to go out and buy or taste anything that was sugary. One man, unwrapping a piece of candy, said, "This time last year, while we were celebrating Christmas, did anyone have the slightest thought that we would be confined in this place as we are today?" His eyes brimmed with tears.

The next morning, to our surprise, the *bodoi* did not come to call the roll and assign work. After a long wait, the order came for everyone to have the day off, to be spent in the camp. As I had some job every day, I had not had occasion until now to see the pitiable sight of my companions who were infected with scabies dragging themselves out onto the cement court to lie in the sun, hoping it would kill the acari and dry their skin. Each had in his hand a small branch with dried leaves clinging to it which he used to chase away flies. Old Mr. Cuc pointed to a youngish man, half-naked like the others, and said, "That fellow over there is Nguyen Ngoc Nhut, son of former Vice President Nguyen Ngoc Tho; he's now contaminated by scabies like anybody else!"

Although we were in the same platoon, I had not paid much attention to him until now. I knew him, however, from my school days. Vice President Tho himself had helped my family obtain permission to bury my mother in the capital's cemetery. If we had not been able to bury my mother there, we would have been at a loss to find a place. We hadn't the means to bring her remains back to our native place and we had not joined any of the societies that would have taken care of the burial. Now, I decided to repay somehow my debt of gratitude, and I approached Nhut to ask about his needs. He told me he belonged to a squad living in the shed near mine. I gave him a few tablets of antibiotic from my provision of medicines and told him to use them as a trial cure against the scabies. The drug alleviated his condition some, but an adequate dose to clear it up would have required a few dozen tablets. After a temporary defeat, the scabies resumed its virulent attack on the poor fellow.

The "epidemic" was such that nobody was fit to go to work. The study monitors told us that measures to be applied to the whole camp were being considered. Perhaps we would be permitted to pool money and appoint somebody to go into town to buy medicine. But the doctors among us said that Xuan Loc would not have enough of a supply to treat every patient in camp. It would be best if we could write home and ask our relatives to buy medicine at a much lower price, considering its availability in Saigon. The monitors thought this was a good idea. To us, it was perfect. This would give us an opportunity to communicate with our families. Since June, when we first reported for reeducation more than six months before—supposedly for only seven days—we had had no chance to write to our families or even let them know that we were still alive. And of course our relatives had no idea of our whereabouts.

Finally, permission was given to us to write home. We were instructed not to write anything that could give a hint as to the location of the camp. "Any letter that appears to have given an indication of where you're now living will not be transmitted," the order said. Anyway, what mattered most to us was the chance to inform our families that we were alive. I believed I could manage to let my wife know of my whereabouts since I had once brought her to Xuan Loc on a visit to a friend of mine, named Hop, and his family. So in my letter I wrote, "Tell Hop and his wife not to worry about the money I owe them; I shall pay them back later." I hoped my wife would guess what I meant to say because I owed no money to Hop. Later, I found that it happened as I had planned, that my wife was able to guess where I was being held. In my letter I said I was not infected with scabies but she might as well send me some antibiotics, just in case.

A week later I was informed that gifts had arrived for me at battalion headquarters. Tet, the Vietnamese New Year, was barely two weeks away, so I was very happy that something had arrived for me, but I was disappointed when I opened the package. Although I had written that I was not affected by scabies, my wife believed I actually was but had been instructed to write the contrary. The package had been limited to three kilos, and more than half was medicine: a potassium permanganate solution, absorbent cotton, a dozen tubes of cream, and about 100 antibiotic tablets. What remained consisted of small quantities of shredded meat, sweets, toothpaste, and sugar. In other words, the edibles were not as plentiful as I had expected.

One of the men, Bay, received, among other things, a green mango wrapped in a small plastic bag. His letter had a postscript saying, "I think you will be allowed to eat this mango while it's still green because I hope the Revolution will not forbid you to eat a mango grown in our garden." The monitor responsible for the censorship of the letters and the checking of the gifts said Bay's wife was nuts, and Bay conceded, "I must confess that she is a little crazy." We all laughed. But afterward Bay confided to me that his wife was very clever, and what she wrote in the postscript was meant to inform him that she knew he was being held in a place not too far away, so that he would receive the mango while it was still green. This was an example among countless others of how we and our families found ways to communicate with one another.

But our ruses were not always possible. The very next time we were allowed to write home, we were instructed to follow a definite formula. It was forbidden to add anything that was not part of the authorized pattern, which was two paragraphs. The first included such sentences as "I am in good health" or "I am sick, I need medicines such as..."; the second was meant to "summon up our families' enthusiasm" with the phrase "every member of the family should contribute to the task of building the new society in order to soon secure welfare and happiness."

Owing to the medicines sent by their relatives, the men afflicted with scabies, which had spread like a forest fire and caused such havoc among them, were quickly cured. Within a week, the sores dried up and crusted over; the men were able to put on their clothes and walk normally without pain.

The whole camp was instructed to make preparations for Tet. Battalion headquarters was to supply a cow for the occasion, and we were told to plan an entertainment program. All this boosted our spirits; how different compared to a few days before when we had to lie in bed and listen to the pitiful moaning and crying of our companions plagued by scabies!

Those among us who had a gift for performance responded enthusiastically; their rehearsals attracted a great number of onlookers, among them many *bodoi*. Many in the camp were well versed in music; one in particular, Ha Van Ngan, specialized in composing scores for church music, and he, along with some others, took care of group singing. Dr. Thuy, who recited poems so beautifully, was responsible for a poetry and dramatic performance. All the creative work had to be submitted to battalion headquarters for censorship, and no impromptu or on-the-spot improvisations were allowed. The Tet preparations alleviated somewhat the sadness of the younger men but did not much change the taciturn and melancholy attitude of the older ones.

On New Year's Day the cow was butchered. An aged lieutenant named Cuong, a native of Nha Trang City, volunteered to do the cutting up. The best cuts, of course, went to the camp command. A piece of meat as large as two finger joints was distributed to each of us. The day before we each were given a few sweets and a share of tobacco as big as a betel nut, and we still had some of the food received from our families that we had saved for the occasion. So everybody was cooking for the great feast. The *bodoi* watched in amazement. One of them pointed to a *lap xuong* (Chinese sausage) and asked, "What kind of dried animal is that?"

Cooking at this camp was not easy. We could not borrow cooking utensils from the kitchen as we were forbidden to go there because we might ask for a drink of the *nuoc com*.[7] But we were well stocked with cans. Before, only a few of us carried aluminum cans, which had once contained powdered milk, and we had used them to cook small quantities of greens that we found. Now most of us had written home to ask for foods to be sent in aluminum cans, and there were plenty of "pots" to cook in. Those whose families lived in the distant highlands or had been lost during the war did not have aluminum cans. They had to use tin cans thrown away by the *bodoi*. Although rusted, these were still usable. My companions joked about wealthy people who could afford to have as many as two aluminum cans or "gos" (short for Guigoz, a popular French brand of powdered milk); as I had two of them, I was mocked and called a "millionaire." Mockery notwithstanding, my two "gos" served me well during my five years of detention in various reeducation camps, whether to fry food, simmer soup, or cook rice gruel.

As we were not allowed to use the camp kitchen, we usually did our cooking—furtively, most of the time—at the foot of various trees. We had to collect every dry leaf, twig, and small branch we could find to use as fuel, and each of us had a bundle of these hidden somewhere near his sleeping place in case we has a chance to light it and cook whatever was edible: a portion of cassava root, a few shoots of amaranth or purslane, or the like. Now, supplied with food from our families, we busied ourselves cooking different dishes; the grassy patch beside our shed was covered with the smoke rising from our fires. The *bodoi*, who usually objected to our cooking, now turned a blind eye, and those on the lookout in the watchtowers sometimes shouted down, "What are you cooking? It smells so good!"

On New Year's Eve, our ad hoc drama and music groups performed first for the *bodoi*; we were to watch the second show, which took place at night. A particular feature of the day was a volleyball match. We had been instructed to mark out part of the yard to serve as a court, and the net and ball were lent to us by the *bodoi*. Old Mr. Cuc, a former sports coach at the Nha Trang Naval Academy, was in his element. Judging by the way he organized the game and umpired the match, everybody agreed he was a real professional. In practice games on previous days, the men who had been selected to play in the match got tired after playing only a short time, blaming a lack of food. The monitors

---

[7]Literally, "rice water," a viscous liquid produced after rice has simmered in water. The *nước cơm* is believed to be highly nutritious and has been used by Vietnamese, especially the poor, to feed infants and the sick.

reported this to battalion headquarters, and it was decided that members of the volleyball teams would be treated to a "special diet" for two days prior to the match, which meant that they were allowed to eat their fill and drink tea sweetened with sugar.

The entertainment on New Year's Eve was appreciated noisily by the *bodoi*, whose loud clapping reached as far as our quarters. When it was our turn to watch, we all acknowledged that our artists had practiced seriously and made careful preparations for the event. Two songs for the chorus, entitled "River Lo" and "No Enemy Can Get in Our Way," were so well scored that the *bodoi* themselves kept commenting, "The *nguy* fellows really know music!" Dr. Thuy's poetry recitation moved us all to tears, and everyone enjoyed the popular "Vong Co" (literally, "Nostalgia of Times Past") sung by a former actor of a "renovated theater" group. But the most entertaining performance came unexpectedly from a scene depicting Tao Quan being received in audience by the Celestial Emperor.[8] Naturally, in this scene Tao Quan reported the offenses committed by the Americans and the *nguy*, and Nam Tao recorded the indictment. Then Tao Quan begged the Celestial Emperor to sympathize with the men undergoing reeducation whose dearest wish was to be allowed to return soon to their families. Upon which, the actor playing the Celestial Emperor delivered an impromptu speech that made the audience both cry and laugh. Responding to Tao Quan's appeal, he said in a voice choking with emotion, "I must confess that I also wish for the same thing! I also hope to be allowed to go back to my wife and children soon!"

The audience clapped and laughed. Many of us burst into tears because of the sorrowful implication of the joke. Even the battalion staff, the monitors, and the *bodoi* sitting in the front row clapped in appreciation, despite the breach of discipline of the improvisation. Another feature of the occasion was "Uncle Ton's[9] Address to the Nation," in which he expressed his best wishes for the New Year. After hearing the speech read by a *bodoi*, we told one another that its words were identical to a lecture we had been given only a few days before. This reminded us of the admonition, "Speak and act according to the teaching of the Revolution." We had often noticed the way the *bodoi* expressed themselves in exactly the same way and had often wondered why. Now we understood: they had been taught that much; therefore they had only that much to say! They all came from the same mold, behaved according to the same model.

---

[8]The Celestial Emperor (also called Jade Emperor) is the supreme ruler of the universe. Táo Quân is a household deity. Each year, on the twenty-third day of the twelfth lunar month, he has to fly up to the celestial court to report on good or bad deeds of the members of the household during the year. Nam Taò is the deity who is a kind of registrar at the celestial court.

[9]Tôn Đức Thắng was the figurehead president of the Democratic Republic of Vietnam in the collective leadership that emerged on the death of Ho Chi Minh in 1979.

The next day, after the forced merriment of the Tet celebration, everyone became his old sullen self again. Our self-pity was even worse, since this was the first Tet spent in a reeducation camp. Now, we waited and worried about our fate. What would happen to us in the days to come? All our jailers had told us was that we could not be released yet. Would they keep us here indefinitely?

Meanwhile, we had practically nothing to do except sweep and clean the camp and chop wood for Logistics. The monitors themselves were at a loss to find work for us to do. They invented small tasks to keep us busy. Finally, they told us to pry loose the slabs of stone in the area before the meeting hall and use them to pave the road leading into the camp. This area had probably been used to park armored cars in the past. The stones were pried loose one by one, put into canvas bags, and carried to the road outside. We were told to do the work without any regard to construction techniques, simply laying down the slabs in a layer covering the road surface. Maybe the *bodoi* thus hoped to avoid having their vehicles sink in the mud when the rainy season came, but a civil engineer among us observed that the stones themselves would sink when it rained, and the road would become a mass of stones and mud. The *bodoi* shouted their vexation. "Get on with your work! Don't try to get out of carrying stones for the road. If you don't work at this, you'll have other things to do anyway."

It was back-breaking work, carrying the heavy bags of stones under the blazing sun. In our undernourished state, we were soon exhausted; the former doctors, in particular, became faint and pale after only a few loads. A *bodoi* asked Dr. Nguyen Khiem, the eye specialist, "Have you ever carried stones before?"

Khiem replied, "No, not until now."

"Then have a go at it, just to taste this kind of work."

The "paving" lasted less than a month because there were no more stones to work with. After a week of waiting for another assignment, we were organized into production teams and instructed to hoe the ground outside the camp for planting maize and sweet potatoes. This promised to be a fairly large-scale undertaking. Beyond the camp perimeter we saw local people also busy hoeing land in preparation for future crops.

Arriving at our new worksite the first day, we began to partition off land into plots that would then be allocated to the various teams. There was plenty of land in that area, and we had the impression that we would be staying a long time, farming it. The team leaders were told to look for inmates who had some farming experience and instruct them to show the rest of us what to do.

On the third day, however, events took an unexpected turn. Local people, mostly women, were gathered at the worksite when we arrived. They demanded to know why their land was being occupied. One of the *bodoi* asked, "Which land is yours?"

A woman standing in the front of the group replied in a loud voice, "This land here! Many generations of local folks have worked hard to make this land productive; we now entirely depend on it for our livelihood."

The *bodoi* retorted, "This is wasteland, and we have been ordered to bring these fellows who are on reeducation to work the land."

The women shouted back, "What order? Who signed it? This land belongs to us. We haven't worked it because it's not time yet. Now that you have hoed the ground, all the fertile soil will be washed away when it rains. We have to wait until there's enough rain to begin any work on this land."

The monitor then intervened, asking, "You say this land belongs to you. Do you have papers or documents? Show them to me!"

A middle-aged woman replied, "As many as you want. You have no right to take possession of our property."

Monitor Hong insisted, "Where are your papers? Show them to me!"

"We don't have them with us! Do farmers in the North carry their papers around with them when they work in the fields?"

At this, everyone laughed.

The monitor, angry now, resorted to threats. "What's your name? I'm going to go to the province commissar to find out whether you really own this land."

"What gives you the right to ask for my name? Go back to the North, maybe there you have the right to ask anybody for his papers. But here in the South, only responsible people are entitled to ask for papers. You said you had your orders; then who signed the paper? What's the date? Have the people been notified of the order through the radio and the newspaper?"

Hong was furious, but he was too baffled to know what to say; all he could do was utter a vague threat. "Very well! If you want to know, you'll know soon enough!"

The women vied with each other to comment, "Pooh! Do *bodoi* now have all the right in the world to take possession of people's land? Don't people have the right to say anything about it?"

Monitor Hong ordered us to assemble to return to camp. On the way back, we talked and laughed about our peasant women. The angry *bodoi* shouted for us to "shut up."

At evening roll call, Monitor Hong himself took the trouble to explain the morning's event. "Don't worry about what happened this morning! Our superiors will take appropriate measures against those stubborn peasants. A preliminary investigation shows that they are landowners who have exploited the poor people for quite a long time. Besides, the local people are very regressive Catholics. They will certainly be punished."

As a result of what had happened, we resumed our wait for new assignments. The *bodoi*, relieved of guarding us at worksites, stayed in the camp, lounged around, and amused themselves. As we had no work, we started making miscellaneous implements and personal articles. Our footwear, which we had worn since reporting for reeducation, had to be repaired or replaced. We made saws out of the metal bands that had secured containers of military equipment, needles from bits of barbed wire, and files from pieces of steel taken from the frames of the "Made in the U.S.A." haversacks most of us had brought along. Our living quarters soon became a busy workshop. Some men sewed pieces of canvas removed from the mudguards of M-113 personnel carriers into bags of various sizes. Others made guitars out of salvaged plywood with steel strands of telephone wire for strings; for low-pitch strings, very thin copper wire taken from the meters of an electric motor was tightly wound around the steel strands. A third group made chisels out of the steel bolts that had secured the links of tank caterpillars, and with these, they chiseled out ornamental articles such as crucifixes or rings from stainless steel mess kits. The young *bodoi*, attracted by the quality of our products, offered to barter their cigarettes or tobacco for aluminum combs or knives.

The making of ornaments appealed to all of us because everyone wanted to have something to bring back as a souvenir to his wife and children. Later, it was the *bodoi* themselves who brought materials for us to work on. We asked them to look for discarded car batteries, the cases of which were sawed into small pieces, then polished by grinding and made into dominoes. They also found pieces of aluminum for combs. At first the monitors wanted to forbid this work, but after seeing the interesting articles we made for the *bodoi*, they too ordered all sorts of things, from aluminum suitcases and trunks to knives, combs, and brooches.

Because of our transactions, I was able to learn from the *bodoi* that the camp administration was in the process of "categorizing" us, based on our accounts of past history. I kept the information to myself. One evening after roll call, the monitor asked us to declare again our military serial numbers. A number of us were questioned again and again, especially those known to be former officers of combat, military intelligence, or military police units. The news on the categorization, which had leaked out, and the business of the serial numbers brought back all our old worries. For a week none of us had enough peace of mind to work at our crafts, but when we didn't hear anything new, we went back to making articles for daily use. Outside the camp, preparations were being made for national assembly elections; every evening loudspeaker vans criss-crossed the town to urge voters to turn out in large numbers.

The *bodoi* spent their leisure inventing new games, one of which consisted of removing the phosphorus component of an artillery shell and throwing it into the air like a piece of fireworks. In fact, they began this game when we showed them how to disassemble the shells so we could get the cases, which we made into women's bracelets. Later, seeing how many shells had been disassembled by the *bodoi*, the monitors forbade us to use any more shell cases. But the order came too late. The stage was set for trouble.

As there was no work to be done, we were ordered to move from the brick houses we had been living in to a crumbling shack. We hurriedly repaired it. A row of brick houses just in front of the shack apparently had served as married quarters, each house built to accommodate one small family. My carpentry team was instructed to make doors and windows for the houses and furnish them with tables, chairs, and beds. Each house then was allocated to two monitors. The first house in the row, having more windows than the others, was reserved for the political commander; the one next door went to the logistics commander and the third one to the military commander. Our transfer to new living quarters probably saved most of us from violent death.

During my whole period of reeducation, many events occurred that I can never forget; they are intensely alive in my memory; they still haunt me and maybe will forever. One of these events happened on the eve of election day, the first election of its kind to be held nationwide since the Northern armies swarmed into the South. It was April 24, 1976. That day, loudspeakers installed on cars and vans were constantly urging the citizens of Xuan Loc to go to vote the next day "for the building of a new Vietnam." The time was around noon; after the midday meal some of us were taking naps in the shade and others like me just resting and daydreaming. I was sitting near the fence, facing the area where the *bodoi* were quartered, and I watched them idly as they joyfully distributed some sugar among themselves. Perhaps the imminent election had called for a celebration. A *bodoi* called out, "Please, comrades in the cell, assemble for the distribution of sugar! And, mind you, this is Cuban sugar!"

Hearing this, old Mr. Cuc, Long, and I, who were resting at the foot of a tree, watched the scene with curiosity. Several young *bodoi* sat in a circle with a basin of tea placed in the center; each had in his hand an enamel bowl, which he usually used for rice. After tea was poured into the bowls, someone spread a sheet of paper on the cement floor and poured out the contents of a small sugar bag. We could not see how much sugar there was, but obviously it wasn't much. The one who poured the sugar out—apparently the squad leader—then invited the others to have some. "Now, comrades, let's have some tea with sugar!"

Each *bodoi* in turn bent forward, took a pinch of sugar with his fingertips, raised his face upward, opened his mouth wide, and let the sugar fall into it; after that, he drank some tea. It was the way people take medicine. Some of them spilled sugar all over their collars. While these *bodoi* were enjoying the sugar, others, standing guard across the alley over what seemed to be a quartermaster store, played at throwing lumps of phosphorus into the air, producing small explosions and bright sparks. One of the *bodoi* in the tea-drinking group swore.

"Damn! That stupid game of theirs is likely to set fire to the sheds. Just wait and see."

One of them cupped his hands to form a sort of loudspeaker and shouted, "If you don't stop your silly game, we'll have to report you. You're still breaking shells to pieces, and its against orders."

The other side shouted back, "Shut up! If you want to report, I'll give you grounds for that. Now, watch!"

A pack of phosphorus was thrown over; it quickly caught fire and zigzagged in the air; white smoke rose from it, and it came forward as if jet-propelled. But the tea-drinking *bodoi* only laughed and talked; they were having too much fun to be bothered. Suddenly, there was a shout from across the alley. "My God! It just shot into the store!"

Seconds later, frightened shouts broke out. "Fire! Fire! Sound the alarm! Sound the fire alarm!"

A minute later, there was a terrifying explosion. A pall of black smoke rose into the air. The *bodoi* cried out to each other, "They've set fire to the ammunition dump! The ammunition dump is on fire!"

When we heard the first shout, we thought only that some shed was on fire and that there was no immediate danger to us, but then the ammunition began exploding, and we called out wildly to each other, "Look out! The ammunition dump has been blown up! The ammunition dump—"

Our cries were drowned out by deafening explosions, and suddenly there was chaos all around. Those who had been taking a midday nap roused from sleep and dashed back and forth in search of shelter. I ran from the fire and took refuge behind the raised concrete floor of a building that we had just repaired. It was covered with corrugated iron sheets, and with its steel frame I thought it would be strong enough to protect us against shellbursts. But there was nothing over my head to protect me from a direct hit. At that instant, I saw Thuong, the one whose personal history account defied any known record for length, run in panic to a clump of banana trees and crouch behind them. I called out to him, "Thuong, come here quick! Can't you see that place is worthless as shelter?"

Thuong bent his back and ran toward me, while around us shells exploded continuously and more and more violently. Then, a shattering explosion, and I was momentarily deafened. The clump of banana trees had disappeared. A shell had landed on the spot and destroyed everything. Thuong was so terrified that he threw himself on the ground, praying aloud to Buddha: *"Na mo A Di Da Phat. . ."* (Hail to Amitabha. . .).

As my ears cleared, I heard the frightening shriek of rockets added to the boom of artillery shells, then the deep, hollow sound of explosions coming from afar. Clearly, the fire had reached the rocket dump. The shrieking noise filled our hearts with terror; I had seen demonstrations of firepower before, but this was far more frightening. After the ammunition dump behind us blew up, there seemed to be explosions all around us. Thousands of rounds of ammunition of all kinds and pieces of miltary equipment of every description whizzed above my head. Rockets still in their packing, AK rifles, and other armaments were zigzagging through the air, and from time to time, mortar shells looking like big pestles landed near us. All the *bodoi* had disappeared, except for Monitor Dong, who seemed not to be afraid of anything in the world. He made a show of being battle-hardened by walking around upright, at the same time shouting to us not to run about but lie motionless on the ground. From our prone position, we saw three mortar shells pop up from behind a shed, then land close to where Dong was standing. A loud explosion and he was nowhere to be seen; maybe he had been blown to smithereens by the blast. Suddenly somebody said, "Monitor Dong has been hit. He's tossing about in that patch of elephant grass over there!"

At the moment nobody thought of going to his rescue, but suddenly one man, heedless of danger, dashed out from our side, grabbed Dong under his arms, and dragged him toward the earthwork where the watchtower stood. Sheltering behind it, he called for help. "Help! *Bodoi* wounded! *Bodoi* wounded!"

He called again and again, in the midst of the deafening, shattering explosions without any *bodoi* appearing. When the explosions abated somewhat, a *bodoi* came from behind the other side of the earthwork, and the two of them carried Dong to a concrete bunker. It was then that I realized that the place was crowded with *bodoi*.

The explosions had begun about 2 P.M. and had only slightly abated by 5. It was not until dusk that we were ordered to assemble for roll call for a casualty count. As we gathered, we found that we had to go to the rescue of men who had jumped into the wells. Four wells had recently been dug, and all four were full of people; fortunately, it was the dry season, and each well contained barely a meter of water, so no one was drowned. A number of us were detailed to make a thorough search of the sheds for missing inmates; we found one body crushed under a pierced steel plate; these plates were the kind used to pave runways, very heavy and pierced with holes to let water through. When we lifted the plate, we saw a man lying underneath with his head crushed so that his eyeballs protruded. It was a ghastly spectacle. It took us a moment to understand what had happened. The plate had been placed on two supports and used as a table. The man had taken shelter under it hoping for the protection of the metal top, not expecting the cement brick supports to collapse from the strength of the blast. Later identified as Tran Dang Duong, a medical officer from Thua Thien Province, he was the only one killed from my sector of the camp.

After roll call, we found the casualties in our part of the camp to be light: one dead and seventeen slightly wounded. Luckiest of all were the fellows in the squad that had just been "evicted" from the brick houses and moved to a shed farther away. The row of brick houses, separated from the ammunition dump by only a narrow metal pathway, was completely destroyed. At the time of the explosion, the battalion staff and most of the study monitors were elsewhere, so they suffered no casualty except for Monitor Dong. He was seriously injured and was taken to the regimental infirmary, where he died. Those who had been wounded and taken to regimental headquarters for emergency treatment told us on their return that Dong had been hit in the thigh by a fragment of mortar shell, had lost a lot of blood, and, as there had been no blood to give him, had passed away during the night. They also told us that there were a great number of wounded among the inmates living in other parts of the camp.

Back in our shed, we discovered that a shell had landed on a spot about two meters from my sleeping place. Clothes, medicines, and food were scattered all over the place, and it took us until late at night to clear up the mess. My reserve of food was gone; fortunately, my clothes and money, carefully tucked away in my bag, were intact.

The next day we were allowed to prepare our mate Duong for a proper burial. In contrast to previous occasions at Trang Lon camp, when our dead companions had been wrapped carelessly in ponchos, Duong was placed in a real coffin purchased from the undertaker in town. This was the first and only time I ever witnessed a reeducation camp inmate being buried in a coffin as if he were an ordinary citizen. On occasions that followed, corpses were wrapped in sleeping mats or placed in rough coffins we made ourselves.

Although it was obvious that the disastrous explosions had occurred because the young *bodoi* had been playing their silly game, loudspeaker vans went around the town that night announcing that the culprits had been caught! The official communiqué read, "Hear this! Hear this! The recent explosion was a sabotage act committed by counterrevolutionary elements. The culprits have been caught by the People's security forces. We ask our fellow citizens to keep calm, go about your business as usual, and prepare to turn out in great numbers to vote at tomorrow's election. The culprits will be severely punished."

The following day, we had to start repairs. The metal walls and roofs of buildings had been pierced by shell fragments so that they looked like beehives. From the roofs of buildings, we saw that the district town of Xuan Loc appeared to have suffered severe damage. Beyond a perimeter about 300 meters from us, most of the houses had had their roofs blown off. Near our camp, a rice-processing factory was completely destroyed. Inside the camp, there was relatively little damage, but farther away, where most of the artillery and mortar shells and the 122mm rockets had landed, a great number of houses had been demolished. There must have been many casualties among the local people and much damage to their property.

Long and I were detailed to clear the house occupied by the battalion staff. We were instructed to put all the furnishings to one side and gather all the broken bricks into a corner. While clearing the kitchen, I chanced upon a bottle of cooking oil and a bottle of rice wine made from black glutinous rice. I was about to put them with the furnishings when Long took the bottle of wine, uncorked it, and drank several mouthfuls. Fearing discovery, I tried to stop him. "If you want to drink wine, pour some into a plastic bag and drink it when we are back in our place. If you drink it here, you'll smell of alcohol and won't be able to hide it."

Long agreed; he found one plastic bag for the wine and another for the cooking oil. That night, pretending we were going out for some fresh air, we chose a deserted spot and, between the two of us, drank the whole bagful of rice wine. I slept soundly that night, until it was clear daylight. As I woke up, I felt very nimble in both body and soul. Long too was more cheerful than usual; he nodded his contentment and said philosopically, "The ancients were right when they said, 'In misfortune, there is luck.'"

About a week after the explosions, we were ordered to assemble in the meeting hall. Political Commander Sau opened the meeting by speaking of the election results, which "had scored a political gain." He concluded with praise for the man who had rescued Monitor Dong. Despite efforts to create a cheerful atmosphere by staging volleyball and soccer games, there were few participants. The majority of us were hungry all the time and had no energy for games. Once again, time dragged. Our crafts work was on the wane for lack of materials and because of low spirits. Some of us started to grow tomatoes and sweet potatoes on the strip of land running alongside the fence; others followed suit, and so there was a general hunt for land on which to grow vegetables and which one could look on as his own. Within ten days, there were no more available pieces of cultivatable land. We spared no efforts to look for small plants to grow and water every day, and soon we were able to improve our diet with sweet potato leaves or green tomatoes. But then our products began to be pilfered. We organized a watch and caught a fellow red-handed; he was Son, the former military police chief of Vung Tau. This was not the first time he had been caught stealing, so we held a meeting and demanded that he do some self-criticism. But afterward, everybody had to concede that the man was a kleptomaniac, therefore incurable.

Spring drew to a close, and the clouds that formed daily promised heavy was prone to minor sicknesses. We tried not to nap at midday to avoid waking up with headaches. Every day at noon, a few of my friends and I would meet to talk; in particular, we liked to indulge in palm reading or horoscope casting. The best palmist among us was Pimply Hieu, an artillery officer whose face was covered with pimples, giving rise to his nickname. His interpretations and forecasts were very exact, most of the time, and he initiated me in the art of palm reading. As for horoscopes, we had to take off our hats to Hao, a former intelligence officer. He was very quick at casting horoscopes and always guessed right. If given the exact hour and date of birth of a person, he would be able to describe the physical appearance and recount events of the person's past; everybody admired him and regarded him as an authority in the art.

Hao had paid particular attention to the horoscope of Dr. Lac, who had just set up a private clinic in Truong Minh Giang Street when the Northern army invaded the South. Hao predicted that Lac would be released within the month, mentioning influence of this and that star to support his forecast. One noon, a few days before the end of the third lunar month, we met as usual for a chat. Hao was held up to mockery because the end of the month was drawing near without any sign of Lac's release, which showed that it was high time for him to "pack up." I asked Dr. Lac, "You know, we have had our horoscopes cast just for fun. Why do you believe so much in them?"

Lac confided that he did not much believe in horoscopes but thought he might be released because Dr. Duong Quynh Hoa[10] was working to get him sent back to his clinic to resume practice. Lac had graduated from a public health course organized by the United Nations World Health Organization, and Dr. Hoa had assured him she would intercede to get his release so he could work for the Revolution. Now, when Hao said he would be released soon, Lac had no doubts about it. And Hao himself said that "if Lac is not released this month and if I do not leave this camp next month, I will give up casting horoscopes for good."

I was amused and, like everybody else, doubtful of his words. There were a great number of people detained at this camp, and the chances for an early release were deemed rather slim. So far, those who had been released were all related to high Hanoi officials. As for the rest of us, if there was no one in our families—even going back for three generations—who had worked for the Revolution, how could we expect to be released at all? Hao, the "astrologer," had been in intelligence and was subject to repeated questioning and investigation; he certainly had not the slightest chance of being allowed to return home! When I asked him about this, he said, "My horoscope indicates very clearly that there will be a 'change' but no 'opening' yet in my condition. That means that I cannot remain in peace here but will be transferred to another place!"

In the midst of our discussion, the gong suddenly sounded, summoning us to a meeting. We assembled, and a *bodoi* called the names of Dr. Lac and Vo Tai, both from my squad. As with those who had left before, they were instructed to go back to their sleeping places and bring out all their belongings; they "must not leave behind anything, be it a bit of thread or a needle." Thus Dr. Lac was released as forecast by Hao.

The release of Lac and Tai was the subject of discussion for several days after

---

[10]Dr. Dương Quỳnh Hoa was minister of health in the Provisional Revolutionary Government of South Vietnam (PRG).

the event. Someone calculated, tongue-in-cheek, that "if every three or four months, one or two men are sent home and there are about 1,200 of us in this camp, an average of eight persons will be released each year. Then the last man will leave in about 100 years." That evening, the joke was brought up by an angry monitor. We had to stand for an hour, cruelly bitten by mosquitoes, listening to his invectives and threats. He concluded, "The Revolution never tires of educating obstinate elements, even if it takes 100 years or more."

The next morning, the kitchen team, returning from the day's rice distribution, informed us that an inmate had escaped from the camp during the night. And the following day the monitor came to our shed with the same news, but added that the escape had failed.

This was the first escape attempt. When we reported for reeducation, most of us had hoped that it would be for a short period. It even could be said that when the *bodoi* first came to occupy the South, everybody believed we would be left in peace; nobody thought of opposing the new government, including people who had experienced communism in the North and had come to the South in 1954. People thought now that the communists had conquered the whole country, they would adopt a less hostile attitude than before—when they still had had to fight against us—if they wanted to extend their influence and consolidate their hold over the country. Those of us who had reported for reeducation had not expected kind treatment, but we had hoped that at least we would be allowed in the end to earn our livelihood and feed our families. That hope had dwindled little by little. The more we listened to the explanations and speeches of high-ranking cadres, the more we felt that we were elements to be kept under strict surveillance and that there was no place open to us in the new society.

The news that one of us had tried to escape but had failed made us more aware of the grim realities of our situation. The feeling that we were de facto prisoners became more acute. The *bodoi* guarding us often reprimanded us for that and forbade us to regard ourselves as prisoners. They said, "You are people on reeducation; after you have completed your reeducation, you will be sent home. You are not prisoners. You are not prisoners because you have reported for reeducation of your own free will. You have not been arrested and detained here." Those words had given us some hope, but one day when we were weeding the area around battalion headquarters, someone looked into the meeting room and saw a slogan written clearly on the blackboard: "Vigilance! And more vigilance! We must absolutely not let any more prisoners escape from the camp!" That slogan, which revealed the true nature of our condition, was made known throughout the whole camp within a day. We no longer considered the monitors and *bodoi* as people responsible for our reeducation. They were prison wardens and we were prison inmates; that much was quite clear!

The person who was caught trying to escape was a young lieutenant. He was locked up in a metal Conex weapons container. When the sun blazed down on the box, the man inside groaned and cried, "Oh! It's very hot in here! Hot like hell! Oh! It's stifling! I can't breathe."

My heart ached when I heard his agonizing cries, almost as if we were being subjected to the same torture. I looked and looked at the box that now served as a prison cell and completely forgot that I was supposed to be weeding. The *bodoi* standing guard came up to me without my noticing it and asked in a low voice, "What are you looking at?"

In my confusion, I could not think what to answer; then I recognized the *bodoi* to be the one who, together with me, had brought Tri to the regimental infirmary for scabies treatment. I saw no better way than to tell the truth. "I must confess that I cannot bear hearing his cries. Granted that attempting to escape is a serious offense; still I'd rather that he was shot than locked in a container under the blazing sun. He will surely die by inches, sooner or later."

The *bodoi* lowered his voice to warn me. "You're lucky it's me you're speaking to. Another person would take disciplinary measures against you. If the fellow in there is suffering, that's just too bad for him. But that doesn't concern you a bit. Now, go back to your weeding." I turned back to pulling weeds from between the rows of sweet potatoes. A moment after, looking back at the scene, I saw the *bodoi* pick up an armful of dried banana leaves and spread them on the top of the box to reduce the heat inside. A day or two later, passing by the box, I noticed that the banana leaves were gone. I listened carefully but there was no longer any moaning. I never learned what happened to the man inside.

The rainy season began with a few scattered showers. One day after the midday meal, the *bodoi* suddenly swarmed into our area, and guards were deployed all around. The monitors ordered us to go in turn into the shed to bring out our belongings, then assemble in the main yard before the meeting hall. The whole move took us by surprise, but it took only a little more than half an hour for all 1,000 or more men to assemble in the yard with our luggage, most of which was bulkier than when we came because of the articles of daily use we had made. A monitor stepped forth to announce that orders had been received to make a thorough search of our belongings. The *bodoi* then came forward and told us to empty our sacks and bags onto blankets or mats spread on the ground. The search was very thorough. Almost everybody had some personal items confiscated; bowls recently shaped from aluminum plates, new combs intended as gifts to wives and daughters, water pipes, and so forth. Only canvas bags were not confiscated. As in the previous searches, I suffered no loss because I was always on my guard against such eventualities. My money was well hidden, and I had the habit of hiding my newly made items away from my sleeping place. The *bodoi* who searched my belongings asked, "Haven't you made some articles for yourself in aluminum or steel?"

"Well, I am not very clever with my hands. I have only been able to sew this canvas bag to put a few things in."

As the *bodoi* left to search the next man, I put my belongings back into my sack and bags. Questions flashed through my mind. I remembered having seen a fairly large number of vehicles stationed beyond the gate in the morning, so I thought that after the search we would be moved to another place. I saw Long putting things back into his knapsack, and knowing that he had been short of money for some time, I surreptitiously handed him some paper money issued by the new regime, saying, "We may be moved to different camps and may not see each other again. So take this, just in case."

Long hurriedly took the money, but replied, "You must be joking! This is just a routine search. I don't think there will be a move after this."

I shook my head to signal that a *bodoi* was approaching.

After the search, we were ordered to stand in perfectly straight lines, and a cadre unknown to us began to read out names from a list. Those called were all doctors or pharmacists. They stood in lines in a separate corner. Then the cadre called out a larger group, men who had been officers of combat units, such as Long (Rangers), Tien (Paratroopers), Hao (Intelligence), Tri (Intelligence), and Son (Military Police), whom I knew by name and with whom I had been living since our Trang Lon days.

Long turned pale when his name was called, probably from shock rather than fear. He looked at me with a wry smile; his eyes wre wet with tears as he said good-bye. "Vu, my dear friend! It's certain that I can no longer live near you. Thank you for everything. I shall never forget you." Wiping his tears, Long shouldered his knapsack and joined the group. I stood among those who would stay behind or would be parts of other special groups, my heart filled with sadness. Normally, Long was no more an intimate of mine than were others, but now with his departure, I realized I had just lost a real friend. I suddenly recalled how he used to discuss his plans and intentions with me, trusting me. I felt bitter remorse because it was too late now even if I had been able to do anything to assist him.

When the cadre finished calling the names on his lists, the *bodoi* ordered us to return to our shed with our luggage. It was obvious that only two groups were to be transferred; a small one composed of doctors and pharmacists and a bigger one made up of those who, in the communist jargon, "owed a debt of blood."

Back in our shed, we hurriedly put our belongings away in their usual places, then stood watching our companions in the courtyard making preparations for the transfer. They remained there until nightfall; even after the food distribution, there was still no sign of movement.

After dark, *bodoi* and monitors came to our shed, ordered us to go to our sleeping places and absolutely forbade anyone to go out into the court. Lying inside our mosquito nets, none of us could sleep. Our ears were alert to the noises outside. It was late when at last we heard the sound of trucks rumbling into the court, then voices calling from one vehicle to another, then quiet and a single voice reading some instructions or giving orders. Finally, there was the sound of engines starting and the trucks began to move out. Above the din of the engines, we heard our companions' voices calling to us.

"Stay here for now, buddies! And good luck to you all!"

"See you in Saigon!"

"Have a good sleep, fellows!"

Suddenly, a voice was heard, very distinctly, "Hey, Vu! Vu! Hey!"

I froze, knowing that Long's truck had just passed by. Old Mr. Cuc, thinking I was asleep, said softly, "Vu! Long was calling you. Did you hear?"

I replied in a low voice, "Yes, I heard."

"I would never have suspected that that young fellow, so tough, could be so sentimental!"

"I can't believe he's so attached to me. To think that there were moments when I suspected him of being an informer, of doing harm to me—"

Mr. Cuc sighed. "In fact, people like him are very honest and sincere. What a pity! I wonder where they are taking them. Probably, to have them pay their 'blood debts'!"

"We'd better get some sleep. The more we speak about this, the more painful it is to us."

We became silent, but it still was difficult to sleep. I was lost in thought; our fate might not be any brighter than theirs! The rumbling of the convoy seemed to linger in my ears. I prayed to God that Long could fall asleep as quickly as he had done during our transfer from Trang Lon to Long Khanh.

The next morning Thé and I talked for a time, mostly about Long. Thé mentioned Long's bad habits, and we laughed over them; indeed, he had behaved like a very intelligent but very mischievous child. Thé said, "You know, Long is very fond of you. He wanted to imitate your quiet manners, but couldn't. Once, when you suspected him of being an informer, he was very upset and very unhappy about it."

I quickly changed the subject. "Oh, that childish fellow was such a babbler! We'd better find out what will happen to us now. Let's go see if the rice gruel has been distributed, and then whether or not there is some work to do."

Old Mr. Cuc used to say that since the Revolution had won, "they must be different now from what they were when they were still living in the jungle." But now, he could not help asking what was the purpose of this classification of camp inmates. No one wanted to suggest an answer. Since permission was first given for us to write home to ask for medicines and food shortly before Tet, we had been allowed to send one letter every month. We could not write anything except about our health, however, and even that had to be done according to a precise formula to facilitate censorship. The letters we received from home also were more or less similar, each letter urging us to make every effort to get good results in reeducation so that we would be allowed to return soon to our families.

Since the attempted escape, we were no longer allowed to go out to cut wood for the kitchen. Contractors now supplied the wood, which their trucks unloaded before the gate, and all we had to do was go to the entrance and carry it into the camp. We thus lost the opportunity to have any contact with the local population.

The rainy season was now in full force with daily downpours. The road we had paved had indeed become a mixture of mud and stones, as predicted. From time to time, we had to help push the *bodoi*'s vehicles when they bogged down in the mire.

We went back to such daily chores as weeding or clearing and cleaning the camp. When it was time to harvest peanuts, all we had to do was pull up the plants, leave them to dry in the sun for a few days, then pick out the nuts. We had a chance to eat some of the nuts surreptitiously, and the *bodoi* also ate a lot of them. Some ate too many of the raw peanuts and got diarrhea.

When the maize crop was harvested, the *bodoi* gave us a number of used cartridge containers in which to cook the ears. After they were cooked, the *bodoi* kept half for themselves and gave us the rest. As there were only three or four *bodoi* to one team of harvesters, they had more to eat; we inmates had only one or two ears, but that was better than nothing. Even those who were sick did not want to deprive themselves of the nourishing cereal, and they tried to join the work parties whenever they could. The maize crop was so abundant that Logistics did not know how to use it all up. Finally, it was decided to distribute the maize to us and deduct the ration from our share of other food. Consequently, we ate maize for breakfast and lunch, but because of our large numbers, we could only eat our fill for a few days. After that, we went back to one bowl of thin gruel in the morning, one bowl of rice at noon, and another one in the evening. Fortunately, we had the sweet potatoes we had planted and were thus able to use the leaves to improve our diet.

Two weeks after the peanut and maize harvests, we were ordered to prepare the ground and plant another crop of each, but on a larger scale this time. We expected good crops at the end of the rainy season, but whether they were or not we never knew because we were not there to harvest what we planted.

One morning we were ordered to assemble with our belongings. Everybody expected another search that would give the *bodoi* the opportunity to appropriate some more of our money. But the search was perfunctory, and after it a *bodoi* said, "We have received the order to make preparations for your transfer to another camp."

We could not believe our ears! There had been no sign of an imminent move.

There had been no telltale agitation at Logistics. The young *bodoi* had made no moves to get ready for transfer as they had done before. Now suddenly, this order to move us!

We were divided into small groups, each escorted by two *bodoi*, who led us toward the back of the camp where an opening had been cleared, apparently as a shortcut. After a twenty-minute walk with our packs on our shoulders, we arrived at our destination. Only then did we realize that our new camp lay just at the other side of Long Khanh stadium where our old camp had been.

During the walk, we had been discouraged, fearing we would have to cover a long distance with our heavy loads. And we spoke of what a waste it was to have planted so much maize and peanuts and not be able to enjoy the crops.

The sight of the new camp with houses complete with doors and windows brought some comfort to us. We told ourselves that a change of camps might bring us luck after all!

Chapter 3

Camp Three: Xuan Loc II

Knapsack on my shoulder and bag in my hand, I walked through the entrance into the new camp. It was crowded with inmates who stood watching us, looking for familiar faces. I kept my head down, raising my eyes quickly from time to time. I did not want to be recognized and have my name called out, as was happening with others. At the last camp, I had got into trouble many times for talking with this or that person, and now I wanted to go through without anyone recognizing me.

But suddenly someone spoke in a loud voice. "There's someone who looks like old man Tran Tri Vu! But this one seems to be thinner and much older. See, the fellow with the gray knapsack on his shoulder, over there!"

I knew I was about to encounter a friend; we had had the habit, among close friends, of addressing one another as "old man." I quickened my pace, but looking up suddenly, I caught sight of a white-haired man with a sickly, haggard face and yellowed skin. We looked at each other. The man shook his head and curled his lips and I walked on. I had not expected to meet such acquaintances in a place like this. The eyes that had just searched my face, whose faded look had made me so uneasy, belonged to Ta Ky. Not long ago, in the general turmoil and confusion of the days preceding the fall of Saigon, Ha Thuong Nhan[1] and I, not knowing what to do to allay our anxieties, went together to the Dui market to find some solace in a bottle of beer. Old man Ta Ky was there, sitting at his usual place as was his habit each evening. His face with its square chin radiated power and energy, which true scholars are known to possess. But all that was gone now; he looked as dejected and forlorn as a tiger confined to a cage. Speech was not needed between us; a shake of the head did just as well. His simple gesture described in an instant his sorrowful state of mind.

I was assigned a place in a shed furnished with plank beds. Half the building was already occupied, the arrangement being that each group would be composed of half old inmates and half new arrivals. The former told us that they had food ready for us. I asked, "Then, you knew in advance that we were coming?"

One of them replied, "Yes, we did. The *bodoi* here are decent fellows. They're not too bad."

---

[1]Both Ta Ky and Nhan were well-known South Vietnamese poets and writers.

97

After putting our belongings at the head of our beds, we went out to have the midday meal. I sat down at the foot of a tree and began eating. The old inmates had already had their meal and were taking a rest. Suddenly, I felt a light tap on my shoulder and heard my name.

"Ah! 'Old man' Vu! How come you are still here? I would have thought a resourceful man like yourself would have been in Guam by now!"

I looked up and recognized a friend, but annoyed by what he said, I replied without humor, "Good heavens! Thang! You talk too much. I'll be in big trouble if your words reach the wrong ears. I've gone through hell at the other camp, just because of informers. Now—"

Before I could finish the sentence, three or four fellows appeared. Recognizing them as old friends in the arts, I could not help but be worried.

"Great heavens! How in hell could all of you manage to get in this place? I pray you, friends! Leave me alone. At my old camp, I suffered enough because of reports by friends. Now, spare me, will you?"

"Damn! Just our luck to have met this old man! What are you so afraid of anyway?"

Confronted with their cheerfulness and surprise at seeing my fear, I relaxed somewhat.

"How many of our gang are here? At the other camp, we were divided into categories, a little less than half the inmates were moved somewhere else and the rest of us brought here. Those who left first were said to 'owe blood debts,' so we believe we are considered to have committed minor offenses. What category are you fellows? If you belong to the 'serious offenders' category, we're all finished!"

"Don't worry, old man! We are not considered 'bad guys.' The psychological-warfare and combat fellows have already been screened and moved out."

"Do you know Mai Chung, by the way?" someone asked.

I looked at the man, recognizing Trinh Cung of the Association of Young Painters. I replied, "Mai Chung? The winner of the prize for sculpture?"

"Yes, that's the one. It seems he has been sent to the North."

"How d'you know? He's too young and all he has done is paint and make statues, not a damn thing to deserve exile to the North! You have to be someone important, don't you? Sending people like you and me to the North would be a waste of petrol."

"Well, that's what a *bodoi* told me and I am taking his words at face value. The day we were categorized, a fellow from battalion headquarters told me that one group would be sent to the North. It's possible that he just wanted to scare the hell out of me."

As we talked, I became more and more convinced that the atmosphere at this camp was much more relaxed than the other. I asked, "Tell me, are you so fearless that you can behave as if you have no regard at all for the 'Sons of the Revolution'? Aren't there informers here?"

"They don't need informers here."

"They use bugs then?"

"Here, the group leaders have to make full reports on all our activities."

"Damn! That makes life all the more difficult! At the other camp, they didn't trust group leaders; they only trusted their own informers."

"Here, we only have to be on our guard against 'self-administration' cadres. Do you know what they are?"

"No."

"They are fellows like you and me, with the difference that they are appointed by the *bodoi* as group leaders or deputy group leaders. They have authority and direct control over us. You cannot question what they say. If you want to beat them up, do it at night, with a blanket pulled over their heads. During the day, you must keep your distance from them."

Our conversation continued in the same vein for some time; then one of them, looking at my can of rice, asked, "What the hell are you eating with your rice?"

Despite the teasing tone of the voice, I replied cheerfully, "Being on reeducation, our usual diet is rice eaten with that most precious substance called salt. What else do you want to eat with your rice?"

"Hold on a minute! I'll be back with some food, just to entertain a bosom friend."

"How about sweet potato leaves fried with garlic?"

I could not help expressing surprise. "Are you fellows undergoing reeducation or are you on holiday here? Doesn't anyone here eat rice with salt? Or are you bastards making fun of a new arrival?"

"Good heavens! You must have been treated badly; you've gotten stupid! Just look around you; there's plenty of sweet potatoes. You're welcome to them any time you want green leaves. But don't eat too much; you could have a bout of arthritic backache."

Trinh Cung said, "This evening, if you still haven't anything to eat with rice, go to the area in the back—way back there—and have your meal with us. We have fish cooked with brine and Chinese sausages; as for vegetables, there are more than enough. By the way, old man, have you managed to hide any money on your person?"

I scratched my head, looking around; I saw only the familiar faces of my friends, so I said, "To tell the truth, I always have some money on me in case I can use it to protect myself."

"Ah! That will do. You have the right to join our club."

The more relaxed atmosphere was obvious here, but "once bitten, twice shy." I still had the feeling of being under surveillance although the people around me now were friends of long standing. The feeling became more distinct as the day wore on, and that evening we were told to prepare a resume for the camp administrators so they could prepare a list of the new arrivals. A rather short, foxy-looking fellow approached me with a smiling face.

"So, old man Vu seems to have met up with old friends again, doesn't he? Fellows here are very pleasant. Relaxed atmosphere, plenty of entertainments! Was it the same at your old camp?"

I was immediately on guard. Here was a complete stranger calling me by name and noticing many details about me, especially my friends' habit of calling me old man Vu. I replied solemnly, "We also had an easy atmosphere, 'elder brother.' The men had much affection for one another and the cadres were understanding people."

The stranger laughed and said, "Don't be too deferential, I beg of you. I am young enough to be your younger brother, so why call me 'elder brother'?"

My new team leader, Khuong, hastened to introduce us.

"This is Bui Quoc Khanh, our deputy group leader for Logistics."

I greeted him and said, "I am Vu, but I guess you already know my name."

Khanh asked, "What were you before?"

"I was a teacher at Chu Van An [a secondary school]."

"I was a teacher too. There's another teacher here, Chinh, who also taught at Chu Van An, but later he worked for Hoang Duc Nha at the Ministry of Information and 'Open Arms.'[2] You know Chinh, don't you? He was one of Nha's clique."

The way Khanh addressed me as if he were my younger brother and spoke about other people—with such indiscretion—made me even more cautious. He said he had been a lieutenant and a teacher at the Army Language School under the former regime. I tried to move the conversation away from the past, and I asked: "What about bathing and washing of clothes here?"

Khanh hastened to reply before my team leader did. "After work you can bathe in the stream. In the camp, you can take a bath at the well over there, but normally there's not much water in it. Usually, after bathing in the stream, the men will carry away some water for later use." Afterwards, I was shown around the camp. I noticed that the latrine area was extremely filthy.

The camp was believed to be the former hospital of Division 18 (of the South Vietnamese Army); some said it had been the hospital of the Long Khanh military sector. The architecture was relatively modern, but now that the place was used as a prison, it was crowded. The operating theater, the laboratory, the

---

[2]The "Open Arms" (Chiêu hồi) policy advocated by the government of South Vietnam aimed at winning over the Viet Cong to the nationalist side. One of President Thieu's cousins, Hoàng Đức Nhã, was at one time the minister in charge of the program.

offices—all had been converted into sleeping rooms. We lay close to one another on rows of plank beds with a passageway about 60 cm wide between the two rows. The various buildings were connected by covered verandahs. All cultivatable areas had been planted with sweet potatoes, so there was no open space left to walk on. A trellis was attached to the front of each building, supporting bitter gourd or cucurbit plants, with the result that the rooms were poorly lighted and airless, quite a contrast with the roomy spacious camp we had just left. On this very first day, I already felt ill at ease because of the crowded living conditions. There was no place to sit down to eat, outside the rain poured down and all I could do was go back to my sleeping place, which was damp and smelled of fish. With the overcast sky and the crowded prisoners eating their meal in the dark and smelly room, my spirits sagged. Indeed, everyone here was sad and pessimistic. The room, five meters wide and seven meters long, held nearly fifty of us who were now sitting on the plank beds with our arms around our knees and looking toward the door, which was the only opening letting in any light. No one uttered a word, and everyone wore the same sullen look.

Unable to stand it any longer, I left the room to look for Thang, probably my dearest friend compared to others in this camp, who was said to live in the same area as mine but at the back corner of the camp enclosure. After asking a number of people, I found him sitting on his plank bed, his arms around his knees. He did not recognize me until I came near him, although I thought he had seen me as soon as I came through the door because, like everyone else, his face was turned toward the entrance.

I asked, "Could it be that you saw me come in but did not recognize me? Have I changed that much?"

Thang replied, "Forgive me! It's not that I didn't recognize you but, in fact, I was not looking at anything in particular. Even when you came up to me, I was not conscious of your presence. But enough of this. Come sit beside me. Don't trespass on the space next to mine. My 'home' is only 60 cm wide."

I hastened to say, "Nevertheless, it's bigger than mine, which is barely 50 cm wide. Fifty people in that small room!"

His neighbor said affably, "Oh, make yourself comfortable; use my space. We're all friends, you know. By the way, don't you recognize me, Vu?"

I looked at him. The face was quite familiar, but I couldn't recall his name. I held out my hand to him and said, "Good Lord! I took you for somebody else. Well? How are you?"

"I can say I'm fine but not very strong."[3]

In the meantime, I searched my memory. Suddenly, his name came back to me. He was Hieu, a pharmacist, the son of Dr. Nguyen Dinh Luyen. His two elder brothers, Lieu and Nang, were close friends of mine and I knew the family

---

[3]In Vietnamese, a play on words.

well. I asked him, "Now, Hieu! What became of your mother, Hien, and Lieu and Nang?"

"Since the event [the fall of the South], I haven't had much news from home. My mother seems to be fine; my sister Hien couldn't leave the country, and I've heard that only my brother Dai has managed to escape."

Seeing that Thang was waiting, I asked his pardon, but he said, "There's no need! The fate and circumstance of every one of us is the same; it is a waste of time to inquire after any particular individual, including me."

Hieu chipped in, "This Mr. Thang has had the luck to meet with his wife, so he's 'better off' than both of us. The thing is, since he met with her, his hair has turned as gray as clouds."

I hastened to ask how he had been able to meet his wife. He replied in his usual measured and quiet manner, and as I listened, I really looked at him for the first time and realized how old he seemed and that he indeed had the gray hair of a sixty-year-old man. A distinguished economist, Thang always had held some economics post through all the many cabinet changes in the government of South Vietnam, specializing in national development planning. Slowly he told his story.

"Remember the explosion of the ammunition dump? We counted ten dead and nearly 100 wounded among us. Usually, the path that runs close to the latrine area of this camp is used by the local people to go to the fields on the other side of the stream. But one day after the explosion, it was crowded with people coming from Saigon to ask for news about their relatives. It was the *bodoi* themselves who told us, 'Your wives and children swarm around this place to ask after you. The enemy has spread the rumor that many inmates died in the explosion at Long Khanh. So, at the moment, the order is that this area is off limits to the Saigon inhabitants.'

"During the next days, I was so anxious that I pretended to have to go often to the latrines so that I could have a look at the path; also, it was a way to pass the time. Suddenly one day, I caught sight of a woman carrying a basket containing several stalks of sugar cane and a few bananas. At first, I didn't pay much attention to her, but as she approached the fence, I noticed she had the light complexion of a city dweller. From the latrine, I stretched up to look over the top of the metal sheet used to hide from view the person squatting inside. I looked at the woman as she looked at me. I nearly burst into tears; it was indeed my wife! I was so happy! I called her name and asked her about our chidren. My wife was so glad that she completely forgot she had disguised herself as a local farmer and came close to the fence. At that moment, the *bodoi* in the watchtower began to shout, and he fired a volley from his machine pistol. The bullets whizzed in our direction. I said hurriedly, 'Go back home! Leave this place! I'm fine.' The *bodoi* fired a few more volleys, probably in the air. I drew back and stayed motionless. Looking out through a crack, I saw my wife run away, her sugar canes and bananas thrown from the basket onto the ground. I quickly slipped out of the latrines and went back to my place. A short moment afterward, a *bodoi* came to our shed to ask, 'Who has gone to the latrines just now?' Nobody admitted to it, so the matter ended there."

Hieu, who sat next to me, continued the account. "Since that night he hasn't been able to get much sleep and, in particular, his hair has become grayer and grayer."

Thang said, "When I met my wife so unexpectedly, I did not feel it as deeply as in moments like this when I think back about it. Within my heart, I feel so much pity for her. Her health is not very good. It was a daring thing for her to go to look for me as she did, and an exhausting business for her considering her health. And then to be scared away by the gunfire without a chance to tell me anything! The worry about her and the memory of that scene kept me sleepless for a whole week." Thang finished his story with a sigh and a wry smile.

Conscious of the sad atmosphere, I tried to switch the conversation to another topic. "At the camp where I was, the discipline was so strict that we dared not do anything. It's more easygoing here, isn't it?"

Thang replied in a low voice, "Well—! Whether it's more easygoing or not, it depends on the individual and the circumstances. You've been given a hard time over there, but has there been any suicide because of it? Here, there already has been a suicide case."

I felt uneasy, and said, "Over there, we weren't desperate enough to think of committing suicide. But who was it who did it anyway? It seemed to me, when I came here that there was so much joking and laughing. All those young artists don't appear to be very downhearted, do they?"

"Well, merrymaking is always possible here; but in the end, this kind of fun proves to be unhealthy, both physically and mentally. Do you know Gia? Once, as I mentioned your brother's home near the highway, Gia said he knew both of you, you and your brother."

Hieu reminded me, "Don't you remember Gia, Dr. Thu's son-in-law? His wife's also a pharmacist, like him. I remember we both were at his wedding party. We were dead drunk that day!"

"Of course," I said, "I knew him well. Where is Gia now? He's here too, isn't he?"

Hieu looked at Thang, who replied, "Yes, he also lived at this camp . . . but he's gone now!"

"He killed himself," Hieu said. "He was buried on the bank of the stream, over there. Anyway, there was no hope for him to be released."

The answer was completely unexpected, and it sent shivers down my spine. I remembered Gia's wit and his sometimes shocking language. The image of a rather skinny and very cheerful young man came to mind. I could not imagine that such a man could deliberately put an end to his life! I said, "There must have been something specific; this life is not bad enough for people to commit suicide."

Hieu got down from the bed, saying, "I leave you two to your conversation. I have to find a partner for chess."

A man sitting in a corner of the room called out to him, "Wait for me, Hieu! A true gentleman like yours truly will find his mind muddled up if he can't indulge in his daily game of chess!"

Seeing that everybody was about to leave the room, Thang hastened to say, "If you all intend to leave us here, I'm afraid we'll have to go too. I dare not stay alone in the room."

I tried to dissuade him, "Let them go! It will be easier for us to talk in private. I want to ask you a lot of questions, but it is difficult with so many people around. What I fear most is an informer. So why leave here for another spot?"

Thang laughed softly but heartily; he still had that particular laugh of his that was so familiar. He said, "The room is said to be haunted. I never have had the courage to stay here alone. Are you afraid of ghosts?"

I could not help laughing, "What do people in our situation have to fear from ghosts or spirits?"

Thang, his smile still lingering, replied, "Take it from me, old man! It's true that the room is haunted. But if you're not afraid and want to stay here, I'll stay too. I am not very fearful but I've seen so many strange things happen that, in the end, I have to believe that ghosts may indeed exist."

"What do they look like?"

"This room was the operating room of the former military hospital. You may have noticed its particular layout. See the enameled tiles on the floor and walls? We didn't pay much attention at first, but it happened that some men who were having siesta in this room were harassed by ghosts, so much so that they cried out. This happened to several men, each time the same. Everyone who took a siesta alone in this room would see himself in his dream pushed, pulled, and beaten up by former patients in this hospital. Each cried out so loudly that his companions came running and woke him up. When questioned, each one said he saw a number of patients dressed in hospital shirts come near him to drive him away from the room. Some daredevil types volunteered to stay and sleep alone in this room, but they were subjected to the same treatment. From then on, no one will take a nap alone in this place. It took several of us to be able to have siesta here without being harassed.

"Have you noticed the ammonia smell around this shed? At night we sometimes are reluctant to walk far away, so we urinate close to the door. You will no doubt notice the smell. If you walk a certain distance from the shed late at night, you will certainly hear sounds of moaning and crying coming from the sweet potato patch or the fence. This place is haunted, no doubt about it! Some of the older men have asked the *bodoi* to buy flowers and bananas to make offerings to the ghosts, and this has had some effect in that the harassment has let up somewhat. But we are still afraid when night comes. Those who are chicken-hearted have to wake up the fellows lying near them so they can go out together to relieve themselves. One night, I suddenly woke up needing to urinate, so I slid quietly from my bed and went out, my head still filled with ghost stories I'd heard during the day. I went toward a drain some steps away, and suddenly I heard an indistinct, strained voice that made my hair stand on end. It was a funny feeling because I have never seen a ghost, nor have I believed in ghosts before. Listening more closely, I decided it was the choking voice of a man moaning and speaking in his sleep, not a ghost at all. Nevertheless, the creepy feeling persisted. I intended to tell the story to the men in the morning. I would tell them that there was no ghost and that when many people slept in the same room, it's not unusual to hear someone speak and cry in his sleep. When I returned to my place, the man who slept beside me said in a low voice, 'Why didn't you call me when you went out?'

"I said, 'If you want to make water, just go. There's nothing to be afraid of.'

"He got down from the bed and left the room. A few minutes later, he clumped back in and said in a low voice, which in the stillness of the night, sounded loud enough to be heard throughout the room, 'Ghosts! There really are ghosts, fellows!'

"There was the sound of soft laughter. Some men, suddenly awakened from sleep, growled. I asked in a soft voice, 'Did you also hear somebody speak in his sleep?'

"'Right! I stood listening for a moment and realized that the moaning sounded regular and persistent, as if produced by a machine. That's not the way people moan in their sleep. You heard that too, didn't you?'

"'Yes. The sound came from the building covered with metal sheets, just in front of me. It was probably someone with a weak heart.'

"'But nobody sleeps there! That's the meeting hall, don't you remember?'

"The next morning, the story that the place was haunted was the subject of discussion for newcomers like myself. Oldtimers added a few details to make the story more frightening. They said the meeting hall was the place where the corpses of the ten inmates killed during the recent explosion at the ammunition dump had lain while waiting for burial. From then on, I never dared go too far at night to have a piss; I just relieved myself at the foot of the trellis supporting the bitter-gourd plants near our building."

I finally felt free from the constant surveillance I had been subjected to at the old camp, and my life became more bearable. I had identified several character-istics of this camp that may have accounted for what seemed to be a more confident, therefore easygoing, administration. First was its position adjoining regimental headquarters, which meant we lived near the quarters of our battalion commanders' immediate superiors. The battalion command building faced the entrance just inside our camp, and at its back the ground sloped down to a stream that sometimes reached a width of five or six meters after heavy rains. The *bodoi* quarters were behind the command building. The latrines were at one side of the enclosure next to the barbed wire; beyond it was the metaled[4] path across which stood the mess and the stadium used as the ammunition dump, the scene of the recent explosion. On the other side, another metal path bordered the camp, and across it was the regimental headquarters.

Another thing was that the inmates here were not treated as roughly as at the other camp. There was no morning roll call, but immediately after reveille everyone had to go out to the yard for a three-minute physical exercise session. In fact, this was a form of roll call. After the exercise, team leaders had to go to the gate to report to the *bodoi* on duty whether or not their teams were at full strength. Two inmates—men who had been combat officers—were said to have escaped from the camp after Tet, but the *bodoi* saw it as an ordinary event and did not blow it out of proportion as their counterparts at the other camp had done. They said the escapees would be caught sooner or later.

After we had settled down to our new life, I suggested that if we needed food and medicines, we might ask the *bodoi* to help. But the oldtimers said there was no need; the *bodoi* often asked inmates to make a few things for them and in exchange they made purchases and brought them right to our barracks. Of course, a little discretion was needed, but everyone understood that and most of the men took part in these transactions.

One peculiarity of this camp was that most of the inmates had been members of the liberal professions and after enlistment in the army had been allowed to serve according to their specialties: teachers had been seconded to educational institutions, doctors and pharmacists to the Army Medical Corps, musicians and painters to the Psychological Warfare Department, etc. As a consequence, there was a decidedly "bohemian" character to their general behavior.

I still remember the Ho Chi Minh birthday anniversary when the battalion decided to hold a big celebration and give us the responsibility of constructing the shrine. In charge of the construction team was an architect named Yen, whom Bui Quoc Khanh had introduced as the "general manager of President Thieu's properties." He made a big beautiful lantern shaped like a lotus flower, and the artists among us decorated the shrine with drawings of their own creation. But after the ceremony, during a review of contributions by the various teams, the shrine construction team came under heavy criticism. They were accused of mischievous intention to distort, for example, "The lotus flower looked like a rocket," or "The slogans were written in letters supposed to look like bamboo, but in reality they looked like pieces of dried bone." The team

---

[4]In Asia, asphalt roads are usually called "metaled."

members were looked upon as "roguish," "critical of the Revolution," and "imagining themselves to be beyond detection by the Revolution." The men who had contributed so much effort to the construction of the shrine felt themselves personally threatened because these criticisms could be entered into their individual records.

The camp's management was also quite different here. Food was distributed to us in a haphazard way, and we were not clear about how much we were entitled to. We had to be content with the quantity we were given, and we were quite ignorant of the principle that governed the distribution. We took delivery of provisions directly from contractors, and our supply of rice was distributed by the *bodoi* weekly, kept in a storeroom, and managed by the deputy group leader, in other words, by us camp inmates.

When our team was on duty, I was often detailed, together with others, to pick up fish from a contractor. Usually in the detail was Dam Quang Khanh, a young former paratroop lieutenant, who dressed in a way intended to set off his musculature and who was well known for his funny and daring words. He always volunteered to receive the goods, a task many of us felt no enthusiasm for because it involved carrying heavy loads. We went to the entrance of the regimental headquarters, and there the contractor weighed the goods, and we carried them back to the battalion. There, we were stopped by the *bodoi*, who selected the fattest fish for their tables; then we brought the rest to the common kitchen for cooking and distribution to the inmates.

The contractor employed three teenage girls, which was the reason for the presence of a great number of *bodoi* and of Dam Quang Khanh whenever deliveries were made. Usually, we were told to stand aside and were forbidden to talk with people from outside the camp, but "Para" Khanh somehow managed to befriend one of the girls. When I first noticed their game, I decided that the two were already much in love with each other. Khanh's duty was to hand jute sacks over to the contractor for him and the girls to fill with fish. Two of us carried each half-filled sack, but on the way back to the camp, Khanh managed to find a letter hidden somewhere in a sack. Everyone praised him for his talent as a wooer because, although he and the girl could not talk to each other and had to look at each other from a distance, they still had managed to establish a romantic rapport. In fact, the girl, whose name was Kim, often helped Khanh by secretly passing him money and gifts.

Each time we took delivery of food, representatives of regimental headquarters were present; thus everything was done in the open, unlike in the other camp. However, after the delivery, the *bodoi* from the battalion never failed to seize part of the provisions for their own use. In spite of this, we thought we were better off than before; besides, food delivery was more regular—once every ten days. Most of the time it consisted of fish; sometimes it was fish sauce. For vegetables, we grew Chinese cabbage and bindweed, which we picked once every few days; and we found we could ask the *bodoi* to buy a few things for us such as sugar, candy, cigarettes, tobacco, etc.

When the weather was fine, we played volleyball. Some played chess. A few of us were able to make a set of mahjong pieces complete with a board, and we played mahjong often under the shade of a big tree. The *bodoi*, attracted by the novelty of the game, were given the perfunctory explanation that it was more or less similar to *to tom*, a kind of card game quite popular in the North. Little did they know that, considering the circumstances, pretty high stakes were being risked: peanuts or, if the "gamblers" were well provided, sweets.

The most popular pastime was cooking. Fish was usually cooked first in brine, then each man, according to his abilities and means, prepared it the way he liked. "Wealthy" ones fried the fish until it was quite dry and ate it up within a few days; "poorer" inmates recooked the fish until all the water had evaporated, then shredded and ground it. This would keep and be gradually consumed while waiting for the next distribution. We also made soup, using sweet potato leaves, amaranth, or other wild edible vegetables. After the evening meal, some men still busied themselves cooking rice gruel; certain fellows were always occupied with the preparation of food of one kind or another.

Work at this camp was also different. At our old camp when we went out to work, some *bodoi* stood guard while others supervised and gave orders to rest or stop work for the day. Here, all work was done on a "piece" basis, and when a job was finished early, we were allowed to go to the stream to bathe and wash our clothes. The *bodoi* themselves wanted to bring us back to camp as soon as possible so they could spend more time downtown. Every time a detail went out to work in the field at the other side of the stream, the *bodoi* in charge reported the total number of men in it to the guard at the gate. When the detail returned, the *bodoi* on duty at the entrance had to count the men, then sign a paper, which he handed to the *bodoi* in charge of the work detachment. Because of this "piece work" arrangement, we usually rushed through a job in a perfunctory manner, sometimes finishing in a little more than an hour. On the banks of the stream many varieties of wild edible vegetables—especially *ngo* plants—could be found. After bathing and washing clothes, we never failed to pick some of these plants to take back to camp to cook.

After work and washing up at the stream, we were permitted to rest at the camp, so we had plenty of leisure. Many spent it by making the combs, knives, and other articles for daily use or to be kept as souvenirs. We made items of steel or aluminum under the guidance of inmates who were painters and sculptors. Their work achieved a highly artistic quality, and the metal products especially had surprisingly beautiful engraving.

The camp was supplied with electricity, so various evening classes were organized. The incentive to organize and teach these ad hoc courses lay in the payment-in-kind from the "students"—sugar, cigarettes, candy, etc. Portrait drawing was popular—many in this class learned to draw very good likenesses of people—but the best attended class was acupuncture. It was taught by a man I will call Tuc, who had just been initiated into some of the techniques of acupuncture by the son-in-law of Dr. Hoang Mong Luong, considered a master of the art in the South. The inmate sleeping arrangements had placed Tuc next to the son-in-law, Dr. Nhiep, and he had pestered the doctor to teach him, which Nhiep did. When Nhiep was transferred out of the camp, Tuc himself began teaching, considering that his "training" had enabled him to master the basics.

One group made smoking pipes, hammering pieces taken from discarded car battery cases into shape and polishing them. The end-product often had a "made in Western countries" look. The best worker in the group was Thach, whom we called Thach Kien Cang.[5] A big man, Thach had won a competition as a top bodybuilder, and despite the present circumstances, his body kept its muscular appearance. Now, whenever he was free, he was seen rubbing and polishing pipes.

In addition to artists and literati, this camp had many well-known doctors among its inmates. Dr. Binh, the only hematologist in South Vietnam, had just completed installing a hematology laboratory at Cho Ray Hospital when he was summoned to report for reeducation, and Dr. Nguyen Xuan Ninh was a young surgeon, who was also known as a person who had succeeded in learning to read and write Chinese in record time. On many occasions I witnessed our doctors performing minor surgery on inmates; the patient was put inside a mosquito net and the surgeon operated with a razor blade.

In short, everyone was busy with some work or hobby to pass the time. What then had happened to drive Gia to suicide? I kept mulling over the question until a man named Hung, who had been Gia's "sleeping neighbor" from the beginning, finally told me the story.

"When we first came here, Gia appeared to be a jolly fellow, believing like the rest of us that reeducation would take only a short time. He behaved normally, although he was sometimes short-tempered. When we realized we had been duped (the instruction to bring a seven-day provision of food and money was the great hoax), Gia's behavior changed entirely. He became sullen; at night he tossed and sighed in his sleep. Once he confided to me that he and his family had had a chance to leave the country before the *bodoi* swarmed into Saigon. He spoke vaguely about it being all his fault that his family was kept back. Another time, he mentioned that his lack of determination had made them miss the opportunity to go abroad. 'It was all because of me,' he said. Whenever he had a minute to himself, he sat thinking, his face showing sadness, despair even. We were afraid he would be driven to commit some desperate act, so we watched

---

[5]Literally, *Kiến càng* means "king ant," characterized by giant mandibles on a thin body.

him very closely. Let me show you the place where he took his own life; you will see how stubborn he was!"

Hung brought me to the front of the camp and pointed to a low, square shed that might have been used as a guardhouse or storeroom or morgue. It was about three meters on each side with a flat roof of metal sheets and supported by columns made of artillery shell cases welded together. I had to bend my head to enter. There were traces of wood fires on the floor, but from when I could not tell. The shed had not been used for any purpose recently because it stood hidden in a corner of the camp that looked down on the *bodoi* quarters. Hung continued.

"Can you imagine? Despite the low roof, Gia hanged himself here. He came at dawn. Nobody paid any attention to him. Hours later, a chap who chanced to pass by discovered the body. Gia had let his body fall in an oblique position so that the noose would tighten and strangle him. That meant that when he began to choke, Gia only had to stand up to escape death. He must have been very determined to have chosen to die in this terrible way."

The knowledge that he had died in such circumstances did not give me much insight into the reasons for his desperate act, and only months later when I too experienced confusion and despair did I arrive at a full understanding of the "question."

On the surface, the camp had a light-hearted atmosphere, with men playing chess or volleyball in their spare time, or making things to keep as souvenirs. The men living in the area close to the gate even played poker, for which they made cards and a box from which to draw them (they were afraid the handmade cards would bear telltale signs). The leader of this group of "gamblers" was Quan, a former quartermaster officer. If one looked closer though, another side of life at camp was clear: the silent group, the large number of inmates who sat with their arms around their knees, listening and meditating.

As for the *bodoi*, their life was characterized for us by two distinct features. They openly tried every means to obtain money for the purchase of things they had been dreaming about: wristwatches, fountain pens, sunglasses, radio sets, cassette recorders, and motorbikes. Second, they cared very little about politics and did not hide the fact that their side was plagued by internal conflict. The battalion commander, Hung, from the South, and the political commander, Tri, a Northerner, opposed each other openly.

Commander Hung liked to visit our area to chat with us. His opinion of his comrades "from the North" was that they were not civilized or educated enough. He relished anecdotes intended to ridicule those "jungly comrades." The *bodoi* from the North got wind of this, and every time "Comrade" Hung left our place, "Comrade" Tri would appear to ask, "What did the bastard tell you?" We took care to disperse quickly when Hung left, and Tri would be very angry to see no one around.

"I know the bastard was here and talked rubbish to you; but where's everybody now?"

We usually answered, "We saw Commander Hung come here, walk around the building, then leave."

We took advantage of the conflict between them to draw interesting information from the more communicative Hung. Expounding the policy of the Revolution, he advanced the argument that we would have to stay on at the camp for a longer period than we might have thought. "After all, you constituted the hard core of the Southern forces. In order to build the new regime in the South without having to face major opposition, we have to detain you here for some time."

When asked how much longer, Hung replied, "According to high-ranking comrades who have attended seminars on reeducation policy, it must last from three to five years."

When we mentioned a newspaper article dealing with reeducation policy that we had heard of but had not read, Hung said, "It's no use trying to find out. Nobody can know in advance what the Revolution intends to do. Even if you have come across some document or paper, that won't get you anywhere. The Revolution is not so stupid as to write down in black and white what it is likely to do. I myself have read a lot of papers, but I can say that there's not any single point I have fully understood. The Revolution often uses the sentence 'Hurricanes and storms are less terrible than Vietnamese syntax.'[6] Have you heard that?"

Some of the men argued that doctors and engineers were people much needed for the reconstruction of the nation, so why detain them here? If released, they would be of much more service to the People. Commander Hung answered, "Doctors? I don't think they are as effective as our rural medical cadres. What doctors usually do is examine the patients, write out prescriptions, and advise hospitalization for serious cases. Our country is poor; we lack medicines; our hospitals have only limited facilities. Without medicines and facilities, doctors can do nothing, and they may create more complications. In contrast, our medical cadres can advise country folks on how to treat their illnesses with medicinal herbs. On balance, who's more useful? Who's needed more?"

Some of us were so irritated by the answer that we could not help voicing doubt as to the possibility of curing serious illness with a few handfuls of medicinal herbs. Hung replied, "You fellows don't have the same outlook on

---

[6]Rendering of the meaning, but not the form, of the Vietnamese sentence "Phong ba bão *táp* không bằng ngữ *pháp* Việt Nam," in which "táp" rhymes with "pháp." The Vietnamese communists have adopted the popular way of expressing ideas, beliefs, etc., by means of phrases and sentences having words rhyming with each other so that they can be easily memorized.

things as the Revolution. The Revolution is more practical than you are. A patient who dies for lack of medicine will cause more unrest among people around him than a very sick person who dies while he is under the care of the medical cadre; that man's death has no political repercussions whatsoever."

We dejectedly shook our heads at this kind of argument. Perhaps a distrust of this "revolutionary outlook" was what caused a number of *bodoi*, whose families in the North had come to visit them at the camp, to ask our doctors for advice and drug prescriptions whenever one of their family members was taken ill.

It became clear that the men who had been in this camp since the beginning had had more opportunity than some of us to realize the hopelessness of our situation. Although life here was more bearable than at the last camp, our despondency and despair were greater. The easier it was for us to get the help or connivance of the *bodoi*, the darker we felt the future of the whole South would be. One of the men said, "Here, we use money in exchange for complaisance. But back home, where can our families find the money to get the same treatment?"

Living as prisoners without any hope of release, a number of inmates developed mental stress to the point that their general behavior changed completely and their bodies became frail. So pitiful! Every one of us must have kept hidden in his mind many questions for which there were no answers: "Should I try to escape from the camp or should I wait? What if I do escape? Would my family get in trouble? Would our neighbors leave us in peace? How long would I have to be in hiding? If I choose to wait, then for how long? Would what I wait for happen? Would something else befall me first?" Nobody was still naïve enough to think that after completing reeducation, we would be allowed to return to a normal existence. The more we "studied," the more convinced we became that we now constituted a special category of people, discriminated against by the new regime and discarded by the new society. And in any case, could we manage to survive until we were released? We were convinced that only a handful of high-caliber technicians such as doctors, engineers, and a few others could hold a slim hope for release. The majority had no way out. Absolutely none.

One memorable characteristic of this camp was the competition forced upon the various teams responsible for growing vegetables. Each team was assigned a plot of land to work, and each was to eat what it produced. In the competition, the quantity of vegetables produced by each team would be weighed and the value estimated. The cash equivalent would then be deducted from the amount reserved for the purchase of food and necessities, which we were entitled to by special favor of the Revolution. This was "revolutionary" logic: the more vegetables we grew, the less money we were given to buy what we needed. Naturally, nobody wanted to put much effort into cultivating and watering plants just to have our food expenses deducted in the end. But the cadres pressured our team leaders to increase productivity, using such promises as an incentive: "Teams or individuals who distinguish themselves by high productivity will be rewarded with entries of outstanding performance in their personal records. This will be taken into consideration when proposals for release are examined."

A number of middle-aged former farmers in my team decided to participate in earnest in the competition. Using half-treated, diluted human body wastes as fertilizer, they watered the plants daily, filling our nearby living quarters with the stench, especially when the sun blazed and the wind blew into our room. As usual, whenever there were body wastes, an army of flies and bluebottles swarmed around in terrifying numbers. We worried about a possible epidemic because a few dysentery cases had already developed. But the cadres said menacingly that those who opposed the use of human manure as fertilizer were considered saboteurs and bourgeois elements accustomed to a life of comfort under the old regime. Due to the fertilizers and adequate watering, the plants ran riot; we had so many of them to eat that we got sick of them, especially of amaranth. Finally, when food was distributed, we left our share of vegetable soup untouched; meanwhile, we looked for wild vegetables to eat instead.

But there was a funny side to the competition business. My team worked most actively at manuring the land; our plants grew luxuriantly, and we thought we would win first place. To our surprise, Quan's team always took the lead. Much later, when we became friends, he revealed his secret. "The members of my team were all gamblers; so in this business, we gambled on winning the competition and knocking your old farmers out. You used human manure to water your vegetables; we made believe we had our own methods. We did a lot of shouting while we worked to give the impression we were competing in earnest. When we gathered our vegetables, we fluffed out the leaves to make the crop look bigger than it was. But our real trick was putting five or six big bolts, each weighing around three kilos—the kind used in heavy construction—into the baskets. The *bodoi* never inspected the baskets, but weighed them. Ours always outweighed yours by at least ten kilos. We all had a good laugh thinking about your team leader and old Mr. Cuong trying to figure this out."

When living in a situation from which there is no escape, it is best to work without letting your mind wander. I believed that the more tired the body, the less heavy the heart will be. From my own experience and the many conversations I had with fellow inmates, I was able to frame a guiding principle to govern life in reeducation camps. I devised for myself a way of thinking that would not accept defeat. I thought that if worse came to worse, I would still be in control of my own destiny. If I ever felt that I could not stand it any longer, I would weigh every possibility to barter my life away advantageously. But as long as I was able to endure this life, I was determined to keep up my spirits until the last possible minute. Thus, during the day I joined the young men and kept busy doing odd jobs; in the evening, I talked or exchanged confidences with some fellows who had earned respect as "thinkers"; they were keen observers, and their judgments were recognized as being very realistic.

My own past had been a succession of study periods and examinations, and I had had a good many unexpected pieces of luck. I became conscious of the fact that I had never had to analyze real problems or think out possible solutions. The "thinkers," after much pondering and arguing, settled on two options that were open to us, based on their analysis of our situation. According to their estimates, the total number of people detained for reeducation amounted to one million or close to it. If each inmate's personal record had to be reviewed to assess the gravity of his offenses, any government would need years to complete the task, much longer if many had to be brought to trial. Then, what should we do in order to get out of the camp?

Only two solutions fit the reality of the situation. Other alternatives were unacceptable either because their execution did not depend on us, or they did not coincide with what we had learned and were still learning about the new regime. The solutions we thought most likely to bring freedom to each individual were either finding outside intercession or escaping. The latter involved seeking safety not only for the individual but also for his family, and we were fully aware that this would entail many difficulties and complications, though not insurmountable ones.

Each night, we gathered in some corner to exchange views, and before going to bed we would try to arrive at some conclusion. Sometimes, we had differences and the discussion became fairly heated; this was, in a way, a pastime. Many of the men were inflexible—decisive in their thinking and definite in their rejection of other people's views. But we were in complete agreement in not encouraging the hope that one day all of us would be released by the Revolution like cadets graduating from a military college. One man said, "It is clear that they have decided to eliminate us from the new society. They don't really want to reeducate us and allow us to participate in the building of the society they have conceived." Another said he had a letter from his family, saying "Everybody back home knows the government plans to resettle the families of reeducation camp inmates in new areas; afterward inmates will be permitted to join their relatives there." We thought that the planned measure was likely. If so, not only we inmates but our families as well would be confined according to some new method—we would be thrown out of the new society. Only much later did we hear about the "New Economic Zones."

After a year of reeducation our mood, which had fluctuated according to each new development in our situation, was now the opposite of the expectant state we had been in when we left home to report to the communist authorities. The new regime had promised to provide us with a new and logical line of reasoning and to train us to live according to the norm set up by true revolutionaries, that is, people with high ideals and armed with revolutionary virtues. Our expectations and hopes of the first days now had been replaced by a self-defense attitude aimed at liberating ourselves from our situation. Even the team and group leaders, themselves inmates who had been given firm promises of early release and good jobs, showed signs of despair.

Our problem then was no longer what to do, but how to do it—how to pull strings to get us out of the camp or how to escape in safety. The experience of the past few releases showed that the surest way out was to have relatives in high positions in the Revolution's hierarchy who would arrange releases. As one man said, "There are now hundreds of thousands of files piled up in the military administration offices, 'public security' headquarters, and at the Ministry of the Interior. The question for each of us is to have somebody ferret out his record from those mountains of files, write on it 'to be released,' and affix his signature to it."

As far as I was concerned, the reeducation camp at the former Long Khanh military hospital was where I began to see the truth as it was and also where I began "to see some light at the end of the tunnel."

Time dragged on. We reaped one more harvest of maize and one of peanuts. One day, Commander Hung stopped to chat with us, and he asked me about the other camp. I told him that what we enjoyed most there was going out to cut wood. "By cutting our own wood for the kitchen," I said, "we helped save money allocated to buy kindling. The contractor charged a high price for kindling but delivered mostly rotten wood." Commander Hung promised to discuss the idea with Logistics, and very soon we were again ordered to go out wood cutting. One of the men made a kind of cart with metal cable reels for wheels, and this enabled us to move a large load of logs with only one man pushing and another pulling the cart. The next day, a *bodoi* from Logistics came to our place. "I've seen many reels like these over there, at the other side of the camp," he said. "As you know how to use them to make carts, I'll get permission for you to take them."

We enthusiastically supported this idea, and the following day the *bodoi* brought us to the warehouse area to gather materials for construction of the carts. This area was the very scene of the explosion a few months before. Only now did we realize the amount of arms and ammunitions stored here. The *bodoi* showed us to the various places where wheels and reels could be found. Big guns were kept here, and one of the men, wanting to show off, said that these were all 37mm antiaircraft guns. The more we discussed it, the more convinced we were that this area must be one of the main ordnance depots—if not *the* ordnance depot—of the Northern army. After the fall of Saigon, there had been orders to collect all ordnance in the area. Here we saw burned artillery pieces that looked ludicrous with their bent tubes; all around lay cases of half-burned AKs. Feigning stupidity, I asked the *bodoi*, "I suppose there are enough weapons here to equip several battalions. Right, comrade cadre?"

The *bodoi* looked at me and said with an air of importance, "What did you say? Several battalions? You're a noncombatant, I guess. This much ordnance can equip several divisions, not battalions!" He then pointed to the spot where ammunition and rockets had been stored.

"See that stretch of ground burned black with the immense hole in the middle? Tons and tons of ammunition and rockets had been unloaded there. That's why it took so long for the ammunition dump to burn out. The men who were on guard duty have been severely punished. Their silly play caused so much damage and many casualties! Luckily, the antiaircraft missiles had been moved to Thu Duc before the explosion. Had they still been here, the number of dead would have been much greater."

I said, "What terrified me most that day was the roar of the rockets!"

The *bodoi* smiled and said with pride, "That's why they are called 'Stalin's organs.'"

We removed a number of wheels with good bearings from the gun carriages and built a number of carts. They were strange-looking things, and when we walked through residential areas, people turned out in large numbers to watch. In our tattered khaki garments, pulling our carts with the metal wheels making a great racket in the streets, we must have been quite a spectacle! As before, each trip gave us the opportunity to make some purchases and post letters. All we had to do was add our home address to a letter and throw it down when the *bodoi* were momentarily out of sight. The townsfolk would pick it up, provide an envelope, write the address, stamp the letter, and post it.

Once I sent a long letter home in which I pressed my wife to "look for doctors and medicines to treat my illness which could not be cured by simply waiting." Much later, she told me that whoever helped to send it had added a postscript that read, "At present, 'they' are greedy for money; so try your best to have strings pulled on your husband's behalf. Many families have succeeded in having their relatives released because they knew how to go about it."

Political studies at this camp usually took place after the evening meal, so fortunately the time allocated for the sessions was limited, and we did not have to stay too long to listen to what we no longer believed in. Besides, the cadres themselves made light of the studies. They only organized political speeches for national observances, and we often found only one cadre, whose name was Tri, and one *bodoi* in charge at the lecture hall. Most of the *bodoi* preferred to walk into town in the evening. For us, this was a more bearable program than the solemn study sessions at our old camp.

Time went by heavily and tediously until the end of the rainy season when, once again, some signs of change appeared. There was in the camp, besides a smithy and a woodworking shop, a metal sheet workshop where the main task was to make the suitcases so favored by the *bodoi*. The workers there said they had been told recently to make more suitcases not only for the *bodoi* at our camp but for their comrades at regimental headquarters, and to finish them as soon as possible.

The smithy, on the other hand, had orders to produce more hoes and large knives supposedly for use in clearing land for cultivation. Workers at the smithy had such privileges as arrangements for outside purchases and a greater share of food, to say nothing of their workplace near the stream, which meant regular bathing and clothes washing and no set working hours. To work at the smithy, one had to grease the palms of one's team leader and the workshop chief. This section included people like the former governor of the National Bank, Le Quang Uyen, and the former manager of one of its branches, Tran Ngoc Diep.

The carpentry shop crew, which I managed to join (after considerable effort) mainly produced furniture for regimental headquarters and was located at its adjoining compound. We too were entitled to certain privileges and advantages; each morning that we were assigned to work there, we were given breakfast, instant noodles cooked in water and rice. The rice was white rice, not the rotten stuff supplied by the PRC and hidden for long periods in the forests.

Working at Regiment, I sometimes had the opportunity to talk with apparently high-ranking officers. When not busy, they would come out and watch us as we sawed, planed, chiseled, and hammered. One day an older officer approached me and asked without any preliminaries, "What would be your wish at present?"

I answered without hesitation, "Each and every one of us would like to return home to live with his family and work at the job that will have been arranged for him by the Revolution."

The officer smiled and shook his head. "All of you, when asked, have only one wish: to return home! That's simply not possible because you have not yet completed your reeducation. You have gone through only a period of political studies. There's another important part of the program that you have yet to study."

Remaining impassive, I asked, "Oh, really! What important part? The communiqué said that we had to report only for reeducation. In the beginning, all of us believed we only had to go for seven days."

The officer laughed out loud. "Again, the story of the seven-day reeducation! Tell me! Who on earth would ever believe that within seven days you can bring about a complete change in your thinking habits and way of life? You are wrong if you think you can! You still have to undergo reeducation through physical labor. Besides, you cannot return home now. Outside, transformations and new developments are taking place at this very moment. The People will not leave you in peace if you go back among them because the People have made much more rapid progress than you. In addition, there are circumstances that could put your own life at risk."

I decided to argue a bit. "Speaking of reeducation through labor, we have been doing just that these last few months."

Again, the officer laughed. "Really! All you've done is plant a small quantity of vegetables for your own use. That is not reeducation through labor. You must work enough land for real production. Here, your work amounts to very little indeed."

"Good God! Then, when do we begin 'reeducation through labor'?"

"When you ask for it, it will be allowed."

"How, whom, and where to ask? Please tell me, comrade cadre!"

"You no doubt will be given a lecture on how to ask. I'm pretty sure that will take place soon."

After that conversation, we waited daily for some development. One day, our team was told to pick some men to go with Logistics people to bring back a supply of rice. Anticipating a fairly long trip and the chance to eat some Chinese soup, I asked to go. This was my first ride in a Molotova truck—it was fairly new and painted navy blue—and we drove off in the direction of Saigon. At a spot where the road forked, we took the branch leading to Tuc Trung and finally drove into a former rubber plantation administrative compound with a number of beautiful French bungalows. We realized we had been here before to collect rice. The driver suddenly pulled up, got down, and said, "Get down if you want to piss."

As we were about to climb back on the truck, the driver signaled us to follow him, saying, "Wait! Come here, I have something to tell you."

We followed him to a spot about five meters away from the truck, where he stopped and gave instructions. "When you're loading rice on the truck, make sure to add two extra sacks, and be sure they are whole and full of rice. Put them on top of the others, toward the rear of the truck. Do I make myself clear? Remember to take good sacks of rice. In a little while, when we get to the marketplace, I'll invite you to have some noodle soup."

We all smiled and replied cheerfully, "Of course, we'll remember, comrade cadre."

We climbed back on the truck and drove into the warehouse, surprisingly big, like a hangar. One of the fellows said this was the place where the plantation rubber was stored. When we had come here earlier in the year to pick up rice, the warehouse had been full, with sacks of rice piled nearly to the roof. Now, it was empty except for one corner; most sacks were broken, and the spilt rice covered with mouse droppings looked like small sandy mounds with black beans spread in a regular pattern. One of the men said to the *bodoi*, "Only a few months and the warehouse is almost empty! Last time we came here, we had to climb high up to get our rice.''

The *bodoi* replied, ''The rice is used up by you, not anybody else. And this is the last of several warehouses that have supplied rice for your meals. When you have eaten this rice up, there will be none left. We don't know yet where we're going to get more rice to feed you. Last month, rice was brought here by my unit for the last time.''

I asked where they brought it from.

''Where on earth could we get it if not from the deep forests. Why?''

''Because the rice we've been getting is quite rotten.''

''Well, it's been stored in caches deep in the forests. There, even people are likely to rot, let alone rice!''

We had orders to load the number of sacks agreed upon by the storekeeper and the driver. The two *bodoi* instructed our team leader to keep count and then left us to ourselves. We worked until we were covered with sweat. Finally, our team leader said, ''Let stop work! I don't care whether or not it's the right amount.''

Surprised at his words, I asked, ''Isn't there enough there?''

''There's enough for the camp, but we forgot to look for the two extra sacks the *bodoi* told us to get for him.''

We then decided to tell the driver his share was included since no one was eager to climb back on the mound to search for unbroken sacks. We went out to wait in the fresh air. Much later the driver returned and we started back toward the truck, but he told us to wait outside while he drove out of the warehouse. Just as our truck was coming out the door, another suddenly appeared from nowhere and headed into the warehouse. The two vehicles grazed each other, but the damage was not serious, just some dents on the front ends of each truck. Both drivers jumped down and rushed toward each other, intent on a fight. The other driver shouted, ''Are you blind?''

Our driver answered with a stream of abuse, ''You s.o.b.! I'm not blind! You drove in without blowing your horn, so I rammed you just like that!''

''Damn you! Don't you dare insult me!''

The two *bodoi* were about to hurl blows when suddenly there was a shout. ''What are you two comrades doing?''

Both turned toward the newcomer, who ran forward; they tried to justify themselves. ''This one drove carelessly and then insulted me!''

''A socialist combatant never uses such language!''

''And a socialist combatant never drives like you!''

The middle-aged stranger said, ''Do the comrades intend to fight it out right here? Do you want to be detained and wait for your unit to come looking for you?''

We watched and could not help laughing. The two *bodoi* continued to argue and the stranger to arbitrate for a long while. Finally, they came to some arrangement, and our driver climbed back on the truck, started the engine, and drove out for us to board.

Reaching Gia Kiem marketplace, the driver pulled up. Without waiting for orders, we climbed down and followed the *bodoi* to a soup seller. Everyone looked at us with surprise, but then they all smiled. One man in my team said to the *bodoi* in a low voice, "I have a few dong; could I have permission to buy some beer?"

"Permission granted."

The *bodoi* then approached the counter where noodles were served and said softly, "Please bring those fellows one bowl of soup each; I'll pay for these. If they want more, they'll have to pay for it out of their own pockets."

The *bodoi*, who seemed to know his way around, went in the back of the shop. A moment later, he came out accompanied by a young man. Looking out, we saw him climb up on the back of the truck, choose a sack of rice, and heave it onto the young man's shoulders. The latter took it away, and a moment later he came back for another sack. A woman brought bowls of soup to the four of us sitting together, and I asked her, "The rice is rotten. Why do you buy it?"

"We have to make do with it. Nowadays rice is a government monopoly, so it's very difficult to find it on the market."

We ordered two bottles of beer. When the shopkeeper opened them and we poured the beer into glasses, it gave forth just a few tiny bubbles. I asked, "Has the beer been kept too long?"

"It would still be good if that was the case," the shopkeeper said, "but this is new beer; it has lost both quality and flavor."

We sampled the beer. It was neither sour nor sweet; it had the disagreeable taste of a soft drink gone bad.

"This beer has gone flat!" one man exclaimed. "There's no fizz and the taste is nasty."

"No, it's not gone flat. That's how the new beer tastes. You're used to the old kind of beer, but now there's only this for sale. It seems they are using maize instead of barley to make it."

The soup, on the other hand, was eaten with great relish and very quickly. We asked for more as all of us had some money in our pockets, and in the end we each had as many as three bowls of the delicious soup. I could not stand the beer, but my companions, reluctant to spend money for nothing, finished both bottles. As we handed money to the seller, she said, "No, I'm not going to take your money. You're camp inmates, you don't have to pay. I'll ask the *bodoi* to pay for one bowl of soup for each of you."

We thanked her and said jokingly, "Why don't you take our money? Is it because you pity reeducation camp prisoners? You know, today is the first chance we've had to taste *pho* [noodle soup] in nearly two years."

The woman asked, "Do you know when you're going to be released?"

"Nobody knows! It looks as if we're going to die in a reeducation camp!"

"Why do they have to hold so many people for so long? Around here, there are nearly 100 families who have had no news from husbands and sons. I tell you this in strict confidence: *they* have a great dislike for the Catholic immigrants resettled in this area. The *bodoi* have their quarters all around here; every five houses, there is a separate group. They don't live in barracks and prefer to mingle with the villagers."

A moment later, the *bodoi* reappeared. He spoke in a low voice with the woman, who handed money to him—probably payment for the rice. We asked to make some purchases and were permitted to go across the street to buy cigarettes, sugar, and sweets. On the way back, we stretched out on the sacks of rice, feeling sleepy. Someone said, "The soup was passable, but the beer did not taste like beer any more."

Another added slowly, "The bottle looked like before, but what was inside was not the same. So are we all. Completely changed!"

A third fellow said with vexation in his voice, "But what a change it has been! A pack of noodles, for instance, previously wrapped in cellophane with chicken, crab, or prawn flavor, has become in just a few months something wrapped in dirty paper with no flavor whatsoever, only the taste of coconut oil and salt. We can't help feeling sad and dejected."

When we got back to camp, dusk had already set in and food had been distributed. Luckily for us, another team was ordered to carry the sacks of rice to the warehouse. We hurried to the well to wash. The other inmates we came across all had the same question: What's new in the outside world? We had to answer it hundreds of times.

That night, we gathered together to discuss what we had seen and heard during the trip. Details such as empty storehouses, *bodoi* stationed among the local people, many families still without news from husbands and sons— together with the discovery that beer was no longer what it had been before— gave us plenty of food for thought and worry.

As the *bodoi* kept pressing us to speed up production of the articles they had requested, we became more and more anxious about possible changes to come. Everyone believed that eventually we would have to leave this place. To keep us here seemed costly and useless. We ourselves saw no reeducation value to this kind of detention, and the communist authorities must have been aware of it too. In fact, for the last year and a half we had done nothing but serve those *bodoi* who hungered for all sorts of things.

From the economic point of view, neither we nor the *bodoi* had done anything that could serve the nation's interest. They engaged only in extravagant destruction. With my own hands, I had helped to destroy a whole block of newly built houses just to get the metal sheets needed for the roof of the meeting hall. I had seen with my own eyes the *bodoi* take apart electrical transformers to get the many-colored wires, which they used to weave into shopping bags. We had helped tear down many houses made of pinewood to get kindling for the kitchen or to get plywood boards for the *bodoi* to sleep on. Vehicles, slightly damaged, had been torn apart to provide steel for the smithy, rubber for sandals, aluminum to make various articles for daily use. Expensive equipment intended for collective use had been made into cheap small items for individuals. The men from the North had shown no sign of constructive spirit; they had no notion of the value of machines and equipment, of materials and labor. If they were intent on anything, it was to collect items of small value, which they hid away in their newly acquired suitcases or bags.

The rain began to let up. The camp was making preparations for planting maize—the last of the season—and we were turning furrows to plant sweet potatoes when orders came to organize study sessions, with a political cadre from Central Government as lecturer. We busied ourselves preparing for an expected big change. Notebooks lent to friends had to be recovered, and those borrowed, returned. We washed our clothes and exchanged home addresses with the promise that whoever was released first would bring news to the homes of those who had to remain.

When the course began and the subject stated by the cadre, we knew that what we had been waiting for had finally happened. The new lesson was entitled "Policy regarding the setting up of New Economic Zones" (NEZ). It had three parts, the first aimed at showing that the NEZ policy was the right response to the needs of the country. The cadre elaborated on the perspicacity of the Party in its assessment of the nation's potential in terms of cultivatable land and manpower. The second part dealt with past experience, with a view to learning the right way to prepare for the establishment of NEZs and to organize the labor force. The third part spoke of the duty of each individual in relation to the NEZ policy.

The lecture on, and subsequent discussion and writing of the "results obtained" paper, lasted one whole week. The last part of the lesson was the most important. The cadre posed the question, "How should reeducation camp inmates respond to the question of setting up New Economic Zones?" We spent many days discussing the topic, but it was hard to concentrate. Soon, it would be Christmas—another Christmas in a reeducation camp! From somewhere church music wafted in, reminding us that the end of the year was near. Memories of the past filled our minds, followed by feelings of sorrow and bitterness.

The cadre kept beating about the bush for a long time; then one day he ordered us "to make a decision and respond positively to the policy adopted by the Party and the government." Before the entire body of camp inmates—including the sick, whatever the illness—the cadre asked a man sitting in the front row, "You, for example! How would you respond positively?"

The man hesitated, then replied, "Well, I would agree to go wherever the Revolution wants me to go in order to build a New Economic Zone."

The cadre shouted in the loudspeaker, "Not much determination in your answer! Tell me, are you or are you not dedicated to respond to the appeal of the Party and the People?"

Only the man who stood facing the cadre answered. "Yes, I am."

The cadre again shouted, "I expected you all to answer the question! Now, have all of you decided to respond?"

Only then were there answers from the audience, a resounding "Yes! We are decided!"

The cadre shook his head and spoke into the loudspeaker. "What a weak response! Too weak!"

Commander Tri walked to the far end of the hall; his voice was harsh as he said, "Are you still asleep at this hour? Don't you want to pay attention, participate actively? You want to stay here forever, right?"

The cadre, sitting at the front said, "Very well! I'll give you time to think it over. From today until the end of the week. On Monday, you will discuss the matter in your own groups; after that, those who respond positively may ask to participate in the building of New Economic Zones. Those who don't want to go are free not to do so. Remember, you're acting in your own interest! If you want to go, the Revolution will consider your request. But I must tell you in advance, not all requests will be accepted by the Revolution. Only those who are sincere and considered worthy will be accepted. You're well aware that you will be released only after you have completed your reeducation through productive labor. So, it's up to you to make the choice." Having finished, the cadre gave us permission to leave.

The audience stood up in noisy confusion. Suddenly a voice rose above the commotion and Comander Tri was seen walking toward the loudspeaker. He shouted, "Wait! Everybody sit down!"

We knew that our political commissar undoubtedly was going to be criticized for our lack of enthusiasm in class. He said, "I strongly criticize your attitude during today's lesson. To bring group discussions under control, all group leaders are to stay to receive instructions on how to organize the discussion. The rest of you may go."

Later I was informed that Tri had repeatedly instructed the group leaders to submit papers from each of their members. Nobody was to be exempt. Writing a paper to volunteer for work in a New Economic Zone was an obligation we could not shirk.

The problem now was to find out where we would be sent. One of the oldtimers at the camp was told by a *bodoi* that on previous occasions inmates had been sent to Ka Tum on the Cambodian border. Most of us wished to go someplace not too far away so that we could contact our families without too much difficulty.

When the deadline arrived for submission of "decision papers," a friend said to me, "Some of the fellows know beforehand that they will not have to go with us. My team leader seems to know something and appears not to be making any preparations. Bui Quoc Khanh, on the other hand, has been seen trying to barter some of his possessions for a pair of good canvas shoes and some warm clothes. He seems to be worried and tense. And Commander Tri summoned Nhon, the painter, to battalion headquarters to paint his portrait. Nhon said that Tri put on his new uniform and lieutenant's badges for the occasion, but when the portrait was finished, Tri was not satisfied with it. He said the background was too light; he wanted it darker to make it look like a photograph! Nhon said that ever since he had regretted his efforts to produce an artistic portrait, which, because of the will of a *bodoi*, was now 'as dark as a dog's muzzle!' "

The days passed as we waited for the order to move out. Then suddenly the carpentry team was given an urgent order to build a shed to receive inmates' relatives who would visit them soon. Although we in the carpentry team were the only ones told, within an hour or two the news was known throughout the camp. After nearly two years of reeducation, this was the first time that we could hope to see our wives and children. Not only did the carpentry team get busy, but the whole camp population was occupied doing one thing or another in anticipation of the event. Some men hastened to make a few objects as gifts for their wives; others appealed to the artists to paint their portraits to be given to their families—"in case I die in camp, my wife and children will have something of me to set out on my shrine." The older men, who until then had been critical of the younger ones' hobby of making things, now also searched for pieces of aluminum and asked the others to make combs or bracelets for them.

Christmas came just as the shed was completed. There was still no word of the arrival of our families, but we consoled ourselves with the new hope of their visit before Tet. Two days after Christmas, we were instructed to write to our homes telling of the decision of the Revolution "allowing families to visit their relatives in camps." We were permitted to give the exact address of the camp, and a list of relatives who would receive permission to visit was attached to the letter. Our relationship with each person had to be specified to prevent persons not related to inmates from coming to the camp. From the moment writing paper was distributed, the whole camp bustled with activity, as if in preparation for a festival. Although the date of the visit was still unknown, some men already had their hair cut and beards shaved. Everybody complained about his emaciated appearance that would no doubt sadden his parents, wife, and children when they saw him; each one of us, therefore, tried to bring some improvement to his appearance.

The night the paper was distributed, we sat up late to write our letters as we had to give them to our team leaders the following morning. We were allowed to write only on one page the size of a school copybook; the second page was reserved for the list of relatives. The *bodoi* advised us to ask our families for some warm clothes and a large piece of plastic material to use as a raincoat or cover if we had to take our meals in the rain. Our joy was now tinged with worry: If a visit was permitted, was it to give us the opportunity to ask for food and clothing in preparation for our transfer to a far-off place where "warm clothes would be needed"? This particular detail haunted us day and night! Did it mean that we were going to be sent to the North? Our letters had to be written in tiny handwriting to convey within that one page both our love and longing for our wives and children and our need for medicines, clothing, shoes, plastic material, and food that would keep for a long time. Since the camp administration had forbidden us to keep money, the business of letting our families know that we really needed money without actually saying so, took care and inspiration. Most of us had to write and rewrite before arriving at something that fully expressed what we wanted to say. Everybody sat up late that night. We kept the finished letters by our beds, ready to submit in the morning.

Shortly after dawn, I was awakened from a deep sleep by confused noise and activity. A voice said, "The *bodoi* have come in great numbers to the room next to ours. I wonder what they're up to!"

Reveille had not sounded yet. A man sleeping near the window looked out and said in a low voice, "Both commanders and the medic are coming."

Curious, we got up though still sleepy, folded our blankets and mosquito nets, and put them in order. Suddenly a voice sounded in the other room, "Go and fetch a doctor!"

A *bodoi* appeared at the door, saying, "Nobody is allowed to leave the room. The doctors among you are requested to report to the commanders."

The first doctor to report was Bui Tran Anh, the jolly surgeon. We could hear him speaking loudly and clearly from the adjoining room. "He has just died; the body is still soft to the touch. Let me try artificial respiration to see if he can be revived."

The man near the window again announced, "Many more of our doctors are coming. It seems that one of us had just died."

The doctors were heard discussing the case. "Does anybody have medicine to give him a shot in the heart? That might save him."

"No way to find the medicine here! Let's ask the *bodoi* if they have it."

"No use asking them!"

Dr. Bui Tran Anh's voice again, "Can you please try to see if there's any hope of reviving him? I've tried artificial respiration for quite a while without result. The body's still soft."

"Just keep trying! At the same time, let's give his arms and legs a vigorous massage."

A moment later, somebody said, "Nothing doing! The arms and legs have already become rigid."

Dr. Bui Tran Anh said, "An examination of his body shows that the man died an hour or two ago. There are no bruises, no tell-tale signs on his body."

The group leader and the two chaps sleeping on either side of the dead man were instructed to write reports that would be used to investigate the circumstances of his death. The man's name was Nguyen Van Dan. His "neighbors" said that he had been speaking and crying fearfully in his sleep during the night. They woke him up, and later he went back to sleep. At dawn one of the men sleeping next to him woke up and tried to wake Dan to get him to move over, but there was no answer. He said Dan appeared to have gone into a coma, but in fact he had alrady passed away. His roommates hastened to report to the group leader and the *bodoi*. The dead man still had his letter to his wife and children placed at the head of his bed. Dan was known to have a large family. We were allowed to make a coffin and bury him that day.

The house for the reception of visitors had been completed. We also made a number of tables and benches and built a kitchen and a latrine area. The preparations had been carefully planned and carried out. A group responsible for making tea and cleaning up the area was organized. At the last minute, as luck would have it, a plank fell on my foot. The injury was not serious, but I was badly bruised and had to limp about.

Tet was drawing near. The *bodoi* began talking about sending New Year's letters early to their families in the North to avoid backed-up mail. We were then given a complete rest. A few young fellows amused themselves by catching swallows, using thin copper wires with great success. They competed with one another in trapping the birds. Some of us gathered from time to time to chat or listen to poetry readings. We liked best the poems composed by Ta Ky. He read to us, among others, a poem entitled "I am sitting here" that he had written in the period when his own group was engaged in polemics against Republic of Vietnam President Thieu. Then followed another poem, more recent, which was like a continuation of the former and was titled "I am still sitting here." It was a long poem fraught with agonizing feelings, yet its tone still bespoke the unyielding spirit of the author.

On many occasions, I had listened to the poems of Ta Ky whose lines, filled with sorrow, had moved us to tears. I particularly liked one titled "The string of blowflies," which he had just composed as the year ended. He was suffering from an attack of hepatitis and serious constipation. The inspiration came to him as he squatted on the filthy latrine, all the while thinking of his wife and looking at the blowflies, some zigzagging in the air and others settling on the barbed-wire strands of the fence in front of him. The poem, as I recall it, is as follows:

Swarms of blowflies perch on the barbed wire;
Clouds of blowflies ascend from the latrines,
    flapping their wings, looking like ripples.
My love for thee is like the tide
    which ebbs and rises.

They're the color of sea water.
Their brown eyes are reminiscent
    of Western lassies' hair
Or of thy eyes of sleepless nights.

Black is the string of blowflies;
As black as the necklace of jet grains
    I bought for thee.
Their buzz sounds like thy voice
    murmuring my name;
Thy voice which said, "The two of us!"

The flies perch on top of each other
Like musical notes in a love song.
But the barbed wire draws an irregular staff
So how can thou sing the song?

The swallows are coming back in flocks,
    but not as harbingers of spring
    because spring's already dead.
They're hunting for flies on barbed wires;
The necklace of jet grains is blown to pieces!
I call thy name again and again.

Ta Ky acknowledged that he also liked this strange poem. He did not expect to find inspiration in that filthy place and at his most desperate moment. He described our situation as that of men bereft of spring. Reality now is only the reality brought by the return of the swallows, not to announce the coming of spring, but simply to hunt for flies. Each of us is now full of regret and longing for his broken necklace of jet grains!

When visitor's day finally came, the sun seemed to rise later than usual; we seemed to wait a long time for dawn to appear. The gong summoning us to morning gymnastics had not sounded yet, but mosquito nets and blankets were already folded up and put neatly away. Everywhere, the inmates were seen checking the gifts they would present to their wives and children. Even the sick were making a great effort to get up, rinse their mouths, and fold blankets and mosquito nets. When the group leaders asked whether anyone was reporting sick, nobody ventured to do so for fear of being deprived of his family's visit. Thang and I were among those who often went to the latrine area now because it was the only place in the whole camp where we could have a good view of the road leading to the visitors' house. By dawn, before the *bodoi* had cleared away the barbed wire "concertina" that blocked the road, many families with small children and babies in their mothers' arms already stood waiting there.

A *bodoi* came and announced that it was not permitted to appear before relatives with torn clothes or uncut hair and beard. Consequently, we appealed to skillful friends to oblige us with a haircut, then waited in turn to use the clippers and razor. The clippers lent by the *bodoi* were blunt, and haircuts were very painful. Fortunately Binh, who worked at the smithy, had succeeded in producing a pair of fairly sharp scissors. As for the razor, its blade had been sharpened so often that it no longer fit its original metal guards and a makeshift metal clip had to be made for it. Despite the difficulties and delays, everybody was at last ready for the visit.

The number of visitors kept growing every minute. Those who lived far away in the countryside were the first to arrive. A few families had spent the night in the houses of local good samaritans, until now strangers to them. At last the *bodoi* began to call inmates' names on their loudspeakers, telling them to present themselves at the gate. There, they were searched thoroughly, but were allowed to keep the gifts intended for wives and children. Only a few of the men, whom the *bodoi* disliked, were told to change their clothes or leave their gifts behind. The inmates took turns at sitting at a table where their relatives were permitted to join them. The camp commanders, reeducation monitors, and a number of *bodoi* walked around, listening to the conversations.

At first, the allotted time for each visit was half an hour, but as the number of visitors became too large the time was reduced to twenty then fifteen minutes. At the end of each visit, the families with gifts for inmates were requested to bring them to a table where a commander or monitor checked them before the inmate was allowed to have them. Control at Commander Tri's table was the most severe. Inmates were not allowed to receive green beans, peanuts, or rice! At other tables inmates were told that such items were forbidden but, as this was the first time, the error was overlooked and they were permitted to take them.

I waited the entire first day without anybody coming to visit me. On the morning of the second day, I impatiently ran back and forth to the latrine area to watch the road. Then, I saw that my family had arrived. From afar, I saw my elder brother and nephews, each carrying a bag in his hand; then my wife with my little daughter in her arms was walking toward the gate. I trembled with excitement.

This was strange. I was about to meet my wife and child, and yet I was afraid that something might happen! I returned to my room to prepare myself for their visit. To maintain my composure, I made my way slowly to the gate, leaning on my friend Thế's shoulder; then I rested for a moment, waiting for my name to be called.

When my turn came, I tried to walk in a natural manner but had to limp a little because of my recent injury. My wife, watching me walk toward her, appeared to be deeply moved. She and our child, together with my brother and nephews, were permitted to enter the area only after I had taken my seat at the table. My wife tried not to cry, but tears kept streaming down her cheeks; she was unable to utter a word. My brother asked about my health, all the time telling me in a low voice that strings were being pulled on my behalf. The difficulty was how to know the right strings to pull. Recently, he said, many people were coming from the North and approaching the families of camp inmates with claims that they could pull strings to obtain releases. Holding my daughter in my arms, I was still uncomfortable. My child sat on my lap but looked ill at ease, as if embarrassed. When I had left her to report for reeducation, she was barely two; now, older and clearly much taller, she answered my few questions indistinctly or with a "yes" or "no." Finally, seeing that the time was nearly up, I got down to business and said hurriedly, "There are so many inmates that it will be very long before anybody's case is considered. Therefore we have to pull strings; but we must not pay in advance." I added that from now on, anytime they wanted to give me news about the "string-pulling" business, they must write, "Uncle has/has not recovered/is going to recover his strength." My wife had regained her calm; in a low voice she spoke to me in French to prevent the *bodoi* from understanding. She said she had placed great hope in a person who could exert influence for my release, someone who had prestige and was entirely trustworthy. She also revealed that she was at the moment working for an organization of a diplomatic character, and she was very hopeful that some help would come from that side. Nevertheless, she was still trying to secure the aid of other influential people. She begged me to look after myself and not to give up hope. Although her words were not exactly meant to reassure me, what she said sounded fairly credible.

While we were still discussing this question of my life and death, the voice of Commander Tri was suddenly heard. "It's time for the families to bring their gifts to the table over there for inspection. As for you inmates, say good-bye to your relatives and wait for the delivery of gifts."

I hastened to kiss my daughter on the head, and I gave her to my wife. I looked at them, unable to keep back my tears. They all tried to put on cheerful faces, but there were tears in everyone's eyes. My wife, brother, and nephews all became more emotional as they prepared to bid farewell to me, and I said hurriedly, "After this visit, it's certain that I'll have to go to another place, probably far away. If we are allowed to write home, I'll try to give you an indication where I am. You'll have to read between the lines."

My wife and brother nodded. My brother said, "Remember the first letter you wrote? We knew at once that you were in the Long Khanh area."

As she left me, my wife said, "Keep yourself in good health. Remember! Your health is the most important. Don't worry about us."

Everyone had parted from his family now except the relatives of a man who worked at the smithy. They were allowed to stay for another fifteen minutes. I could not help feeling frustrated and somewhat envious of him.

I queued up at a table away from Commander Tri. But as everyone was trying to avoid him, Tri diverted the end of a line waiting before a table controlled by a *bodoi* to his own. I was among those moved to Commander Tri's table—sheer bad luck! When our turn came, my wife and brother poured the contents of their bags out upon the table. There were sweets, sugar, condensed milk, dried bananas, shredded meat, salted biscuits, and other edibles that could be kept for a long period. Tri selected among them such articles as salted ground sesame and sugar and put them in the bag I was holding in my hand. When he picked up the two parcels of shredded meat, he hesitated, then said to my wife, "Bring these back home and keep them for your daughter. There's no shortage of meat here."

I was painfully disappointed at this loss. Those parcels of dried meat could have lasted me quite a while. Next, Tri rejected a pack of peanuts, and then he returned a box of cooked white rice. "Do you think that your husband doesn't have rice to eat here?"

Unable to keep quiet, my wife replied, "I brought along this handful of rice to serve us as a meal, but now I want to share it with my husband. I am sure that what I am doing is not against the rules. I ask you to allow my husband to have it."

My wife's voice was so pitiful that he could not do otherwise than hand the rice to me, as he said, "Time's up. You can take this and leave now."

I began to put the parcels I was allowed to take into my bag. My wife packed up the ones that had been rejected, making a show of arranging the parcels while deftly pushing one pack of shredded meat toward my side. The *bodoi* began to urge our group of inmates back inside the camp. I turned and waved to my child and wife, and they watched me move away, their eyes filled with tears. Raising the bag of supplies onto my shoulder, I tried to put on a cheerful appearance, but my heart was seized by complete despair. I did not know whether I would have a chance to see my family ever again.

I felt utterly miserable after I got back inside the camp. No one had suspected that peace could be like this. Nobody ever imagined that the new regime could detain so many people. I had reported for reeducation—though warned by friends and acquaintances—like the naïve, stupid fellow that I was. I believed it was unthinkable that hundreds of thousands of people could be detained at one time, that there wouldn't be enough prisons to keep them in or enough rice and food to feed so many.

Before the visit, each of us had been filled with impatience and expectation. Afterward, we fell into despair and perplexity. We had longed for some white rice and a piece of meat prepared by our wives, but now that we had them in our hands, we found that we had no appetite. Those delicacies now had the taste of a last meal for a condemned man because we all understood that now we were due to depart for another camp.

Acting from experience, I proceeded at once to open my parcels and sort out the foods I had to consume immediately and those I could preserve. But the main purpose for my haste was to look for money and a letter. I found those treasures hidden in a most unexpected place. I put the letter in a safe spot, intending to find a quiet corner and read it when night came. As for the money, I had found a way to hide it that would permit me to get at it when needed and, at the same time, protect it from detection and theft. I shared the perishable food with my friends, especially those who shared their food with me, and then with those who had lost contact with their families and had no hope of receiving any visits or any food parcels.

My wife's letter informed me that she had done everything possible, based on the advice of our neighbors, to secure my release. These friends had also held a meeting to draft a request for my release because "I had lived an honest life and always assisted my neighbors." The person who advised my wife on what to do was a neighbor whom I had helped with the formalities required for admission of his children to a public school. Besides, the local administrative council had issued to my family a certificate attesting that I had been a teacher under the former regime and a good citizen. My wife had also asked an acquaintance of ours to introduce her to a high-ranking cadre who recently had come from the North, and she asked that person to use his influence to obtain my release. He had promised to intercede and assured my wife of positive results. My family had great confidence in that individual because he had declared he would accept payment only after my release. Moreover, my wife had asked the organization she was working for to make a request on my behalf to the Ministry of Foreign Affairs of the new regime. She added that one of her present duties was to act as interpreter during the daily contacts between her employer and high-ranking cadres of the new government. After I had finished reading, I felt that my morale had been given a real boost. My wife could not have done better!

As for my friends at the camp, they became more dejected, more pessimistic after the visit than they had been before. The only ones to show some optimism were those who had been assured by their relatives that they had pulled the right strings to obtain their releases. Some men were informed by parents that their wives and children had tried to flee the country and had been reported missing. Others learned that parents, brothers, and sisters had attempted to escape but had been caught. A number of inmates learned that relatives had been evicted from their homes by local authorities and told to move to New Economic Zones "if they wanted their families to be reunited soon." Other men's wives had agreed to resettle in New Economic Zones upon the promise by authorities that their husbands would be released in the near future to join them at the new places.

The visitors also told about the many difficulties created by the new regime. In any contact with authorities, the ordinary citizen was now required to produce his resumé. To apply for the sale of a car or house or for a travel permit, a resumé had to be attached to the application. If the social category of the family was listed as "member of the *nguy* army" or "member of the *nguy* administration," refusal was certain. Students had to declare the "social category" to which their families belonged, and if a family was *nguy*, the children would have no hope of passing their examinations or being admitted to an institution of higher education, however intelligent, gifted, or hard-working they might be. Thus, everything required that palms be greased. Anything, however difficult it proved to be, was always feasible if money could be had. One person was said to have offered a cadre a simple radio set; in exchange, he was issued an official paper certifying that he had served the Revolution well. Thanks to that certificate, his son, a detainee at a reeducation camp, was released less than six months afterward.

Without contact with the outside world, we had believed that people everywhere, especially in the countryside, were active supporters of the new regime, but now we knew that most people evaded the laws and regulations imposed by the new administration. Trading no longer took place in shops, but furtively in the streets or alleyways to avoid control by the authorities. Life was chaotic under the regulations enforced by the new civil servants. People connected to the former regime were selling their possessions to get enough money to flee the country or bribe someone to get husbands or sons released. Meanwhile, the officers of the new regime were looking for all sorts of things to buy because they had nothing and craved everything.

Every day, each family had to appoint one member to attend a study session at the block or subdistrict office. People who attended study sessions at their workplace during the day were nevertheless required to go to evening sessions in their neighborhoods as well. "People's" organizations mushroomed. Women, children, youth, elderly people, everyone was dragged into some organization. The more measures of control devised by the administration, the more opportunities for bribery were presented to the cadres. No one could foresee where the present chaos would end, and no one wanted to think about the future in the long term.

We pieced together all these bits of information given by our relatives and they brewed like a storm in our consciousness. We were worried and bewildered. If life outside the camp was that chaotic, when could we expect it to stabilize? On the other hand, thanks to the supplies in our gift parcels, the sick had their medicines, the weak had more to eat, and everyone was feeling much better.

Tet was drawing near, and Logistics gave instructions for us to prepare to make *banh chung*[7] for the holiday. The cadre promised to distribute enough glutinous rice to provide one *banh chung* for every two inmates. The few pigs raised by the camp administration would be killed to provide the meat. In the midst of this preparation for Tet, orders came for us to hand over all papers, magazines, and books in our possession. Many of us had been given books and magazines in our gift parcels, and the orders stressed that it was absolutely forbidden to keep books written in a foreign language. I had a Bible, which I had brought along when I first left home and which I kept hidden in a safe place, but now I had to hand it over because many people had seen me reading it. The doctors among us had received a number of medical books from their relatives; they now saw these confiscated without having had a chance to read them. But something unexpected happened to me. I was summoned to the camp administration office one day, and told, "At the other camp, you asked to purchase Lenin's selected works. The books have arrived. You can have them. The price is 1.70 dong. Can you pay for it now, or do you want us to debit the amount you left in our custody?"

I felt uneasy as I did not know whether they were trying to find out if I had money hidden about me. I replied, "I don't have any money, but I can ask my friends to lend me some. Let me go back and borrow the money."

But the cadre allowed me to leave with the books—five paperback volumes. I had to conceal them from my friends; if they knew I had bought Marxist books, they would suspect me of being an informer. Those five books, published in the USSR, cost less than two packs of instant noodles, a bargain indeed! Later on, something very special happened to me because of those books.

New Year's Eve arrived. We were allowed to gather in the meeting hall to watch television. From what we saw, people outside seemed to be celebrating Tet with much zest and activity. At our meal that evening, we had a treat of pork cooked with brine. Before going to bed, we gathered in small groups in our favorite spots to enjoy sweets, cakes, and the other delicacies given by our families and also to speak about the past. Our group listened to poetry readings, and, as usual, we most appreciated Ta Ky's poems. When the gong sounded, we

---

[7]Traditional Vietnamese New Year's cake made of glutinous rice with a filling of green beans and meat with some fat and wrapped in banana leaves. The *bánh chưng* is cylindrical in shape; in the original Southern style, it is called *bánh tét*.

dispersed and went to our beds, but we could not sleep. Most of us kept chatting with those lying alongside. Outside, the *bodoi* were heard celebrating. In drunken voices, they expressed their merriment by singing or shouting, and at midnight they welcomed the New Year by firing guns in the air. We also heard the cracking noise of firecrackers from the town. Earlier in the evening a communiqué had been read on television forbidding the aimless shooting of guns, but now rifle fire was heard all around, mingled from time to time with the boom of bigger guns. Through the window, I saw flares lighting the sky.

On New Year's day, the inmates played a volleyball match, and at noon the *banh chung* was distributed. In the afternoon, there was musical entertainment. But all of this was more form than substance compared with the Tet observance at the other camp last year. The men here liked to sit around chatting instead of attending events aimed at collective entertainment. The *bodoi* had to urge us to join the spectators at the volleyball game and to attend the musical show. We were given a complete rest from work during the three days of the traditional Tet celebration.

On the fourth day, there was renewed activity in the air; Logistics told us to turn in the aluminum basins they had lent, the camp commander asked me to pay for the books, and the inmates, acting on information gathered from somewhere, began to pack their belongings. The fifth day passed; at noon on the sixth day we were summoned to the meeting hall.

A cadre from Regiment spoke. "My superiors have examined your requests and selected a number of you considered to be worthy of performing productive labor duty. You are aware that labor is glory and productive labor is the main stage of your reeducation. I am going to read the names of those who have been selected; the name of each person will be followed by his serial number. If I make a mistake, the person concerned should stand up and request correction at once."

The assembly in the meeting hall—over a thousand men—listened in silence. The cadre read from a list for more than an hour before my name was called. Just listening to the reading of names, we were able to get an idea of how the selection had been made. We had been categorized and classified long enough now to be in a position to make such judgments. More than sixty doctors were in the camp, but less than ten of them were "selected." The majority of those who were making suitcases for the *bodoi*, as well as the engineers who repaired radios for them, were not on the list; neither were those who had frequently bribed the *bodoi*. The doctors whose names were called—Bui Tran Anh, Nguyen Khac Cung, Tran Ngoc Khue, and others—were known to be disliked by the *bodoi*. Generally speaking, the inmates who were "selected" were those who had committed more "serious offenses" than those who were not named.

Finally, the list was completed, and another cadre from Regiment was introduced; he was to take charge of us, and said: "Greetings and best wishes to those of you who have just been designated to follow me to a new camp. I have a few words of advice for you which are as follows. The place you're going to is hot in the daytime and cold at night; I tell you this so you may barter for warm clothes with your friends who are staying behind. Medicines should be brought along, just in case. In particular, we advise you to settle all pending matters before leaving this camp. When you arrive at the new camp, we will consider no matter relating to your old camp. Therefore, I have to emphasize the need for you to settle your affairs—all of them without exception—with this camp."

Only then did Commander Tri appear, and he said, "Before telling you to disperse, I want to say good-bye to those of you who have been selected to go to the new camp. I wish you much progress in your reeducation so that you can return to your families soon."

We returned to our rooms to prepare for departure. In fact, we were all ready to go; what was left was to say good-bye to friends who stayed. They came to shake hands with us. I then learned that, once again, a number of us had been reported on, and this had proved harmful to us. For example, Dr. Tran Ngoc Khue, a candid young man, had been "selected" because someone had reported that he belonged to a family "suspicious to the Revolution." As for Dr. Anh, he had been the medical officer of a marine battalion.

Among those who stayed behind was the former governor of the National Bank, Le Quang Uyen. Also, one physician had been released; it was said that his father, who lived in France, had interceded directly with Hanoi on his behalf. A number of detainees had witnessed his family's car arriving at the camp to pick him up. This reinforced my belief that without outside intervention detainees like me had not the slightest chance of getting released!

The meal that day was prepared earlier than usual to be distributed to those who were going to leave the camp. The cadre who had come to take charge of us appeared to really care for our interests; he chatted in a friendly manner, and, among other things, he induced us to "ask Logistics to pay back the money they would have spent for your food and at the same time, settle all their debts with you." He also said to "try to collect as many planks, nails, as much electric wire as you can, and everything that can be used to construct dwellings because as yet there's nothing where you're going." One fellow said that some time ago we had pooled money to purchase a TV set that had been installed in the meeting hall. Now we did not know what to do about it.

The cadre said, "You have to demand that they settle the matter; it's in your interest. If they don't, insist on bringing the set with you. I shall support your claim."

On the recommendation of the camp commander, Bui Quoc Khanh was promoted to be the leader of the departing group. He busied himself organizing a work party to dismantle the kitchen, as we were entitled to part of its equipment, which included woks, aluminum basins, and jute sacks in good condition. When the cadre spoke to Khanh about claiming the money we had contributed for the TV, Khanh revealed that our share of rice had not been used up because the camp command had ordered part of it hidden near the kitchen area. He also disclosed that the money for purchasing food each month had not all been spent, that each month there was some money left. The cadre wrote down every item that the camp command was holding that rightfully should have been turned over to us.

He said, "Khanh! Follow me to Logistics to claim these items. We won't stop until we obtain satisfaction."

Khanh shrank back. "I beg you," he said, "not to tell them that I gave you the information. They will enter something very harmful in my personal record. Please say that this is what the majority of the men have told you."

The cadre said, "Don't be afraid! I'll protect you. Be forthright in making the claim. Nothing will happen to you."

We had not realized until then that Bui Quoc Khanh had been appointed deputy group leader for Logistics because he had been conniving with the camp command to cheat us out of our share of rice and food money to profit the command. Now that he had to go, he disclosed the dealings out of spite.

At around five in the afternoon, we were ordered to bring our belongings and gather in the meeting hall for the last time before making our way to the trucks. Picking up our bags and the additional articles we had made for ourselves in this camp, we walked to the hall. After roll call, the cadre in charge of the departing inmates said, "I repeat in your presence and the commander's that if any one of you has any query, he should state it now. If not, we shall proceed to the trucks. After this, no question or complaint will be considered."

The men became noisy, but no one dared stand up and speak for fear of reprisals. The cadre again urged us to speak out.

"A moment ago, you had so many questions. Why don't you raise them now? Come on! Speak out!"

Quan, a fellow known for his hot temper and outspoken manner, stood up. "We who are leaving the camp are the majority compared with our companions who stay. We have pooled money for the purchase of the TV set, so now we ask to bring it along with us. We also ask to be given back the rice and money which are ours by rights."

The whole group followed his lead. "That's right! Quite right!"

Everyone applauded. Commander Tri turned pale with anger. He stood, embarrassed, for a long moment before us. Finally, he ordered us to be silent and said, "The TV set is not entirely your own property because there's also the money contributed by those who left in the previous transfer. You're going to a place without electricity, so there's no point in bringing the set with you. Let me ask Logistics to settle the account so that there can be no loss for you. Where's Khanh? Come with me to Logistics to work that out right away!"

The cadre said, "The commander has guaranteed that you will be given a fair deal. Let's have a round of applause for him! After that, let's begin to board the trucks."

At first, we were allowed to pass through an opening we made in the fence near our barracks to provide a shortcut to the trucks parked near regimental headquarters. I was among the lucky ones who got through before some *bodoi* came and blocked the opening. The rest of the men had to go through the gate at battalion command, then through the regiment command area to reach the parking lot. The walk was tiring for them, loaded down with bags and cases, and we had no idea why the sudden change in route. Another moment and more *bodoi* came; they shouted at us to give back all the boards and sheets of rubber we had been using to sleep on, which we were now bringing with us. We had to unload from the truck all our cases and other belongings to get at the boards and rubber, which had been placed underneath. This tiresome work occupied us until dark.

Only later did we understand the reason for all the fuss. Because of Bui Quoc Khanh's disclosure of cheating on our share of rice and money, the equivalent of which had to be refunded, battalion commanders were very angry. They turned against us and forced the long walk to the parking lot and the return of the boards and sheets of rubber. But we did get twenty sacks of rice as our compensation. We did not appreciate the full value of the rice then, feeling only resentment at the trouble brought down on us by our claim.

Everyone was finally on board the trucks waiting for departure. We could not help feeling sad when we looked back at our old camp. A number of those who stayed behind stood near the fence, looking in our direction. Each time we were categorized and transferred, the same moving scene took place.

The question that kept popping up in our minds was, "Where to now?" I was sitting beside Thé and old Mr. Cuc. Looking around, I saw only the familiar faces of those who had been my companions in various camps since the day we first reported for reeducation.

Thé said, "It seems that we who are leaving are considered to have committed more serious offenses than those who are staying!"

I searched around, then pointed at Hoang Xuan Hai. "Serious my foot! You can see here a genuine son of the Revolution among us!"

Hai laughed. "Don't say that, for pity's sake! My bastard of an uncle promised to vouch for me to get me out. But he's an authentic communist and therefore cannot be relied upon. Besides, there are a lot of fellows here who have very high caliber guarantors, and yet they have to go. Fellows like Dr. Cung and Dr. Thieu, for instance, have high-ranking influential people to vouch for them, as you all know."

I made a quick mental check of my friends "of the arts" whom I had met at this "military hospital" camp and found that all of them were staying, among them Ta Ky, Trinh Cung, Do Thanh Nhon, to mention only a few. The general feeling was that those who remained were luckier than those who left. We discussed where we were likely to go, examining such details as those told us by the cadre, as "It's hot in the daytime but cold at night." The fact that we had to bring along woks and rice could only mean that we would not be going too far because there was no reason why those items were not available in the North. One knowledgeable fellow advanced a well-founded argument. "We are under the administration of the 7th Regiment of the 5th Division. This regiment specializes in logistics, and its area of responsibility is in the South. Cadres and soldiers from the regiment are now travelling with us; this means that we'll be living in the vicinity of the 5th Division."

I saw no point in prolonging the discussion, so I said, "Let's wait until we reach National Route No. 1. If the convoy turns left, there's a good chance we'll go to the Midlands or the North; if it turns right, that'll mean we're to remain in the South."

A jeep from regiment command appeared, both headlights on, and all the trucks, Molotovas, and Red Flags started their engines. We settled ourselves firmly on our seats and tried to position our legs and feet so they would not get numb.

The trucks began to move; old Mr. Cuc raised his hand and crossed himself. I thought, "It helps to have faith. To be protected by God is better than to be protected by top brass under this regime or that regime." For some reason, I laughed quietly to myself. Suddenly, the vehicle veered to the right. We looked at one another and nodded; we were going southward. Everybody was happy and cheerful. Good-bye Long Khanh! Good-bye Xuan Loc! We would have no further occasion to return to this place.

I had first reported for reeducation toward the end of June 1975; it was now February 1977. What had I learned about the new regime? What had I learned about the communists? I could think of nothing. In fact, I had not learned anything of value during all this time. And above all, my hopes of the first days had now completely vanished!

Chapter 4

Camp Four: Bu Gia Map

The convoy rumbled through the town of Xuan Loc. Although the streets were lighted by electricity, oil lamps were used in most of the houses. In many of them, pots of chrysanthemums and branches of yellow wild cherry, which traditionally decorate Vietnamese homes at Tet, were still on display. Soon, the convoy left the lights behind and plunged into the dark mantle of night. We seemed to be heading for some destination in the South, but it was still possible that the convoy would take Highway 20 going to the Central Highlands. This was a good tarred road, so the vehicles sped along smoothly. Everybody felt sleepy; the day had been very tiring and filled with tension. After about an hour, the trucks slowed, we heard voices and laughter, and the lights along the road indicated that we were in Trang Bom, an area inhabited by Catholic villagers originally from the North. The convoy was now moving toward Bien Hoa. Arriving at the junction, bright in the blue light of mercury lamps, the convoy turned off for the motorway. Everyone became wide awake, whispering, "It's very likely that we are going to pay a visit to Saigon!"

We repeated softly to one another the names of familiar places along the highway. But the convoy left the Bien Hoa area, turning onto Highway 30, and moments later we realized we were driving along Highway 13 leading to Ben Cat and Lai Khe. It was well into the night. The air was dry, and the *bodoi* sitting at the rear of the truck opened the tarpaulin fully. The light of the truck behind us was bright enough for us to see places we passed—crossroads, bridges, and, from time to time, a vestige of war, such as a small post, almost completely destroyed, the only remnant of a low crumbling wall that in the shadows vaguely resembled a headless man on his knees.

The truck moved along the bumpy road. We tried to recognize a few landmarks and guess where we were headed. At a crossroad, which most of us thought was Chon Thanh, the convoy turned toward Dong Xoai, driving on Highway 14. There was no sign of habitation on either side of the road, which became bumpier and bumpier as we drove. We racked our brains to try to remember if there was in the area a military base big enough to accommodate a thousand inmates. We estimated there might be that many of us because another convoy was waiting when we got to the Chon Thanh crossroads. When we passed them, a *bodoi* was heard calling out, "You comrades go ahead; we'll follow you."

One of the men said that big bases in this area had been abandoned long ago. Later, when the war became more violent, B-52s often bombed this jungle-covered area known to be a key point at which many communication lines converged and led eventually to the Ho Chi Minh Trail. We concluded that there were no big installations left here; indeed, those we saw had been reduced to ruins. From time to time we came across a guard post at the side of the road.

Suddenly the convoy turned into a road that had been metaled long ago, then abandoned; now what remained were a few piles of road metals in between the potholes and clumps of grass. Behind us, the sky began to lighten. On both sides of the road, only reeds were to be seen and, in the distance, jungle and more jungle. Suddenly, a horn sounded somewhere ahead of us, and the convoy pulled to a stop. The *bodoi* at the rear jumped down, saying, "Stay where you are and wait for orders!"

We noisily asked to get down to urinate, and finally a *bodoi* called out, "Please, comrades, get down to stand guard and let them relieve themselves."

After climbing down, we found we were standing on a road alongside the slope of a hill with no vegetation or building on either side. I stretched my arms and legs to ease my muscles and found that the air was cold but refreshing. There was no sign of a human being, nothing to show that people had been living in this place before.

In about twenty minutes, the *bodoi* ordered us back on the trucks. We waited a long time while they had their morning meal. After much effort, we managed to get at some edibles such as pieces of dried bread or noodles inside our bags, which were fairly crushed from being sat upon. We had a quick bite and took a swig at our hipflasks.

The day had grown much lighter when the trucks restarted their engines. After about an hour's driving, the convoy began to climb a steep slope; the landscape around us had all the characteristics of a mountainous region. Some said this road led toward Phuoc Binh. The sun, rising above the horizon, shone through clouds of dust stirred up by the wheels of our trucks. Although the convoy moved slowly, the dust was heavy and dark from the laterite soil of the area. Everyone's face was covered with the red dust.

The road became more and more winding as we climbed. The convoy slowed further, the engines roaring as the trucks attacked a steep grade. The descent was nerve-wracking; the drivers blew their horns constantly to warn one another and try to keep a safe distance between vehicles. The surface of the laterite road, traveled by so many vehicles, became a thick layer of dust, and at times the trucks were clearly slipping. Suddenly we pulled up, and we heard our driver ask, "What's the matter?"

A voice answered, "A driver ahead of us slammed on his brakes, the truck behind hit him, and both went into the hillside."

We resumed our descent, passing the scene of the accident. A group of detainees stood on the side of the road with two injured men lying on the ground. The *bodoi* sitting at the rear asked, "What're you waiting for?"

"The trucks at the tail end of the convoy. They still have enough room for us. We have two casualties here with serious chest wounds."

Soon we reached a level section of road skirting a big hill. To one side, the ground sloped down toward a wide stream, then up a hill. Suddenly, there were voices and hand clapping. "Hey buddies! Many of us! Many, many more of us!"

We were passing an area with newly built thatched houses, completely surrounded by a bamboo fence. It was no doubt a reeducation camp. No one was on the outside, but behind the fence a great many people were waving at us.

The convoy skirted many dark hills, and we counted some twenty such camps scattered along a stretch of about a dozen kilometers.

The convoy moved up a gentle slope toward a dark forest on a road that seemed newly built. Tree branches swept against the tops of the trucks. Looking out, we saw nothing except intertwining lianas and foliage so dense that it shut out the sun. We were moving very slowly on the bumpy road, and after about half an hour we emerged from the forest into an open, sunlit space. Some *bodoi* ran out to meet us as the convoy stopped, asking our driver, "Why are you so late?"

"We started early last night," he answered. "The going was hard over the mountain roads, and there was an accident on the descent."

The *bodoi* lowered the tail gate to let us out. They were sloppily dressed and all were pale looking. We jumped down and looked around in a daze. There was no sign of habitation. We stood in an open plot of land that appeared to have been cleared very recently, surrounded by a dense, dark forest. We took down our luggage, then lined up ready for inspection. The convoy turned around slowly and left us in the clearing, which was about 200 meters wide and 500 meters deep. We stood in straight lines, looking extremely dirty with our faces and clothes covered with the red dust. Looking around, we saw *bodoi* cooking with various sorts of utensils placed on a few stones. In a corner, some hammocks were slung between wooden poles. Each *bodoi* wore a scarf around his neck. The cadre who had come to fetch us at Xuan Loc, whom we now knew as Commander Tuyet, made his appearance. Having driven in a car with glass windows, he was not covered with dust. He did not look like a soldier. He went up to a man who looked paler than the others and said, "Begging to report to the commander that I have brought the inmates to perform productive labor. The total was 1,112 when we started and composed of inmates from the two camps at Xuan Loc. On the way here, one vehicle met with an accident; two wounded men had to be brought to Phuoc Binh hospital. So there are now 1,110 inmates present."

The cadre addressed as commander cleared his throat several times before speaking.

"On behalf of the People and your families, I now convey to you their warmest greetings. I very much hope that you will eagerly perform your 'productive labor' duty at this camp and will soon be granted back your citizens' rights and allowed to return to your families. You, as well as I and my men, shall have to build everything from scratch to turn this place into an area that will contribute to the wealth and prosperity of our fatherland. Now, there are various urgent tasks to be done before it gets dark. I'd like to remind you that you must absolutely comply with the rules here. As you can see, we are surrounded by jungle; you cannot survive if you leave this place. So I ask you to make every effort to overcome the difficulties that may arise in the initial period. You will become accustomed to them afterward. Now, you may take a rest; wash yourselves and relax."

Later, we were informed that the man was a regimental political cadre. We were taken down a steep path to a small stream at the foot of the hill. Looking at the terrain around us, we discovered we were standing at the bottom of a hill that was relatively lower than the surrounding ones; the stream closely followed its contour. We waded into clear water that soon turned a reddish color as we washed ourselves. Dust and dirt had settled in a thick layer on our skin and clothes, and it was hard to wash off. Soon, the shrill "woman's" voice of Bui Quoc Khanh was heard callling us to assemble. We expected to be taken to a camp somewhere in the forest. Khanh accompanied Monitor Chuong for a review of our ranks to select a number of able-bodied men. He hesitated in front of me for a moment before asking, "Can you cut trees, Vu?"

"Of course I can."

More than a hudnred of us were picked to follow a *bodoi* along a path into the forest. This was my first such experience. On this sunny midday, the tiny trail looked like a snake winding its way into the shadows. After a long while, we arrived at a thatched hut walled with bamboo. The *bodoi* said, "Go in there, pick out a machete each, and come back here; we're going to organize into work parties and get to work right away."

The hut smelled of mold. It was used as a storeroom with a pile of machetes and coils of copper wire on the earthen floor; they probably had been there for a long time. I began choosing a knife, but they were all blunt. They had been roughly forged and had handles made of iron. The cutting edges had never been sharpened and were not fit for cutting or chopping wood. Finally, I chose one with a relatively polished handle, hoping I would not hurt my hand much. Everybody complained that the knives were too blunt, and the *bodoi* said, "There's nothing here that is ready for use. When you want to use something, you have to produce it with your own hands. We lack everything here. You should learn how to overcome difficulties to obtain the things you need. If your knife is blunt, you must try to turn it into a sharp one. Do you know how? Go to the stream, find an appropriate stone, and sharpen your knife. Don't work too hard! If you work on your knife every day, there will be a time when it becomes really sharp."

Listening to him, we were worried but, at the same time, felt like laughing. The *bodoi* continued. "Now, divide yourselves up into groups of five each. You're to cut trees to build a shed for rice storage. This is an urgent task because if you leave the rice sacks on the ground, the termites will eat the rice by tonight. The first day I was here, I forgot and put my bag of clothes on the ground before going to sleep; the next morning, I couldn't find it anywhere. A comrade *bodoi* who had been living here for a long time showed me a termitarium, its earth still fresh. Digging into it, I found my clothes full of holes and looking like beehives. Now, get to work. Choose small trees, no bigger than your wrists. Don't try to cut big ones; you won't be able to get them down. And remember to cut trees on this side of the stream only. It's absolutely forbidden to go to the other side. Do I make myself clear?"

"Yes," we all said in unison.

"Each of you has to bring me one tree trunk. The sooner you finish your work, the earlier you'll be allowed to rest."

We moved forward into the forest. My group of five included Thé, who seemed to have some experience in this kind of work. He said, "We have to keep together and help one another cut trees. It will be very hard if we work alone."

Another member of the group was Le Duong, a former civil servant. He was the most solidly built fellow among us. Duong said, "It's up to each of us to choose either to team up with others or work alone. As for myself, I'll go alone. I have to try to bring back a tree soon, then go find something to eat."

He set to work alone; the remaining four of us went together. Thé was elected "team leader." As this was timber forest, there were plenty of big trees, but smaller ones were hard to find. We finally found a spot with a few scattered small trees, and we started work. It took us a long time with our blunt machetes, and in less than half an hour our hands were covered with blisters. After we had cut through the trunk, we felt exhilarated, as if we had just paid up a debt. But our joy was short-lived for the trunk stood its ground. It moved but did not fall down. Looking closely, we saw that lianas had wound around the foliage at the tree tops, binding them together. The four of us tried to pull down the tree, but it hung there like a pendulum. We finally gave up on that one and tackled another, but in the end we did not succeed in pulling down one single tree. Two hours had elapsed since we began work. We looked at one another in complete amazement, to say nothing of being tired, disappointed, and very hungry. We had thought it would take just minutes to fell a small tree!

Finally, I volunteered to climb one of the smaller trees already cut so I could chop through the foliage and free the trunk. My companions thought this was risking a fall, but there was no other way. So I climbed the tree while my companions held the trunk. The foliage was not too thick; only a few small branches had lianas curled around them, and I quickly cut them away. As the tree began to slip downward, I threw my machete and jumped safely. My companions pulled the tree down; one credit to our account! Trieu Minh Chau, a former navy man, followed suit. He climbed another tree, chopped off the top, and nearly fell, but we all managed to steady the tree. Suddenly, a loud voice called us to assemble for the midday meal. Coming back to the open space, we saw that about forty trees had been cut by the other groups.

We lined up for the distribution of food. Each man's share was similar to that at the Xuan Loc camp, which meant two half-bowls of rice and a pinch of salt. But now there was a difference; after we had eaten, we felt that our stomachs were as empty as before. That was what manual labor meant! Our bodies required more food. I had to take out some pieces of dried bread from my bag and drink half a can of water before I felt I had somewhat satisfied my hunger.

We compared notes on the easiest way to cut trees—how to find the right ones and the difficulties in pulling them back through the dense trees, fallen branches, creepers, bushes, and undergrowth. An hour after the meal, we resumed work. We still owed two trees. As for Le Duong, perhaps owing to his considerable strength, he had single-handedly cut his tree soon after starting work. To avoid cheating, each man who brought back a tree had his name entered on a piece of paper by Bui Quoc Khanh.

We walked along the bank of the stream looking for suitable trees. When we saw a clump of thinly scattered trees on the other side of the stream, Thé said, "What the hell! Let's go cut those trees on the other side, bring them back and take a rest. Otherwise, no telling how long we'll have to search."

We all agreed. The work was done in no time. We carried the tree trunks across the stream, put them down on the ground, and jumped into the water. A great number of fish, the size of a little finger, came to nibble around us. We thrust out our hands to catch them, but they flitted away with unexpected swiftness. After bathing, we carried the trees back to camp and hoped for a rest. But when we delivered them, Khanh said, "Go give the men a hand with the shed; it'll be dark soon"

We did not say anything, but walked to where a number of inmates were building a shed to store rice. In fact, the "shed" was just a small hut built over a floor of freshly cut tree trunks, closely spaced; its roof was made of a few torn pieces of canvas. Le Duong was working, his face and body covered with sweat. Chau said to me in a low voice, "I thought if we came back early we would be able to rest for a while. Look at Le Duong; he came back before the midday meal, and he's still sweating like a bull."

Thé said, "The lesson from this is, when you have piece work to do, only finish at the last minute."

The hut finished, we carried in the sacks of rice that had been unloaded from the trucks and stacked them on the floor, hoping to thwart the white ants. Afterward, we were allowed to bathe in the stream. It was then four or five in the afternoon. The *bodoi* guarding us, armed with rifles, wore sandals and stockings into which they tucked their trousers. A scarf was wound around their necks, perhaps to protect against mosquito bites.

The team responsible for cooking summoned us to the evening meal. A *bodoi* supervised the distribution. Each person, in addition to his share of food, was given a tablet that he was told to take after the meal. It was quinine, very bitter to the taste. After the meal, we were ordered to assemble for a meeting to listen to a cadre's comment on the day's work.

He began by saying that a meeting was to be held each afternoon to review the day's work and the spirit shown and to commend those who had done especially well. "Although tired after a long trip, most of you have earnestly and actively tried to compete against time and have achieved very good results. Some of you have shown a high spirit for the work. That's the positive aspect. There's also a negative aspect. Some teams disobeyed instructions. For example, the team composed of Vu, Thé, Chau, and Thinh went to the other side of the stream to cut the trees. Afterward, instead of carrying the trunks right back to camp, they bathed in the stream. To bathe during working hours is to evade work, which shows lack of discipline."

Standing in the ranks, we were completely taken aback by the unexpected criticism. The forest was deserted, no *bodoi* accompanied us; even if there had been one, he could not have known our names so soon. Again there must have been some informer among us.

Concluding the review, a number of men were voted "outstanding workers." Naturally, Le Duong was among those commended. He was cited by the cadre in these terms, "Duong was the first to cut his tree and carry it back. Moreover, to 'save' our rice, he sacrificed his rest to help build the storeroom. Let's cheer him with a round of applause."

We applauded perfunctorily because we were tired from standing and listening to the cadre. Now he said, "Since we have not yet had time to build houses, you have to make the best of it and sleep in the open. Tomorrow, we shall complete, with all possible speed, a number of shanties for you to sleep in until houses can be built. For now, content yourselves with sleeping here, and not too near the trees to avoid termites and snakes. You will dig temporary latrines in each area allotted to you; we'll build regular latrines later. I also remind you that there are plenty of mosquitoes here, so every day you will be given an antimalaria tablet; you must take it every day for seven days. However, it is best if you don't get bitten. You must boil your drinking water. Tomorrow we'll get the distribution of drinking water organized. Now, follow your team leaders to the lots assigned to you for sleeping tonight. After that, the team leaders will meet with the cadres to organize tomorrow's work and work parties."

My group was assigned an area of the open space. Several of us were detailed to dig latrines. We sat beside our bags of clothes, looking at our new campsite: an expanse of red earth surrounded by forests. Above, the evening sky still had a bluish color, but all around us it was dark, gloomy, and mysterious. Here sat a group of men, haggard, exhausted, and confused. Where were these forests? What on earth could we raise here?

We made our sleeping arrangements. Spreading our pieces of plastic on the ground, we decided to use half of each piece to sleep on and pull the other half over us as a blanket and also as protection against rain and mosquitoes. Everyone was tired. We kept looking up at the sky and avoided turning our eyes toward the dark forest around us. People in other places, looking at that same sky, those masses of clouds, could never know that here, in this godforsaken place, there existed wretched creatures lying on the ground and looking skyward, not knowing what was in store for them! Would we be able to survive? We would no doubt suffer from malaria like those *bodoi*; our skin would become livid and yellowish like theirs. The image in my mind's eye brought up forebodings for the future, and so as not to let my thoughts wander, I began to watch my companions to see what they were doing. Old Mr. Cuc was quietly saying his beads. Only a few men were talking with each other; one was singing to himself, "O, native land of mine! Where the afternoon sun shines so serenely." Suddenly, I caught sight of Thé, just as he was looking at me. As if caught red-handed committing some forbidden act, I smiled wryly. Thé also smiled as he whispered, "Very soon we'll have to clear trees to have land for cultivation. It will be very hard work. This region must be very unhealthful; no one has tried to make a living here. Perhaps . . ."

I cut him short. "Not a word more, please! You had better rest. If the *bodoi* can live in this place, so can we."

The sky was darker now, and all around it grew quiet. Last night, I had not had a wink of sleep in the crammed lorry. And although I had not done so much work today, I was aching all over. I felt pain everywhere in my body. I hoped to be able to get a good sleep to recover my strength. The buzz of mosquitoes sounded louder and louder, and to protect my face I covered it with the plastic material, which made me feel very hot. Then my breathing condensed on the plastic and I had to shake it from time to time to fan myself dry and to chase away the mosquitoes that buzzed around my ears. I don't know how long this went on before I finally fell asleep.

I woke up with a feeling of cold in my feet. Using one foot to scratch the other, I found out that one of them was all wet. I soon discovered that the water was, in fact, the night dew that had condensed on the plastic and run down to my feet. I wanted to get up as there was noise around me, but I couldn't raise myself. My whole body felt stiff as if paralyzed. Not until I had moved all my limbs and back could I finally manage to sit up. The damp from the ground rose up around our sleeping area. A number of people who had got up before me were sitting with their arms around their knees waiting for daybreak. Old Mr. Cuc seemed to be saying his morning prayers. I asked in a low voice, "Uncle, did you sleep last night?"

"I've had some sleep. But my spine got so cold that I had to sit up to be more comfortable. You and Thé seemed to sleep so soundly!"

A voice said crossly, "If you don't want to sleep, please keep quiet and let other people sleep."

From time to time, a fresh wind blew through the trees with a rustling sound. I too sat with my arms around my knees to wait for daylight. Only when a number of fellows began to walk away to relieve themselves did I dare to pick up my can of water and walk slowly toward the edge of the forest to rinse my mouth and wash my face. Group leader Khanh was heard calling out to the kitchen team to begin cooking the morning gruel. Everybody was now awake. The whole camp was suddenly noisy. By dawn, everybody was sitting at his appointed place, ready for another day. Mats and plastic sheets were already rolled up and put away. I took out of my bag a few slices of dried bread. Chewing it, I thought to myself, "There's no point saving this for the future. I have to eat now to give me enough strength to do manual work. If I save this until I become too weak, it will only be harmful to my health. Still, if I eat this up, there will be nothing left to fortify myself against sickness." I had thought the parcels of food received from my family would last me a few months at least, on condition that they be consumed only in case of sickness or during rest periods. If I make a habit of eating them regularly, how long would they last?

Group leader Khanh was busy looking for people and assigning work. Four men, amid smoke from the damp wood, were trying to keep the fire burning to cook the gruel. We soon learned we had to fan the fire continuously to keep it going. Finally, the gruel was ready, and each of us, armed with a can, queued up for the distribution. It was a thin mixture; I blew on it to cool it, then drank it down.

As we assembled for work orders, we found that a number of men still lay on the ground and were feverish. A cadre asked, "Who gave them permission to stay down? Tell them to get up for the roll call. They cannot rest until the nurse examines them and gives them permission to rest. But they must absolutely not lie down. They must sit—not lie down—in the shade."

Group leader Khanh called to the sick to get up and join us. About ten of them stayed where they were. Khanh made his report. "Beg leave to report to the cadre: there are a few of them who have high fever and cannot get up."

The cadre did not react in any way to this but went on. "Now, get on with the distribution of work. I have to remind you that everything you do must be done seriously. You must absolutely not go beyond the area assigned to you. The *bodoi* who will lead you to the place of work will show you where to cut elephant grass, bamboo, or trees. I also want to remind you that around this place there are other camps. If you trespass upon their areas, you will be detained until someone comes for you." Khanh began to read out the names in each team. One team was detailed to cut elephant grass, another bamboo, and a third trees. I was assigned to the bamboo team. Before we set out, I suggested that we go to the stream to sharpen our knives, which was approved.

The water was as cold as ice. The sharpened machetes looked better than when we first got them. A *bodoi* came and led us to a bamboo thicket not too far away. The team that was to cut elephant grass had to climb to the top of a high hill. After we arrived at the site, the *bodoi* asked, "Have you cut bamboo before?"

"No, never," we all said at once.

"I'll demonstrate. Pay close attention to the way I chop. Be very, very careful! Don't let the bamboo bounce back. It could disembowl you." He grasped a machete and chose a bamboo that looked as if it could be cut fairly easily. He struck at a spot below a curve in the trunk; the bamboo doubled over but was not yet severed. The *bodoi* then said, "This is the mortally dangerous moment! You have to stand to one side and leave enough room for the bamboo to spring back. If you stand too close, you can be killed!"

The tree, which was cut close to its foot, was stretched dangerously taut by the sheer weight of its ten-meter length, so taut that the section of the trunk where it bent had split open. Before striking the final blow, the *bodoi* shouted, "Look!" The machete came down; there was a sharp crack and the lower part of the bamboo, freed from its foot, sprang as high as our heads. At the cut, it was pointed and frightfully sharp. This was a special kind of bamboo, similar to the *nua* species, with a hollow trunk and long joints, called *lo o*. In this region of the South, the *lo o* thickets are scattered throughout the forests. Where other trees are growing, there are absolutely no *lo o*, and in *lo o* areas of the forest no other tree is found. Nature has clearly defined the area where each species is to grow!

The top of the *lo o* had many branches and a profusion of long leaves. When cut, it fell obliquely, its foliage still tangled with that of the surrounding trees. Again, we had to pool our strength to pull it free, and again this required hard, sometimes futile efforts. Our quota was six 4-meter sections of *lo o* each. The felling, pulling down, and cutting of the bamboo was exhausting in itself, but the main obstacle was hunger. We panted after every exertion, our arms and legs seemed to have no strength, the canful of thin gruel we had this morning had long since disappeared from our stomachs. Two bamboo were the most we could cut before we had to sit down and gasp for breath. After a while, even a simple movement like standing up required great effort. On that morning, we cut only two bamboo. At first I thought I could easily carry back four *lo o* sections, but now, carrying only two, I found I had to stop to rest several times. My shoulders felt hot under their weight and soon became painful from the up and down movement of the poles. When one shoulder became too painful, I shifted the bamboo to the other. Back at camp, pale from hunger and exhaustion, I took off my shirt and saw that both my shoulders were already bruised. This showed how city people performed, working for their living in the jungle.

In the afternoon, made wiser by experience, I brought along a few slices of dried bread and a can of water. The *bodoi* no longer accompanied us. Since this was the first time most of us had had to live so primitively, the cadres probably decided no one would dare to go too far away from the area. We cut two more bamboo; it was easier to carry them back than in the morning.

After the evening meal, we gathered for our meeting, which began with a song, "Solidarity," accompanied by the clapping of hands. Monitor Chuong, who spoke with a drawl, opened the session.

"Reviewing today's work, I would first like to commend some of you who have done their work in a positive manner. But there are among you a great number of persons who have not tried their best to fulfill the norms. You were instructed to cut six trees, but some only cut four or five. If the norm for bamboo cutting is six per head and you cut only four, this shows lack of self-discipline. Why is it that while the share of rice is the same for each of you, some of you carried back four trees and others only two? We have orders to pay close attention to your work, and it may be that we shall have to change the way rice and food are distributed. Those who work hard should be entitled to a bigger share than those who are lazy." Finally came the recommendations for citing those who had done outstanding work. Le Duong was among these outstanding individuals since he had surpassed the norms. How we hated him! He was strong and could do the work, so why couldn't he be satisfied with that? Why try to surpass the norms and bring criticism on the rest of us? We felt both tired and angry. Monitor Chuong was a long-winded, boring speaker, and at last I no longer paid any attention to what he said. Only when my companions started clapping in accompaniment to the song, did I know that the meeting was over.

I went back to the place where I had put my sack of clothes and sat down; my "home" now was where my belongings were! This sack of clothes was my property; sitting beside it gave me a feeling of intimacy. Based on last night's experience, I spread my plastic sheet on the ground, then took out all my clothes and laid them on top. This padding would keep my back from getting too cold. Looking around, I saw that Cuc, Thé, and the others were "making their beds" in like fashion. Thé was the one among us to be pitied the most; his family lived far up in Central Vietnam, so no one had come to see him, nor had he received any parcels. How could a young man like him sustain himself with a diet like the one we had at the moment? I often invited him to help himself to some of my provisions of dried bread, but he always refused. Today when I offered him something, he said, "You go ahead, I am not hungry. To tell the truth, I came from a region where people are accustomed to shortages. You keep what you have for later use. We need proper nourishment here. With this kind of work, if you're undernourished and you get a bout of malaria, you can never recover your strength. You'll be like an invalid. It's no joking matter, I tell you!"

"Well, I simply asked you to share something with me, just for fun. These few slices of bread can't be so nutritious, can they?"

"You haven't known shortages, so you cannot imagine what they really are. At a certain moment, a slice of bread like this one can save a life. If you have high fever and, at the same time, are hungry and weak, drugs you might take will only rack your body. Instead of being cured, you're likely to join your ancestors for good. I'm telling the truth. Save the bread in case of an emergency, especially when you feel that your strength is giving out. Under the circumstances, I see there is serious danger that this is going to happen here."

"I agree with you on that point. But how long can these few slices of bread last? Right now, I'm so famished I could eat a horse, so how can I hold on to food for the future? By the way, I've noticed that the *bodoi*, while guarding us, are also picking greens or digging up plants. It seems that they too are looking for something to eat. Do you have any experience in finding edible plants?"

"Well, I've been watching the *bodoi*, too, as well as looking at the plants and grass that grow here. There are many edibles of fairly high nutritive value. Believe me, there's not as much scarcity here as you think."

Old Cuc was praying as usual, but his ears were sharp enough to overhear our conversation. Nodding his approval, he quickly made the sign of the cross as if to ask God's permission to interrupt his prayer, then said, "I've seen near the *lo o* thicket many bushes whose leaves resemble the *lot* leaves people usually use to wrap slices of beef before grilling. Cooked, those leaves could be very nourishing and refreshing, if indeed they are *lot* leaves."

Thé teased him about interrupting his prayers, but Cuc only smiled. He went on, "This is what I'd like to suggest. Tomorrow, whenever we find something that is edible, we'll try to gather as much as possible so we can share it among ourselves. This way, everyone will be able to add to his diet. There is real danger if we continue as we are now. Our urine has begun to turn yellow, with a reddish tint; that means our bodies have started their debilitating processes."

Behind Thé, a voice said, "Right!" It was Dr. Anh, a former medical officer in a marine battalion. "A normal body that is overworked will discharge urine of a reddish-yellow color," he said. "This is because the body is then feeding on itself. In medical circles, we call this phenomenon autoconsumption. You're right to be worried. But edible things are not lacking here, and we're worried because we don't know what or where they are. There must be some mountain people's hamlet around here. They usually get more food from nature than from cultivation. The question for us now is to learn what we can pick, dig up, or catch. I know for sure that there are plenty of rats here. Jungle rats are very good to eat; they are not at all filthy like gutter rats. Foxes are not scarce either. And tubers—there are plenty of yams; if we have time to dig for them, we'll have enough to eat. Forest yams sometimes weigh three or four kilos."

As Dr. Anh spoke, almost everyone around listened with the attention one would pay to an important lecture. Anh was a very short man, and despite our circumstances, he had kept a rather plump appearance. At the Xuan Loc camp, where I had often seen him playing mahjong with others, I had thought he was merely a city playboy, not a survival expert. He probably had been thoroughly trained in the marine corps, which had been one of the finest fighting units under the former regime.

The discussion on what kinds of food to look for continued until a *bodoi* raised his voice in warning, "Go to sleep if you want to recover enough strength for tomorrow's work!"

Thanks to the layer of clothing under me, I felt warm and comfortable. I also fixed a crude roof over my head with the plastic and drove sticks of wood into the ground so that my head just fit between them. The plastic cover was thus kept away from my face. Sleep came quickly and soon was so deep that I neither heard anybody shouting in his sleep, nor talking, nor any other noise as I had the night before. When I woke at daybreak, the morning fog was so thick that I could not see beyond three or four meters. Above my head was an opalescent thickness; beyond the edge of the clearing was complete darkness. Even with full daylight the fog had not lifted. I picked up my can of water, walked out to have a wash, and moments later a voice summoned the team leaders to dole out the morning gruel. Today, each team received two full basins, and the gruel was then ladled out to individuals, a much quicker process than with yesterday's long queue.

Coming back from a quick wash, Thé whispered in my ear, "Someone has got away!" Hearing this, I was immediately alert. I answered in a low voice, "I wouldn't discuss that here."

I pressed Thé's hand and shook my head. He understood and returned to his sleeping place to put his things in order. Shortly after, we got our work orders. Today I was assigned to the grass-cutting team. The quota was one *ganh*[1] per person in the morning and one in the afternoon. Each *ganh* must consist of two armfuls of grass, the circumference equaling that of both arms joined together with fingertips touching. We were told, "If you miss your quota, you'll have to go back to cut more until the quota is filled."

Now I was on the team that had to walk a long way and climb a high bare hill. Simply to carry the bamboo pole and the coil of ties (which were, in fact, lianas)

---

[1]A load consisting of two full baskets, or equivalent, of some product that can be attached to or suspended from both ends of a pole and carried over the shoulder.

was almost all I could do. We cut the grass with blunt sickles. I intended to cheat by tying a very loose sheaf to make it look bigger, but of course when I stood it upright, all the grass slid off onto the ground. I had to cut more and tie up the bundle again. When I had the two sheaves ready—fairly presentable although not exactly up to the standard set by the cadre—I thrust the pointed ends of the pole into them and shouldered the load. The *ganh* of fresh grass was heavy and the descent down the hill difficult. At first the sheaves were about half a meter above the ground; after a bit, they slid down until they dragged along the path. I had to stop to tie them up again. Guong, a man nearing retirement age and known to have much experience in this kind of work, showed me how to tie the sheaves the right way and suggested that I carry the load with the pole placed at the back of my neck and over both shoulders to distribute the weight.

At the foot of the hill, we stopped to rest, and conversation turned immediately to last night's escape. The escapee was a man of Indian and Vietnamese origin. He was born in Vietnam of a Vietnamese mother. For the sake of adventure, he said, he had volunteered for an officer training course. When the South fell, he reported for reeducation out of fear and the belief he would be released when his family obtained recognition as Indian citizens. His Vietnamese name was Son, but his companions called him Ali, his Indian name. He had been greatly disturbed since the day his family visited him at the Xuan Loc camp. His parents and wife had told him that the Indian Red Cross had interceded on their behalf and the whole family was due to return to India soon. "Now, Ali is perhaps trying to find his own way back to India," someone said with a laugh.

The fact was that finding one's way out of this jungle to the national highway would have been quite an achievement in itself. Someone said, "But why go to the national highway; this region is near the border.[2] You know . . ."

At this point, many voices rose to warn, "No more of that commentary please!" "You're talking nonsense again!"

Most of us, fearful of consequences, hurriedly shouldered our loads and plodded along back to camp. One idea kept recurring in my mind: "This is a border region!" I believed many of my companions were also tortured by that idea.

While still at the Xuan Loc camp, we had heard of the about-face of the Cambodians who had begun to attack the Hanoi forces along the border between Cambodia and Vietnam. Before that, at the Trang Lon camp, there had been many nights when heavy gunfire was heard in the distance, but at that time we did not know who was fighting. There were only the sounds made by Soviet AK rifles, the bursts harsher and sharper than the deep staccato of our M-16s, so we

---

[2]Between Vietnam and Cambodia.

knew it was a fight between communists. Now that we knew, our worry was what kind of treatment we would get if we did escape across the border.

The blue sky was without a single cloud, and the sun blazed down on us. I was sweating profusely as I carried the load of grass down the bare hillside. I stopped several times to rest in the shade of the sheaves and to munch a few slices of dried bread. When we arrived back at camp, it was past the time of food distribution, and the *bodoi* shouted at the stragglers.

As I rested after the meal, I suddenly felt an itch on my neck. I picked off an insect that Thé identified as a grass bug, similar to a tick, with a flat round body and six legs like those of a crab. Since I snatched it off without thinking, its mandibles remained in the bite and the next day I had a slight fever. Even a few years later, that bug bite still looked reddish and itched.

In the afternoon, leaders were appointed for all the work parties to see to it that every worker returned to camp at the same time. Clearly, this was intended to keep us under surveillance; Ali's escape had made the *bodoi* more cautious. The afternoon crop was smaller than the morning's as we were urged to get back to camp on time, and also because of our hunger and exhaustion. The group leader was not satisfied with our performance. At the evening meeting, we expected to be blamed, but fortunately, the new monitor, Quang, seemed to be an easy-going fellow. He only said briefly that many of us had not worked well. "If you maintain that attitude, our future will be badly affected."

At the end of the session, the cadre asked, "Have you anything to say or ask?"

Many inmates raised their hands. One of them was allowed to "express his view." "We have to work hard, but we do not have enough to eat. We request to be allowed to have more food."

The cadre replied, "My superiors are well aware of the problem, and they are trying to buy more foodstuffs for you. But it is not easy to find something to buy in this area. They are now busy considering which solution to adopt."

After the evening distribution of rice, we did not eat it right away. Everybody tried to cook something extra. The Guigoz can with a handle added made of a piece of steel wire, which we brought along during the day to serve as a drinking cup, now became a cooking utensil. We fetched stones from the stream to make a kind of stand to hold the cans over a fire. Others hung their cans above the fire between two vertical sticks cut from tree branches. With all of us blowing hard on the many fires of damp wood, the place was soon shrouded in smoke and everyone's eyes were red.

By the third day at the camp, we all knew how to improve our daily diet with wild vegetables. We gathered the greens pointed out to us by some of the men, although we did not know what they were. They tasted a trifle bitter, but were definitely edible. Most of my companions cooked their vegetables with a little salt and a pinch of monosodium glutamate. My soup was of a better quality due to the addition of some shredded meat from my pack. With two half-bowls of rice and a canful of vegetable soup in my stomach, I felt fuller than usual. And I slept more soundly.

After three nights of sleeping on the ground, the group responsible for building the *lang* (shanties) had completed their task. Each *lang* had a low thatched roof, which opened at either end. It was divided by a narrow passageway with sleeping platforms on both sides; each platform was framed with tree trunks upon which lengths of *lo o,* opened up and spread flat, were placed and tied down. Although the platforms had rough surfaces, they were raised about half a meter above the ground, and this would protect us from the cold. With a roof above us, we were able to hang our mosquito nets. The simple construction of the *lang* and the speed with which they were built meant that it took only three days for the construction group to provide accommodations for more than a thousand people. Each of us was allotted a space measuring about sixty centimeters.

With the *lang* completed, the inmates were divided into two groups, one assigned to clear the jungle and prepare the land for cultivation, the other to build houses and barracks in the camp. As a member of the carpentry team, I was permitted to "stay home" to work on frames for the houses. Some team members went out to cut trees, which had to be of the right size and very straight. Others were detailed to cut rattan stems to be used as lashings. This was the first time we had to build thatched wooden houses without using a single nail!

The *bodoi* showed us how to make tenons and mortises to join the beams and rafters of the frameworks. Carpentry tools were lent by regiment command. The battalion commander himself, the very cadre who had brought us here from Xuan Loc, directed the construction of the first house in the camp. He had much experience and claimed to have built many three-unit buildings using rare timber. We were shown how to select the right kind of wood, how to saw and chisel it and fit tenons and mortises. We had to work very carefully and were spared the task of going out to cut trees. After the *lang* construction I was exhausted, and this work gave me a temporary relief. Meanwhile, those who were clearing the land returned from work so tired that some of them could not help crying. When they saw me and my teammates doing carpentry work but not having to fell trees, clear jungle, or cut elephant grass, many of them could not hide their envy. The result was that after two days, group leader Khanh tried to equalize the labor somewhat by rotating members of the different work teams. Fortunately for me, the commander did not agree with Khanh's order; he insisted that the carpentry team should remain unchanged because we already had been shown how to do the work. From then on, Khanh made no secret of his dislike for the carpentry team, but from time to time, we also had to cut trees, and this was as hard as any other work. It took as many as four persons to cut and bring back a perfectly straight tree of good-quality wood. I sometimes volunteered for the job so I could dig up some yams.

There were no more yams in the camp neighborhood because they had been dug up by the *bodoi*. We had to go deeper into the forest to find them; sometimes a half-day passed before we came across any plants. Yams are a climbing plant with long roots. With makeshift spades made from a section of *lo o*, we would dig until the hole was about one meter deep before we even saw the tip of a yam. Then, so as not to break the tuber, we would dig around the yam for one more meter; when it began to loosen, we had to pull it up gently and slowly or we would end up with half a yam at the most. In fact, that was what usually happened to most of us. To be sure of getting the whole yam, we had to dig down more than two meters, but as we went deeper into the red soil, it became softer and easier to dig. The main thing was to be patient.

Usually we brought back at least one yam, which we shared. A small-sized one could fill up four Guigoz cans and provide extra food for two days. Yams are more friable when cooked, they cook easier and taste better than sweet potatoes, and they are easily digested. At first, only a few of us looked for them; soon everyone did it. At noon, we asked to go to work earlier than usual to have time to dig for yams, and before long deep holes were seen along both sides of every path and trail crisscrossing the jungle. We were not the only ones digging; the *bodoi* vied with one another in the hunt for this tuber. Sometimes we left a yam half dug, intending to get it next day, but when we returned, someone had dug it out before us.

We hoped we would gradually accustom ourselves to the hard life of the forest, but more and more people fell sick every day. Some came down with malaria. The food and medicine given by our families were used up within a week. Here, we had no contact whatsoever with inhabited areas that might exist in the vicinity of our camp. About four kilometers from the camp was a small hamlet of mountain people. We had seen some of them from a distance but had not had a chance to approach them. One day, on one of our forays to cut trees, we chanced to meet an old Montagnard. I greeted him. "Where are you going, sir?"

He did not reply, but made a gesture with his pipe in the direction of a spot far in front of him. A moment later, he asked me in heavily accented Vietnamese, "You are reeducation detainees, aren't you?"

I nodded, then asked, "Have you any food you could sell us?"

"I have nothing to sell. I had some hens, but they were sold to the *bodoi*. The ones that are left are still too small."

"Well, buy some rice to sell to us. If you pay one dong for the rice, we'll pay you two dong; if you pay two, we'll offer you three. Is it agreed?"

The old man shook his head and said, "No, I'm not selling for money, but I'm willing to exchange it for a shirt."

I was so pleased that I said immediately, "It's a deal. Here's your shirt."

I took off my shirt as I spoke. The Montagnard shook his head with a smile. "No, that shirt won't do; it's all tattered."

"Come back here this afternoon; I'll bring you a new shirt. Do you agree?"

"At the moment, I have no more rice. But soon I'll have enough to trade."

Despite the missed opportunity, I still believed that some purchase would be possible if we could get near this tribal hamlet. One day, I volunteered to go and look for perfectly straight trees to be used as front columns. I walked quickly upstream, on my way to the Montagnards' hamlet. When I came near, I heard children calling to one another. A young man ran out; he looked at me in surprise and asked in a voice that did not sound much different from that of a Vietnamese, "Where are you going? What leads you to this place?"

I replied, "Is it forbidden to come here?"

"No. But reeducation prisoners rarely come here. Since prisoners were brought here to clear the jungle, you're the first one I've ever met. You're an officer of the ARVN, aren't you?"

Afraid that if I told the truth and he reported on this meeting, someone would tell the *bodoi*, I said, "Private. By the way, how do you happen to speak such good Vietnamese?"

"I was also a soldier in the ARVN. The *bodoi* sent me to a reeducation camp; I came back from there only recently. Anyway, being a private, why were you sent to a camp?"

"Because they disliked me. But you, why were you sent? To my knowledge, only officers have to go to reeducation camps."

"I was forced to go by the local cadre. He arrested me, then took me to Phuoc Binh where I was detained by the *bodoi* for more than one year. I've just been released because I have to take my whole tribe to another area. But I don't intend to go there; I shall take my family to Blao instead."

I asked in surprise, "Where? Would Blao be the same as Bao Loc? Anyway, why go so far? Besides, it would be very bad for you if you didn't obey their orders!"

"Yes, Bao Loc. It will take us a few weeks to get there. If we leave before the *bodoi* arrive, they won't know where we're going."

"How will you go that it will take as long as a few weeks to get there?"

"Well, we'll follow the forest trails. We're used to traveling that way. It won't be too far. Have you anything to cure stomach ache? It's for my child; he has stomach ache, but we have no medicine. Before, when the camp holding majors was still here, it was easy to ask them for medicine. But they've been taken somewhere else."

"Oh, really! Is there another camp around here?"

"There's another camp uphill from where the regiment's barracks are being built. There were also many doctors detained there. The camp where the army majors were held is near here. It's empty now, except for the grave of Major Tran Manh Dan."

"How can you know this?"

"He was buried by his fellow prisoners; over his grave they hung a metal plate with 'Major Tran Manh Dan' punched out with a nail. He was buried at the foot of the hill; I pass the spot each time I go to work at the clearing."

"Are there *bodoi* in your village?"

"No, but every few days, two *bodoi* come here to take down the names of those present and teach children to sing revolutionary songs. Male teenagers and adults have to have their names entered on a list. Sometimes, we are told to put out flags or hang banners."

"Is there any food in your village you could sell us? We have some money, but nobody is selling anything around here. At our old camp we lived near the local folks, and it was easier to buy things."

"Did they really allow you to buy things outside the camp? Here it's forbidden. The officers who were here tried to buy chickens. They were caught and bound hand and foot."

As we talked, many children and some old people came and stood around us. Realizing that it was risky to stay too long, I was about to leave when I noticed that two old women had festering hands; on closer look, I saw that all their fingers were missing.

The young man saw my look and said, "The old women had their fingers eaten by leprosy. Before, when medicine was still given to them, the skin remained dry. But now, as the Revolution has no medicine, their whole hands are being eaten away. We asked the doctors among the detainees for medicine, but no one had this kind to give them."

About to beat a hasty retreat, I said, "I'm afraid I have to go and look for trees to cut. If you want medicine against stomach ache, go where we're working at clearing the forest. There are many doctors among us; they have medicine, but I don't know if they are willing to give it away. Anyway, I'm sure that if you bring some rice or chickens, they will agree to barter. It's because all of us are hungry; we have little to eat, and we have to work very hard."

"I think I can bring some rice and I hope to get some medicine."

At the mention of rice, I was tempted to buy some but shrank from the idea because of the presence of lepers in the hamlet. Back in camp, I suddenly realized that the hamlet was situated upstream from us. The water from their washing flowed down to where we bathed and washed our rice and vegetables. I intended to tell my companions, but in doing so, I would reveal my visit to the tribal hamlet, so I kept the information to myself.

About thirty detainees worked at constructing houses for battalion command, and more than one hundred were building barracks for inmates. The rest worked at clearing the jungle, particularly around the space marked off for construction of the camp. In this dry season, the felled trees and brush dried very quickly. Within a few days, the place became a mountain of dried leaves, and battalion command decided to burn the whole lot. Many parts of the surrounding area had been devastated by forest fires apparently started by sparks coming from other jungle camps. One night we were awakened by explosions as if there were fighting in the distance; it was the *lo o* forest section going up in flames. On some nights, the sky was brilliantly lit up by distant fires.

As the wind began to blow in our direction, battalion command decided to burn the leaves and partly dried trees earlier than planned. If fires from other areas spread to this place, everything, including the *lang* where we slept, would go up in a flash.

Preparation for the burning was a big job as we had to clear an encircling belt. The day of the burning we were deployed in the forest surrounding the clearing to stamp out falling sparks or pieces of burning brush. Once the fire was under way, we witnessed for the first time in our lives the spectacle of a fire spouting smoke and flames with stormlike force; the wind fanned the flames, which burst forth with a roar. Even at a distance we felt the incredible heat. But the stronger the fire, the quicker it died out. After about two hours, an area of some dozen acres had been leveled; each end was visible from the other as now nothing blocked the view. Only the blackened remnants of a few big trees lay scattered on the ground, which was covered with dark gray ashes. Now we had to look for and stamp out smoldering fires. At dusk, we stopped for a wash and a bite to eat. Suddenly, the wind rose again and flames erupted in several spots but were quickly put out. That night, the whole camp was organized into groups to keep watch for new fires.

The battalion command's house was finished. The rafters, made of tree trunks with the bark stripped off, looked very beautiful when mounted on the framework, but when covered with thatch, the house became ugly because it was so dark. It had walls of wattle and was partitioned into three separate rooms; the floor was made of bamboo. Furnished with tables, chairs, and beds, everything in the house was well arranged to the satisfaction of Commander Tuyet. He gave each member of the carpentry team a Vam Co cigarette as a reward. Most of us smoked shredded tobacco; therefore, a cigarette was a valuable gift. But the Vam Co cigarettes had an acrid taste; perhaps the tobacco had not been properly cured. Having completed the battalion command's building, we started on the house for the monitors. Nobody bothered to supervise our work now. Commander Tuyet asked the monitors to do so themselves, but they all said, "They can do as they please, provided that the house is fit to live in. We're not as particular as the comrade commander."

One day Commander Tuyet came to our worksite to chat with us and also to say good-bye. "I wish you good results in productive labor. I've been assigned to the administrative committee of a district in Ho Chi Minh City. I'll be leaving the camp tomorrow."

Monitor Quang, a jovial and easy-going fellow, said, "The commander is surely very clever. He brought us here to the middle of the jungle, and now he manages to be appointed to a post in the city!"

Commander Tuyet tried to explain himself, "How wrong you are, comrade! This is an order from our superiors; we cannot ask for transfers, you know that."

Monitor Quang said, "It's no use pretending! If you didn't maneuver, how could our superiors know of your presence here to transfer you to a new job?"

The commander tried to change the subject. "Well, I think you will have every amenity here in the future. Soon this place will be provided with electricity, like in the cities."

Quang argued, "If we are going to have all the amenities of modern life in this place, why did you decide to go? We can wait till kingdom come, and we still won't get any electricity here. I myself am going to find ways to be transferred. I won't be sitting and waiting for the coming of electricity!"

The man who replaced Tuyet was Commissar Thinh. This *bodoi* seemed more fond of showing off his authority than his predecessor. The day he arrived, he came to watch as we worked on the house for the monitors. He criticized our work, saying it lacked "quality." He added that inmates at other camps had built better houses and had higher technical skills. As he spoke, he took out a filter-tipped cigarette and began to smoke in a manner that was intended to show he was "classy." Commissar Thinh also liked to convene his monitors frequently to give them instructions; therefore, even the *bodoi* did not like him. One of them told me that he was not the real battalion commander. The person having higher responsibility and greater power should be the political commissar, whereas Thinh was only the military commander.

As soon as we had completed the monitors' house, we were called upon to construct a disciplinary cell as regiment had just informed the camp command that Ali had been apprehended by the territorials (regional militia) and was going to be turned in to battalion. The disciplinary cell was to be a small hut with strong bamboo walls. A *bodoi* took great pains to show us how to build it; his know-how showed that he had had much experience in constructing prison huts. The walls were made of thick bamboo lengths, each about three meters long, buried one meter deep into the ground. There was one opening about seventy centimeters wide. The roof was also made of bamboo trunks, and all were secured with the rattan lashings. The cell measured about two meters by four and could shut in a maximum of six persons. At the end of the bamboo floor opposite the door was a long, solid piece of wood with holes in it, used to lock in the prisoners' feet. This device had a long wooden bar going through to the outside. To shackle a prisoner, the bar was simply raised to let the poor fellow put his foot through a hole, then lowered and the protruding ends of the two pieces of wood fastened with a peg. There were only three holes on each side of the narrow passageway that ran through the middle of the floor, which meant that each of the six prisoners would have only one foot locked. We were surprised at this device, which seemed so antiquated, but later on, at every place we were taken to, we saw prisoners punished by having one of their feet shackled in the same way.

Son, alias Ali, was brought back one night. No one saw him arrive. Each day, a member of his team had to bring food to him; he was only entitled to a half-ration. For his bodily functions he had to use a can placed beside him on the floor. The man who brought his meal had to empty the can and clean it. After Ali had been confined for one week, we were told one afternoon to assemble to hear about the decision on the disciplinary measure taken against him. Commander Thinh spoke at length to let us know that under the revolutionary regime it was no use trying to escape "even if we went as far as the sky." Then Thinh read the order returning Ali to his team and group for "control and education purposes." In particular, the group and team leaders and the two inmates lying next to him in the *lang* were to be entirely responsible for him. The order was signed by Thinh himself.

From then on, Ali had to work at clearing the forest like everyone else. My friend Thé approached him to try to find out how he had been caught. At first, Ali only smiled without answering, but when pressed, he agreed to tell his story. He said that when he reached a populated area, he asked the way to Saigon and thus disclosed himself as an escapee. He said that if he had walked in the direction of the Delta, nobody would have paid any attention to him as there were always crowds of people cutting trees at the edge of the forests. Thé relayed this to me and, in a moment when nobody was around, said, "Based on his account, an escape toward the plain is possible, provided we have enough strength and food."

I answered, "In my opinion, what's difficult is not how to escape, but how to live unnoticed afterward. We cannot remain in hiding forever. Besides, when the camp command reports our escape, will our families be left alone? Won't they be kept under surveillance?"

Thé also told me that Ali said the folks outside knew he was an escapee; they were kind to him and fed him. Only because he had the bad luck to ask his way from a territorial was he immediately chased and caught.

The carpentry team had to work at jungle clearing after we had finished the command's houses. The quota was 100 square meters per inmate every day. Trees bigger than those that an arm could encircle were to be cut later. The difficult part again was the lianas entwining all the small trees. Hunger and exhaustion kept us from filling our norm, and to speed up, we resigned ourselves to cutting trees no bigger around than a wrist. Even then, we were completely exhausted and still under quota, except when, by sheer luck, we were assigned to work on a plot without too many trees and thus no need to cut lianas.

One day we reached an expanse of heathland with thinly scattered trees, and thought we could easily meet the norm, but then the *bodoi* increased it to 250 square meters for the day. In the end, we were exhausted all the time, yet we could never fulfill the norms.

After a month of this life in the forest, every one of us had become skin and bone. Even the *bodoi* took pity on us and allowed us to have more rest than permitted. Usually, we were given a five-minute rest after one hour of work. We would have a drink of water, and those who had shredded tobacco would roll themselves a cigarette; others who had waterpipe tobacco drew on their pipes before drinking water. But the majority tried to eat some wild vegetables to appease their hunger.

Each morning at dawn, after hurriedly swallowing a few mouthfuls of thin gruel, we gathered in a group and set out for the clearing site, which was never anywhere near the camp. The cadre responsible for selection of land for cultivation usually ordered us to clear areas that he hoped, after burning the cut trees, would have plenty of ashes to fertilize the new fields. Sometimes, it took us over an hour to reach our place of work. The walk alone was tiring enough; when we set to work, we had no strength, but we tried to look as though we were working in order not to be reprimanded.

On the way to work, we were as vigilant as wild animals on the prowl; we lost no opportunity to snatch the first shoot of edible wild greens or the budding "tweezer" leaves[3] we came across. Sometimes, the struggle to get the greens led to harsh exchanges that could turn into fights if others did not intervene. "Tweezers" were relatively easy to find. The mountain people had taught us the use of these leaves that could be eaten raw or cooked; cooked, they had a taste reminiscent of the *rau ngot* found in Saigon vegetable markets. Each pair of leaves grew on both sides of the stalk and were, therefore, easily recognizable. Sometimes, we dug wild tubers and ate them, although nobody knew what they were. Out of hunger and attracted by their fragrant and refreshing smell, some men took the risk of cooking and eating them; when no harm came to them, everybody followed suit. Like yams, they also came from a climbing plant growing on spongy soil, but these came out easily. By pulling slightly on the stem, we sometimes came across a tuber the size of a wrist and about 20 centimeters long. We named it "vine bulb." When everybody took to eating vine bulbs, the *bodoi* also hunted and ate them.

Bodoi behavior toward us changed with each individual. In general, the young *bodoi* watched us only to prevent escape but made no remark on our work; the guards who were over twenty-five years old were very domineering. On the way to work, they forced us to walk fast and forbade us to stop to pick wild greens or dig tubers. We had to work the appointed hours and could rest only when it was time. On those days, we were more exhausted and hungry than

---

[3]Edible leaves growing in pairs, each looking like a pair of tweezers.

usual, and the work, in spite of the rigor, did not improve a bit. Actually, the *bodoi* guarding us were as tired as we were. During breaks, when we cooked wild greens, they watched us from a distance with hungry looks.

The *bodoi*'s quarters were disposed so as to surround the camp. By this time, the inmates' barracks also had been completed, and we had moved into them. At night, the *bodoi* stood guard, two at each post, and they were not allowed to sit down. At mealtime, each squad sent two or three *bodoi* to the camp command kitchen to carry back a basin of rice, another of either *nuoc mam* (fish sauce) or dried fish, and a third of soup when it was available. Back in their quarters, they would add some wild vegetables or a roasted bird or fox if they had shot or trapped one. They called such additions *cai thien*.[4]. Those who were resourceful and experienced ate better than others who had to be content with a daily fare of rice and dried fish or fish sauce. Because of their hard life, we saw no chance of any kind of help from them. The young *bodoi*, who were kind to us, were teenagers from the North who recently had been drafted; the others, who had long been in the army, not only bullied us but were tricky and full of complexes. They got angry when we laughed, thinking we were making fun of them. Sometimes we came across a few *bodoi* from the South, who were less severe than their Northern counterparts and quite frank when answering our questions. It was they who showed us how to take preventive measures against malaria and told us it was dangerous to bathe too long in the stream when coming back from work. They called the *bodoi* from the North *mây thang dó*.[5] Sometimes when we were resting a bit longer than usual, a Southern *bodoi* suddenly appeared to warn us, "Stand up quickly! *May thang do* are coming."

Because he knew there was sympathy between *bodoi* from the South and the detainees, Commander Thinh often came to the clearing site when Southern guards were on duty. Arriving unexpectedly, he would ask, "Where's the comrade in charge?"

When the *bodoi* ran forward, he ordered in a way that forestalled argument, "Tell everyone to resume work, will you? They have rested long enough."

Sometimes, the Southerner would retort, "I have no watch and have just given them leave to rest. Believe me, they have taken no more rest than allowed."

Having said that, he continued to let us sit and rest. Commander Thinh grumbled but left. One day I asked a Southern *bodoi* whether this way of farming was any good. One of our team members was an agricultural engineer, and he had told us that farming by clearing forests and burning trees was a poor

---

[4]Sino-Vietnamese word meaning "to improve" or "improvement." The use of Sino-Vietnamese words (usually to express abstract or complex ideas, situations, events) in such a mundane situation sounds pedantic to the Southern ear.

[5]Term of contempt replacing them, they, or those guys.

practice. Further, because the clearings were so far apart, we would not be able to use machinery to the best advantage if we later acquired it. Another difficulty would be transporting crops to granaries, with no roads over the hilly terrain. The *bodoi* said, "*May thang do* don't know a damn thing. They are accustomed to living in the poorest regions, and their farming method is very backward. They believe that if the trees they cut and burn leave plenty of ashes, they can be sure of good results from the soil. But this is effective for only a few crops; then they have to move on to new fields."

I asked why they chose an area so remote from communication routes; they would have to build a road with many bridges to reach the existing highways before crops could be brought in. The *bodoi* explained that they wanted to develop an area that had been a guerrilla base during the war. In fact, the region we were now clearing was part of the Dac O secret war zone. We were shown craters made by B-52 bombs scattered all along the banks of the stream.

During the war the Northern commanders stationed their troops near natural watering places. In the dry season they could easily get water by digging a well. That was why there were a number of crumbling huts along the banks of our stream, which had served to store a variety of hoes, knives, steel wires, and other implements. The area around these tiny warehouses was dotted with bomb craters, now hidden by vegetation. This compelled us to move cautiously, but at the bottom of the craters we often found another source of food—big frogs. A godsend as far as we were concerned.

As we went deeper and deeper into the jungle, the work got harder and the route to the worksite more difficult. At the point when we were the most tired and low in spirits, an unexpected event took place. We were busy cutting trees in the deep forest one day when a *bodoi* appeared and ordered us to return to camp for a meeting. We hastened back at a brisk pace, hoping this meant someone was going to be released. We really did not expect it for ourselves, but the scene of any inmates being released was always a happy event. We arrived at the camp command in an hour, the roll was called, and we waited. There were more roll calls while the monitors searched our barracks. At last we understood that someone had escaped. We were ordered to return to our barracks to bring out all our belongings and wait for another roll call. We were told specifically not to bring out belongings of the men sleeping alongside us. When we had done as ordered and were lined up, each within his own squad and platoon, Bui Quoc Khanh asked, "Where are the two persons who usually sleep beside Le Duong? Has any of you seen him anywhere?"

Only then did we notice that Le Duong, who had left for work with another team, was not among us. The two inmates who slept beside him were led to the battalion office for a "working session." They returned at dusk. The only conversation that night was about Le Duong's achievement. He had always been an outstanding worker. We wrongly believed that he had been wholeheartedly won over to the new regime; we disliked him because he always exceeded the norms and made our lives more difficult. Whether it was cutting bamboo, clearing land, or laying the foundation for a house, Duong always tried to please the *bodoi* by his work. But now he had vanished into thin air. He had left a few clothes behind but nothing of worth; as for his medicines and other "valuables," he apparently had hidden them earlier in the forest. This morning he had taken only a machete and a can of water with him when he left for work. Everyone now praised Duong for his secretiveness. Not only had he hidden any sign of opposition whatsoever against the new regime; he had also behaved in such a way that the camp commander and, especially the group leader Khanh, had fully trusted him. As time passed, we became more and more certain that, unlike Ali, Duong had succeeded in his escape, and this rekindled our desire to carry out the plan everyone had been brooding over but had not dared to carry out.

Just when I was sweating blood clearing jungle and preparing land for cultivation, I was transferred to the carpentry team working at the area's regimental command. Regiment was building a number of barracks intended for one of its component services, which was to be transferred from Xuan Loc. Other barracks were being built on a hill overlooking a dirt road leading to other camps in the area. I was appointed leader of a team responsible for the joining and mounting of rafters and beams made by inmates of the former camp for army majors. The task was difficult because we did not understand what those earlier workers had in mind and we had no drawings of structures they intended to build. We had to modify the beams and rafters a great deal before we could mortise and mount them in our accustomed way.

But working at regimental command had its bright side: breakfasts of sweet potatoes and drinks of an infusion of forest leaves. The *bodoi* who had lived here a long time were fond of a beverage made of an infusion of the root of a small shrub they called *sam* (ginseng). It had a fragrant and refreshing taste similar to that of the *Nhi Hong* ginseng sold at Chinese pharmacies. From time to time they gave us an infusion of *ngu gia bi* (aralia) bark or *ha thu o* leaves[6] to drink, which also was refreshing and had a tonic effect. However, I believe that what really gave us strength was the few boiled potatoes we had for breakfast. We found a certain solace in the fact that our work was not too hard and our daily fare was supplemented by sweet potatoes. Our bodies then were very quick to respond: a roasted rat or a boiled sweet potato was all that was required to make us feel stronger, breathe deeper, sleep more soundly, and have sharper ears. It was then

---

[6]Plant growing in the forests of Northern and Central Vietnam; its tubers contain an alkaloid that possesses the property of regularizing blood circulation and reviving tired tissues. Because of this, it was believed to be the "plant of youth."

that we were able to fully understand the realistic expression used by our forefathers, *met tho hoi tai* (lit., exhausted to the point of exhaling air through the ears). When we did not eat enough and still had to work to exhaustion, our hearing became dull, and we were not even capable of drawing air deep into our lungs. In those dark hours we all believed that our bodies would rot away in the forest; we had no hope of surviving until some distant day of release. Because of that, we were constantly haunted by the thought of escape.

One day, the regiment's political commissar asked us to erect a portico—he wanted it to be very beautiful—in front of the meeting hall. The hall had been built with great care by inmates of another camp. Its red columns were perfectly straight; its high ceiling was made of thin bamboo wattle, which gave the hall a modern look. There was seating room for a thousand persons. We were instructed to erect the portico at the foot of the hill and cut steps leading up to the hall in such a way that the whole construction should be a beautiful sight to look at. Each of us went off in a different direction to search for rare and perfectly straight trees. I went to the west, and as I was climbing a hill on the top of which I saw a few solitary trees, perfectly straight with small round leaves, I suddenly caught sight of a red brick guard post beyond the hill. A red flag was flying on top of the post and, half hidden in its folds was not the yellow star of Vietnam's communist regime, but the picture of three towers, side by side! I immediately realized that over there was Cambodia, a country that now opposed the Hanoi government. In a flitting moment, the image of myself escaping was in my mind's eye. Feelings of anxiety and elation seemed to drive me crazy. I trembled and felt chilled to the bone. I did not know why the idea of escape brought such strange reactions. As the crow flies, the guard post was no more than two kilometers from where I stood, but at closer look, I saw layer upon layer of forest between us, and at the foot of the hill stood a *bodoi*'s guard post flying a red flag adorned with a yellow star. I hurriedly ran back down the hill, fearful of being accused of attempting to cross the border in case someone had seen me at that spot. I waded across the stream and returned to the dirt road and did not stop until I met up with my teammates; only then was I able to recover my calm. I helped my companions bring back the trees they had cut, my heart filled with joy as if I had recently discovered a hidden treasure.

After a month, our work at regimental command was completed, but they still wanted us to come back daily to do chores in the barracks. We were told to cut bamboo, chop wood, make chicken coops, and do other small jobs. One day, while cutting bamboo, a man had his arm horribly ripped open by the knife edge of the tree he had just cut. He was probably caught by the bamboo springing up, and the flesh of his arm was torn from the elbow to the shoulder. Blood spouted from the wound. The regimental nurse bandaged the cut, but blood still oozed out. He was allowed to stay at headquarters to await transfer to the regiment's infirmary. Months later, he returned to the camp, all skin and bone; his yellow complexion giving the impression that he had no more blood in his veins. He had become an invalid, incapable of any more physical work.

Because of the accident or for some other reason, we were no longer ordered to work at regimental headquarters. My team went back to clearing land, which became much harder as the dry season progressed and we had to walk very far to the worksite. From the day that I knew the border was only about ten kilometers away from camp, I constantly nursed the idea of escape. Many others also knew that the border was nearby. One day, about to leave for work, we were ordered to stay in the camp instead. A bit later a convoy of military vehicles crowded with *bodoi* was seen on the dirt road skirting a high hill we could see from our camp. An inmate, detailed to do chores at the camp command, informed us that the district assault force was operating in the area. A truck drove into our camp, and about twenty fierce-looking *bodoi* got out. Seeing us looking at them, they swore, "Sons of bitches! Are we so strange that you keep staring at us?"

"Who else among you also wants to escape? You'll see, this time I'm going to send you all to hell!"

A monitor led the assault team around the camp toward the forest at the back. They returned late in the afternoon. One *bodoi* carried a small deer on his shoulders. They cooked, ate, then climbed on their truck and left. Later we learned that the assault force was in our area because as many as fourteen inmates had escaped from a nearby camp. Despite the scale of the operation, no one was caught.

Now, a number of measures to prevent escape were enacted in our camp. We were ordered to cut *lo o* and fence in the entire area, except for one gate leading to battalion headquarters and one opening into the latrine area. At night we had to organize guard duty. Each house was provided with an oil lamp; the man on guard duty sat in the middle of the passageway and whoever wanted to go out to urinate had to report to him, going and returning. A nameplate was posted at each sleeping place, and it was absolutely forbidden to sleep anywhere but at one's designated place. Each inmate had to stand watch for two hours; his replacement would be the man sleeping to his right. Guard duty lasted from the moment the gong signaled bedtime to the moment when it sounded reveille and the call to morning gymnastics. It was then that the group leaders took the roll and reported to the camp command.

At day's end, after getting our ration for the evening meal, we busied ourselves cooking vegetables to add to the rice and we did not eat until six or seven o'clock. If we ate earlier, we were unable to sleep because of hunger. When we finished our meal, we had to cook a can of vegetables or wild tubers to eat when we woke up in the morning, along with the meager breakfast provided for us.

Most of our free time was spent trying to get more food. Not unlike animals, we only thought of eating . . . eating. There were days when we could not find anything edible to cook at night. Going to bed with an almost empty stomach, which kept rumbling over and over, we could not sleep. Many a night, trying to answer the demands of my stomach, I kept a few grains of salt in my mouth until they melted, drank some water, and managed to fall asleep. But then I woke up very early in the morning, hungry and chilled to the bone. My body, which had been tossing on the bamboo bed, ached all over and kept shaking like a leaf. The only way to relieve the cold and pain was to get up, go out to urinate, then come back and sit with my arms around my knees and a blanket wrapped around my shoulders until daylight. Most of us got little sleep because of hunger. The quicker we fell asleep at night, the earlier we woke up in the morning.

The worst times were when we were sick. A mere cold could confine a person to bed for several days, not to speak of a case of malaria. Some people did not recover even after a full month. Quinine tablets caused all sorts of frightening sensations on half-empty stomachs, and most of us did not dare eat the wild greens and tubers when we were sick.

Not a single night passed when I was not awakened by the moaning of a sick man or an inmate crying in his sleep. The weaker ones among us became more pessimistic than ever, the sound of laughter had become a thing of the past. Those who used to make jokes no longer had the heart for it. I made every effort not to sink into despair. I thought that at the worst, I would try to escape across the border; there might be a chance of getting assistance there. Compared to my companions, I was not much stronger, but I felt that I had been a bit luckier on more than one occasion. Even my body tended to function in a healthy manner on its own. There were nights when I was very hungry, but in my sleep I often saw myself living my former normal life. Once I was taking my wife and child to an ice cream shop; I still recall vividly that it was a shop my family frequented in Cholon. When I woke up, I felt both joyful and frustrated; the sweet and fragrant taste of the ice cream seemed to linger in my mouth. I did not know why I often dreamed of happy events and delicious food; perhaps it was because I was not so low in spirits as some of my companions. But sometimes I was oppressed by a feeling of shame and humiliation that I could not share with anyone. Seeing my companions steal from one another, do harm to one another in a vile manner, or fight with one another over trifles so disgusted me that I no longer knew whom to trust or confide in.

One day as I sat absorbed in my thoughts, I caught sight of Yen, an architect I had known since the days of the Xuan Loc camp, also sitting deep in thought. At that moment, I was trying to devise ways to cross the border in such a way as to be able to convince those on the other side that I was not a *bodoi*. Suddenly, Yen looked at me and smiled in a most unexpected and strange manner. I was worried. Was it possible that he was reading my mind?

Then one night just as we had laid down but were not yet asleep, we heard the sound of a large number of *bodoi* approaching. Soon after, we heard many shouts and then the voice of group leader Bui Quoc Khanh respectfully addressing a *bodoi*.

"Comrade cadre." A moment later, we were being told to roll up our mosquito nets and sit with our legs drawn up, each at his own sleeping place; nobody was allowed to put his feet on the floor. A monitor, escorted by a *bodoi* and group leader Khanh, went from place to place to check each man's presence and ask where his belongings were. While this was going on, there were many footsteps passing by outside, then *bodoi*'s voices sounding like they had arrested someone as they moved from the latrine area at the back of the camp toward the camp command's office. We heard sounds of a beating and a man's voice imploring, "I beseech you, comrade cadre," accompanied by thumping, which could be heard very clearly through the wattle. Then there was silence. We hung up our mosquito nets again and lay down. I wondered what had happened, who had been caught and beaten. And why the beating?

So far, we had done nothing that might be construed as an act of opposition to the *bodoi*, nothing that could be cause for a beating. We did not have enough to eat, we worked until we were exhausted, our bodies had become terribly thin, we were in tatters, and many of us had no footwear left. We had to walk barefoot in the jungle on stony ground and through thorny bushes. In other words, we were in the most wretched and humiliating condition, not one likely to lead to beatings, given our passive attitude. It was not until the next afternoon that we were given some idea of what had happened. Four inmates living in the barracks next to ours, as soon as it got dark, had attempted to escape as a group. They were caught immediately; in fact the *bodoi* were waiting for them. I knew two of them, Yen and Dr. Thieu, fairly well. What we did not quite understand was how Yen, who was over forty and seemed to have mature judgment, could be so careless as to let himself be caught in this way. Everyone knew that it was best to try to escape in broad daylight while we were at work, especially when we went to a work site alone and unsupervised. The escape would not be discovered for several hours.

We expected the captured men to be brought to regimental headquarters, so we were very surprised to see Dr. Thieu detained in the camp disciplinary cell. He was confined for three days; after that, the camp command assembled the group he belonged to and read a decision returning him to its supervision—"as he had shown repentance for his offense." Thieu said that Yen had induced him to escape. Much later when I was sent to work at regimental headquarters, I found that Yen was there; he had been spared confinement and was kept at regiment to work. He told me he had been betrayed by Dr. Thieu, who had informed the *bodoi* of the escape plan. When the four of them crept out of the bamboo fence through a narrow opening they had made in advance, the *bodoi* who had been lying in ambush right outside caught them one by one. Because of that, Thieu had not been punished. Yen did not entirely despair of his situation. He said that his family had pulled some strings, and he still hoped that he would be released earlier than the other inmates.

Eventually, the whole camp knew of Thieu's sordid betrayal of his companions. This caused all of us to be on our guard; no one dared trust anybody. Thieu's was not the only attempt to acquire merit in the eyes of the Revolution by such means. A monitor had disclosed that the camp command had received orders to examine and assess personal records and make recommendations to Division for the release of a number of detainees on the occasion of big national celebrations—Ho Chi Minh's birthday, Independence Day, the Party's anniversary, the People's Army anniversary, etc. This news had induced many detainees to report on their companions in the hope of proving themselves to the *bodoi*. A number of so-called educated people had been vile enough to try to harm others in the hope of an early release. As for me, I guessed that because our spirits were so low, the camp command spread the rumor about an assessment of personal records to encourage us to work harder for fear of being poorly rated.

After two months of clearing work, the number of sick had increased considerably. Every morning at roll call, each barracks was full of men remaining in bed. The nurse who came to examine them acknowledged that they were indeed sick. None of us wanted to stay at "home," because this would mean a missed opportunity to find wild vegetables and roots to add to that day's ration.

After the patches of jungle we had cleared of trees and bamboo had dried to a whitish color in the sun, the camp command gave the order to burn them. Only then did we fully realize the consequences of our sloppy work. When we set fire to those plots, only the dead leaves and branches on top burned; the bushes that had been left and were pressed down beneath merely withered. We had to wade through those partially burned masses to completely clear out the undergrowth, which we made into piles and set afire. We had to chop close to the ground in order to sever a bush; the sun beat down, and the ashes flew about like a duststorm each time the wind came up. In that cloud of ash, to breathe or not to breathe brought equal misery. With our bodies bathed in sweat, we turned into thin, tattered scarecrows, darkened by the dust. No work was harder than this clearing and burning of the forests. Hunger and exhaustion, combined with the dirt and itching, nearly drove us crazy. I tried to keep calm, but many of my teammates kept swearing while they worked, which aggravated their nervous tension.

One day, a man piled up the branches he had cut at a little distance from the stump of a big tree. The heap of branches and twigs, all quite dry, looked like a giant bird's nest. His teammates were surprised at what he did; our instructions were to pile everything right around the stumps so they would burn along with the branches. Otherwise shoots would spring up from the stumps when it rained. Normally, an order was needed to set fire to the piles; this usually came only five minutes before work breaks because when every pile was on fire, the heat was so intense, it was impossible to stay within the area. Using a lighted tinder, we'd kindle the bottom of the piles, then run to windward. That day, we did as usual. After the break, we returned to check the results, and a horrible scene lay before our eyes. In a pile of smoldering ashes lay a half-burned, twisted body; there was the same fishy stench of burned human flesh that I had smelled once before. It was nauseating. The body lay in the center of the heap of ash. Apparently, the man had built a pyre for himself, lighted it, then climbed onto the stump nearby and jumped into the fire. We hurried to inform the *bodoi*, but they said little except to advise us to be cautious and not let such an "accident at work" happen again. The camp command sent a *bodoi* to make a rapid examination, then ordered the body wrapped in a piece of plastic and buried at an unfrequented spot on the side of a hill. This luckless man—I do not recall his name—was our first casualty since we began to build our camp in the jungle.

There were other ways in which life here was taking its toll. Many no longer tried to conceal their anger; when exhausted by work, they gave vent to obscene oaths. One day our guard—a fierce-looking *bodoi*—leveled his rifle at a middle-aged detainee and threatened to shoot him. The man said imploringly, "May I request the comrade cadre to shoot me in the head. I'd rather die than live this life. I will stand at the roadside. Here. This way, you can say that you had to shoot me because I was trying to escape. I only ask you to aim at my head so I can die quickly."

The *bodoi* was very angry but did not know what to do. He turned his AK the other way round and threatened to beat the man. But he left, saying, "Get on with your work! You talk like a crazy man."

The *bodoi* always stood guard at some distance from us; the worksite was full of dust and small insects, and we were not much different from animals, with the number of tiny fleas and ticks setting up house in our clothes. The itching, especially when lying down to sleep, was unbearable, and sometimes we would have to get up, take off our clothes, and try to shake out the tiny parasites. Most irritating of them all were the gnats that kept buzzing about, getting in our eyes. We all firmly believed that, having prepared the land, we would have no strength left to cultivate it. Many of the men told the monitors straight out that because we did not eat enough, we were completely exhausted and incapable of work. Still, the norms kept being raised. The camp command thought only in terms of the maximum area of cultivation "in order to reap the best possible first crop." But our capacity for work flagged more and more with each passing day.

One day, some men detailed to do chores at battalion headquarters returned with the good news that our daily ration would be increased to permit greater effort in the production of the first crop. They said Commander Thinh had had a meeting with his study monitors and arrived at the recommendation that cassava (manioc) should be bought and distributed as additional fare and that some rice should be borrowed for us, which would be deducted from our ration after the harvest. According to their calculations we would produce enough cassava in about eight months to meet our needs; our ration of rice could then be reduced because the only work left to do would be to weed the crop and wait for the harvest.

The next day, the camp command ordered us to assemble for a "working session." Commander Thinh began with a speech intended to boost our spirits.

"The Revolution always cares for your health; it's because it considers human beings as precious assets. Next week, my superiors will send out people to buy cassava to add to your daily fare. They are also contemplating the possibility of increasing your rice ration. There is one point I'd like to make clear to you: It is not true that the Revolution doesn't know of your problems; it does. Now, do you agree to the purchase of cassava and the increase of your rice ration?"

We replied with shouts, "Agreed! Agreed! Hurrah!"

Suddenly, someone cried out, "Allow us to write home! Please, allow us to write home!"

"We request permission for our families to visit us. We're so hungry! We're sick and running out of medicines!"

Commander Thinh raised his arm for silence, then said with a smile, "If you want to write home, you can do so next week. As for visits from families, we shall try to build a visitors' shed in record time, but only after the land has been cultivated. We have to make very careful preparations before inviting your wives, children, and parents to come here to see the results of your work. It's not proper to have them here while we're still unprepared, is it?"

The prospect of receiving cassava and some more rice, of being allowed to write home, and of being visited by our families in the near future was a great boost to our spirits. Clearly, the *bodoi* were trying to relieve our pessimism and despair.

A few days later, a number of men were ordered to make preparations to pick cassava roots, departing in the morning and returning in the afternoon. I volunteered to go, hoping I might be able to make some purchases in an inhabited area. Our party of more than twenty people left the camp before dawn. I thought we would be driven to our destination because from time to time a truck from regiment would come to battalion headquarters and drive the *bodoi* to market. But we walked, first passing regimental headquarters, then, half an hour later, passing another reeducation camp. The inmates evidently had not yet left for worksites as we saw a great number of them walking about the enclosure.

I judged the distance between our two camps at a little over five kilometers. As far as we knew, there were only three camps in the area. We walked until the sun was fairly high above the horizon and then began to see hill after hill planted with cassava; in the distance, we caught sight of a few local people. The *bodoi* told us to stop, and one said, "In a moment, you're going to enter the village; bear in mind that it's absolutely forbidden to 'communicate' with the villagers without permission. You must walk in a straight line; you must not break rank and walk ahead of the line or trail behind. Now, listen carefully. The inhabitants of this place are 'progressive' people; they have no great love for you. Do I make myself clear?"

"Yes!"

We were led down a dirt path to a flat expanse of ground below. An old wooden portico displayed a slogan that read "Nothing is more precious than Independence and Freedom," from which the paint had begun to peel off. Behind the gate was a courtyard with a flagpole in the middle. This was probably the village center, a few dilapidated thatched houses denoting utter poverty. We stopped and were instructed to wait; the monitor and *bodoi* walked off. We had waited about half an hour when we saw a group of villagers, including old people, women, and children, coming out of the village toward us; they uttered a few discordant shouts, "Down with the *nguy* army! Down with the *nguy* administration!"

To each shout, the children responded, "Down with them!" three times. Some of my companions burst out laughing at the so-called demonstration, but we hastened to silence them.

"This is a demonstration against us. It's dangerous to laugh at them!"

The group consisted of about thirty people, more than half of them children who sat astride their older siblings' shoulders. Standing at a distance from us, they continued to shout the slogans a few more times, then stood silent. A brat picked up a lump of earth and threw it in our direction; it broke to pieces in the middle of the open space between us and the group of villagers. A moment after, they decided to disperse, one following the other. Only a few children, some carrying younger ones in their arms, stayed behind. Soon, one of them walked slowly toward us, the others following cautiously. One of my companions asked, "Aren't you here under orders to demonstrate against us?"

The child tightened his lips as if to keep from laughing and nodded. An older boy, about fifteen, approached and shouted in an accent that was unmistakably Central, "You think you know something, don't you? Go back! Off with you!"

With these words, he drove the other children away. Thé, using the same accent, hastened to ask him, "You come from the Center, don't you?"

Surprised, the boy looked at Thé for a moment before answering, "We came from Quang Binh Province. Are you also from there?"

Thé nodded, then asked, "How long have you been here?"

"Long enough. Those children you saw were all born here."

"Here come the *bodoi*," someone warned.

The boy left, and the monitor and the two *bodoi* returned with a guide. They said cheerfully, "As you can see, all progressive people hate you. You must be very careful; otherwise they will put on another demonstration against you. Now, follow me! We'll go and pick cassava roots."

We were led out of the small hamlet to the fields, all planted with cassava, which surrounded the huts. Each plant was almost three meters high, which meant that the cassava must be more than one year old. A *bodoi* asked the guide, "Comrade, why haven't you pulled them up at the right time? Why let them grow so old?"

The man shook his head and answered, "What's the good of it? We cannot store them too long. There's no one to sell them to. We planned to carry the roots to the city but have no means of transport."

The monitor asked, "Why not barter? If goods can be transported here, they can be exchanged for your cassava, which will be carried back to the city by the same vehicles."

Again, the man shook his head, "It's not as simple as that. If they bring expensive goods, we cannot pay for them with cassava, and we have no money. On the other hand, we cannot claim payment for the petrol used to transport our cassava. From time to time, some vehicles come here for rare wood, but there is nothing else to barter away. It's very hard to get anywhere from this place. The district authorities have provided us with one bus that runs between here and the district town, but it's so unreliable; one day it runs, another day it doesn't. Today, it just sits there."

We were ordered to root up the cassava; we gathered the roots and also the stems that would be used to grow new plants. The *hom* (cuttings) must be taken from relatively young plants, and we were brought to a patch of cassava that were about the right size. The soil was spongy, but this being the dry season, the surface was hard. After we had worked for an hour, the sun was at its zenith and very hot.

An old woman from the village appeared carrying two big pots suspended from a bamboo yoke across her shoulder; she was followed by a young girl carrying two tin containers of water in the same manner. The woman said to the monitor, "Could you let these men boil water for tea and cook some cassava roots to eat? You and the comrade *bodoi* are invited to eat with us in the village."

The monitor hastened to reply, "No thank you, Mother.[7] It's just as well we share the meal with the party."

The old woman did not say anything; she prepared to return to the village

---

[7]*Bộđội* and cadres usually addressed women as *chị* (sister) and *má* or *mẹ* (mother), using the familiar form to endear themselves to the common people.

followed by the silent girl. The two *bodoi*, mimicking the Central accent, teased the girl, who looked away shyly. The old woman laughed and said, "She's a grown girl, but she's very bashful with boys."

The monitor as well as the *bodoi* burst into laughter.

We stopped working. Some of us dug a pit to cook cassava roots, others went to look for kindling wood, the rest peeled the tubers. We did our cooking in the middle of the cassava field to prevent sparks from our fire from being blown too far afield. When the water was boiled and the cassava roots cooked, we offered some to the *bodoi*. They ate gleefully. For us, this was a chance to eat our fill. The *bodoi* had nothing in which to drink water, so they borrowed our cans. Taking advantage of the relaxed atmosphere, I suggested, "After we have finished eating, could the comrade cadre allow us to go into the village to buy some waterpipe and shredded tobacco?"

The *bodoi* and the monitor discussed the matter; finally, the monitor came over and asked, "Who has some money on him?"

We all raised our hands. The monitor laughed. "How daring of you! Who gave you permission to keep money on you? Well, I'll overlook it for the time being. Now, take some rest and afterward divide yourselves into two teams. One team will gather the *hom* into bunches that one man can carry; the other will pick up the roots and pile them at the roadside. You will then delegate one of you to follow me into the village to see if there is something to buy. But we won't start before we've had a short rest."

The monitor and the two *bodoi* left to go into the village, and we sat down to relax. One man began to snore within minutes. After a while, we set to work—just a few men to tie the *hom* into bunches, the rest carrying the cassava roots to the road. We intended to bring back as many as possible to feed the many inmates in the camp.

When the monitor and the two *bodoi* came back, they rebuked us for having taken too many tubers, for the main purpose of the trip was to bring back cuttings for new plants. The men had to go back to the field to gather more, but I had been appointed to go into the village to buy whatever I could find. Everyone wanted to give me money.

"There's no use bringing too much money," the monitor said. "You can't expect to find goods to buy here. Ten dong will be more than enough."

But everyone wanted to hand me either a 5-dong or a 10-dong note of the new currency. I had to take 50 dong from the five fellows nearest me; finally I said, "Let me take only this much. When I return, we'll share everything equally among us, be it a needle or a piece of thread."

My friends laughed. "Agreed!" "Unanimous!"[8]

---

[8]Instead of saying *dồng ý* (agreed), the North Vietnamese preferred the words *nhất trí* (lit., all of one mind). The camp inmates, in this case, used the jargon in jest.

Easy-going Monitor Quang said, "Ah! You want to make fun of the Revolution, don't you?"

As he and I were about to leave, the men said, "Buy anything! Don't bring back the money! You'll fail us if you do. And if there's rice wine, buy it, by all means."

The monitor led me to the front of a house and told me to wait outside. A moment later he returned with a middle-aged man and said to him, "Comrade, see if you have anything to sell these fellows. Since they came here, they have been deprived of almost everything. At their old camp, they were able to buy some goods from time to time. Now, they have absolutely nothing left."

The man said, "I'll bring you to the village shop. You can buy what they have, but I don't think there's much."

We went to a thatched house with bamboo walls, the upper part of openwork and the lower part completely closed. At the entrance was a wooden board with the words *Cua Hang Mau Dich* (lit., Trading Shop) written in beautiful letters. The villager walked in and inquired, "Where's everybody?"

A woman came from the back of the shop, her hands covered with soil. She asked, "What is it, comrades?"

"I bring you these customers. The comrade *bodoi* from the reeducation camp came to buy our cassava. He would like to see if there's something to buy in your shop."

"We're not open today. In any case, there's nothing worth buying. There are only some discarded things nobody wants."

The monitor asked pleasantly, "Don't you have any edibles? Cakes or sweets, or perhaps some sugar? Or cigarettes or waterpipe tobacco?"

"I'm afraid there are no sweets or food, but we do have some waterpipe tobacco left. And there are some sweets no one cares to buy. Please wait until I have washed my hands; then you can come in and have a look."

Our guide said, "Well then, comrade! Please come in and look around. I've got to go to the field now."

The monitor led me into the shop. It was divided into two compartments; one side served as an office, the other had bamboo shelves placed against the walls. On the top of a high shelf, there were several parcels wrapped in paper. In one corner stood a few piles of roughly made stone bowls. Large baskets, one on top of another, were stacked on the ground. The woman came back, and the monitor said, "I've brought this camp inmate here to see if there's something to buy. They have some money, but they haven't met anyone who could sell them anything. They are short of everything, from tobacco to sweets."

The woman answered, speaking in the Northern accent, "Most of the folks here provide their own food, so we seldom sell edibles. From time to time, when the district store sells us some inexpensive goods that we can resell at very low prices, we distribute them to the families in the village. When the goods arrive, we notify the people, and the goods will be gone in a jiffy. After that, there's nothing left to show on the shelves. As of now, there are only a few unsold tobacco cakes we don't know what to do with. Could the comrade ask whether they want to buy them? Ah! There are also a few parcels of sweets left."

I was disappointed by the poverty of the shop, but when I heard that there were some sweets, I hastened to say, "We could do with the tobacco and sweets. It would even be better if you had some salt or fish sauce."

The monitor added, "I've seen quite a few hens and chickens in the yards. Is it possible to buy some chickens or eggs?"

As he spoke, he looked at me; I eagerly nodded my agreement. The woman showed her understanding of the situation by replying cheerfully, "That kind of merchandise is reserved for sale to the district store. Private sales are not allowed here. Anyway, you have to ask the owners; they may want to sell."

The monitor picked up a cake of tobacco and sniffed it. "Ugh! What a bitter smell! Indeed, they don't know how to cure tobacco down here! Up North, just the smell of our tobacco is enough to intoxicate us, let alone smoke it. By the way, have you been here long? Is your family here with you?"

"I have lived here since 1968," the woman said. "I was then serving at the battlefront, bringing supplies to the fighting units. We came as far as this area but could not return to the North because B-52s were heavily bombing the supply route. The Party decided that we should stay and organize a 'fighting village' in this place. I married here. I am the only one from the North, the rest of the people came from Quang Binh Province. I always hope to be able to return to my native village, but I have not had the means. Recently, I received a letter from my parents in the North, which made me miss them even more."

The monitor said, "You have your own family here now, so what's the point of going back North? Besides, it's easier to earn your living here."

The woman shook her head. "Everybody says so, but I think that life here is as difficult as in the North; things are not much different. Anyway, my parents believe the rumor that everybody in the South is living in prosperity, so they asked me to send them such luxuries as an electric fan and a bicycle!"

The monitor hastened to interrupt. "I grant you that we're not prosperous now, but in the future, when this area has become an agroindustrial complex, you'll have everything you want."

The woman replied with a wry face, "Please, comrade, enough of that! What you say won't happen soon. The other day, a comrade from District came here on a visit, and I asked him for a coach ticket to go home and visit my parents, but he said that if I went now, it would be a very long trip. He told me to wait until the road along the Vietnamese highlands range was built, then the distance to travel will be much shorter. But from what I've seen, things would not be that easy. When we took supplies to the troops down here, I thought I would die on that one trip along the trail [Ho Chi Minh Trail]. If I wait to go North until a proper road is built, I'm sure I will wait for a very long time. My husband says that the work force has been expanded by a great number of reeducation detainees, but what does that mean? If we build a road without road metals to pave it, no vehicle will be able to drive on it after only a few rainy seasons."

The monitor said as if he was well informed, "I've heard comrades from the transport unit say that hundreds of kilometers of road have already been tarred. And on both sides of that road, people from other places are being moved in and resettled, gradually as planned. The construction work will undoubtedly be completed soon."

The woman shook her head and did not disguise her contempt. "Comrade. Have you ever been on that road? If and when they finish it, I'm afraid I'll be too old to go. My parents will be dead and I'll have no more relatives to visit."

Afraid an argument would start, I took a chance and asked, "How much are these tobacco cakes, madam?"

She did not answer; instead she went to a shelf and picked up two parcels— supposedly containing sweets—carefully wrapped in cellophane. When she opened them, we found that only one was intact and the other had about half its contents left. She asked, "Do you want to buy these sweets?"

I replied quickly, "Thank you, madam. I'll buy anything you have because my companions have given me as much as sixty dong."

The woman laughed, "What's all that much money for? The tobacco is seven dong a cake. I'll ask seven and a half dong for the parcels of sweets."

As I picked up the tobacco cakes, I felt a little worried. Wrapped in dried banana leaves, each must have weighed more than one kilogram. Three cakes might be too much. But I told myself that there would be more than enough people to share them. I paid for the items and said, "My friends told me to try to buy some edibles, but I can see that they are not available here."

The woman took the money, and as she looked for change, she said, "The folks here are also in poor circumstances. Sometimes District asks whether we want to buy high-quality goods, but no one can find enough money for that. If we manage to raise a litter of piglets or a few chickens, we have to sell them to the district store at the official price, which means that we won't get much."

The monitor interrupted. "Then comrade, tell the people to sell them under the counter to these men. It's possible to sell at a little higher price."

The woman smiled; she spoke in a low voice as if afraid that somebody might overhear what she said. "Well, I was going to tell the comrade to bring this fellow to see the village folks. He can ask them to sell him some things without anyone being the wiser!"

The monitor laughed. "Well, has everything here been paid up? I'm going with him to see if he can buy a few chickens."

Clutching the tobacco cakes and parcels of sweets under my arm, I followed the monitor, my heart filled with hope. If, on top of what I already had, I could buy some chickens, that would be something beyond all our expectations. It suddenly occurred to me that bringing them back to the camp might be risky. What if the camp command would not allow us to eat them. An idea popped into my mind; I asked Quang, "Comrade cadre, could we be reprimanded for buying chickens?"

"What would be the reason for that? But why not kill them here and wrap them up; nobody will pay any attention."

I did not expect the monitor to come up with such an idea. I had intended to suggest that we say we bought the chickens to keep to lay eggs and to permit us to raise a brood of chicks. This would be a form of "increasing production" and would probably sound more constructive.

When we got to the row of huts, I stopped to let the monitor precede me; among the people here could be some of those who had "demonstrated" against us. The monitor asked, "What are you stopping for?"

"I am afraid of being hooted at."

"Nonsense! You've nothing to fear when you're with me. Let's go in to bargain with them!"

He came near a house and asked in a loud voice, "Anybody home? Where is everybody?"

An old woman came out from a house, surprise showing on her face. She asked in a Central Vietnam accent, "What's that?"

The monitor said, "I've inquired at the village shop. They told me to come here to buy a few chickens to prepare some chicken porridge to treat guests from District."

The old woman shook her head and made a gesture of denial. "It's forbidden to sell this way! If District knew, we would be severely reprimanded!"

The monitor laughed; he came near the woman and spoke close to her ear, but I was able to hear what he said. "The truth is, I brought these camp inmates to the village to pick cassava. They would like to buy some chickens 'under the counter.' Sell them some. The people at the village shop told me to come here; there's nothing to fear."

The old woman still hesitated; she said, "My family has no chickens to sell. Others may have some. I have none left."

The monitor said as if he really believed her, "All right, I'll have to go there," pointing to the next house.

As we moved away, the old woman said, "I think I'd better tell the folks to bring the chickens to you. Where are you picking cassava? Just go back there; in a while, people will come with chickens. It's hard to chase after the chickens now; it's too noisy. By the way, how many do you want to buy?"

The monitor turned to me for the answer. I asked, "How much is a chicken, madam?"

"Probably over ten dong each. It depends on the size."

"Very well! Please tell them we would like to buy about five chickens."

I followed the monitor back to the field and found that my companions had already finished their work. Neat bunches of *hom* stood by the side of the road. My friends were sitting on the ground eating manioc. Seeing me, they noisily demanded to know the result of my "mission." I handed the tobacco cakes and parcels of sweets to one of them and said, "Divide this up among you. The whole lot cost 28½ dong. I suggest we divide this into three parts now, and we can divide it individually when we get back to camp. Now, if anyone wants to buy chickens, have the money ready; they'll bring the chickens out here very shortly."

The men were overjoyed when they heard this. "We'll have chicken porridge tonight," several exclaimed at once.

The monitor was smiling and talking in a low voice to the two *bodoi*; they were looking in our direction, and seemed to be discussing this business of buying chickens.

As I was eating my share of manioc, two women appeared, carrying two small bags—the kind which, filled with sand, were used to construct fortifications. They approached the monitor who pointed in our direction. They came toward us and asked, "Who wants to buy chickens?"

A number of men stepped forward and took hold of the bags as if to prevent others from getting them. From where I sat, I hurried to intervene. "Don't fight over the chickens! We have agreed to an equal distribution, remember!"

They restrained themselves, and I proposed that only one person take care of the purchase. Both parties haggled earnestly over the price. One of the women said, "The price is fifteen dong each. You're free to take it or leave it."

The monitor picked up a chicken and balanced it in his hand. "This chicken is rather small," he said, "it's not big enough for the price you've asked. These fellows want to buy quite a few chickens, so it's in your interest to ask a more reasonable price."

The tone of the woman's voice changed. "For you, comrade, I am willing to cut the price down to ten dong a chicken."

The men cheerfully produced two ten-dong notes. The women pocketed the money, joy showing on their faces. The monitor waited until they were out of earshot, then he shook his head and said, "Why were you in such a hurry? Why didn't you try to pay them seven dong a chicken? They would have agreed to that price. This village has reached the status of a socialist community, it's true, but those women are still trailing behind; if there's a chance, they never fail to ask an exorbitant price for what they sell."

As we examined the chickens by parting their feathers to expose the skin, several more people came with their fowls. They did not carry them in bags but held them upside down by the legs, which were secured with a piece of string. This time there were a lot of chickens; we did not know exactly how many.

Before leaving us to make the purchase, the monitor again advised us "to bargain for cheaper prices." We gathered around the villagers and began bargaining. This chicken was too skinny, that one too tough, etc. Finally, we agreed to pay fifty dong for seven chickens, and we pushed our advantage by asking them to tie the chickens for easy transport. The women talked to us as they worked. I said, "How mischievous you were a while ago! We have been so miserable; we were brought here to do forced labor, and you had the heart to hoot at us! What was all that for?"

One of the women replied, "We have been ordered to do that by the Party. As for us, we cannot make head or tail of it. Here, we have to do whatever the Party tells us to do. We know that you inmates have a very hard life. And we have no hatred whatsoever for you."

A man asked, "Is there a market in this village or around here?"

"This is a 'fighting village'; therefore, there's no market here. There's no other village in the area except ours. And there's nothing to buy and sell either. As we already have a 'trading shop,' we are not allowed to hold market here."

I said, "Why don't you come to our camp to sell your goods to us? When we were still in the camp near the town of Xuan Loc, it was very easy for the people there to trade with us. At night, there was much activity around the camp."

The woman shook her head. "We cannot do such things here; it would be against regulations. Only the trading shop workers have the right to trade with the village people, and the villagers' only job is to produce goods. Distribution is the duty of the trading service. If we buy goods from the government without selling our products to them, we'll get severe criticism."

One of the men insisted, "Then why did you sell chickens to us?"

The women laughed and replied, "It was to help you."

Another fellow said teasingly, "Now look! You booed us but you also sold us chickens as a sign of support. In the future, how can we know when you want to hoot at us and when you're giving us support?"

The women giggled. Seeing this, the monitor came over and asked, "Have you finished? If you have, there's nothing more to discuss. If somebody saw you 'communicate' with one another like this, it wouldn't be any good for either party."

The women stood up and returned to the village. We discussed how to carry the chickens discreetly back to camp. Finally, the monitor ordered us to strangle the whole lot and put them in a sack. I regretted the waste because some of the fowls seemed ready to lay eggs, which would have been very nourishing to eat.

At four in the afternoon a truck came from regiment. We loaded the cassava roots on first, then piled the bunches of cuttings on top and tied up the whole load. The monitor sat in the cab with the driver, and he allowed one of us to ride back to camp with the sack of chickens. The rest of us walked, accompanied by the two *bodoi*. We had barely got started when we heard someone running after us. It was the fifteen-year-old boy who had been among this morning's group of hecklers. He came running up with a chicken in a bag and offered it for sale. No one had any money left except me. I asked the *bodoi*'s permission, and they agreed, so I said to the boy, "I have no money left except this five-dong note." The boy followed us for a while, then said, "I also ask only seven dong for my chicken, like the other people."

Turning to those walking beside me, I asked, "Does anybody have two one-dong notes?" But these had been used in our purchases; everyone tried to hide higher denomination money. I shook my head and told the boy, "I'm afraid you'll have to bring it back. Nobody has the change to pay you seven dong. That will be for next time then."

The boy handed me the bag, saying, "Well, you can have it for five dong." I gave him the money; the boy took the note and ran quickly away. The chicken stayed motionless in the bag.

We reached regimental headquarters at dusk, and it was completely dark when we got back to camp. The men noisily distributed the tobacco and sweets, and within minutes a group was preparing the chickens for cooking. I unobtrusively hung the bag containing the live chicken close to the thatch roof of our barracks. My friends at camp had taken delivery of the midday and evening rations for me. Thé came to say, "The men who are cooking are calling for those who want to contribute their share of rice for chicken porridge. If you want to join, go in the back."

I brought my share of rice; that night, Thé and I and many others had a meal of delicious chicken porridge. This was the first time we had had such a good meal since we had reported for reeducation! Although I was not a waterpipe smoker, I still claimed my share and exchanged it for shredded tobacco. I finished my meal with a cigarette and found that life still had some flavor to it. In other circumstances, people would take for granted such things as chicken gruel and shredded tobacco cigarettes, but here at this moment to be able to afford such "delicacies" was like a miracle. I felt much stronger suddenly, and in higher spirits. Even the cigarette had a special flavor, different from the taste it had after a meal of rice gruel mixed with wild greens. Indeed, happiness was only a relative feeling!

The next day it was the turn of other detainees to go to pick cassava. Although the work was tiring, to go was now a privilege. In the evening, the men came back with tobacco cakes, sweets, sugar, and live chickens. The camp commanders chose to close their eyes to our purchase of chickens. The live ones were shut up in small pens around our quarters. When I went out to work, I tied the legs of my chicken and entrusted it to the care of the kitchen team. When I returned, I brought it back to the barracks and fed it with a handful of insects of all kinds. Later, I built a hen house for it, small but very strong, to guard against foxes. I had developed a sort of affection for the chicken. Daily, I took care of it as if it were my own child.

Since we had been allowed to add manioc to our daily fare and especially to buy food items at the village, life had become more bearable. Surveillance by the *bodoi* seemed to slack off a bit. When we worked on the land, they went off searching for yams. But this relaxation was short-lived; it ended a little more than a week after it had begun.

Returning from work one evening, we found that another inmate was missing. The group leader maintained that everybody was present when roll was called at the worksite just before the walk back to camp, but at the food distribution there was one ration too many. Later, I learned that Dr. Anh had disappeared. The result of this was that surveillance and roll call became as strict as before, and we were no longer allowed to pick cassava. There may have been other reasons for that. It seems that our purchases had caused a great disruption in the lives of the local people. The *bodoi* told us that we had "bought up the village goods, so the purchasing section has no more chickens to buy for the trading shop."

By now, we had cleared a fairly wide area. The neighboring hills and flat expanses in the valleys were ready for cultivation. The cassava cuttings were piled on the bank of the stream. We began to plant. Walking abreast of each other, we dug holes about forty centimeters apart with our hoes. A second group following us planted the cuttings, pushed the soil around them, and stamped it down with their feet. The cuttings had been chopped down to the proper length of three joints each. In this dry season, the men working with the hoes had the hardest job because the surface of the ground was hard. In fact, we expected all the cassava cuttings to die. But a few days later when we passed the fields, red sprouts were visible above the surface of the earth. The planting proved to be almost as hard work as the clearing of the forests. In these open spaces, the sun blazed down on us, and when we were allowed to rest, we could not find a single tree to shade us. Our daily fare also had suffered a change for the worse; we were no longer allowed to eat fresh cassava, and since no more cuttings were required, we had no opportunity to go to the village to buy edibles.

After a week of hoeing and planting, the number of sick increased, and almost everyone was obsessed with the idea of escaping across the border. Besides, the informers among us had perhaps dressed up their reports with the result that roll calls became more frequent and surveillance more strict. At night, when someone went out to relieve himself and did not immediately return, the *bodoi* on guard near the fence would yell out to drive him back into the barracks. The fear of detainees escaping became an obsession with the *bodoi*. From time to time they spread the rumor that "a great number of inmates would be released shortly" and said "it would be stupid to escape from camp now because that would be a complete waste of so many months of reeducation." Those "disclosures" no longer attracted our attention, and my companions cursed when they had to listen to them.

Clouds began to appear each day now, announcing the approach of the rainy season. The camp command's plan was to plant rice on dry fields after the cassava planting was completed. One day I was summoned to repair the battalion's barracks; the roof had been covered with freshly cut thatch that had shrunk during the dry season, and there were now many small holes and slits, especially around the lashings. From inside, those holes looked like so many stars studded on the dark background of the roof. As I sat on the roof tying bunches of thatch to fill up the slits, I was able to overhear a discussion about rice planting.

Commander Thinh was a scheming fellow, always optimistic. He told the group of study monitors assembled for the session, "If we plan our work well, we'll surely carry off the flag[9] this time!"

The study monitors all protested. "Really! If we can do our work so as not to be criticized, that will be the best we can hope for. It's not that easy to carry off the flag! The men are so hungry and weather conditions so severe that even fulfilling the norms will be hard."

Thinh burst into laughter; but he replied firmly, "Don't you worry, comrades. We have the experience. If we want to carry off the flag, we'll be able to do it. Wait and see!"

"By dressing up your report again, no doubt!"

Thinh shouted back, "Who do you say has presented false reports, comrade? When was it? Young comrade, don't be insolent!"

The voice of Political Commander Tu was heard above the confusion, "You don't know Comrade Thinh yet! He has more than one trick up his sleeve; if he wants something, he'll get it. Comrade Thinh, tell the comrades how you plan to carry off the flag. Let's see if they think it's feasible. As for me, I think it's going to be quite difficult."

Thinh answered, "I plan to see to it that we attain a production of two and a half tons of paddy per hectare and that we carry off the flag. Last year, in Kontum, they took the regional prize with only two tons per hectare."

"Good God!" This was Monitor Quang's voice. "I didn't expect to hear such wishful thinking! Is this land fertile for rice? We have no fertilizers and no insecticide and the work force is too weak to work properly. To speak of two and a half tons per hectare in such conditions would be . . ."

[9]Carry off the prize (in the form of a flag).

Thinh laughed still louder. "Ha! Ha! The comrade doesn't believe me? Let him wait and see! I have made my plan. I say that we'll carry off the flag. You want to bet?"

"I have nothing to risk in a bet against you, but if you can manage to produce two and a half tons per hectare, I'll volunteer to clean your behind each time you go to the latrine."

Everybody roared with laughter. Sitting in the shadow near the wall tying bunches of thatch, I could not restrain myself so I ran off silently to a stand of elephant grass a little distance away to laugh out loud. Monitor Quang was known to be a joker; it was like him to react in such a manner. A moment later, I returned to my place near the wall. The discussion was still going on, and Commander Tu was talking. "Like I said, Comrade Thinh is a scheming fellow. I am sure he has a plan that will work."

"Those guys are too hungry and too weak. We cannot force them to work any harder."

Thinh said, "Just maintain the present level. That'll be sufficient."

Monitor Quang replied, "I cannot believe you. I am a peasant. I am sure that rice planted on cleared land with such labor cannot reach such productivity."

Thinh said, "I can't make you believe me. There's no need for further discussion for the time being, but you'll see. To be quite frank, I think you're still too green. Ha! Ha!"

That evening, I told Thé about the camp command's discussion. He was flabbergasted. "What! Production of two and a half tons with this land! They can wait till kingdom come! My family used to plant rice on cleared land. Even if the soil and the seeds are right and the weather favorable, the maximum productivity was 1.7 or 1.8 tons per hectare. Maybe their estimates were wrong."

"They will probably force us to sweat blood!"

"That won't do any good! Hard labor doesn't necessarily mean an increase in productivity. It also depends on the quality of the seeds, on fertilizers, and the soil. The seeds I've seen in the stores at logistics section are the ordinary kind."

I only discussed the matter with Thé, but a few days later one of my friends said complainingly, "I've heard that 'they' have a plan to outdo the other units in productivity in order to carry off the flag. We'll surely be dead before the harvest season arrives."

I chuckled to myself. Thé was a very discreet fellow, and I was sure that if he had discussed my story with someone, it had been only with a reliable friend. In any case, it took just three days for the story to go the rounds of the camp!

Perhaps to realize the plan for planting cassava, group leader Bui Quoc Khanh was instructed to raise the work norms set for each stage of the process, aggravating our hardships. Without the cassava roots to eat, we were hungry again; having planted the plots near the camp, we now had to start out very early each morning for the other fields, which were about three kilometers away. The weather was stifling despite an overcast sky, the usual climate just before the rains started. To make matters worse, there was now this business of raising the norms!

We got up early while the sky was still dark and cooked a can of greens or tubers, which was not easy. The wood was green, the cooking place wet; we put our heads close to the ground and blew on the fire to stoke it up, just enough to cook what we had. The smoke was dense, and by the time we finished cooking, our eyes were red and our bodies covered with sweat. The younger men constantly uttered profane oaths while they cooked and blew on the fire. Later, we washed, then went to take delivery of our midday ration, a half-bowl of rice and a handful of dried manioc slices. These slices had not been properly dried, and they had turned brown and had a sour smell; cooked with a pinch of salt, they seemed to stick in our throats the moment we swallowed. After we had eaten, we could not stop belching from the acid gas in our stomachs. The men who suffered from stomach trouble were afraid to eat this stuff and gave it away.

As we became weaker, the *bodoi* and even the group and team leaders appeared to become more severe. They were obsessed by the fear of a drop in productivity. As far as we were concerned, eating was the only important thing on earth. We had arrived at a point where no one was able to find enough wild greens or roots to eat his fill, and because of that nobody dared to eat up his entire ration and what edibles he could find during the day's work. In the morning we ate just enough to have strength to go to the field. Upon arrival, we had another bite and continued to have a bite after each hour of work. At noon, we ate up what was left of what we had brought with us, then hastened to go in search of tubers or wild greens.

Knowing that this was the only way for us to fill our stomachs, the *bodoi* closed their eyes to our hunt for extra food. Our subsistence for the evening and the next day depended on the results of our picking and digging during the midday rest. The team of *bodoi* standing guard in the morning was replaced at noon by another team. The afternoon team was most anxious to get back on time because they were looking forward to their meal and rest. So when the day's work was finished, we were urged to leave at once, shouted at, and forbidden to linger to look for greens and roots. Even when we came to the stream to wash, we were rushed. We had two alternatives: either have a quick wash in order to have enough time to wash our clothes, or bathe and clean ourselves carefully and then put on the same clothes we had worn during the day. Most of us preferred to bathe long in the stream because this time spent in the clear water at the end of the day was for us the most invigorating, pleasant, and relaxing in the whole day. Our bodies were clean, and we were free of the itching from the tiny insects that got into our clothes and fed on us. If the young ones saw someone wash his clothes without bathing in the stream, they would tease, "Relax, buddy! Enjoy the hour while you still have time!"

But when the whistle summoned us to assemble for the walk to camp, followed by the shouts of those standing guard where we bathed, we had to hurry and put on our smelly clothes again. The discomfort and irritation returned. We felt like animals with the ever-present ticks swarming over our bodies.

While dragging out this wretched existence, it was no wonder that the propaganda speeches of the political cadres aimed at boosting our morale became an ironic and impudent comedy. The *bodoi* themselves were aware of this, and they did not prolong any more than necessary the political study sessions, as they had done at the Xuan Loc camp. Whenever there was a topic that regiment wanted us to study, the session was completed within one afternoon, that is, we worked in the morning, had a wash at noon, rested until 3 P.M., then went to the courtyard in front of battalion headquarters where we sat in the shade of the trees to listen to the lesson. The political cadre from regiment, in fact, only read from his documents, then asked, "Do you have something to add?"

We replied unanimously, "No!"

After that, we had a fifteen-minute break, then a discussion period. Groups of fifteen sat in a circle to talk, and at around half past four the group leaders met with the political cadre to report on the results obtained at the "workshops." Generally speaking, everybody reported that "the men agreed 100 percent with the comrade speaker." Then the political cadre made a remark on our attitude vis-à-vis political studies, and naturally "there were still some elements who did not show enough eagerness; their comrades should urge them to make more efforts so that everybody could progress at the same pace. . . . Otherwise, those very persons who would surely be released later than the others would harbor resentment against the regime."

At this moment, when the study session was about to end, the political cadre usually would begin his disinformation task by imparting some news that later on would become a serious topic of discussion among the inmates. On one occasion, he disclosed that "all reeducation camps at Ka Tum had been disbanded because the inmates there had successfully completed their reeducation and had been allowed to return to their families"; at another time, he said that "more than one hundred inmates of the camp uphill from this one had been released because they had worked well, despite the fact that we were in the midst of the cultivation season."

In such moments, when "secrets" were imparted, some of the fellows trapped the cadre with seemingly stupid or unexpected questions. One day, a man began a lengthy exchange. "At the very beginning of our reeducation, many high-ranking cadres told us that our offenses were relatively less serious than those committed by field-grade officers and civil servants above the rank of director. Is that right?"

The cadre replied without hesitation, "That's right! No doubt about it! You can see for yourselves that you have not been beaten or ill-treated at all."

"Then why were we compelled to plead guilty to crimes punishable by death when we were asked to write an account of our past history? With such serious crimes, how long do we have to stay in reeducation camps?"

Obviously embarrassed, the cadre replied with a forced smile, "Well, we must call a spade a spade! There's no other way to describe a crime punishable by death. Anyway, compared with people of higher rank, your crimes are less serious; consequently, you will be released earlier."

"How soon is 'earlier'? How many years of detention? To which article of the Penal Code can we refer to know the number of years we are supposed to be detained?"

Carried along by his own momentum, the cadre replied, "How can we know how long you're supposed to be detained? You'll only know when you're released."

"Then why did the regiment commander say one day that if we were not released yet, it was because the present situation did not permit it?"

"That is also right. The situation at the border is at the moment very tense. Can't you see that?"

"Then which principle or policy is in force to deal with our offenses? According to the law or the situation outside the camp?"

"According to both the law and the situation at the moment."

"If that is so, how can you know in advance that many detainees will be released?"

A young inmate interrupted, saying bluntly, "Then, what you've said was only guesswork, comrade cadre! We've heard plenty of that stuff before."

Vexed, the cadre replied, "I didn't guess. It was regiment command that instructed me to disclose the news to you. We only want you to keep up your spirits so you can complete your reeducation; if you give up hope now, everything will go wrong."

A fellow retorted, "At the Xuan Loc camp where we were, a regiment commander invoked his honor as a Communist Party member to assert that we would not be detained too long. It has been two years since, and still we cannot know the day when we will be released. So who can we trust now?"

The cadre hesitated, then gathered his papers and prepared to leave. Then he said, "A period of two years cannot be considered a very long time."

At this, the men protested loudly, "Then what is considered as 'long'? How many years?" and "Good God! Already two years of detention and yet it's not enough! Then what is enough?" and "Oh, what difference does it make. You can detain us here until we die, for all I care!"

The cadre shook his head, made a vague gesture with his hand, then left to go to battalion headquarters. We were ordered to disperse and return to our barracks.

From that afternoon on, we talked about that study session. Everyone acknowledged that it was quite clear now that we were to be detained indefinitely, according to an undefined policy without any legal grounds. Our fate depended on a few decisions made by the authorities. "If you obtain good results in reeducation, you will be released soon!" But what could be considered "good results"? We were living under vague, inconsistent regulations and the maxim, "hurricanes and storms are not as dangerous as Vietnamese syntax," came to mind. In truth, the Vietnamese language does not lack words to express definite and concise ideas, but the men and women of the new regime had created a new and tricky way to speak it, as in, "Bring a provision of money or foodstuff required for seven days of reeducation!" or "If you obtain good results, you'll be released soon!"

We continued the daily task of planting cassava. The carpentry team to which I belonged, having built the required number of buildings for the whole camp, was now instructed to saw tree trunks to make tables and chairs for the camp command. Also, each study monitor was entitled to a wardrobe trunk in which to put his clothes and other personal belongings, and each *bodoi* was allocated a real bed instead of boards placed on a trestle as before. We were given more to eat than our companions who worked in the fields; in addition to our daily ration, the ten of us were given two basins of rice and two basins of noodle soup—instant noodles cooked in water—each morning. The *bodoi* did not have to eat rice mixed with maize or manioc; it seemed that they had more white rice than they could consume. There was always uneaten rice thrown in the pigsty.

After finishing the beds, we were ordered to work at sawing high-quality wood that was thought to exist in large amounts in this part of the jungle. Commander Thinh or some of the study monitors would lead us to a spot where the trees were believed to be of the right kind. A temporary shed covered with wattle was built for us in the carpentry team to work in. We felled the trees, then cut the wood into boards about ten centimeters thick. Sawing the newly cut trees was very hard work, but we were always aware that we were having an easier time than the men planting cassava on the hills under the blazing sun, trying to fulfill impossible norms. After sawing, the boards were stood upright and covered with branches to prevent them from cracking if exposed to direct sunlight. Each time a truck from regiment came with supplies for the camp, we had to carry the boards to the dirt road for the truck to pick them up and take them away. Moving the heavy boards through the dense growth of the forest was a job in itself. Every time a load was dispatched, we were each given a few days later a packet of Vam Co cigarettes, the new brand that, though bitter, "was better than nothing."

One day, coming back to camp from such a trip, we found animated discussions going on about the escape some days ago of Dr. Bui Tran Anh, taking with him only his knapsack and leaving all his clothes behind. Dr. Anh was nicknamed Bi Tran Ai[10] because he was a joker, did not pay much attention to hygiene and rarely washed himself or his clothes, and always smelled of waterpipe tobacco. Most of the men thought him somewhat crazy: How was such a fellow able to escape from the camp? But I believed he was a thoughtful person. He pretended to be a joker and a bit "nuts," but his words revealed that he had a deep understanding of our situation and had thought seriously about it.

The day after his escape, when everybody was out working with only a few inmates remaining in camp, Dr. Anh was suddenly seen returning with his knapsack on his shoulders. The *bodoi* surrounded him and pushed him toward the battalion office. Those who witnessed the scene said Dr. Anh claimed he intended to escape but was seized by remorse and decided to come back. As the camp commander was absent, the *bodoi* kept him in the disciplinary cell, which meant that one of his legs was fettered. The knapsack he carried over his shoulders was full of rice. The following day, Commander Thinh ordered him to reconstruct his escape. He related every detail, and it turned out to be a very simple story. At dawn he left his barracks, pretending to go to the latrines, his knapsack clutched under his armpit. He followed the path leading to battalion headquarters, openly, without trying to conceal himself. Arriving at the rice storehouse, he went round to the back, got in by climbing over the wall, filled his sack with rice, threw it outside, climbed back out, and followed the path toward the dirt road. But seeing this route guarded by *bodoi*, he returned to the storehouse and hid himself in it with the intention of finding his way out that night. It was then almost daylight. He spent the whole day sleeping. That midnight, he got out and went across the adjacent cassava field toward the road. But after a day without food or water, he realized he could not go very far, so he hid himself in a bush on the deserted hill facing the camp and waited to make his way back to camp until there was no one around. He also said that when he hid in the warehouse, he clearly heard the *bodoi* discussing their search for him.

Perhaps because he seemed somewhat irrational, Dr. Anh was kept in the disciplinary cell only one week; after that he was returned to his group for

---

[10]A play on words. "Bùi" became "Bi" (used mainly as a component of several compound words that convey ideas of sadness, sorrow, pessimism, compassion, pity, etc.). "Trần Anh" became "Trần Ai" (hardship). However, the pun was meant as a joke, as can be seen in the context.

"education" and surveillance. To his teammates' laughing questions, Anh replied jestingly, "I intended to escape, but I forgot to bring along my packet of waterpipe tobacco and I just couldn't do without it, so I returned to camp." Many believed his answer to be perfectly sincere—although most of us knew it was a joke—because Dr. Anh was known to be a pipe addict; he was also known for being able to draw on his pipe longer than anyone in the whole camp.

All the events at the camp outside the daily routine came with unexpected suddenness. One night not long after Dr. Anh's comical escape attempt, another strange event took place. As we were ready to go to sleep, we suddenly saw the beam of a flashlight flickering as the man holding it made his way toward our barracks. Behind him loomed the silhouettes of a number of *bodoi*. As they came closer, we saw that it was Commander Thinh followed by several study monitors. Suddenly a voice said, "Where's Khanh? Ask the men to assemble quickly."

We were told to assemble into groups and to stand in front of one of the barracks, which were situated fairly far apart from one another. Monitor Quang asked, "Do you know why you have been summoned here?"

A voice answered, "For roll call."

Monitor Quang went on cheerfully, "You guess wrong! There's no roll call. Now, when somebody's name is called, he is to present himself before me; after that he is to stand to my left. Is that clear?"

"Yes."

The first man whose name was called approached Quang and by the light of the flashlight saw in his hand a pack of letters. He cried out, "Letters! Letters for us!"

The men standing in the lines were so happy that they suddenly became noisy and disorderly. Within me—and probably within the hearts of the other men— was joy mixed with anxiety; these must be letters from home. We had not received any for a long time. Was there one for me?

After a number of names had been read, I heard my own called out. The night was dark, and though I moved cautiously on the wooden clogs I had made for myself, I kept stumbling again and again. The monitor handed me a letter, then said, "Wait, here's another one!" I joined the group of inmates who had received letters and waited. Like a blindman I felt my two letters with my hands, my heart filled with great joy as if I were actually holding my wife and child in my arms. A multitude of thoughts churned in my mind. I no longer paid any attention to what was happening around me. I did not know which of my friends had got letters and which ones had not. I remained detached from my surround- ings until a shout from the monitor reminded me where I was. One man was complaining that he had been given only an empty envelope, which meant that his letter had fallen out somewhere or was in someone else's envelope. The monitor said, "All of you who have received letters, please check to see whether you have been given other people's by mistake." The reason for the confusion, of course, was that our letters had been opened and perhaps censored.

When we were told to disperse, we lighted a number of thoroughly dried pieces of wood—the kind we only used as tinder to start a fire—and in small groups we sat around the flickering light of the fires to read our letters from home. Both of mine began in the same way, "I and our daughter are both in good health," and added in parentheses, "Actually in good health; I mean it." The reason for the additional assurance was that now everyone had to write letters according to compulsory standards aimed at "mutually boosting each party's morale" or else, it was warned, the letters wouldn't arrive at their destination. If that happened, the fault would be entirely the writer's who did not comply with the directive that letters be written with "eagerness and enthusiasm"[11] in the heart and mind. But reading a letter full of "enthusiasm and eagerness," we often could not bring ourselves to believe what it said. The vernacular of the moment differed so much from what we had been accustomed to! What I was looking for was found at the end of my letters. Added as a postscript to the first one was the sentence, "Uncle will surely get well because he has come across a very good doctor, a graduate from a medical school in the Soviet Union. He firmly believes that Uncle's illness can be cured." In the second letter, my wife also added a postscript that read, "Uncle has great hopes of recovering from his illness very shortly because his doctor is entirely devoted to him. At present, we have made arrangements for the doctor to live near us and are meeting him every day." So I knew my family had been working on my behalf and believed they had gone to the right place. The detail about the arrangement made for the doctor to live near by worried me a bit. There were plenty of stories going around concerning Northern cadres who, because of their craving for wealth and comfort, did not hesitate to promise us the moon! While we read, the inmate whose letter was lost went from one group to another, his empty envelope in his hand, begging us to check to see whether his letter had got mixed with ours.

Having read my letters again and again, I still failed to understand the hidden meaning of some of the sentences. For example, when my wife wrote that "our daughter has grown up now and no longer insists on having her milk," did she want to express motherly pride in our daughter's rapid growth, or did she mean to complain about the shortage of milk? And did "Every day, I work actively" mean that she still had a job or that she was working very hard? She wrote that "The lady next door has asked me to give you her regards. At present, she's full of 'enthusiasm' because all her sons have passed the *tú tai* [baccalaureat] exam." In fact, all her sons were well over thirty, forty even. Surely, my

---

[11]A rendering of the short catchy phrase, *Phấn Khởi Hồ Hởi*, the word *Khởi* rhyming with the word *Hởi*, one among many phrases that the Vietnamese communists are particularly fond of.

wife wanted to say they had been *tái tù*[12] (sent back to prison); if so, the word "enthusiasm" must be understood to mean the opposite.

My wife also sent me her New Year's wishes for "good labor, good studies, and good health." Looking at the dates, I found that the letters had been written more than seven months ago, and the address on the envelopes was that of the Xuan Loc camp. The two had been written about two months apart; there must have been many changes since. If she had not written to me since, it was because she had had no replies from me. These letters must have been kept at battalion headquarters for a long time. But why wait until now to distribute them? As I was reading and rereading those sentences full of riddles, there was a shout from the *bodoi*. "Put out all the fires! Everybody must go to sleep now! The gong sounded long ago for you to turn in. Haven't you heard?"

Two *bodoi*, their AKs slung on their shoulders, yelled as they passed. We stood up and put out the fires with our feet. I returned to my sleeping place, but my eyes stayed wide open as my mind struggled with unanswered questions. A moment later, Thé slid into his place beside me.

I asked in a low voice, "Have you got a letter?"

"I've had no news from home since I reported for reeducation. No visit, no letter. Maybe my father has died."

"Nonsense! Don't be sad and don't lose faith! You'll get your letters some day!"

"I am not sad! Better this than be like Sinh, the one who got an envelope without a letter. It's pitiful to see him sit there, holding his head in his hands."

"Go to sleep now! We have to be able to work tomorrow."

The next day, the letters were the only thing the men would talk about. In the afternoon, we were told to stop work early and go back to camp to wash up and have a rest. We looked at one another as if to say we expected something new and unusual to happen. That evening, we were ordered to assemble in the open space where the meeting hall was to be built. The study monitors seemed to be cheerful, which surprised us. It was doubtful that anything pleasant was coming. Commander Thinh arrived, and a monitor shouted, "Attention," then presented himself before the commander.

"Request permission to report, commander. Assembly of inmates completed."

Commander Thinh was all smiles. As usual, he relished this kind of formality. He began to play the role of a man who took great care of people committed to his charge. "Most of you have received letters from home, right? And most of you are no doubt pleased with the news your families gave you. As for the rest, although you have not for the moment received any letters, you will hear from your families soon. I shall make the recommendation that from now on

---

[12] A play on words in which the order is inverted.

you will be allowed to write home regularly, and, naturally, you will receive letters from home regularly, at least once a month. Do you agree to that?" There was no answer from the assembled detainees. Thinh forced a smile, then continued, "Lately, I have been very busy and have had no time to talk with you. I had to carry out the plan for cultivation of the area reserved for cassava. Now, as the work has made good progress, I have gathered you here to speak about two subjects. The first is related to preparations to be made in anticipation of your relatives' visit, and the second to the proposed change regarding your daily fare."

He explained that we would have to build a house in which to receive our families. Construction would begin the following week. He did not move directly into the second subject, but began with a lengthy introduction, "What with the many difficulties our fatherland is now facing—the destruction caused by the Chinese "expansionists" on both our southwestern and northern borders, the ravages of recent typhoons, and the loss of crops to insect pests in many parts of the country—your existence must be directly affected by those factors." After further enumeration of the hardships that led to the famine that people outside were enduring at present, Thinh announced, "Beginning tomorrow, there will be a change in your rice ration. To facilitate the work of the kitchen team, you will have rice twice a week, the same quantity each time. For the rest of the week, we shall eat sweet potatoes and manioc. You will have to exercise determination to win against all difficulties and join the People in the common effort to produce more rice for the nation. When we have rice in sufficient quantity, naturally we'll change the ration again, for the better."

Hearing that we were to get less rice, we could not help complaining and cursing under our breath. The silent group of *bodoi* standing around did not shout us down as they usually did. In an attempt to change our mood, Thinh said, "By the way, I forgot to inform you of some good news. Tomorrow night and the following night, the film projection crew of the People's Army will be here to entertain you. Now, before you go, let's sing a song!"

A voice called out,"Where's Khuyen? Come up here and set the tone for the song. Ah! Khuyen's sick? Then, any of you who's willing, set the tone, will you? Remember, we will have a rest after this."

One of the inmates was urged to stand up. He asked, "What song shall we sing?"

Someone answered in a low voice, "What else? 'As if Uncle Ho was present.'"

Reluctantly, we sang to our irregular hand clapping. Then, for no reason, a laugh was suddenly heard, and the men began to sing louder; the hand clapping became more regular. Thinh also sang and clapped his hands in time, visibly pleased. When we had finished the song, he clapped his hands as a sign for us to sing again. And we did, at the top of our voices,

As if Uncle Ho was present at the Great Victory Celebration! His word has come true and we have achieved glorious victory! After thirty years of struggle for national independence, thirty years under the Democratic Republic, our fight has ended in Victory! Vietnam Ho Chi Minh, Vietnam Ho Chi Minh!

The song finished, we clapped our hands and roared with laughter.

Chapter 5

Camp Four: Bu Gia Map (cont.)

The next day, we were permitted to stop work early and go back to camp to have our meal, then prepare to go and watch the movie. At dusk, we were ordered to fall into lines and make our way to regimental headquarters. A fairly large number of inmates, upon learning that we had to go to regiment, asked to remain "home" on the pretext that they were not able to see clearly at night. As for me, I said I wanted to go just to see what the film was like, but my real aim was to take the opportunity of possibly meeting friends or acquaintances from other camps. But when we arrived at the headquarters, night had fallen; there was a new moon and not enough light to allow us to recognize anyone. We knew that inmates from as many as three camps were gathered to watch the film. The space allotted to each camp had been carefully planned with some distance between them, and we were watched closely by the *bodoi*. Before the film began, we were reminded of the rules to be observed: We were not allowed to stand up or to walk to and fro; if we wanted to go to the latrine, we had to inform our group leaders, then go to the place as directed.

A cadre of the film projection crew welcomed us, speaking through his loudspeaker in these terms: "The People's film projection crew of the province of Song Be has the pleasure of conveying to the comrades and camp inmates here present the greetings of our superior officers. We have been instructed to come here to entertain the comrades and camp inmates for two nights. Tonight, we are going to show the film entitled *Remember Your Own Name!* produced in the Democratic Republic of Germany."

The film related the story of a young boy separated from his parents, who were detained by the Nazis in a concentration camp. There were scenes of despotic German soldiers, of cold and hunger, rare visits by relatives, and strict inspection of parcels of gifts. In other words, what was being shown before our eyes to expose the criminal doings of the German fascists were the very things to which we had been subjected. The film had no subtitles; instead, there was dubbing in Vietnamese added to (but not replacing) the words the actors were speaking. For example, when a German SS soldier yelled at a prisoner who was too tired to walk fast, the Vietnamese speaker also shouted, "Can't you walk faster?"

From the audience, somebody clapped his hands and said loudly, "Perfectly identical!"

When the prison warden compelled an old lady to open her parcel of gifts, the speaker yelled in Vietnamese, "Open all your parcels, big and small!"

Again, we clapped our hands and voiced loud agreement, "How very similar! Rice, green beans, and peanuts should be 'taken back'!"

The irony of the evening was that the film affected us in a way entirely different from that expected of it. On the way back to camp, some of the men disclosed that while going to and from the latrine, they had been able to make contact with detainees from the other two camps. Apparently, the number of inmates who had escaped from those camps was much greater than from our own. According to the inmates from those camps, it was quite easy to escape across the border. They said that when making the escape, one simply needed to "hide away in the forest and wait a few days until the border guards' vigilance slacked off, then slide across."

The following day, we went to regimental headquarters again to see another film, *The Boy from Hanoi*. Most of us had seen it both at Trang Lon and Xuan Loc. We tried again to talk to people from the other camps when we went to relieve ourselves. They said that detainees of a camp in our vicinity had been transferred to an unknown destination because a great number among them had made their escape. They also informed us that a cadre had told them the reeducation camps in this area would sooner or later be moved farther inland because of the tense situation along the border.

Our daily work routine now went on as usual but the atmosphere worsened. The food provided to us consisted mainly of dried sliced manioc cooked with a little salt, which very few of us cared to eat because it was covered with mold; only those who were not able to find any wild greens or tubers were forced to eat it. Twice a week, on Thursday and Sunday, we were given rice; each of us was entitled to a half-bowl, obviously less than the portion we had received before. Many of the inmates paired off to draw lots with winners having the right to eat both rations. The majority of us moved toward self-sufficiency with wild greens and roots. As the number of detainees reporting sick grew, requests for rice gruel increased. But the rice was limited, and the gruel got thinner all the time. Those who were seriously sick and unable to consume anything other than porridge lost patience and began to curse others, less sick, who claimed a share. But they all knew the gruel was too thin to do them much good.

In this change of fare, there was an unexpected victim. Thanh, the inmate who led us in singing the night the commander told us of the cut in rations, was thrown in the disciplinary cell immediately afterward. It appeared that he was accused of intentionally ridiculing the Revolution by inciting the detainees to sing "As if Uncle Ho was present at the Great Victory Celebration," just when the ration cut was announced. A monitor claimed he saw Thanh wink to signal the men to sing as loud as they could. It was an entire month before the poor fellow was finally set free!

The carpentry team was greatly reinforced to build the meeting hall and a visitors' house. The cassava planting was done, and there remained only the land reserved for rice. I was now assigned to a team constructing a power line leading from regimental headquarters to the camp. Our every movement was strictly controlled; the *bodoi* kept constant watch over each work party. We were no longer allowed to go by ourselves to search for trees to fell. The line connecting the camp to regiment ran for about three kilometers through hills and valleys. The wire used, the *bodoi* said, was made in the Soviet Union and had been brought to this area during the war to be used to install a telephone network. It appeared to be a special category of wire—bare, with a thin copper sheath on the outside and a steel core. The *bodoi* said the line would bring electricity from regiment, which was going to be equipped with an electric generator, to the camp to operate a television set here. But it turned out to be only a telephone line. When it was operative, the *bodoi* complained that since telephone communication had been established, there were nightly alarms, sometimes intended as a drill, sometimes to alert the *bodoi* to go out and search for escapees.

We now continued with construction of the meeting hall. We were given complete liberty to do the planning. Based on our past experience, we first erected a perfectly straight high frame, then built secondary rafters and beams for the two ends of the framework. The final result was a structure entirely built of bamboo, roofed over with *lo o* because the dry season had withered all kinds of grass, including the elephant grass usually used for roofs.

Soon after the hall was built, the first heavy rain of the season poured down furiously. All the buildings in the camp except battalion headquarters leaked, and we had to stop all other work to repair the roofs. The barracks housing battalion no longer needed thatch for its roof because a number of metal sheets had been found for it. The day we were sent to fetch the sheets was another opportunity for us to learn about the life of people outside the camp.

We were driven in a truck, which had brought a load of dried manioc to camp, toward the road that had once been tarred but was now all high grass and potholes. After bumping along for a while, the truck turned onto a red dirt road that seemed newly constructed. We drove slowly along, fairly far into the forest, until we came across a number of scattered derelict houses. The place was completely deserted and appeared to be an abandoned hamlet. One house, which seemed to have been the administrative office of the hamlet, had metal sheets still in good condition on its roof. We were ordered to get on the roof and dismantle it. The work was easy because the wooden rafters to which the metal sheets had been nailed had already rotted. We used a bamboo pole to push the sheets off and the work was soon done. The *bodoi*, the monitor, and the driver had all gone to inspect the houses, so we went in search of something we could eat. Behind each house was a plot of land planted with lemon grass and hot peppers as well as patches of verdant cassava. As we busily dug up cassava roots, picked hot peppers and Indian spinach, we suddenly heard voices. A group of old women clothed in tattered uniforms of the former Southern army and carrying empty baskets on their shoulders appeared. They asked in surprise, "What are you doing, my dear sirs? Why do you destroy our houses?"

Also completely surprised, we answered, "We were ordered by the *bodoi* to come here to remove the metal sheets from the roof of this house."

At this point, the *bodoi* and monitor came back, one of them carrying a metal chair in his arms. Seeing this, the women walked toward him and, angry now, asked loudly, "Why do you take away the belongings of the People?"

A long discussion followed, with the result that the *bodoi* had to leave empty-handed. We stacked the metal sheets on the truck, then asked to be allowed to pick some more cassava roots. The monitor said, "No, if you pick their cassava, they will come out and quarrel with you. Those women are very bad. They must be townsfolk driven out because of their reactionary attitude."

A detainee, regretting the lost opportunity, insisted, "Well, just now I asked them, and they said we could take as much as we wanted."

The monitor replied, "I've said no and that's final! Why are you so obstinate?"

We climbed on the truck in silence. Each of us had in his pockets only a few hot peppers. The bunches of vegetables and cassava roots we had picked had to be left behind. The truck took more than an hour to drive back to camp. Commander Thinh invited the driver to stay and have a meal of chicken porridge with him, and the monitor reappeared to give us a basinful of uncooked cassava roots.

The house we had built for battalion had been handsome when it was just completed. Now, after only a half-year, it leaned to the side. We had to dismantle the thatched roof, reset the columns, and add extra braces to the frame. Then we covered it with the corrugated metal sheets. Doing the repair work, we discovered what had caused the building to slant—all its columns were being eaten away at the bottom by termites. In the forests, termites and ants—thousands of millions of them—were everywhere.

With the start of the rain, we had to postpone all other work to concentrate our efforts on preparing the land for rice planting. The former *lo o* forests that had been cleared and burned had left a thick layer of ash on the ground, and under it were the live shrubs and plants that we had to hoe up or pull up just as in the cassava fields. The planting area still appeared insufficient, and we were pressed with the utmost urgency to clear more land. Our food became worse and worse every day, but in the midst of this general misery, I found a new source of supply. I could steal rice meant for the pigs.

One day, when I was called upon to repair the roof of the pigsty, I realized that the *bodoi* took better care of their pigs than anything else. The pigsty was built near the battalion kitchen, and a member of the kitchen team was detailed to feed and wash the pigs and clean the sty. This task was assigned to a *bodoi*, but he usually called on a detainee to do the work under his direction. Every chore, from cutting vegetables, cooking them, and mixing them with bran, to washing the pigs and cleaning the pigsty, was done by the detainee. The two pigs in the sty had only to eat, empty their bowels, sleep, and grow fat! While I was at work on the roof, I chanced to see the *bodoi* pour into a basin a heap of the whitest white rice and put it down for the pigs! They drew near, sniffed at the rice, then knocked over the basin, spilling rice all over the ground. While we inmates suffered from hunger, while a mouthful of rice was more precious to us than gold, this was beyond endurance.

I climbed down and said, "Good heavens! How can they turn up their noses at such rice?"

The *bodoi* hastened to explain, "These last days, since it has been raining, the pigs have got stomachache due to chill, so I do not dare give them vegetables to eat. They have not recovered yet, that's why they refuse the rice."

Having said this, the *bodoi* left. I went to where the rice had been spilled on the ground near the wall, picked up a handful, and sniffed at it. The rice smelled good just as freshly cooked rice should. I hurriedly picked up my water can and dipped it into the heap of rice, filling the can to the top. I put on the lid and hid the can in the stack of thatch. When I had finished repairing the roof, I approached the *bodoi*.

"The roof has been repaired, comrade cadre."

The *bodoi* looked about fifteen or sixteen years old. When I addressed him as "comrade cadre," he seemed very pleased. In fact, only the commander and the study monitors, that is, members of the battalion staff, were entitled to be called cadre. But we all addressed young *bodoi* who liked to give themselves airs as "cadre," just for fun. This one too was filled with his own importance.

"Can you guarantee the quality of your work?" he asked.

I replied, "Just get on the roof and see for yourself. I was very careful. From here you can see that no light is getting through. I did my work very conscientiously!"

The young *bodoi* gave me further instructions, "All right! But it's still early for you to leave. Stay here for the rest of the day to do some work in the kitchen. Now, have a bite of this, then chop me some wood."

He handed me an aluminum basin containing about one bowlful of white rice and a dried fish still hot from the grill! I thanked him and enjoyed my meal right on the spot. When I had eaten, he gave me a can of warm tea made from wild tea leaves. Late in the afternoon, the *bodoi* told me to stop working and prepare to go back to my barracks. Before leaving, I carried the chopped wood into the kitchen and arranged it neatly in a corner. I said good-bye to him and asked permission to take the decayed cabbage leaves I saw in the kitchen that had been discarded.

I said, "Today, the pigs are not well, so this much cabbage is going to be thrown away. Could the cadre allow me to have it?"

The *bodoi* hesitated. "These leaves are already rotten; they're not good to eat. But take them if you want. Go and get a rest. What's your name? If I need more help in the kitchen, I'll ask for you."

I gave my name, thanked him, said, "Good-bye, comrade cadre," and left. I went to the stream to wash up. I took off my shirt, wrapped the cabbage leaves in it, then took it into the stream to wash away the rotten part without losing the small pieces, still hard and unaffected by the decay. That evening, I managed to cook three cans of porridge with the rice I had taken from the pigs and mixed it with the cabbage I had saved. The porridge had a particularly delicious flavor; rarely had I ever had the occasion to taste white rice porridge flavored with the famous Dalat cabbage! I shared this meal with Thé and told him of the possibility of finding something to eat at the pigsty.

He said, "I am now working at the construction of a charcoal kiln to produce charcoal for the smithy. It's near the pigsty, so it would be easy for me to get there." From that day on, Thé and I often stole and ate rice reserved for the pigs.

To get more land for cultivation, we now had to clear areas where big trees grew. The work was extremely hard, our bodies did not have the strength and resistance of our first days at the camp, and we were not able to fulfill the norms. Everyone was discouraged, including our guards. Many of the *bodoi* were exhausted; the young ones who had recently come from the North also suffered from malaria. After a few bouts of the fever, they were as pale as a budding leaf. From time to time, out of pity, the young guards allowed us to rest longer than was usually permitted, and sometimes they approached middle-aged inmates to comfort them and assure them that they found no pleasure in seeing them forced into reeducation camps. There was no lack of pessimism among the *bodoi* themselves, who were fed up with the present situation and who disagreed with the policy of the present regime.

The prospect of rice planting brought its share of gloom. The *bodoi* seemed very worried. They made us stop work on the visitors' house and concentrate on clearing land. More rain fell, and the number of sick inmates increased. Morale got so low that no one cared to make jokes any more. One evening at rice distribution, there was again an unclaimed ration, again an emergency assembly and roll call. To our great surprise, Dr. Bui Tran Anh was found once more to have gone! Somebody said that he would surely reappear the following morning on some pretext that there had been too much rain or too many mosquitoes. But he did not come back this time, and after a while, no one spoke of him any more.

We had not yet stopped talking about Dr. Anh's escape when two more inmates living in the far end of the barracks opposite ours were found missing one morning. The camp command apparently concluded that the atmosphere was promoting escapes, for it suddenly changed the work program. The carpentry team was ordered to complete the visitors' house without delay, and all of us were allowed to write home to inform our relatives of permission to come and visit us.

For the first time, we learned the precise location of our camp—northwest Song Be Province—so we could tell our families. Letters were posted, and our morale improved. Everyone hoped that his family would bring medicine and especially food. While waiting for our families, we worked at a snail's pace in the fields, but this dilatoriness earned no reprimand from the guards.

When all the land had been cleared and was almost ready for sowing, Khanh chose some of his most trusted hands to go out to measure the area. Later on it was reported to us that the plots totaled over seventy hectares; someone also said that the measuring team had left some small pieces of cleared land unrecorded. It rained more frequently, and we got orders to sow the rice. We were divided into teams of six each, three using pointed sticks to make holes in the soil and three following behind putting five to ten seeds into each hole, then covering them with earth. The method was primitive and slow. From time to time, a guard would dig up a hole to check if the number of seeds was as specified since most of us were unfamiliar with this kind of work. It soon became obvious that very few of us had fulfilled the norms set by the camp authority. We pointed out that digging holes with a pointed stick was slow and that the holes got too small, which made it hard to sow the correct number of seeds. We suggested that hoes would get better results. Commander Thinh and most study monitors retorted that we were not in any position to give opinions on farming matters, and Monitor Thang, who was known as an experienced peasant, added: "What the hell do you know about farming to dare suggest a new method?"

We had to remain silent then, but the next day some of us set out for work bringing hoes along. The handles had pointed ends that could be used like the sticks when the guards were watching and turned around to be used as hoes when they were out of sight. With the hoes, the work was indeed quicker and easier, and the sowing more accurate. These hoes had been made by us in the camp's only workshop; the metal blades were only as wide as the palm of my hand, just right for our pitiful strength. My work team was able to fulfill its norm every day, with all of us using hoes. Most others followed suit. Finally, the news reached the ears of the study monitors, and they and Commander Thinh promptly turned up at the field. Monitor Thang took charge.

"You are such a headstrong, disobedient lot! I challenge your method. I myself will use a pointed stick to make holes in the soil for one of my men to plant, and two of you will use your so-called new method. Let's see which is quicker!"

He was so cocksure. Some of us began to lose confidence. One man stepped forward and said, "I volunteer to show our method. Please let me choose my partner."

This was greeted with applause and relaxed laughter as we sensed some excitement. Thang picked a confident-looking *bodoi*. We chose one of our best men to join the brave fellow who had volunteered. They hoed and planted, expertly and accurately. Meanwhile, the *bodoi* had to stoop over every time to get the seeds inside the deep and very small holes made by that pointed stick.

At first, both sides moved at the same pace, but gradually the inmates gained ground. Some *bodoi* even checked their results, as if trying to find some fault. The two *bodoi* were left farther and farther behind. There were triumphant laughter and applause in the inmates' ranks and silence on the other side. Finally, somebody shouted, "That's enough. You can have your own way from now on, but make sure you do it correctly." We thought we had won a victory, but it turned out to our disadvantage; our quota was stepped up, and we ended up doing more work!

The rainy season brought a new hazard. A downpour often came suddenly when we were toiling in the open fields; the cold rainwater soaked our perspiring bodies, and we caught colds easily. Those who had had malaria went first. The labor force dropped markedly, and finally we were allowed to take shelter whenever the rain started. We were ordered to stay indoors whenever it rained in the early morning, even if it meant no work at all was being done that day. It was noted that this unusual practice made escape more difficult. Several escapes had taken place during rains when everyone was scattering, seeking shelter over a wide area. It took the guards a while to regroup us, and by that time the escapees had covered quite a distance.

Cassava plants were growing in response to the abundant rainfall; some were over a meter high, and the camp was surrounded by the fresh color of the cassava leaves.

The carpentry team partitioned separate living quarters in the visitors' house and also built latrines, bathhouses, and a large common room for the expected visitors. We were also instructed to build a big wooden porch, which we were just finishing when the first visitors arrived. But the excitement turned to shock and worry when we learned what had happened to them.

I was putting the finishing touches on a wooden plaque when I saw a dilapidated coach approaching; it pulled up at the porch to let out a couple of older people and a boy of about fifteen. They looked frightened and were empty-handed. The old man asked, "Is this Camp 3721 of Song Be Province?"

The guard, who had been supervising us at a distance, rushed up shouting, "You're not allowed to talk to each other without permission! Visitors, get to your quarters! Yes, this is Camp 3721."

As I was standing behind the guard, I signaled the boy asking him why they were not bringing anything. He understood and replied in a low voice but loud enough for everyone to hear, "We were robbed on the way."

We were amazed. Even the guard was taken aback. "Why? When? Where were you robbed?" he asked.

The boy answered, "We were robbed this morning on Highway 14. We were stopped and searched by local militiamen, who stole all our cash. They also took all our parcels of gifts that we brought for my father."

The old man hurriedly corrected the boy for fear of offending the servants of the Revolution. "They said they were local militiamen who had orders to search for smuggled goods such as rice, tins of condensed milk, etc., but I think they were actually robbers. The parcels actually did contain such smuggled goods. After this we thought of returning, but our fellow passengers advised us to go on since we were near our destination. We got to the town of Phuoc Binh and changed to another coach."

"That's enough," the guard stopped him short. "Now get to the visitors' quarters. Someone else will meet with you in a minute."

News of visitors being robbed spread like wildfire through the camp that evening, and it remained the main topic of conversation for several days. Thé had somehow pieced together the information that travelers everywhere were rumored to be subject to searches and indiscriminate confiscation of goods. The bus had been stopped and the passengers robbed in the early hours of the morning on a deserted stretch of Highway 14.

The air was heavy with worry. More visitors turned up the next day, but they had had an uneventful journey on a different route direct from Saigon. However, they had passed a coach that had started much earlier and had been robbed. We all feared that our own families might meet the same fate on their journey.

The study monitor who came to our quarters in the evening to call the roll let us know that the camp command had informed "higher command" about these incidents and asked them to put the situation right. The number of visitors increased as the days passed. Some inmates began to cook the food brought in by their families, the whole camp bustled with activity, and our mood brightened.

Every day saw about twenty families arriving. We told them about the amount of visiting time allocated to each inmate. This business of time allocation caused a lot of anger among us; some were allowed to see their visitors for a few hours. Some for only a half-hour, while others were allowed to stay overnight with their families in the visitors' quarters.

We complained to the camp command about this discrepancy in treatment. It was noted that those we suspected of being informers were the most favored and those who were given only half-hour visits were those well known for their negative comments on the Revolution. When the truth finally dawned on us, those like me, who had been closely monitored and frequently reported on, grew very anxious.

One day an inmate who had been too ill to do outdoor work set about, out of boredom, stealing some newspapers and books from group leader Khanh, who had been able to borrow the reading material from the *bodoi*. This fellow came across a small notebook hidden in Khanh's rucksack; it contained details of inmates' activities, together with such comments as "belonging to pro-American family," "has a tendency to vilify the Revolution," "lazy, avoiding labor," etc. The discovery of Khanh as a callous informer spread among us like a plague, all the more so because his status ensured his effectiveness in reporting on us. Our reaction was mixed; some worried because they had quarreled with Khanh, some were disgusted, and others tried to gain merit with him by giving him gifts or food. Hao, well known for his fiery temper, was furious with Khanh because he suspected he may have had something to do with his visiting time being cut short. Hao confronted the group leader, swore at him, and called him all sorts of abusive names, which Khanh tolerated since he feared what Hao might do in retaliation if he dared challenge him.

Visitors kept coming. One family was so disturbed at the condition of their son that they continued to visit him every two weeks to bring him medicine and supplies. To obtain an official travel permit each time, they had to find a plausible motive for the visit.

One day I returned from the fields to hear that my wife, daughter, and sister-in-law were there. How good it would be to see my loved ones again! I waited and waited for somebody from the camp command to call me; night was falling, but my name was not called and some others had even been allowed out twice! Thé said to me, "It's obvious that you have somehow been blacklisted!"

He then went off to see Duoc, the fellow who had come across Khanh's evil notebook, and was informed that my name was indeed in that notebook although Duoc could not recall what had been written about me. Hearing this, I was outraged. My family, who had endured many hardships to get here only to be told that I was not available, could only witness the happiness of others' reunion. I could not even manage to steal a look at them as the visitors' quarters was near the camp command and therefore closely guarded. I hoped against hope that my turn would come the next day.

But in the morning to my intense disappointment I was given a work assignment as usual. Anger gave me courage, and I went straight to see Khanh.

"I beg the group leader to tell Commander Thinh that I wouldn't mind being punished for whatever crime I have committed, but my wife and daughter are innocent. They shouldn't have to wait forever to see me, witnessing other people's reunions, and not knowing whether they will see me at all."

My voice quavered with barely controlled emotion, and seeing that I meant business, Khanh quickly gave in. "I was not aware that your wife and daughter are here! I'll see the commander right away! Please do not believe what has been said about me. It's only because some foul-mouthed people want to destroy me because I happen to be appointed camp leader!" He then went off in the direction of the command center and came back after a while to tell me to put on my best clothes and go to see my visitors. My anger evaporated as fast as it had come over me.

I reported to the command center and was met by Monitor Chuong, who was famous for his lack of generosity. He said, "You are granted half-an-hour's visiting time. You've got to report for work after that. You will be allowed to see them again in the evening." Again I was overcome with anger and indignation; most people had been spared a whole day's work in order to be with their visitors. I could only say yes, as at this moment there was nothing else I could do.

A fine screen of mist had descended over the visitors' quarters. My legs could barely carry me fast enough. At last I found them—my wife, my little daughter, and my sister-in-law and two of her children. My daughter was still asleep, lying on the dirty floor. She looked so innocent! My wife had changed; she was thin and pale. I felt heartbroken! My wife could not control her tears and could hardly speak at the sight of me. My sister-in-law and her children moved out to leave us some privacy. All my wife could say was, "How are you?" I only nodded. I rushed to my daughter and picked her up, hugging her. She woke up, gazed at me, and then her face broke into a smile. I asked my wife, "How have you managed to feed yourselves? Have you been ill recently; you don't look well! I have only half-an-hour's visiting time now, and then I'll have to go out to work. I have somehow been cursed! If you have anything important to say, say it now."

"We have been trying to get you out," said my wife. "It's hopeful because our patron holds an important government post. He has promised to arrange for your release. We have also applied to an international organization to lobby for your release, among our other efforts. A high official has promised that the matter would be dealt with in due course. Therefore, you've got to keep up your spirits! Don't ever try to escape! We all believe that you will be released soon; there's no need to do anything extreme!"

My sister-in-law and her children came back. I asked her, "How have you managed with so many mouths to feed?"

"Well, we have to eat sweet potatoes and maize to supplement the rice;

there's not much we can do. Everyone is in the same boat, hungry and miserable. There's no way to find a job; they've all been reserved for the Revolution's followers. Even our technical specialists are unemployed. Those who have been to the New Economic Zones have had to return to the city, mostly due to all sorts of illnesses. The people were forced to move to these zones; they are remote and inaccessible areas, and there is no sanitation whatsoever. By now, everyone is afraid of going there. We have asked for permission to stay in Saigon because we have young children who would not be able to endure life in a New Economic Zone. Had it not been for our large number of children, we would have been kicked out of our own home! All these Northerners want is to get rid of us so that their families up there can move in and stay here forever!"[1]

When I asked about their education, my nephew and niece told me that the time for academic subjects had been reduced to make room for compulsory labor, learning revolutionary songs, and political education. Labor consisted of planting cassava plants in the schoolyard, sweeping public roads, building a porch onto the school building, and so on. Political education consisted of lectures about socialism and imperialism and in taking part in government-sponsored demonstrations, painting slogans, and similar activities.

Seeing that visiting time was nearly up, I turned to my five-year-old daughter and asked, "What do you do at home?"

"I go to school every day, and I have lots of friends there!" She was, by far, the most cheerful of us all.

Finally I stood up, preparing to leave. "I have to go to work now. I'll see you in the evening. Prepare your meal now."

My wife hastily went through a bag and brought out a *banh tet*. Now, I noted that she had brought me two bags full of food. I presented myself at the command center as required, then went to see Thé to ask him to smuggle in the food. Thé was working at the forge, which happened to be near the visitors' quarters; he had smuggled in supplies from visitors before by hiding them in bags of charcoal.

My head was filled with thoughts of my loved ones; I went about my work like a robot. My stomach was full thanks to that nourishing piece of *banh tet*. That afternoon, again donning my best clothes, I waited to be called. Time dragged by and nothing happened. At last, deciding I had had enough, I went to the command center and was met by Monitor Thang.

"I was promised by a study monitor that I would be allowed to see my visitors again this evening," I said.

---

[1]After the fall of South Vietnam, many North Vietnamese saw the South as a rich country with unlimited opportunities. It was actually a government policy to move North Vietnamese cadres south to fill the newly created government posts. With this came the practice of taking over living quarters formerly belonging to Southern owners.

"Which study monitor?"

"Study Monitor Chuong, cadre!"

Thang looked convinced, but he leafed through a small notebook until he came across something, at which he paused, then read slowly and carefully. Eventually he said, "You are granted an hour's visit; after that, bring whatever gift you have from your visitors here to be examined. I repeat, one hour's visit. I am counting the time now; off you go!"

I thought of protesting, but decided it would be a waste of time. Whatever was in that notebook of his must be very important! I thanked him and hurried off. Thang called after me, "Don't forget to tell your visitors to leave tomorrow to make room for others!"

I told my wife that we would have only one hour together since I had somehow been damned. "Why is it that one man spent last night with his family here and now he is here again, while you have only been granted two hours so far!"

I shrugged. "That's the way it is here! The whole business is entirely dependent on the study monitors' whims. I am still more fortunate than those who are allowed only a half-hour's visiting time!"

We sat down to supper. It had been nearly three years since I had last had a hot meal like this. How delicious a proper meal tasted! My wife and my sister-in-law ate very little, leaving most of the food for me and the children. My wife had somehow regained her composure. She told me that she still kept in touch with her relatives in France; they sent her some supplies and medicine once in a while, and the latter she had put aside for me and and actually brought with her. I felt somewhat consoled to know that my family was still better off than most others I had heard about. We talked on, the main topic being ways to get my release as early as possible.

"How stupid we were," said my sister-in-law. "If only we had bought some sort of paper certifying that we had positively contributed to the Revolution; it could be used as a means to win your release. It's the only thing that works nowadays!"

"I am not so sure about that," I said, "but it's become clear that such things as a sudden amnesty or the intervention of some high official is just rubbish. The only thing we can do is wait and see until we're overcome from illness and exhaustion. Then someone may be released for medical treatment. Otherwise, we will have to be here forever, which we are all convinced is the case."

My sister-in-law comforted me. "Don't let your thoughts destroy your hopes! You've got to believe in something. They just can't keep so many people like this forever!"

"That's exactly what we thought when we first registered for reeducation. We deceived ourselves by reasoning that it would be impossible to detain millions of people because there wouldn't be enough space to hold them! Now look what you see here. There is plenty of space to hold millions of people in these vast jungles. It has even been rumored that we might have to build a pan-Vietnamese route, not just clear a few jungle plots like this!"

"No! You will be released soon! The person we are cultivating is a very, very important government official. In addition, the international organization I've told you about has also promised us! Other people may have to stay here, but you will be out! Don't be so dejected!"

"Don't worry! I'm not dejected! You can go on with your 'lobbying,' but be cautious! I am not losing hope because I didn't have hope in the first place! What's important is to take care of yourselves. For my part, I will stand up to the hardships and will be out of here sooner or later! It's obvious that we are meant to be here for a long, long time. Who will clear the jungles! Who will tend the land if all of us are released tomorrow!"

"Somehow my instinct keeps telling me that you will be out soon," my wife said. "I sometimes talk to high-ranking officials while working as an interpreter for foreign delegations; they all confirm that you junior officers will be released soon."

"I only hope that your instinct and your information are right! Our will power tells us that we can endure all sorts of hardships, but we can't control our bodies indefinitely. Some who have been seriously ill are waiting to die; a few can't even move about at all! Some doctor-inmates say this is due to a lack of vitamin B. But even one of these chaps manages to tell jokes or sing now and then. If one is destined to die young, one has to accept it! Some of those who are seriously ill have gone through periods of raving fever, alternating with lucid periods of relative health; they've been like this for months. Whenever we come across them, instead of asking how they are, we ask if they are ready for their release! We mean being released once and for all!"

My sister-in-law forced a smile at my attempt to brighten up the atmosphere. "How can you joke in this condition?" she said. "If you two have something important to say, say it now before the time is up; also try to eat some more!"

"I really want to have some more, but I just can't! We've all got used to eating less."

"You have really been 'reeducated' in some sense. My children always complain of being hungry although they eat quite a lot!"

"That's because they are still growing. They need extra nourishment, not just rice and sweet potatoes. Here we are kept in a state of perpetual hunger, sometimes so hungry that we do not have the strength to lift a hoe. Therefore, we have to find some way to keep our stomachs full in order to have the strength to work at all."

"Maybe I'll have to apply your method to my children!"

"No way! They're not inmates like us. Now, let's be serious. I think the time is up."

I embraced my little daughter, asking her teasingly, "Did you enjoy being here?" She shook her head. I caught my wife signaling her not to do that; the little girl turned to her mother in puzzlement, and to my amazement, she said, "I don't want to be here! I am afraid of dying!"

"It's because the journey was so rough," my wife explained. "At one time the coach was just tumbling downhill as if out of control because the road was slippery with mud; we were all terrified. We spent that night in Phuoc Binh, sleeping on the stalls in the market as there was no inn. We had to take turns watching our luggage—there were beggars hanging around. It poured rain, and the thunder was so loud that the poor child hid herself in my lap and kept crying, 'I am so afraid.' That's how the idea of death came to her, I think."

I handed my daughter back to her mother and kissed my nephew and niece. My wife whispered in my ear, "Don't ever try to escape, will you?"

"Don't be silly! Have I ever talked about escaping? Why do you keep worrying about that?"

"You know why! Some of our neighbors who were being 'reeducated' have managed to escape, and their families back home have been questioned by the police, followed by them day and night, forced to report periodically at police stations. Their homes were even searched by the police in the middle of the night. One night when the police swooped down on the home of one escapee, hoping to catch him by surprise, they found only an empty house. Everything was intact, but no one was in sight! No one knows where the whole family has gone!"

My sister-in-law added, "Although life here is surely difficult, you have more or less settled down. At home, some people who held only minor government posts are now the worst off. They have been subjected to all sorts of harassment. They have to do compulsory labor starting at 4 A.M. They are shunned at public meetings like lepers; they are constantly reminded that they should show their gratitude to the Revolution for sparing them from reeducation; they have to show up when called to do any kind of work, day or night! There's nothing they can do. Some who dared to protest were whisked away for some periods of 'local reeducation' where they had to pay all expenses themselves! They also received 'special treatment' at these 'local reeducation centers.'"

This was the first time that I heard of "local reeducation centers." I tried to calm them down. "Don't worry! I won't try to do any silly thing. As for you, don't hesitate when an opportunity comes along. Think of yourself and our daughter first; try to forget me as if I didn't exist at all! I really mean it! I wouldn't mind suffering so long as I knew both of you were safe and happy. No, I won't be content to be kept here forever. Once you have settled down, I will be free to do whatever I've planned . . ."

"No! You don't have to plan anything," interrupted my wife, shaking her head. "I don't want to do anything for my own benefit. I can see that you've already made up your mind, haven't you?"

Seeing that I would not budge an inch, she turned to my sister-in-law, who advised me not to "try anything silly. We will try our best to get you out. There's still hope; our contacts are reliable. Don't let your impatience interfere with our efforts!"

Suddenly, we heard the hateful voice of group leader Khanh. "Time is up. All inmates return for work immediately."

Gently pushing our little girl toward me, my wife told her to give me a big kiss. "Daddy's going to leave for work now."

Giving me a long kiss and hug, she mumbled, "Daddy, go with me, don't stay here."

My heart ached. I trembled, feeling a lump in my throat. Trying to hold my tears, I tightly embraced my wife and my little daughter. At last I forced a smile, "I'll be with you again soon."

I ran all the way back. Group leader Khanh was already there, giving out assignments. He stopped me and ordered, "Vu, you take the carpentry team to the command center to do some repairs. Arrange among yourselves how to carry that heap of bamboo I have selected. Once you get there, somebody will supervise you."

I went about grouping the carpentry team without saying a word. Seeing my gloom, one fellow asked, "Chief, why are you so glum? How is your family?"

"Now, leave him alone," intervened another. "You know nobody is cheerful right after parting from his family."

I turned to the task. "Let's see how we're going to carry these damn bamboo."

There were fifteen of us and forty-five bamboo trunks, each about seven meters long. This kind of bamboo was almost solid and thus quite heavy; one would be a real load for a normal person; here it was intended for each of us to carry three at once! On the way to the worksite, we had to pass the visitors' quarters. I suddenly realized that every member whom Khanh had assigned to the team happened to have his wife, his children, or his parents staying in the visitors' quarters at that moment! We hoisted the loads on our shoulders and made our way toward battalion command. As we passed the visitors' house, we saw them all there looking at us from a mere five meters away. I saw the pain on my wife's face. My sister-in-law, my nephew, and niece also caught a glimpse of me, and they stood motionless and silent. I forced a smile, one hand balancing the bamboo, the other waving at them. My body involuntarily bent under the heavy load. I quickened my pace. Out of the sight of my loved ones, I let my tears fall. Obviously, the whole scene had somehow been arranged! I did not mind the humiliation and suffering on my own, but it was different to have my loved ones share it.

As experience had taught us, the first thing I did later that evening after repairing the command center roof was to organize my new supplies. Perishable food items were handed out to closest friends; this was more calculation than altruism, for I could rest in the sure knowledge that the food would be "returned" to me when a friend received his "gifts" from his visitors. However, altruism did extend to those who had lost contact with their families and were thus deprived of any of these luxuries.

Like me, others who had received visitors that day were disturbed at what they had learned about life outside. Our morale had not been raised after seeing our families. Why was it that things were worse off now that the long war had ended and the country had finally been united? At least life should have returned to normal, promises should have materialized. And what would become of *us?* We had learned nothing concrete from our visitors regarding the new government's policy toward reeducation camp inmates.

The guards' routine had been interrupted, especially by the presence of the female visitors. Most of the *bodoi* were mere teenagers. They tended to drift toward the visitors' quarters just to look at the women. Some visitors and guards even managed to talk a bit. One day, escorting the carpentry team to its worksite, a young *bodoi* ventured, "I saw your wife and children the other day; they were so lively and friendly; but I noted that you weren't that cheerful. Why is that? You are quite fortunate to have a family like that! You've no need to be so glum; you will be able to rejoin them once your reeducation has been completed."

"I've got only a little daughter. The other children are my niece and nephew. Did you actually talk to them?"

"Yes, I did. I was attracted to that lively bunch of kids. Your wife told me some very interesting things about Saigon. You are more fortunate than me because you at least have visitors. I haven't seen my family for four years, since being moved south. I have been trying to get leave, but it's not yet my turn! It's nearly impossible to get any gift parcels from the North. You can get everything here easily because it's a rich country. Over there it's a real problem to earn one's own bread, let alone send gifts to relatives. Visits are impossible."

"It's true that my own family is not being hard-pressed at the moment, but they will be in the long run if I have to stay here."

"Why? Can't your wife work? If your brother can manage with that number of kids, why can't your wife with only one child?"

"She says that those who have had something to do with the previous regime find it impossible to get a job. We have to draw on our savings or sell our belongings, but they won't last forever."

"Don't worry! The Party and the Revolution will take care of everything!"

Seeing that the talk was about to turn into a propaganda session, I changed the subject. "I've just received some good coffee from my wife. Would you like to share it with us? Please come to see us in the evening. Sometimes I'd like to chat with the *bodoi*, but there seem to be orders for you not to."

"There's no such order! Of course we'll come over if we are free."

He hurried off, and someone said, "It would be a waste of coffee."

"Never mind. Just dilute it. Let's have some fun with them. Just imagine, they might never have had coffee before! They are not much better off than us. All they have day after day are dried fish and rice."

"Bullshit! You have feelings for those damned communists? Even those dried fish and rice are beyond our reach! I knew you must have been up to something when you invited him; I can't imagine you're feeling sorry for them!"

"Well, you seem to know everything."

That evening I confided to Thé and Chiêu. "I've invited some young soldiers for coffee. Let's make some now, diluted of course. We'll meet at that spot near the chicken coop where we can talk safely."

Thé shook his head knowingly. "You must have been talked into this by that cunning Hung. Is he the one who has a coarse voice and used to hang around the workshop?"

"No, that's not the one! This one seems to be innocent enough, judging from his look. I know full well who Hung is."

The ground coffee was wrapped with a piece of cloth and then boiled to produce a brownish liquid. Tasting it, Thé complained that it was rather thin; he added some salt after putting sugar into it.

"What the hell are you doing," exclaimed Chiêu, "putting salt into good coffee?"

"Diluted coffee will pass only if salt is added after sugar," I explained. "We will serve proper coffee when we have our own café!"

At the spot where we were to meet, there were some low bamboo stools. The place had been carefully chosen so that meetings could be held out of hearing of suspected moles; clothes had also been deliberately hung up here to dry. As we talked, two *bodoi* were seen discreetly approaching us from behind the hut. Seeing that they were rather hesitant, I spoke first. "Please come here. We've been waiting for you."

"Where have you been? It took us quite a while to find you! I've asked comrade Lam to come along as well."

I got up to show them they should sit a little distance from us; this was the result of an incident at our previous camp in which a *bodoi* had been reprimanded for having shaken hands with an inmate—"a person who has been stripped of his citizenship," in the words of the *bodoi*'s superiors.

In the firelight we could see that Lam was baring his forearm, showing off a watch, although this was mosquito feeding time when it was essential for everyone to cover his body from head to toe. He also sported a big radio set, an item the *bodoi* associated with wealth.

"May I introduce myself," I said. "My name is Vu. This is Chiêu, and this is Thé."

"My name is Ty. I have just been assigned here. I used to have some talks with inmates at a camp for majors of the former regime. They have been moved elsewhere; now this is the only camp in this region. To be honest, we sometimes want to have a chat with you, just to exchange viewpoints or to kill time."

"So do we! And we all want to complete our reeducation as early as possible so that we can rejoin our families."

"Everytime I see you fellows, I always hear the same thing! Have you made enough progress to deserve that?"

"Oh yes, we have. We all now know how to grow rice and vegetables, to find edible roots and leaves in the jungle, and so on. We have really made progress! All we want now is to be given a piece of this jungle land, clear it, and make a living out of it with our families. Without our loved ones, life is quite boring here. I must say that you're quite amazing, being able to live in the midst of a jungle for ages, with little hope of visiting your families."

"We do feel homesick sometimes, but we've got to carry out our duties to the State and the Party."

"If I were you, I would have to 'disappear' once in a while, just to go back to some town where there is civilization. We are running the risk of being turned into apes, staying in this corner of the jungle as we are now. Why haven't you tried to go to town sometimes? Are you content to stay in camp day after day, even on holidays? Don't you ever have leave? When I was with the former armed forces, I used to go to town whenever I was on leave; otherwise I would go nuts!"

"Who doesn't want to go to town?" sighed Ty. "But it depends on one's means. Although we say that we'd rather sacrifice our leaves to carry out our duties, it's really because we don't have the means to do anything else. I don't have enough to go to a town, nor any relatives in the South. Comrade Lam here has been on leave twice this year because he has relatives in Saigon. The first time he came back he had a watch, the second time a radio set!"

"I've got a rich uncle in Saigon," Lam explained with a smile. "He always seems to have some relatives visiting from the North."

Chiêu, who had been silent, now interrupted. "Can your set tune in to a Saigon station?"

As if annoyed, Lam replied, "My set can tune in to Hanoi, VOA—let alone a Saigon station!"

"We used to borrow a radio set from a cadre when we were at the first camp in Xuan Loc," said Chiêu. "We have been out of touch with the outside world since we came here. Even the commander's set doesn't help; it's too weak. Could you now tune in to some music, just to see what it's like?"

Consulting his watch in the firelight, Lam said, "It's nearly time for the BBC world news."

Hearing that, Chiêu jumped up, moving closer to the *bodoi*. "Please let us listen to the BBC for a while! Can you really tune in? Isn't it hard to tune in to the BBC?"

Lam twisted a dial, then that familiar opening theme was heard, clearly. "That's indeed the BBC," I said. "It's clear. I think it has been relayed by satellite."

The tune came to an end, followed by a few seconds of silence. Then we heard a woman's voice speaking in English over the crackling of atmospheric interference: "This is the Asian service of the BBC . . ." We jumped up, ". . . broadcasting from London." Our hearts beat harder as the words rang in our ears. Suddenly Lam switched the set off. Chiêu groaned. "Oh, God! Please let us listen to it for a few minutes. Why do you . . ."

"No, no, I can't," interrupted Lam, pointing behind him.

"The special guards are near here," explained Ty. "They are deployed to ambush anyone trying to escape. The sound of the radio can be heard quite a distance on a still night like this one, and you know what would happen to us if we are caught red-handed."

Knowing that he was right, Thé joked, "Well, what's the point of listening to the BBC; the Hanoi station is much more reliable. Let's have some coffee."

Chiêu just sat there without saying a word, his eyes fixed on the set, while we poured out the coffee. Ty told us about his one trip to the town of Phuoc Binh. One Sunday, unable to resist the temptation of going to town, he set out early in the morning on foot, as there was no available transport. It took him the whole morning to get there. He spent his savings of fifteen dong on a sandwich, a bowl of soup, and a glass of sugarcane juice, and he spent his time hanging around the town's main marketplace, which was under preparation for the New Year holiday. He then walked all the way back, reaching camp at midnight. He reckoned he had covered altogether more than sixty kilometers, including a trek through a forest. He was exhausted, and it took him a few days to recover. Ty said he would never repeat the trip; he was not the only one to go to Phuoc Binh, he added, but others had hitchhiked to the town and then returned on foot.

Eventually, we got to the main point: finding out whether the *bodoi* would buy scarce items for us. To our relief, they quickly consented. As they were about to leave, Chiêu ventured a proposal: "When we were at Xuan Loc camp a *bodoi* took pity on us and lent us his radio set. We paid for the batteries since they were expensive. We were very grateful to him. Now, is it possible for you to lend us your set for one day? We promise that we'll take good care of it, and of course we'll pay for the batteries."

Ty looked at Lam, asking, "What do you think?"

"What would happen to me if our superiors learned of this?" said Lam, hesitating. "I don't see what good it can do you. Besides, you would certainly be punished if you were caught listening to foreign broadcasts. Thank you for the coffee!"

"It's nothing. We really enjoyed the talk. Please feel free to come again whenever you like."

Ty told us to extinguish the fire as it was near bedtime, and they left. We stayed on a bit after the *bodoi* were out of sight.

"Well, we have exchanged the coffee for a useful piece of information," I remarked. "Now that we know special guards are deployed beyond that fence, we will be more cautious with our private conversation."

Still fuming over his missed chance to listen to the BBC, Chiêu said, "I nearly went mad when that guy switched off the set, the bastard! Believe me, I will somehow manage to lay my hands on it one day. I used to be able to listen to the BBC and VOA at Xuan Loc in return for repairs and maintenance work for a friend of mine. It's a shame that these *bodoi* here are so poor!"

The main topic of conversation in camp still centered around what we had learned from our visitors about life outside. One inmate disclosed to me that his sponsor—in fact his only hope—had been placed under house arrest. This man was none other than the lawyer Trinh Dinh Thao, a leader of the People's Movement for Peace, which was one of the constituents of the National Liberation Front, the South Vietnamese communist organizational apparatus. It was clear that the conflict between North and South Vietnamese communists had now come out in the open. Ironically, this was also a cause for despair for some inmates who had high hopes pinned on relatives who were South Vietnamese communists.

Our physical well-being was improved day by day thanks to the extra food brought by our visitors. The results were most conspicuous among those who had been immobilized for weeks by serious illness. It took the worst cases about two weeks to fully recover after receiving proper medicines.

The rice fields had been sowed, leaving the cassava fields to be weeded. The abominable weeds had been growing at an alarming rate after the rainfall. We had to worm our way through tracts of cassava to pull the weeds; the work was as back-breaking as hoeing. Early morning rainy spells were greeted with joy as we were then ordered to stay indoors. Bad days were when the rains caught us at work in the fields in the jungle. Hunger was then added to our misery because it was nearly impossible to keep a fire going in the wet to cook anything. We protected ourselves from the rain to a certain extent with raincoats or sheets of plastic, except when the wind came with the rain and tore at our bodies. It was cold and damp everywhere, even inside.

Reading material was in great demand on these rainy days. As time went by, books became, after food, the most sought-after item. We also had been trying our best to hold on to our last pieces of paper. Almost any type of paper had become scarce as there was no place to get any, isolated as we were. Finding toilet paper was especially difficult. Eventually we had none at all. Some followed the *bodoi*'s example by using leaves, but the most common practice was to carry a bottle of water with which to clean ourselves.

I was lucky to have bought the *Selected Works of Lenin*. Every sheet of the thick volumes was made of high-quality paper manufactured in the Soviet Union. I had bought them out of a desire to learn something about the theory of communism, with no idea of their actual value. The last volume was sacrificed first, then the next to the last, and so on. I did not recall how many of the books had been used in this way nor what they were about as I did not have time to read them. All I knew was that the paper was quite tough, and I would crumple a piece of it over and over again until it became as soft as a piece of cloth. It was quite consoling to know that I still had some luxury, unlike most others.

One rainy day as we sat on the floor with our arms around our knees, brooding, I felt an urge to read. I went through my bag. As soon as I produced a book, eager eyes were directed at me; it was the first volume of the *Selected Works of Lenin*. The more I read, the more I wondered why I had not read it before; everything in the book fitted in perfectly with what had happened so far. For example, the Great Leader preached that in the first phase of a newly formed State of the Proletariat, it would be possible for its cadres to possess only basic skills, such as reading, writing, and fundamental arithmetic, to run the government. No wonder, I thought, that they detained scientific and technical specialists, medical doctors, engineers, and even schoolteachers.

It gradually became our habit to discuss the pros and cons of Marxism-Leninism on rainy days as we could not venture outdoors. Spare time on better days was devoted to gathering leaves and roots, setting traps for mice or squirrels, or mending clothes. Nevertheless, having read the *Selected Works,* we became more and more thoughtful. We openly discussed politics, something we had not attempted before for fear of being reported on by informers. At first, under our new government, most of us felt obliged to conform in order to adapt to a new way of life, having accepted that it was impossible to "turn back the tide." We had naively believed that life would be easier for us once we conformed. That illusion had long since been shattered by reality.

It had become clear to us that not only we but also our families were being subjected to systematic discrimination, having been labeled as *nguy* elements. They were forced to move to the isolated, desolate New Economic Zones where it was nearly impossible to eke out a living. And all these acts had been carried out according to the "sound, scientific" teachings of Lenin. The more we dug into Leninism, the more apparent it became to us that such terms as "class struggle," "revolutionary alertness," "maintenance of the dictatorship of the proletariat," and so on were not merely academic ideas but were being translated into actions and controls by the new rulers, at least as far as we were concerned. It was terrifying to think that millions of people, from children to the aged, were being systematically subjected to discrimination, harassment, and deprivation of citizens' rights—apart from those already in detention—because of a dogma called Marxism-Leninism.

It was even more frustrating to realize that there was nothing we could do to change the fact that we had become "pariahs" in our own country, at least as long as we were stuck here. It occurred to me that we were arguing among ourselves about the validity of a theory brought out at the turn of the century by some fanatics as if we were actually able to shape our circumstances by changing that theory, thereby bringing forth changes in the new government's policies. Some of us being more pragmatic, gave up arguing for argument's sake and turned to humor as a means of maintaining our spirits.

Sometimes we preferred laboring in the fields to staying indoors. Idleness encouraged depressing thoughts as well as reminding us of our imprisonment, humiliation, and hopelessness. Besides, going to the fields gave us an opportunity to pursue our main preoccupation: securing the next meal. Going about our work, our eyes were alert for signs of anything edible—leaves, a stump or a vine that might indicate the presence of a root, footprints of rodents, and holes that might indicate the lairs of snakes or mice.

Hearing the call "break time," groups of obviously weary inmates would suddenly turn active. Some headed for spots that had been spotted; holes were then dug until roots were found. Some tried to smoke out a snake or rodent from a hole, while others built a fire. Still others would head for traps they had laid earlier. Our trapping was a simple business—a length of wire made into a noose at one end with the other connected to the top of a small tree; the tree would then be bent and held down by impaling the noose on the ground, so that once the whole contraption was disturbed, the tree would snap back, with the noose trapping the animal. Some men even attached an empty tin with a few small stones to act as a sort of bell, which announced that something had been caught.

The greatest joy to hungry inmates was the sight of a big prey; it would not be long before the animal's body was chopped up into pieces and roasting over a fire. The aroma was mouth-watering, and when finished, this freshly cooked meat needed only some salt for taste. We felt the strength-giving properties of such fresh meat for several days.

One day I was invited to have some roasted "wood pigeons" with friends. The taste was like that of roasted birds, and the bones were tiny, birdlike. Enhanced by spices, the meat was delicious, and I praised their cookery, asking, "How did you catch wood pigeons?"

"Oh, easy! These are wingless wood pigeons." He then pointed at a spot where, to my horror, I saw a heap of fresh rat skins, heads, and tails.

But wild rats were gradually accepted as the best dish available, as long as one did not have to prepare them.

A break officially was to last five minutes, but invariably it would be at least a quarter of an hour. The guards simply turned a blind eye as they knew full well that we could not work without more time to rest. The one-hour lunch break often lasted up to two hours, and our success or failure in staving off hunger that day would be determined by our efforts during this time.

Family visits suddenly became commonplace. Some relatives were allowed to visit every month. Some wives even managed to turn up every fortnight, with or without permission, since their husbands needed medication. We had in fact, arrived at the point of making arrangements among ourselves for staggering visits or bringing in supplies. Then we shared the food. Chiêu's wife was among the frequent visitors, and our daily diet improved. Even books and textbooks were smuggled in. It became the fashion for some of us to study a foreign language, and some inmates received gifts as payment for English tutoring and handcopying textbooks.

One day Trong was caught by Monitor Tung in the process of producing English-language textbooks. Trong explained that the books had nothing to do with politics, Western decadence, or anything reactionary; that they were merely about the daily lives of a family; and that they were currently in use on the outside. In the end, Tung asked Trong to teach him English! He attended classes regularly every Sunday at lunch time.

On my lucky days when my wife visited me and brought food, I did not have to go foraging for it, and I ate it during lunch breaks. On one such day some of us hung hammocks in the shade and relaxed. It suddenly appeared to me that the surrounding scenery was quite beautiful. The land stretched to the horizon in undulating tree-clad hills. Magnificently tall pines rose on the hilltops, and a clear stream wound its way around the bottom of the hillside where we were. Here and there, colorful tropical birds perched on branches preening their feathers.

"What a view!" said someone. "How good the land is! I would be content to settle down here once I have been released."

"All this vast region lies on a well-known belt of basaltic soil," said someone else. "This kind of soil was loved by the French colonists who set up so many plantations in this region. It's an irony that our countrymen are poverty-stricken on these rich lands through no fault of their own. First the war for independence, then the long struggle for unification of the country, and now there are rumors that we will have to carry out 'international duties' among others." Thus, we were brought back to sad thoughts and reality.

With the frequent coming and going of visitors, some new situations and problems arose. One inmate had been allowed to stay overnight with his wife several times due to her resourcefulness in courting the camp commander's sympathy; it was not long before it was known that she was pregnant. But what attracted most attention was Bui Quoc Khanh's wife, who, on her first visit, brought along a pretty girl, whom she introduced as her cousin. The camp commander and study monitors were seen frequenting the visitors' quarters day and night while the "cousin" was there. The guards were ordered to stay out and keep a watchful eye on the inmates, all of whom understood exactly what was going on. The young guards even told us that a study monitor had boasted to them that he received "physiological support" from the "cousin." Later we noted that every time she visited, which she did quite regularly, Khanh's wife brought along a pretty "relative." Discipline among the guards became so atypically relaxed that young female visitors were being approached and even molested by them. The wives reacted by staying together in a room when their husbands were not with them—always more than two in each room. This situation was so well known that wives were forwarned when they bought tickets at the bus station.

Quite a few unpermitted visits took place, and the reason for this came out by accident later. Relations between inmates and guards improved considerably due to the presence of the families and the gifts they brought for the guards. Visitors were even permitted to carry inmates' mail to and from relatives at home, and some kind-hearted people even brought our letters personally to our families. My wife had asked Chiêu's wife to bring food for me on her visits, and I now also received letters from her almost every week. She kept comforting me that I would "probably be released soon."

With all of this, our morale was up, and we revived musical activities. Our "theater" often remained open late with the tacit approval of the guards; they sometimes even asked us to sing them "golden songs" (their own words), which were actually melodies that used to be popular under the former government of South Vietnam. One young fellow had previously been employed by the DaNang Broadcasting Authority as a professional singer, and his performance was highly appreciated by the young guards, who asked him to write down his songs for them. Singers' fees were paid with sweets, biscuits, or other snacks.

One evening while we were enjoying ourselves in the "theater," *bodoi* Lam approached me, took me to a corner, and said, "I shall be stationed near where you live tomorrow night. I may be able to lend you my radio set."

"Thank you very much," I said joyfully. "Please bring it along. We promise to take good care of it."

"Don't forget to pay for the batteries."

"Of course! That goes without saying."

Lam hurried off, and, looking around, I saw only familiar faces. I gambled that even if there was a mole among us, he would be too eager to listen to foreign programs to report on us. So I said in a low voice, "I have the pleasure to inform you that that *bodoi* has just offered to lend his radio set to us. In return for some fees, of course."

We agreed that the battery cost should be high enough to encourage Lam to lend the radio again—five dong each time, a large sum for the *bodoi* since their net monthly salary was about seven dong.

That evening we waited for Lam at the same spot near the chicken coop until we saw him silently emerging from the dark behind us, having obviously climbed the bamboo fence. He accepted the money from Chiêu and was about to leave when he said, "Keep the volume low. Remember to switch it off and return it to me at once when you hear my signal, when I hit the fence with a bamboo stick."

Six eager prisoners surrounded the set. "Let me keep the set," said Chiêu; "the rest must be on the alert. If you see any stranger sing loudly while I try to hide it, okay?"

He then tuned into the BBC; we heard interference noises, then that familiar opening theme. "That's it!" exclaimed Chiêu.

We sat there motionless, hearing clearly the sounds of our own breathing. The tune came to an end, followed by a few seconds of silence and then a voice speaking in English. "This is the Asian service of the BBC broadcasting from London."

Our ears were glued to the set, our hearts beating. It was as if we were hearing from a long-lost friend. Chiêu increased the volume. An angry shout was heard from beyond the fence—"Not that loud!"

As we listened, there were simultaneous exclamations as if on cue: "What?" "Bloody hell!" "How strange!"

The newscaster announced the visit to Israel by Egyptian President Sadat; this came as a total surprise as we had known the two countries were enemies. But what attracted most of our attention was the news about "boat people" escaping from Vietnam. We had heard of this, but did not expect the number to be so great that it attracted international attention. Besides, we believed that the rest of the world had forgotten Vietnam after the communist takeover in 1975. No sooner had the program come to an end than we tried to tune in VOA. But Lam reappeared.

"That's enough! Give it back to me," he said in a worried voice. "You'll have it again tomorrow but not now; I know a patrol will be around here soon."

"We have listened for only half an hour; that's not enough," complained one of the men. "Now we only want to tune in to some music, not foreign broadcasts."

"Don't worry," said Lam knowingly. "Half-an-hour's listening every day is quite adequate. You won't have to pay for it tomorrow because you've paid more than enough today. I am not against your listening to anything, but it's very likely that you will be caught if you continue to listen now. Not only you but I too will be punished then, and my set would certainly be confiscated. I'll see you tomorrow."

Lam lent us the set the next evening as promised, and he continued to do so for months until we ran low on funds. By then, the set was "rented" only on Saturdays. We finally put an end to it all out of fear on our part that the whole affair would become known to the authorities, as the number of listeners had increased.

The more information gathered from visitors concerning reeducation, the more confused and worried we became. It was now understood that our release would not take place in the foreseeable future, "as the situation did not permit it," in the words of the government. From visitors we learned that a purge was going on in the ranks of the communists, but most disturbing were reports that all aspects of the former ways of life were being aggressively eradicated by the new rulers. Among those hardest hit were the financially powerful Chinese merchants, who up until now still had some control of the economy.

August was drawing to a close, and all sorts of vegetation seemed to have been given a new lease on life after months of rainfall. Green leaves were everywhere. We began gathering a kind of gourd that we called highlanders' gourds on the assumption that they had been cultivated by the highland people, which explained their widespread abundance. We also secretly gathered young manioc roots, as the *bodoi* did openly, although it was not yet harvest time. We became experts at judging the age of a cassava plant by looking at it. This was the first time our stomachs were kept filled regularly. The most common dish was a soup made from cassava roots and their leaves; the young leaves had to be boiled over and over and the boiled water discarded each time to remove their poisonous resin. This soup would then be enhanced, according to one's "wealth," with dried shrimps, sodium glutamate, or just plain salt.

Important holidays were drawing near, the most awaited occasions because releases were anticipated. The anniversaries of the August Revolution and Independence Day (September 2) were about to be celebrated by communists all over Vietnam. These days in camp would be celebrated at meetings where inmates were supposed to study their significance.

Work was suspended one afternoon, and we were called to the camp command to attend "classes." A big grin was on Commander Thinh's face. He started by saying, "Let's sing a song," and we began that familiar song, "As if Uncle Ho was present," the same song that had once caused an inmate to be shackled. The inmates sang unusually loud and earnestly.

"They seem to be so happy! Maybe they are well fed," remarked someone.

A man sitting next to me whispered, "Do you know why they sing that loud? It's because they have somehow been tipped off that about twenty inmates will be released this time!"

I turned to him at once. He looked sober and sincere. A beam of hope flashed through my mind. "Maybe my luck would finally change," I thought. My wife had been repeating in her letters that "the doctor who studied in the Soviet Union is quite competent; he's promised to cure my uncle's ailment" (meaning me, of course). "Maybe the uncle is going to be discharged soon," I mused.

Hearing the noisy applause at the end of the song, Thinh looked on with an approving smile. "Are you happy?" he asked.

Back came a chorus of seemingly jubilant voices, "Very, very happy! We nearly die of joy!"

The study monitors surrounding Thinh shouted them down. "Be quiet! Don't you know how to keep discipline?"

Commander Thinh then put on a serious air. "You must learn how to enjoy yourselves in a disciplined manner! To commemorate these two important holidays of our people, we are going to read to you a newspaper article commenting on the significance of these two occasions. Now, let's be quiet!"

An inmate was appointed to read the article. He cleared his throat and began to read aloud. Murmured conversation started up among the inmates, stopping when a *bodoi* approached. At the end, to our disappointment, there came the usual order, "Let's sing another song to close the meeting." We sang "Let's unite!" and then were dismissed. There was no release announcement. So they knew what we expected of them and they were playing on our suffering! Especially that acting performance by Thinh!

A friend teased me, "You're still naïve for your age."

"I am not the only one, you know! I wonder who that bastard is, the one who spread the rumor about twenty inmates getting released soon!"

Next day there was work as usual, as if there were no holiday. Coming back from the field, I saw Thé running toward me. "We are going to have some celebration after all," he said with a smile.

"What celebration? The holiday is over, isn't it?"

"No! A *bodoi* I know told me that it was because special provisions for the occasion had arrived late. But that's nothing compared to this! He confirmed that there was indeed a list of about twenty inmates who were to be let out. He said he had personally taken the message over the phone and that it came from higher command. Now, let's keep it to ourselves; otherwise some mole will learn of it, and that *bodoi* won't dare tell me anything in the future. He gave me the impression that he was serious."

I just looked at Thé and forced a smile. As if he could read my mind, he said, "I know you don't believe me! But I am sure it's true!"

"No way! Well, maybe your name is on the list."

"No, I think your name is! Oh, maybe mine too! I've got a relative who is very, very high in the government. I call him uncle and so do you. Uncle Ho! Ha, ha, ha!"

Back in the hut, I heard that "the celebration provisions" had been spotted: beer, cooking oil, sacks of wheat flour, and two small pigs. But there was no announcement concerning a celebration that evening, and the next morning we assembled in the yard to receive assignments as usual. Study monitors and guards were nowhere in sight. Then came Bui Quoc Khanh, hurrying toward us from the command center. He said in an excited voice, "There's no work today.

Get back to your barracks to put away the tools and be back as soon as you can for a meeting."

Excited voices were heard in the scramble, "Move on!" "Hurry up!" "Somebody's going to be released this time!" "No, they'll be let out temporarily!"

The event of inmates being let out, even temporarily on "leave," caused much excitement. We were told to form into lines in the meeting hall. The minutes ticked away as we waited. Although outwardly indifferent, inside I was excited and hopeful.

Thinh and his *bodoi* came in. One study monitor barked, "Stand up! Form into lines. Now, sit down!"

With that permanent grin locked onto his face and behaving as if he were about to open a ceremony, Thinh walked slowly to a spot in front of us, leather briefcase under one arm. Slowly, deliberately, he unwrapped a packet of cigarettes, picked one out, and put it in a corner of his mouth. He then produced a brand-new gas lighter and slowly and deliberately lit his cigarette while his *bodoi* watched in admiration.

The whole act, especially showing off his lighter, was greeted with sarcastic smiles and even open laughter by the inmates. Seeing this, Thinh said defensively, "I've got to smoke to remain calm so I can announce good news."

To our applause, Thinh's mouth opened into a big grin and the *bodoi* burst into laughter. They knew full well what we were waiting for, how anxious we were.

Finally, Thinh produced some leaflets from his briefcase. He spoke slowly before a silent, pitiful audience.

"The first good news is that we are going to celebrate the two important holidays at the same time today. Now, at the end of this meeting all of you will be given wheat flour, Cuban sugar, cigarettes, and also some cooking oil. The distribution will be made by the camp leader, his deputies, group leaders, and their assistants under the supervision of the study monitors. This is the first time we have received wheat flour; therefore, methods of preparing it should be discussed among yourselves. Don't worry! We will overcome any difficulty that may arise in preparing this wheat flour."

Holding the leaflets high so that they could be seen by everyone, Thinh said with a smile, "But the main news, which I believe has been eagerly awaited, is contained in these sheets of paper. Before reading them, I must emphasize to you several points."

He raised his arm and went on. "Although confronted with all sorts of difficulties, the Party and the State still take the trouble to look after you. The proof is that you are receiving special supplies for celebration, even though these items are in short supply at the moment. Among the items brought here are those that have been given to us as gifts from friendly nations. They were not intended for you, but the Party and the State are so generous that they took the trouble to bring them here for you. Imagine the difficulties in transporting these supplies all the way here! Do you think you deserve this favor?"

That buzzing noise of voices among the audience grew louder, then an angry curse was heard clearly over the noise, "F . . . it!"

We shrugged and shook our heads in resignation on hearing this.

As if he had not heard, Thinh went on. "Most of you don't! Others, however, have shown genuine repentance, have made obvious progress, and have indicated their desire to adopt revolutionary ways of life. To them, the Party has responded favorably. Although the situation does not permit their release at the present time, to reward their own progressiveness as well as to help their families, the Party and State have made the following decisions."

He slowly and deliberately unfolded a sheet of paper and gave it a long look. From below, necks were straining to look, and voices were heard, "Bloody hell! What decisions if we are not to be released?"

"What are they up to? Transfer to a better camp?"

"Maybe 'the following' will be promoted to be servants of the camp command's personnel!"

The reaction was so noisy that a study monitor had to shout at us. "Be quiet! You there, what have you just said?"

Thinh began to read: "The Socialist Republic of Vietnam—Independence, Freedom, Happiness. It has been decided that the following are granted short leaves of up to ten days, including travel time. The authority of Camp 3721 must ensure that this duration is adhered to. Signed, Commander Thinh."

This document clearly had been prepared by Thinh himself, obviously to show his authority. He then went on to read out the names of the lucky ones. Among them was Bui Minh Duong, formerly an air force lieutenant who had specialized in radar systems, stationed at Pleiku. He once boasted that he had repaired the radar systems formerly under his charge and trained *bodoi* to use them. He thought because of this he would not have to undergo reeducation, although he was later advised that a "short reeducation period" would be in his best interest. His family had also managed to find some sponsor for him. Also on the list were Ha The Ruyet, formerly a university lecturer whose brother was a high-ranking Party official, and Nguyen Khac Cung who had an important sponsor. Finally there was Hoang Xuan Hai, formerly an artillery lieutenant whose uncle was a propaganda commissar. There were eighteen of them altogether. We were ordered to sing the song "Let's Unite" at the end, and Thinh and some of his *bodoi* left. A study monitor took over. He told those who had just been named to go to the command center to get travel permits, associated documents, and money. The rest of us, he said, should get back to our living quarters to prepare for the food distribution.

"Each of you should have something to hold the sugar and wheat flour and a tin for the cooking oil, I repeat, a tinful of cooking oil. Everything will be handed over to your group leaders, deputies, and team leaders first. They will redistribute the food to you later on, except for the oil, which will be distributed to individuals at the command center. Now, hurry up!"

So the present policy was that inmates would be let out temporarily on short leaves instead of being released once and for all, important though their sponsors might be!

Some of the young inmates who had been helping unload supplies told us that there was very little cooking oil, not enough for the *bodoi*'s use, let alone for us who numbered over a thousand. But it had been said at the meeting that each would receive a tinful of oil. The sugar and wheat flour were allocated right at our barracks. Each man was to get a tinful of pure, granulated sugar and two tinfuls of wheat flour. It was the first time that we had received that much. The distribution was carried out expertly and without fuss. Sugar and wheat flour were ladled out in standard-size tins, and no tamping down of flour into the tin was allowed; each tin was leveled off by a stick. Allotments for platoon-sized groups were made in this manner, and representatives of platoons then drew lots for their batch. In this way no one could complain of unfair treatment. The food would later be redistributed to individuals in the same way. The method was subsequently to be adopted by the whole camp since it worked so well.

The promise that we would each receive a tinful of cooking oil was met by pouring the oil into a barrel full of water, stirring the mixture, and giving a tinful of this oily concoction to each inmate. The *bodoi* supervising this affair said that the "oil" would enhance our soups.

At first, I joined the queue, but when my turn came I saw that there was only a trace of oil in the water, so I declined and left. Once in the tin, traces of the oil would be impossible to remove without soap, a rarity among us. I had once received a tiny morsel of fatty beef and the smell of it did not leave my tin for months as I had no soap. A tin was the only cooking utensil we were allowed to keep; it served as kettle, pot, and rice bowl. My declining that "oil" turned out to be a grave blunder. I was later accused of "showing contempt toward the Revolution" for refusing to accept this gift. I learned of the accusation through a friendly study monitor.

The wheat flour was prepared in many ways. Some simply made porridge out of it; some turned it into noodles; some went further by wrapping the dough around a ball of dried shrimps, boiling them, and serving them in soup. Even bread was made by a resourceful fellow, who used bicarbonate of soda in lieu of yeast; the bread was pronounced identical to ordinary bread.

This "celebration mood" lasted until the young *bodoi* who had been socializing with us were reprimanded by their superiors for having lost "the awareness of their class." As revolutionaries, they must not associate with inmates, the counterrevolutionary elements!

One day Study Monitor Tung informed me that he was being transferred. I asked him if this was because he had been socializing with us. "We've heard that quite a few of you have been reprimanded for that."

"No, that's not the reason! Some young *bodoi* and I are being transferred to the battlefront because there have been skirmishes along the western border. This has nothing to do with you. However, most young *bodoi* see their combat assignments as punishment. Be patient. It won't be long before you are released. I wish you all my best."

"We also wish you and your young comrades all our best. When you have finished your assignment and come back here, you will probably find that we are still here."

"Don't be depressed. Try to keep up your spirit and be brave. I will always remember you despite what you are. We may be able to meet again in the future, when you have finished your term here."

"I hope that day will come."

Tung then left, a look of genuine sadness on his face.

A truck arrived on the same day bringing in a new group of *bodoi* and taking the others away. Most of the newcomers were in their late twenties, one was middle-aged. They gave us sullen and even hostile looks. We later learned that they had been wounded in battle with the armed forces of the previous regime but remained in service because their wounds were not serious. We tried to do our best whenever they stood guard over us; nevertheless, they always managed to find some fault and thus had a chance to let loose a barrage of abuse.

The work was less arduous now as it consisted mainly of second-time weeding of young, weak weeds. But new work was immediately given out as soon as the weeding appeared to be done. We were ordered to prepare land for forty hectares of sweet potatoes and to gather bamboo shoots "for export." A new hazard also came up after the abundant rains: jungle leeches. They had laid dormant everywhere there was vegetation during the dry season, and now they became active.

One would suddenly feel a tickling sensation on the neck or legs and, searching for it, find something wet and very tender, almost watery. Jungle leeches would find their way to some soft spot on the victim's skin and then suck his warm blood, refusing to let go until they were full. Only then would their presence be felt. They became so numerous that we had to search ourselves every now and then, and we found some every time we did. There was no way to protect ourselves against them. They always managed to reach our skin, crawling through all sorts of thick clothing and socks. They even dropped on our heads from tree branches!

Not a day passed that we were not molested by jungle leeches. The clothes of those hardest hit became blood-stained. The jungle was totally infested, especially where bamboo shoots grew, and shoot-gathering trips came to be known as "blood donating trips." At first one group of inmates was to gather bamboo shoots while others were assigned elsewhere; however, the same people could not continue the work because they lost too much blood to the leeches. It was decided that each of us would have to undergo the experience; therefore, everyone had to gather bamboo shoots twice every month. Initially, the quota was twenty kilograms of young shoots apiece; this was later increased to thirty kilograms due to the eagerness of those who wanted to show their "progressiveness" to the camp authority. The harvest of shoots was so widespread that we had to venture farther and farther into the jungle.

Besides leeches, there were mosquitoes in unimaginable numbers. A cloud of mosquitoes would descend on any warm-blooded animal that happened to be around. Worst of all, they would hurl themselves at our eyes, noses, and mouths and not hesitate to rush deep inside if those mouths were open. Their number literally stifled us. We had asked our relatives for mosquito repellant, but it did not help much. Finally, we fashioned masks of mosquito net fabric and wore thick clothes and socks. These helped against mosquitoes but were useless against the leeches. Each trip was a nightmare, and some even caught fever.

Our plight was not helped by the attitude of those inmates who checked the shoots, which were thoroughly weighed and inspected. Shoots judged too old would be discarded, and the unlucky picker would have to try again to fill his quota. The inspection team was hand-picked by the camp authority and consisted mostly of those who had important sponsors. Cung, formerly a medical doctor, proved to be a monster to his fellow inmates.

The bamboo shoots were cut into slices and dried for storage. After just over a month, the amount of processed shoots was recorded as over two tons. On one shoot-gathering trip, while on my own, I tried to find a way to the border with Cambodia in preparation for a possible future escape. To my despair, the jungle proved impenetrable with the dense vegetation that multiplied after the rainy season. I found that the cultivated areas where one could cross easily at night were studded with sentry posts. Obviously, the *bodoi* were on alert along the border.

After several such trips, I was laid up for more than a week with a high fever. At first everyone, including me, thought I had malaria, and they made me take quinine tablets, to no avail. I tried another antimalaria treatment, Fancida, which had been brought by my wife. I only ended up passing a reddish-colored urine. The *bodoi* medic insisted that I keep on taking quinine. I finally consulted an inmate doctor, Tran Ngoc Khue, who told me that I had contracted "a version of typhoid." Unlike malaria, my fever did not alternate with chills. Following his advice, I took Tifomicine, which my best friend, Thé, helped me exchange for certain medicines that I had. It worked! My head gradually became clearer, and I could feel the weariness in my bones and the flow of blood through my veins. I felt as if my bones stuck through the thin skin and glued themselves to the hard bamboo bed. I supplemented the daily diet of thin rice porridge with what remained of the food my wife had brought on her last visit. To my frustration, I was so weak that I needed help when I went to the latrine. My recovery was fairly quick, compared with others who had been laid up for months.

By the time I was strong enough to work, it was time to harvest the rice. Those inmates who had been on "leave" now came back; most had exceeded the specified time, but no one was reprimanded. One man was missing. We learned later that he was Hoang Quoc Viet, who took advantage of the opportunity to escape from the country (I came across him on the streets of London early in 1984). To our eager enquiries about life outside, the collective response was less than illuminating: People were "optimistically and enthusiastically building a new society." They gave the impression that they had been briefed on how to answer our questions. Most of these inmates betrayed an air of depression that we took to be a feeling of homesickness at having seen their homes and families and then been forced to leave them again.

One day, in response to my persistent though friendly questioning about life outside, Hoang Xuan Hai confided that "everything looked strange to me because many changes have taken place. Although the same people and the same streets were there, they appeared different to me! Even my own family has changed! Eating and food have become the common topic of conversation; the main concern nowadays is how to obtain rice and other items. Almost all the big shops have been closed, but vendors abound on the streets selling everything. Maybe people have to sell things from their houses to make ends meet."

To my inquiry about his sponsor, he grimaced. "I can't place much hope on him anymore! My own uncle has been keeping his distance from us in spite of the fact that my family has pampered him with everything he's asked for."

I pressed on. "I'm sure you'll be released soon. Your uncle *did* intervene on your behalf for your recent 'leave.' Once you get home, after being released, will they give you some help? How will you make a living?"

"Help?" retorted Hai, as if I was an idiot. "All these Northerners think that we have enjoyed all the luxuries in the world, so now it's their turn! Don't you know how poor they are? They want everything! It's a fact of life that their main concern is how to get hold of accommodations here so that their families can move South! That's why so many people here have been forced to give up their homes to move to New Economic Zones. Most squatters who have been living in makeshift huts along sewer canals are allowed to stay on, although they have a farming background; on the other hand, city dwellers who have never touched a hoe before are being urged to move away to the zones. Those Northerners are being shunned by the people here. I've never seen such intensity of hatred! As for government cadres, there are grumblings of discontent among many communist Southerners, although outwardly they appear united. In fact, this New Economic Zones policy has been opposed by many of them. Most of those who have been to these places and whose houses have been 'requisitioned by the State' are now returning to the city and being put up by their relatives. Some are even sleeping right in front of their former homes! Now, I've gone a bit too far. You must not tell this to anyone else if you are my friend."

"Of course I won't. You know me, don't you? I must thank you for telling me all this. Don't worry. You're not the only one to do this, I suppose."

"All the others are just like me. They have been briefed by the camp authority on how to answer questions 'in such a way as to boost your morale' and not to say anything that may affect the credibility of the Revolution. We all promised to cooperate. And now I've gone too far. My chance of being released early may be affected if they find out about this."

"If your chance is affected, what will our chances be? Will we have to stay here forever?"

Not knowing what to say, Hai consoled me. "You will certainly be released in the end, but it may take some time. Sorry, I must leave now."

He hurried off, leaving me feeling hopeless and pessimistic. How could my wife hope to buy back my freedom when even influence and connections failed, as with Hai?

Thanks to weeks of sunshine, the rice crop ripened and was nearly ready for harvest. Exuberant shrubs of rice plants shot up everywhere, especially on low ground where water had accumulated. Some plants reached as high as our shoulders, their stems bent under the weight of the swollen rice ears. Because I was still weak, I was assigned the task of guarding the fields, watching out for birds and wild animals that would be attracted to a ready food supply. Watchtowers, some three meters high, had been erected along the edge of the jungle next to the cultivated land. We were to stand guard in these towers and beat metal gongs to scare off marauders.

One morning I set out for my post accompanied by a group of *bodoi*, who would be deployed in the area to ambush anyone attempting to escape. We left before dawn. I was taken to a watchtower at a deserted spot, far from the camp and next to the jungle, and told to remain there until sundown when they would fetch me on their way home. I climbed into the tower, put aside my packed lunch of a bunch of manioc roots and a tin of water, and settled down. The wind carried an early morning chill that seeped through my bony body. I wrapped myself with a piece of tarpaulin to ward off the cold. Time went by; there was nothing to do. What a waste of time, I thought. Wild animals come out only at night to search for food. I was about to hit the gong, mostly to please some *bodoi* who might be around, when I heard a noise that sounded like rustling tree branches, but there was no wind. I looked to see where the noise was coming from and a small wild pig moved out of the bushes into view, its hind legs kicking as it moved in a threatening way as if it was about to rush at a target. The thin, dark animal was about the size of an average dog. It looked around cautiously before heading for the rice field. Then two more pigs emerged from the bushes, following the first. I reached for the iron bar and was about to strike the gong when all of a sudden wild pigs of all sizes poured out from the bushes. They kept running out of the jungle as if in a stampede. They ran toward me or, to be more precise, toward the rice field. I sat there frozen, fearing that the sound of the gong might panic them and bring them stampeding into the poles supporting my watchtower.

The whole herd dived into the rice plants, using their snouts to bring down the plants and then devouring the ears of rice. They seemed to do this expertly, as if they were familiar with the process. Some stopped now and then, tensely looking around for any sign of danger. The whole herd would follow suit every time this happened. Suddenly, the iron bar fell from my hand, and the herd turned around and headed swiftly toward the jungle. Instinctively, I shouted at the top of my voice, sounding ridiculously weak in the noise and commotion. When they were out of sight, I went down to fetch the iron bar and hit hard at the gong to draw someone's attention. After a while some inmates approached on their way to the field, and I asked them to report the presence of a large herd of wild pigs to the *bodoi*.

To my surprise two guards turned up a few minutes later. They were among the ones who had recently been brought in and were hostile to us. One came up to me and asked curtly, "You there! Did you ring the gong? Did you say there was a herd of wild pigs? Where are they now?"

I pointed at the spot where most of them had come out of the jungle and then pointed to the ravaged shrubs of rice plants. "On hearing my gong, they went back where they came from," I said. "I think they are deep in the jungle by now."

One *bodoi* looked down at the footprints, then asked, "How many of them do you think there were?"

"About thirty, maybe more."

The *bodoi* followed the footprints and called back to me, "You there! We are going to hunt them. When you hear gunshots, hit the gong hard and try to make as much noise as you can. You will have your share when we get back, okay? Now, wait until you hear my shots."

I waited and waited. It seemed an infinity. I thought the *bodoi* had given up. Suddenly there were shots in the distance. I hit the gong until my hands were numb. The shooting went on for a while, then stopped. Maybe the herd had gotten too far away to be caught. Then more shots were fired, one by one at first and then a barrage from an automatic rifle. I went on hitting the gong as instructed until I was worn out.

The two *bodoi* emerged from the jungle at noon, each carrying a young pig weighing about four kilograms. One said to me with a smile, "You were right! There were too many of them. I used up the whole magazine. These two were the lightest. You can have a leg if you've got a knife on you. If you want more, go in there and help yourself. There must be some dead ones here and there, deep inside. Don't be put off by the distance."

They seemed good-natured enough so I proposed, "Why don't you bring the lot back to sell to the inmates? They are ravenous for meat."

His face brightened. "Really? Have any *bodoi* sold anything to you before?"

"Good God!" I said. "The meat of wild pig is the best! They will pay any price for it. A study monitor once sold us a big deer for nearly one hundred dong."

The two looked at each other, grinning. They talked for a while. Finally, one said to me, "You keep an eye on these two. We'll go back and try to find some more. If only I had known I could sell them to you." They walked off.

I picked up the smaller pig, trying to guess its weight. It was rather heavy for its size. The meat seemed quite lean. Suddenly I saw a group of *bodoi* and a study monitor coming toward me.

"Who fired the guns, Vu?" asked one of them. "Oh, I see! They've been hunting for wild pigs. I thought there was fighting."

I related the entire incident with the result that this whole group decided to go to look for the pigs. One said, "Don't go that way! We'll go this way, skirting the rice field and crossing a stream to a spot where there are many bushes. The wounded pigs might have hidden themselves there. I know this place like the palm of my hand."

While I was eating lunch, the two *bodoi* came back, carrying a big boar. I told them about the other group. One swore angrily, "F . . . them! We must dispose of these three pigs right away; otherwise, they will demand a share of these too."

"If you want to sell them to us," I said, "please take them to our barracks and leave them there until the rest of us come back in the evening. You will then get your money. We used to deal with other *bodoi* this way."

The two talked it over. At last they left, without telling me what they had decided, carrying the three pigs with them in the direction of the camp. A few minutes later the other group came back with its bag: a big boar and a smaller pig. Study Monitor Chuong asked me if I would like to buy some meat.

I replied without hesitating, "I am afraid I don't have the money."

"Don't have the money? I can't believe it!"

Surmising that I had been under some sort of surveillance, I added quickly,

"I really mean it! I spent all my savings on medicine when I had fever. Frankly I'd like to have some meat as I am still convalescing."

"In that case you can pay me later."

"Thanks a lot, but I'm afraid it will be some time before my wife visits me again."

Chuong raised his voice. "How can you hide the truth from us? Your wife drove here in her own car to visit you, and now you're saying you can't afford a morsel of meat?"

Sensing his mood, I dared not answer back. I just smiled stupidly. Obviously I had been under surveillance. The car had been chartered by others as well as my wife, but now they think it is our own.

The light guard work lasted several days until I was assigned to join those weaving large bamboo trays to be used to hold rice grains being dried in the sun. The work appeared easy at first, but it was also easy to make a mess of it. After I had worked for a while, I had to tear the jumble apart and start all over again. Meanwhile, the job was being handled efficiently and in a relaxed way by those who had been peasants. After a day of frustration, my back was nearly breaking because of the sitting position required for this work. I asked to be transferred to some outdoor job, despite the state of my health.

The rice was now ready for harvest, and the weather became very hot. Field after field of golden brown rice plants were spread all over the place like giant carpets. The harvesting and subsequent care of the fresh grain were being carried out by predetermined teams under the watchful eyes of our supervisors.

On the starting day, as if we were in his native communist North, Commander Thinh ordered the inmates to shout slogans such as, "We are determined to complete the harvest as early as possible," "a grain of rice is as valuable as a grain of gold," "quick cutting, quick storing," and so on. Our daily diet of manioc roots was supplemented by boiled wheat flour.

Sheaves of rice were threshed on the spot after cutting. The grain was then carried in baskets to a common yard for drying. It would be dried on the large trays during the day and stored away in the evening to keep off the dew. The next day it would be dried again, and the process continued until the grain was ready for storage in the granary that had been built by the carpentry team.

I was assigned to one of the teams whose task was to transport—in baskets carried on our backs—the newly threshed grain to the common yard in the camp. Each basketful of grain weighed about twenty kilograms. At first, I was given a full basket to carry over a distance of about 200 meters. I was to pass the basket to the person waiting there, who would relay it to another over the same distance. After covering a mere thirty meters, I had to stop to regain my strength. I dared not sit down as I could never have hoisted the basket up again. I noticed that most of the others did not fare any better. Even the guards' angry shouts did not help.

Eventually the load was reduced and the relay distance shortened to about fifty meters. Still, we were all exhausted.

The first evening, checking the results, Thinh was angry; he warned that "your chance of release is based on your performance in this rice harvest." This was greeted with indifference as we no longer believed in such promises. Besides, we were too weary to try any harder.

As the harvest proceeded on fields farther and farther away from the camp and up and down hills, the job of transporting the grain to the drying yard became much harder, to the point that the camp authority was forced to reduce the load again and lower the relay distance to thirty meters.

Every evening after work, the study monitors checked our numbers and exhorted us to keep up our efforts. One day near the end of the harvest, Study Monitor Chuong disclosed that we had achieved a result never seen before in this province. According to him, the yield per hectare was nearly three tons. He also promised that we would have a "resting period" after the harvest, although we would have to do some light work such as repairing buildings and weeding fields until the New Year holidays. Then it would be time to prepare the land for the next rice crop.

He added,"From now on we should try to build up musical and sporting activities."

The response was bursts of sarcastic laughter from the assembled inmates.

"What the hell are you laughing about?" demanded Chuong. "You there! Tell me why you are laughing."

"Oh . . . it's just that we are too sick, too tired, too hungry to have any interest in sports or musical activities."

"Why are you always complaining of hard work and hunger?" said Chuong. "You must learn to overcome them! During the war, although we were sometimes too hungry to stand on our feet, we would try to enjoy ourselves as though everything were normal."

Again, raucous laughter was heard at the words, "enjoy ourselves." Chuong looked annoyed but only said, "That's enough! Now you are dismissed."

That extraordinary rice crop yield was talked about over and over again. "How could a hectare of *dry* rice field produce nearly three tons of grain?"

"Three tons per hectare is a top yield for a paddy field."

"Maybe they've said this to make us feel that we have achieved something despite our weakness."

Thé, who slept near me, added, "Perhaps 'revolutionary rice' is heavier than ordinary rice, which is why the yield is so high. In my opinion this kind of rice could only yield 1.7 to 1.8 tons at the most."

"But Commander Thinh had said categorically that the yield would be over two tons per hectare," I said. "He must have had some reason to be so cocksure."

"If it's true that these dry fields could yield three tons of rice per hectare, then we have broken all international records," said Thé. "I'm going to try to have a look at how they go about weighing the grain. We 'blacksmiths' haven't been able to lay our hands on a balance. I've heard that Bui Quoc Khanh was in charge of the weighing. That tricky bloke might have had a foot on the scale."

The next day we returned early, having reaped the last patches of rice. We were immediately assigned to a group whose task was sifting and grading the grain. Seeing the scale for the first time, I eagerly asked the young *bodoi* who was supervising us to let me use it for a moment to weigh myself. "I've never had a chance to do that since I first came for reeducation."

"How can you do that with this kind of hanging balance?" retorted the *bodoi*.

I showed him how to do it by hanging the balance on a sturdy tree branch by the pivot end point. I then clung to the hook with my legs up while a friend moved the small weight until the beam was balanced. He said, "You weigh nearly 47 kilograms, which is still less than that pig we had for the celebration the other day."

My friend then asked me to read his weight; it was just 45½ kilograms. Recognizing an opportunity, others rushed over to demand a turn. Most of them weighed under 46 kilograms. One fellow, Toan, who was at least 1.8 meters tall, weighed only 47 kilograms. We joked that we had become "lengths of wire."

Finally, there were so many inmates clamoring to be weighed that the *bodoi* shouted, "That's enough! Wait until the break. We'll be reprimanded if the commander sees this."

When I first registered for reeducation, I weighed just over 60 kilograms, which I then thought was under my normal weight; now here I was at only 47 kilograms! No wonder I had had to use a string as a makeshift belt to hold up my pants.

I was next assigned to the team whose job was recording the amount of grain as it was brought into camp. We were to build a 50-kilogram wooden container for volume measure, and I did this by putting the correct amount of grain into an existing box, measuring its exact dimensions up to the level of the grain, and using these measurements to build a wooden container of the exact size. After drying, the grain would be sifted, graded, and taken to the granary where the amount would be checked again.

The harvest came to an end. Preparations for storage took another two weeks. Thinh's trick to achieve that extraordinary yield was becoming clear: The total amount of rice harvested was 137 tons on a total area of 40 hectares, giving a yield of 3.4 tons per hectare. This was clearly impossible and resulted in a row between Commander Thinh and the study monitors. Most of them argued there must have been measuring errors or downright cheating to inflate the figures. Thinh was reported to have said, "I have personally checked the measuring. No error could have occurred as far as I am concerned. Why can't you believe in this yield when all the grain is right there in the barn?"

I was called to the command center to explain the weighing and volume-measuring methods. I stated that when we measured volume, we actually pressed the grains down into the container; therefore, the real amount must be higher than 137 tons.

"There you see, comrades," said Thinh triumphantly! "Do you agree that no measuring error could have occurred?"

"This whole business has been masterminded by comrade Thinh alone. Therefore, I have no comment," said political cadre Tu. "I will report to the regiment's command and wait to see what they will do about this."

A few days later, I was called up to meet a cadre sent in by the regimental command. I repeated the explanation about the weighing and volume-measuring methods, stressing that there could not have been any error.

The cadre said, "I have been sent here not to penalize the measuring team but to investigate probable sources of error. It's unscientific and certainly impossible for a hectare of dry field to yield over three tons of grain. I've been monitoring the rice crop all over this region, and I have noted that the crop in this particular area has not been that good. Therefore, in my opinion this exceptionally high yield is impossible."

The investigation went on for three days. All we knew about it was that the *bodoi* kept coming to our quarters to "borrow" our chickens "to entertain the comrade from Regiment." Finally, word leaked out that the cadre had reduced the yield to 2½ tons per hectare, which amazed us as we were sure that that was still impossible.

A few days later, having finished work at the forge near the command center, Thé came home to give me the news that "the 'bug' associated with that extraordinary yield has been identified."

I jumped as though I myself were implicated. "Is the total amount not 137 tons?"

Thé said with a smile, "We have all been fooled by Thinh! That cadre from regiment is quite clever. He grilled Khanh about the measurement of the land, and then he personally went out to do some measuring of the fields himself. Finally, Thinh had to admit that he had cheated, and he tried to appease the cadre by entertaining him with special meals among other things."

I did not follow this. I said, "It's still not clear to me how he managed to cheat. And how did you learn all this?"

"The whole story was related to me by that cunning Hung, who has been supervising us at the forge," said Thé. "He said that the measuring team led by Khanh had left some cleared land unrecorded on orders from Thinh; this means that the total cultivated area was recorded as 40 hectares instead of about seventy, which is the real figure. Seed for the extra area was obtained by claiming replacement seeds were needed to make up for loses due to rotting. Because both Thinh and Khanh were too ignorant of farming matters to adjust the yield to a reasonable figure, that agricultural expert was sent in to investigate the claim. If only they had adjusted the area to, say, 60 hectares, they might have gotten away with it."

"Good Lord," I said, "that's why! No wonder they made nearly a thousand of us work like hell to achieve their ends. No wonder '40 hectares of land' looks so vast."

"Hung also told me that the cadre really scared the shit out of Thinh," Thé said with relish. "But luckily for him, the cadre happened to be a friend of Tu, the political cadre, and therefore agreed to report a reasonable figure to his superiors. Hung also said that as soon as the cadre was out of sight, Tu let loose a barrage on Thinh, who just said he was sorry and smiled stupidly."

We were granted two days of rest to celebrate a good harvest. Study Monitor Chuong was hanging around the inmates' quarters, and I feigned a worried look and told him I was concerned about being involved in errors during the weighing process.

"Never mind about that," interrupted Chuong. "It's all over now, and it's not your fault. Don't worry! Forget it! It's all because of some 'clever thinking' by Thinh. Everything has settled down now. We'll still receive some prize for that achievement, and there may even be some celebration."

Taking advantage of the spare time, some of the young inmates played volleyball, some sang and played on homemade musical instruments, while the majority, being more practical, quietly set about mending their clothes and repairing tools. It was the first time that I had had a chance to wash my mosquito net; it was disgusting.

Orders came to assemble in the meeting hall, which produced the usual hopes and expectations of release or leave. Thinh stood in front of the assemblage and said with a smile, "Let's sing a song before we discuss business!"

The song, "Let's Celebrate the Rice Crop," was sung dispiritedly as it had hardly been rehearsed. Ignoring the ridiculous performance, Thinh went on. "The camp authority highly appreciates your hard work, which has resulted in exceeding our quota. This exceptional feat has been reported to higher command, and we have been promised that your hard work will be rewarded. At the moment, we are waiting for other camps to complete their harvests before all the results are tallied. However, it's clear that our camp is the winner of the whole region! While waiting for the official confirmation and for delivery of the prize, I suggest that we applaud our achievment!"

The ensuing applause was unusually loud, as the inmates knew how that "exceptional achievement" had been brought about. There were even bursts of laughter from the audience.

Thinh intoned, "The main purpose of this meeting is to relay to you an important message." The whole place went quiet. He went on.

"The dry season is about to begin and our superiors have asked us to start the sweet potato crop as soon as possible. The young plants will not survive the hot, dry weather if they are planted late. Therefore, we will start planting the vines tomorrow. The quicker the job is completed, the sooner you will be able to rest!"

The norms were set very high at first. With considerable effort, they could be met where the soil was soft and where there was plenty of decaying vegetation to be used as fertilizer. In other places, we would have to work extra hours. The spot for each potato bed first had to be worked by hoeing. A layer of dead vegetation was then shoveled on top, then more soil heaped up until the whole thing was turned into a sort of platform with about a three-foot base. The follow-up team then planted potato vines in the pile, positioning the lengths of vine as required. We went about the work like robots, trying to fulfill the norms, often cheating along the way. Few people managed to meet their quota. It was getting hotter and sunnier, but productivity increased as people got used to their jobs. I fell sick again after a fortnight of work; apparently, I had not fully recovered from my recent illness.

One morning when we were about to set out for work, orders came for us to go back to our barracks "to prepare for an imminent examination of your personal belongings." We were forbidden to keep sharp metallic objects as well as items made of glass. Thinh went to every barracks shouting, "Those who disobey the orders will be punished and their belongings except clothing will be confiscated!"

We displayed our wares on mats and sheets of plastic in a common yard— clothes, tins, pots, and baskets of all sizes to hold miscellaneous items. Such searches provided the *bodoi* with opportunities to pocket their favorites: copies of melodies, nail clippers, steel combs, and carved metal souvenirs. We seemed to wait an eternity, but no *bodoi* was in sight. Suddenly, we heard the noise of trucks in the distance. A convoy was approaching in a cloud of dust. The truth finally dawned: We were about to be moved again!

The whole place buzzed with conversation. By then, we noticed that the *bodoi* themselves were also making preparations for departure. At long last, Study Monitors Chuong and Thang came to announce, "We have orders to move camp. Some will be traveling on trucks while the rest will have to make it on foot as the number of vehicles is limited. Only those with the least amount of luggage will be allowed into the trucks, that is, one bag apiece, which may contain anything they like."

Most of us had rather a lot of miscellaneous articles that were really indispensable to us. One man asked, "How long will the trip take?"

Thang replied with a smile. "It will take a few hours by truck. If I walk with a bagful of belongings, it will probably take me more than twenty-four hours to get there without stopping on the way."

We all knew how fit Thang was, and I began to think of what I would have to discard so I would be allowed into a vehicle. It seemed to me that I could not shed anything; nearly everything I owned had been obtained through sweat and tears! Especially my hen, who had laid many eggs that had literally saved my life after bouts of illness. I finally decided to leave everything behind except my clothing and the hen. I noted that most people were having a hard time making these painful decisions.

Suddenly Chuong turned to me and said, "Oh, I nearly forgot, Vu. Get the carpentry team together and take them to the command center; bring all your luggage with you as well."

It took me some time to assemble the whole team, as most of them were scattered and busy making preparations for departure. I went on ahead to battalion, and by the time I got there, Thinh and his colleagues were packing up. They had dismantled their bedding and made it into bundles, and their rucksacks were bulging. There were also wooden cases, baskets, and plastic bags that had not been brought with them to this camp; in fact, most of their wooden items had been produced by the carpentry team.

I said, "We in the carpentry team have been summoned here. Could you tell me what we are to do and how many people will be needed?"

Thinh turned to us, "There you are, Vu! Get me half a dozen men to load all these cases onto a truck, and then remove the corrugated sheets on the roofs and load them onto another one. Leave your luggage here; you will travel with us in those vehicles."

My worries vanished. I would not have to travel on foot! I rushed back to the inmates' quarters and chose five healthy-looking men. "The camp commander has summoned you to the command center to receive some assignment. Bring your luggage with you."

Some looked reluctant until they saw my wink. I met Thé on the way back and said to him, "Come with me if you want to travel by truck."

Thé replied in his funny heavily accented dialect, "There's no need for that. I've got my own transport. We blacksmiths have our own Molotova to transport all that bulky stuff. If you have anything heavy, just give it to me."

Back at the command center we loaded all the boxes and cases and covered them up carefully; our luggage was jammed in at the back. A thought suddenly occurred to me. I took my hen and went to find Thé. "Please look after this hen for me," I said "as I don't think it will be safe in that jumble of heavy pieces in the truck. Please take care of it; it has saved my life many times."

As if it understood what was being said, the bird cackled, "Cooc . . . cooc . . . cooc . . ." from within the bag.

Reaching out for it, Thé said, "Of course I will. But what if we are moved to different camps?"

"Well, in that case I still have to part with it."

Thé whispered to me, "Don't worry! That talkative Hung has told me that unlike before, all of us will be moved to the same location. I hope he was right."

I rushed back to the command center and joined the others to load Thinh's bed onto a truck; it was unusually heavy. On inspection, we found a large storage compartment cleverly concealed under it; when moved about, it sounded like it was full of stones.

The furniture and miscellaneous pieces were loaded, and we climbed to the roofs to remove the corrugated sheets. From the roofs we could see the yard where inmates were assembled to board the vehicles. Voices were shouting orders; the new *bodoi* did not hesitate to let loose abuse on the inmates. "This f . . . ing one! Leave all those bundles behind! Do you want to travel on foot?" "All these chickens! Throw them out! They would certainly be crushed to death in this truck." "And all these. . . . Throw them away! I said throw them away, you f . . . bastards!"

All this loading and reloading lasted until midday. Those who had been reluctant to shed their cherished belongings were forced to get off the trucks, worry showing on their faces. The engines started, and the convoy began to move. Those lucky enough to be on board were laughing and joking. They waved at those left behind. "Take care!" "Good-bye!" they yelled. "Try to make it on foot!"

At the command center, two truckloads of *bodoi* and goods arrived. The vehicles pulled up and let out a group of tough-looking *bodoi* armed to the teeth with automatic rifles, heavy machine guns, and B-40 rocket launchers. Their tattered clothes indicated that they had just seen battle activity. A lieutenant with sunburned face came forward to meet Thinh, saying, "I have orders to take over this site, Comrade. Take your time to clear up your things as we are in no hurry. We will live in that bank of houses. By the way, bring all your corrugated sheets with you as we have our own."

I looked down from my vantage point and saw that the twelve or so *bodoi* were unloading their belongings and equipment, including a stack of corrugated sheets. So the roofs had to be removed by us to be replaced by the newcomers! This illogical practice was characteristic of the *bodoi*.

Finally, everything was neatly stacked to await the trucks, which were to return for us. We were given a nice lunch for all our efforts—rice, roasted fish, and tea.

The newcomers were having their siesta in a house, their cases and weapons next to them.

We also rested in the shade. Thé and the other blacksmiths waited with us. We lay on the ground looking up at the cloudless blue sky.

"I rather regret leaving this place. It was easy to gather extra food and catch wild animals in the jungle," said Thé.

We talked of the good times.

"I will really miss that stream," I said. "It's clear and teeming with fish."

"I wonder what the new place will be like."

"Never mind about that," said Thé. "It's all the same everywhere—jungle, hard labor, hunger, illness. There's no point in worrying anymore; we know our fates are sealed."

I added, "I think we have got used to these sudden moves and are not so afraid of facing unfamiliar circumstnces anymore. We'll certainly meet the same things everywhere. However, this move is quite unexpected."

We were interrupted by the sounds of the returning convoy. Other inmates still in camp were obviously relieved to see the empty vehicles.

The *bodoi*'s luggage was loaded under Thinh's watchful eye. Heavy pieces had to be cushioned with straw pads. Next came our own things, kitchen utensils for the *bodoi*, and finally two trussed-up pigs. There was still enough room left for everyone to sit and to move his legs about. We used the straw as mattresses; it was newly cut and gave off a soothing smell.

Farther off, at the inmates' quarters, the men boarded the trucks. Those items previously left behind were now retrieved as there was still enough room.

The vehicle convoy moved out, camp commanders in the lead, followed by inmates and goods, and brought up in the rear by a truckful of armed guards. The vehicles lurched along the potholed road, slowly negotiated a ramp, then moved onto the "highway." We looked back at the vast camp left behind. There stood the command center, the living quarters of the commander and his study monitors, their canteen, kitchen, and stores. And beyond, on the other side of the stream, were the inmate quarters; the U-shape of five longhouses enclosing a central meeting hall. All this had been built with our own sweat out of bamboo, wood, and rattan lashings. Not a single metal nail had been used.

The road snaked through the bare rice fields, hill after hill patterned with potato, and cassava crops. These too were the result of our sweat, blood, tears, and humiliation. Now they were slowly being lost to sight as the convoy rumbled away.

Chapter 6

Camp Five: Bu Loi

The convoy moved slowly on a road which the rains had reduced to a rutted track. Lurching like a boat on rough seas, our truck negotiated the potholes and drove past field after field of cassava, interspersed now and then by stubbled rice fields. We saw signs of abandoned reeducation camps suggesting mass transportation of the whole region's inmates to new sites. We had wound our way through the fields and hills for about fifty kilometers when we heard the din of horns from the front of the convoy, then the sound of people talking and laughing. We were passing a group of inmates lining the sides of the road; they wore hats and had tied towels over their faces to ward off the cloud of red dust raised by the trucks. I realized that these were men from our camp who had gone on the early convoy that morning. Apparently they were made to get off so that the trucks could return to pick up the camp officials, the equipment, and the remaining inmates.

One passenger shouted to his waving pals by the road, "Your belongings that you left behind were loaded on this truck; you don't have to worry anymore!"

Somebody shouted back at him, "What about mine? Did you only help your friends?"

We drove on and finally turned onto a gravel road. I suddenly noticed signs of habitation: trussed-up bundles of firewood were neatly placed here and there along the road as if they were to be transported. Then we saw axe-carrying Montagnards[1] standing along the road looking on at the moving convoy. We told each other we were soon going to reach an inhabited area.

After about half an hour, the convoy turned onto a wide dirt track that was still in good condition, as though it had just been built. Huge timber logs were lying on both sides of the track, indicating logging on a large scale. The farther we moved off the main roads, the more people we saw. The area was quite different from that around Bu Gia Map. One man who knew this region said we were in an inhabited area of Phuoc Binh Province. Had we stayed on the gravel road, we would now have been on Route 14. As the only outgoing road led to the town of Phuoc Binh, it was beyond doubt that we were being moved to another jungle area, possibly a logging site. Our main concern, however, was whether we were nearer or farther away from Saigon.

---

[1]The aboriginal people of the highlands of Central Vietnam. They belong to dozens of ethnic and linguistic groups separate from the majority Vietnamese.

The knowledgeable fellow pointed out that "nearer" or "farther away" depended on what you mean by it. "If our new camp lies near a main road with plenty of traffic, then Saigon would be easily accessible even if it's a long distance from here. On the other hand, if the new camp is near Saigon but in an uninhabited and isolated area, it would be considered 'far away' from the city."

There was a sigh, "What's the point of talking? Do you really think they are moving us to a place near a main road? We are destined to be buried in some jungle." The atmosphere turned suddenly heavy.

Now we were on a stretch of road full of potholes. There was empty space all around us as though this part of the jungle had previously been cleared for cultivation. Soon, what looked like a Montagnard hamlet came into view. The convoy wound its way past clusters of stilted huts and came to a stop some minutes later. There were cheerful murmurs among the passengers: "If this is the new camp, we will be near some villages!"

The childish-looking *bodoi*, who had been drowsing in a corner, careless of his submachine gun, started as the truck pulled up; he looked around, realized the journey was over, and moved to climb down. We were ordered to get off and line up. It was already dark. A group of study monitors arrived to check the number of inmates, and afterward we were ordered to assemble our luggage for the trip to our new home. Following a group of armed guards, we walked on a narrow trail, too narrow to accommodate any vehicle. The vegetation around us was young and sparse.

We arrived at a cluster of derelict thatched huts in a clearing and were ordered to put down our belongings and wait. Being the first to arrive, we were spared the task of unloading the battalion's equipment and furniture. The teams arriving after us had to leave their personal possessions piled near the trucks and carry the beds, chairs, pots and pans, and sacks of rice belonging to battalion to a spot near the cluster of houses. I asked permission to relieve myself and went to the edge of the open space to look around. I saw no other sign of habitation. I went back and ate a few slices of dried bread. An hour later, we were told to assemble to receive orders. Areas of rest were allocated and the men, being tired and sleepy, eagerly cleaned up their assigned places, secured their belongings, and prepared for the night. Thé and I also prepared places for our friends who were still on their way; they arrived earlier than expected as they had been picked up by the trucks that were not fully loaded.

No sooner had we settled down to sleep than orders came for us to report to the "command post" at the other end of the clearing. Commander Thinh was already there. He smiled and greeted us with a question, "Did you notice anything unusual on the way here?" Everyone looked at one another, puzzled, but there was no answer.

Thinh smiled on, "Of course you must have! But you dare not tell me! The unusual thing about this camp is that it is near the People. Do you know why you are brought here to be near the People? You should have asked yourselves the question and found out by now. However, I must emphasize one thing: You are prohibited from socializing with them. You must prove that our superiors' trust in you is well founded, especially after that exceptional harvest! You will find that this will be a short stay, but that still is something you should be glad about. It would therefore be regrettable for any one of you to commit a breach of discipline while in this camp. We shall start building more huts tomorrow even if you will not be here long. Now, you can go."

"The old fox obviously tried to boost our morale," I thought. But it consoled me somewhat to know that we were not the only inhabitants of this corner of the world. Once more, we had to sleep on the ground on a piece of plastic, but this time we were not as miserable or pitiful a lot as on the first night in the dark jungle of Bu Gia Map.

Sleep took over quickly, but I was awakened by the sound of a baby crying in the distance. Someone else heard it too and remarked on it. I said, "It has been a long time since I last heard a baby's cry. How comforted it makes me feel hearing that sound." I could tell that it was a young baby; it went on for a while, then gradually quieted down, probably soothed by its mother. To a prisoner deprived of the happiness of family life, the long-forgotten sound of a baby's crying seemed to be the sweetest melody in the world.

The whole place bustled with activity before dawn; some were tidying up their "beds," others were washing themselves. We quickly organized into teams to boil water and cook manioc roots. Breakfast was finished almost as soon as it had started. We waited for a long time before being assembled for the day's assignments, but finally a few of us were told to choose sites for the new huts, while others were to look for straw to thatch the roofs. Later, we ventured into the jungle to find small trees to cut for building frames. We had reached an agreement with the camp authorities that we would build longhouses on stilts, the floors about one meter above the ground to keep us away from the damp and cold. The suitable trees near the campsite had already been cut, so we had to go deeper and deeper into the jungle.

As we wandered around, we came across a group of young men who were obviously looking for something. Our first thought was that they were *bodoi*, but their tattered, dirty clothes suggested otherwise. We waved at them in a friendly way, but they just stared back at us, some even with hostility. Then they hurried off without saying a word.

Each of us had been given the quota of six small trees a day to carry back to the campsite. We decided at the start that it would be easiest to cut all the trees at one time, stack them up by the trail, and then all together carry them back to the camp in the afternoon when the quotas were filled. We finished cutting by noon and carried the logs to the trailside. The freshly cut logs were heavy with sap, and we were exhausted. After the lunch break we returned to the spot where we had left the logs only to find nothing there. Assuming that we had lost our way, we fanned out to search for our day's quota, but it was no use. At last we gave up, gloomily going back to start cutting all over again. When we finally got back to camp, there was a commotion; others were angrily reporting to the study monitors that their harvest had been stolen!

"Bloody hell!" exploded a study monitor. "This must be the work of those Volunteer Youths from Thai Binh! Who else could have done it?"

So that group of young men who shunned us this morning are volunteers from that famous poverty-stricken province in the North, I thought. They had been sent here, I later learned, to pave the way for bringing in immigrants from their province. We were advised to have several inmates stand guard over the newly cut logs from then on to discourage the thieves.

It took us three days to erect the frameworks for our houses. We then went to the nearby Montagnard villages to ask for straw to thatch the roofs. The new camp took shape within four days after we had first moved in. The new shelters, two parallel rows of longhouses, had thick, wind-blocking walls made of bamboo wattle. Since it was not possible to build a high fence around the camp perimeter, the *bodoi* had to be stationed all around the area every night. We noted that they took care to change their positions each night, but they always betrayed their presence by talking and laughing, especially the younger ones.

It was barely a week before we were ordered to start clearing forests for future rice and sweet potato crops. By now I was consistently regarded as a carpenter and was immediately assigned the less arduous task of building houses for the *bodoi*. Their present accommodation could barely stand the weather, and they were insisting on spacious, sturdy buildings on raised foundations of beaten earth. The frameworks had to be of good quality wood and the roofs covered with corrugated iron.

Venturing farther and farther away from the camp while working in the forest, we encountered one day a bunch of kids, some as young as six or seven years, offering their wares for sale: bananas, jackfruits, glutinous rice cakes, and even the favorite *banh cuon*.[2] Each carried on his or her head a basket containing a meager amount, just enough to sell to a few customers. We asked where they came from. One replied, "I come from the village of Minh Hung about two hours' walk from here. My mother made these cakes for me to sell to inmates of nearby camps."

"Are you not afraid of being arrested by the *bodoi*?" I asked.

"We are! If we are caught trading with ordinary people, we will be harshly punished."

---

[2]A kind of steamed or boiled dumpling made of rice flour and stuffed with pork, mushroom, onion, and spices and eaten hot with diluted fish sauce (*nướ c mắm*).

But the young girl said calmly, "Don't worry! I know the authorities of other camps around here have let their inmates buy things from the peasants. They have to let them so they can stay healthy to work for them. As for us, we know how to make friends with the most difficult *bodoi*."

Seeing that she was not particularly sympathetic to the new regime, I teased, "Don't you dare talk like this! What class are you in? Have you been accepted into the Red Scarves Youth League?"

"Why should I be afraid of them?" she laughingly replied with a mischievous twinkle in her eyes. "I used to go to school, but we can't afford it anymore. I have to help my mother feed our family by selling a few things. Besides, there's no point in going to school now. Most of the time it's devoted to political education instead of real studies."

"Even children as young as you have to take political education?"

"Of course, everybody has to! We used to start with a political lesson every morning on the duties of children, how to build a socialist society, how to denounce the reactionaries, and on our duty to inform the authorities about agents left behind by the Americans. I learned a lot, but I also forgot a lot! I stopped going to school more than a year ago. My father used to be a lieutenant in the former army, and he's also being reeducated somewhere. So I also belong to the *nguy* elements. I didn't like what I learned at school, so I told my mother and she said it was a waste of time. Besides, she can teach me at home, so I stayed home."

Asking the price of the rice cakes, I found it was cutthroat. Each small cake costing one dong could be devoured in two bites!

This trading flourished over the next weeks to the point where even the main staple—rice—was on sale. Our diet improved for a while until our savings ran out. It was my impression and from what I gathered from friends that the *bodoi* here were rather easygoing. This considerably boosted morale and gave us hope for release before too long.

One day at work, I was called to the command center. To my great relief I found out that I would be included in a team about to take over a nearby granary. My task would be to measure the rice stored there as I had done with our famous crop in the last camp. We were led by Tu, the political cadre. And to my disappointment, we set out on foot escorted by two submachine-gun-toting guards. After some ten kilometers we met a group of children who looked like the young vendors we had previously done business with, and I thought we might be heading for the village of Minh Hung. We went on for a time and then turned onto a newly built trail. The path had been brutally cut into the red soil; bulldozed trees lay in heaps all over, their broken branches and roots pointing in all directions.

We soon walked into a camp full of uniformed young men in their late teens, who we later learned were conscripts. We were ordered not to communicate with them. However, once we got into the hastily built granary, we were surrounded by these young men eager to talk. They said that most of them were from Saigon. I asked why the granary had to be handed over to the camp management.

"We are going to be sent to the battlefront to fight Pol Pot," one replied, "so we have to leave this rice which we grew ourselves with our sweat. We don't know why we have not been allowed to eat it. God knows how much effort has been spent to produce all this rice!"

I asked another one if they'd had the proper training to go to the battlefront. They all tried to talk at once, apparently needing to vent their feelings.

"What training are you talking about? All we have learned so far has been basic drills. We have not even been allowed to practice shooting; maybe we shall have our first shooting lesson at the battlefront!"

A cadre appeared from nowhere, shouting, "Get back to your class!" They left and went into some derelict thatched houses on the hillside. The hilltop had been leveled into a miniature soccer field with two pairs of poles at the ends of the field for goalposts. The whole place looked like a dirt-poor village rather than a military training camp.

A ridiculous incident occurred when we got into the granary itself. Its keepers insisted that we measure out the grain, bushel by bushel, onto large pieces of wattle spread on the ground in the yard. The trouble with this, of course, was that it would take us days to finish the job. We suggested instead that we could level off the surface of the stored grain, measure its dimensions, and get the volume. Then a container of known capacity could be filled up and weighed, giving us the density from which the total weight of the stored grain could be calculated very quickly. But this all fell on deaf ears. Commissar Tu smiled and said, "Both sides must somehow reach an agreement on how to measure the weight of the grain in storage."

"It will take ages to measure it bushel by bushel since we will have to take it out and then bring it back into the storeroom," I said. "The rice is in cylindrical bins made of wattle casing, and we can calculate its volume accurately enough and then arrive at the total weight."

My argument sounded convincing, so Tu finally told the granary keepers, "Comrades, we are wasting time! Let them have a go with their method; then we can compare their results with your own figures; if the discrepancy is too great, we will then do it your way."

They debated the pros and cons for a while and finally concluded it was up to them to decide. "You will have to measure out bushel by bushel as we have done in the past."

But we were already measuring the dimensions of the grain bins as if unaware of their decision. It took us about half an hour to arrive at the total amount, which was just over thirty-nine tons.

One inmate whispered, "We will have to settle for just over forty tons as I'm sure they have inflated their crop yield. I only hope they did not inflate it too much this time!"

The two results were compared, and the *bodoi* just looked blankly at each other. Finally one said, "You've nearly matched our result! Well, in this case you've achieved your goal. What do you think, comrade Tu?"

Tu hesitated, asking us, "Can you guarantee that your result is correct? Tell me how you arrived at it."

We showed him a piece of paper with all the figures on it and tried to explain the problem. He listened with a bewildered look on his face and at long last uttered, "Very well, that will do. But you will have to take the blame if later on somebody finds out there is an error."

He was answered by a unanimous chorus, "Of course we guarantee that our result is quite correct," as we were anxious to finish with this business.

One inmate whispered "Blame or not, we've got nothing to lose."

We were then given manioc roots for lunch. Tu naturally was invited to have lunch with those in charge of the camp. Later, when he returned, smiling—obviously having had a nice meal—we took advantage of his mood to ask, "We have heard that there's a market near here; may we please go there to do some shopping? It's been a long time since we last went to a shop."

The two young guards put in a word, "We want to go there too! Just to see the market! Please let us escort them."

His eyes twinkled mischievously, "No, comrades. You can't. As we have just taken over the granary, it's your duty to stay here to guard it. I'll escort these guys back to the camp."

"There's no need to guard it," protested the two youngsters. "Comrade Commander, why not enjoy yourself here? Leave the escorting to us young men. Besides, it's too hot now for the long walk home."

"All right! Off you go! Be careful not to run into the regiment's cadres."

We cheerfully set out with a guide provided by the training camp. We took a shortcut through garden plots, crossing some footbridges and skirting a hillside, arriving at a cluster of thatched huts with orchards at the back. We crossed an orchard and took a path leading to the main road that ran through the open market. An old bus stood there, its top being loaded with huge jackfruits. Its presence indicated that the place was not as isolated as we had first thought.

The first thing we had to do was to invite the two young guards to have some nice treat. Only drinks seemed to be available, and I ordered a glass of chilled lemon juice while others settled for coffee, which they found to have little taste. The only chewable stuff was a kind of biscuit meant for young children. I asked permission to go to the market to buy some sugar for tonight.

"Of course you can," the older of the two said amicably. "Don't forget to come back here!"

From where we stood, we commanded a view of the whole market. About thirty meters away was a tiny shop, at the front of which hung several rolls of bread wrapped in plastic. I went to it, and my odd clothing immediately caught the attention of the shop's elderly owner.

"Where do you come from with those funny-looking clothes?" she asked.

"I am from a nearby reeducation camp."

"Oh! So you are an inmate! Are you in Bu Loi? I've heard from young vendors who have been there that an enormous number of inmates are building a new camp. How are you getting on? I know you men have a hell of a time out there!"

"Yes, we do. But there's nothing we can do to change that. Do you sell any sugar?"

I bought half a kilogram of brown sugar for seven dong. When I was about to leave, she asked, "Do you want to send some letters home? My grandchildren can handle it. We have helped inmates post letters in the past. Replies can also be brought to you in the camp by the children."

Taken by surprise and instantly suspicious, I said, "How could this be possible? Isn't there an informer here?"

"All of us have been forced to come here from Saigon," said the old lady; "therefore, we are sympathetic to you. There's no such thing as an informer in this village."

Although glad to learn of this, I decided it paid to stay on guard. "Thank you very much for your offer, but I can't use your service just now. I have already sent my letters." I bid her good-bye and left.

Seeing that sugar was available, others asked the guards for permission to buy it and a few other items. Just as we were about to leave, the two *bodoi* bought some sugarcanes and gave each of us a length. One said, "This will quench your thirst on the way back. Now, off you go!"

It took us about half an hour to get back to the training camp. One of our guards stayed on at the granary, and the rest followed Tu back to our own camp.

That night all we talked about was the morning trip, the surrounding area, and the nearby reeducation camps. As I was dropping off to sleep, Thé said, "Do you remember that baby crying that night in the Montagnard hamlet? A group of *bodoi* went to see that family this morning to 'ask' them to move. The head of the family was very reluctant as his rice crop was not yet harvested, so we were called on to help speed up the eviction. I asked the man why he had not harvested the crop because it *was* ready; why leave it for the birds? He said that was better than spending back-breaking hours harvesting it only to have the rice requisitioned by the Montagnard *bodoi*. He used to go out to gather just enough for his family's daily needs."

I was deeply involved in building houses for the *bodoi*. The majority of inmates toiled in the bamboo forests preparing land for the rice crop. To get a high yield, Commander Thinh insisted on the "slash-and-burn" technique, in which whole bamboo forests were burned to leave a thick layer of ash as fertilizer. The main problem was that these forests were quite a distance from the camp. I also was forced to venture deeper and deeper into the jungle to find suitable timber for construction. In this way I discovered the existence of two other reeducation camps, one about five and the other ten kilometers away from our camp—in addition to the nearby camp occupied by the Thai Binh "volunteer youths."

One day, searching for large trees to use as posts, we came to a thick forest quite far from the camp, and there we ran into an odd trio: a young woman and two boys, each about ten years old. They wore dirty, tattered clothes, and their hands were covered with scabies sores. They tried to run away from us, but they could not move very fast through the dense forest. As we approached, they looked on, frightened; hunger and exhaustion showed on their faces.

I asked, "What are you doing here in this forest?"

They just stared at us; then the two boys ran off. I called after them, "We are reeducation inmates. There's no need to run away!"

The young woman burst into tears and said, "We come from Phu Van collective farm. We are trying to find our way back to Saigon; we can no longer stand the life in that place! First we're trying to get to some hamlet to ask for money for the bus fares. I know that some have made it before."

Seeing that we did not mean any harm, the boys stopped and looked back from where they stood. The woman waved at them. "Come back! Don't be afraid; these men are inmates."

She then told us that Phu Van collective farm was actually a rehabilitation center for delinquent youths—shiftless beggars and vagrants, pickpockets, thieves, men who used to roam the streets of Saigon, as well as for prostitutes and other petty offenders. At first, the center was officially named "dignity restoring center" but now was known as Phu Van collective farm.

Her eyes fixed on our bags. She finally asked if we had anything to eat. We gave her slices of boiled manioc roots, our daily rations. She put all of them into a plastic bag that she replaced in her pack and silently slung the pack over her shoulder. She said, "Thank you very much. I have to save food for the long trip to Saigon; these boys are too young to think about going hungry in the days ahead. I've heard that there are two other rehabilitation centers in this province for 'social outcasts' from Saigon-Cholon. The one near Xuan Loc is supposed to be much better as it is a model center visited by foreigners. Nobody knows about Phu Van. Maybe it is deliberately isolated to suit the harsh conditions. There are about seventy youngsters there and just over two hundred women. Even the children have to do compulsory labor."

One of the boys interrupted her, "The *bodoi* forced us to hoe the earth like adults. Some cried and refused to go on, but they were threatened that they would lose their rations. We all had to do it."

The woman said the boys used to live with their families in Khanh Hoi.

"They happened to be sleeping outside when the police came around scooping up young delinquents. They insisted that they had families, but nobody believed them since that's what all the real delinquents also said. These two were caught trying to escape, and to punish them, the commune authority put them in a dry well for nearly a week where they got the scabies." She pointed to the sores on their hands and feet.

We grew more and more shocked at this treatment of children. "How did such a practice get started?"

"The dry well was invented by the authorities to punish the older boys who were really stubborn. It's true there were some reckless delinquents who refused to do any hard work. They laughed at the *bodoi*'s threat of letting them go hungry. They even shouted abuse at the *bodoi*, who then tied them up. The farm authorities finally came up with the idea of putting them in a three-meter-deep dry well covered by thick planks and weighted with heavy logs; even the loudest cries were muffled. From then on, the dry well was used often. The stench of excrement and urine down there is unbearable, although it has been cleaned up every now and then."

Going on with her story, the woman described the collective farm as organized along the lines of other reeducation camps in one respect: A camp leader was elected who received orders from the farm authority and then would give out assignments to groups of inmates.

"Our first camp leader was Bich, a very pretty woman. She used to be called up to the command center to 'receive orders' every evening. Sometimes she had to stay there until midnight. One night, when she was about to go to bed after a long 'briefing meeting,' she was summoned by a group of *bodoi* and was not allowed back until the next morning. This went on for a while until early one morning her body was discovered hanging from a rope in the latrines. I think she decided she had had enough. There was no official inquiry into her death, but the *bodoi*'s attitude toward the young women at the farm changed somewhat from that day."

Moved by her account, we tried our best to show her the way to the Minh Hung village and to make some suggestions.

"If you come across a group of young vendors, try to mix in with them to become less noticeable," one of us said.

Another added, "Once you get to Saigon, find some other clothes, as these show who you are."

We were depressed by this chance meeting and all the more worried for our own fate, as it indicated how the "building a new society" was being carried out by the new rulers.

Eventually, as the buildings were completed and we we well settled, there came the business of compiling "self-histories." By now we were well prepared for this step as we had found out that this tricky self-criticism business would be required every time we changed camp, no matter how long it was delayed. One day we were ordered to stay home instead of going out to work. Our first thoughts were about leaves for the "progressives" or transfers to harsher camps for the "unrepentant," but the truth finally dawned when stacks of blank paper and bundles of pens were distributed.

By now, we had memorized details to be declared to ensure that each new version of self-history was consistent with previous ones. We had also learned to keep the details as concise as possible, for by now we no longer believed that lengthy, self-criticizing self-histories would speed up our release. Therefore, sentences such as "lackeys of the feudal colonialist French" previously applied to our civil servant fathers or "agents of the imperialist Americans" to describe our relatives were now absent from our accounts. What once were twenty-to-thirty-page-long histories were now a quarter that length.

We were each given a sheet of blank paper to be attached to our self-histories, the only entry on it apart from our name and personal particulars was the title, "Assessment by Camp Authority." Thinh and his study monitors flatly declared that from now on our fates would be decided by the nature of these assessments.

It was around this time that we learned from a *bodoi* that our presence here was part of a government policy of replacing Montagnard tribal villages that lay along the Vietnamese-Cambodian border with reeducation camps and especially with "pioneer villages" for immigrants from the North, "for only these true socialists have the necessary determination to defend our sacred border."

The fields left by the relocated Montagnards had been carelessly exploited and lacked the minerals needed to support vigorous plant life. Since they were now useless, we were forced to reclaim virgin bamboo forests farther away from the camp, using the same slash-and-burn technique that had caused the ruination of the old fields. Every morning we set out at seven carrying our daily rations of manioc roots. We followed winding footpaths through the dense, leech-infested jungle to reach the great stands of bamboo. Our first job when we reached our destination was to undress and check for leeches; few were spared. By this time, the burning sun would be high in the sky, and we had to stop to replenish our energy with slices of manioc before starting work. The bamboo to be cut had short joints and was full of a sharp, metallic residue that caused severe itching once it got on the skin. The more we scratched the more it itched, to the point of driving us mad. All we could do to protect ourselves was to wear layers of thick clothes from head to foot that could be washed at the end of the day. But we got unbearably hot and sweaty in those layers of clothes, so were miserable either way.

Under these conditions we were exhausted as usual, and now illness became more and more a problem, worse that it had been at Bu Gia Map. In addition to the omnipresent malaria, there were diarrhea brought on by the polluted water supply and a kind of fever characterized by dizziness, aching, and high temperatures. The first person to fall seriously ill was the former musician, Khuyen, who had been chief carpenter at a camp near Xuan Loc. From the day he was moved to this camp, Khuyen had suffered from some kind of intestinal disease in addition to indigestion. He became weaker and weaker until it seemed he was only awaiting death. Another patient was Ha Phuoc Sanh, who had been as big and healthy as an ox, an oddity among the camp inmates. An "early bird," he always exercised every morning before anyone else was up. All of a sudden, he fell ill and was completely laid up, obviously with some liver trouble as his face was jaundiced. Fortunately, his brother was also in the camp, and he tried his best to look after him. However, we all knew that it was only a matter of time before both of these men would die, for no drugs were available apart from some malaria tablets. At this time, we were kept out of touch with our relatives who might have been able to bring in medicine. A depressing atmosphere hung over the camp as more and more inmates were laid up with all kinds of ailments.

One evening, while I was listening to a friend playing his guitar, Thé came in with a big smile on his face. "I've just seen *bodoi* Hung. He told me there was a long list of people on leave. He claimed he had seen this list himself!"

I could not hold back a laugh. "This must be Thinh's latest trick to bolster our morale. Otherwise we'd never fill his quotas."

"Do you think I am an idiot? I promise you it's true this time. You know that cunning Hung comes from my village, don't you? He always tells me the truth. He also said that Thinh had to delay the announcement because he feared that if this many people were let out too soon, there would not be enough of us left to do the work."

Unable to stand any more of this, I retorted, "You sound as if you were among those going on leave! Maybe you are. But my turn will never come. Don't be so naïve. You need more 'reeducation' to see the truth."

"It's a waste of time talking to you!" Thé looked annoyed. "I have never believed the commies, but I do believe Hung because I know him well. He's not much different from us; he doesn't really believe in communism. He was conscripted; he didn't voluntarily join their army. When he first saw me, he recognized me immediatly. His family lives only a few kilometers from mine. From the first, he has been quite sympathetic to me. He also told me that Thinh was asking his superiors to keep us here for a few more months until the land is ready since logistics still has plenty of provisions for us."

"Impossible! How come they have a surplus of food? We would be lucky not to have a shortage, let alone any surplus."

"Remember that time at Xuan Loc? Bui Quoc Khanh once disclosed that the camp authority had managed to 'save' some rice by reducing our rations. A precaution against late delivery! Probably they're doing the same thing here. Do you still remember that truckful of supplies when we first came here? You're not familiar with their practices! They always try to falsify records to skim off something for themselves. Just wait and see; we will be released as soon as we finish this surplus rice, believe me. We'll soon be out! We'll be free!"

I could not share Thé's optimism. That night, lying near him, I sensed he could not sleep for excitement. He woke me up once, whispering, "It won't be long. It won't be long now."

A few days later, having received our daily rations, we waited for the guards to take us to the fields as usual. No one was seen. Anticipation grew. Then Commander Thinh appeared with his study monitors and the guards. We looked at one another, hoping against hope that they brought good news with them.

The younger inmates could not contain their excitement. "It's true! We're going to be out! The list is there!"

And it was! Thinh held up a list and read out the names of those lucky inmates—none other than the same ones who went on leave last time! They were led off to a separate corner and the rest of us were escorted away by the guards as usual to the bamboo forests.

Loud swearing was heard. "Bloody hell! I wonder who that bastard is who spread the rumor that a lot of people would be released this time!"

Back from work that evening, we rushed to see the sick ones who were spared labor and allowed to stay indoors. We asked them if those selected for leave had gone. One said, "After coming back to collect their luggage, they made off for the command center where they waited for transport until noon. I've heard from the cooks that each of them also carried a hoe!"

A man swore, "F . . . them! Why are they carrying a hoe home? I don't understand!"

Another put in, "These guys must have influential sponsors, or they must have bribed someone millions of dong or kilograms of gold!"

Sitting around that evening, Thé suddenly said, "Believe me! That long list of people on leave does exist, despite what's happened so far."

"I wish you were right! Stop thinking about this. Try to catch some sleep for tomorrow's work."

The same routine—work, eat, sleep—repeated itself over and over. However, the depressing monotony was relieved by some exciting and worrisome news we heard one day from the inmate cooks. "Those assessment forms are now being filled in by the study monitors."

One day I was relieved from tree cutting to do repair work at the regiment's command center. Several of us went early to our camp's command center to wait for transport, and there in front of our eyes were the study monitors, each at a desk behind piles of paper—our "self-histories"—laboriously filling in the damned assessment forms. "Go to the main gate to wait for your transport, not here," a guard shouted.

So it was true! We were being assessed. This was the first time we had ever known for sure that our files were being examined, although we had handled wrapped-up bundles of files every time we changed camp. We spent the next days talking of nothing else but the assessments; the air was tense with anxiety, anticipation. Time dragged by, but nothing happened.

Tracts of bamboo forest had now been cleared, ready for burning. The dry vegetation caught fire as easily as tinder, and vast areas were engulfed in flames. As soon as the ash had sufficienty cooled down, we moved in to clear the underbrush. Again the dry, warm ash, stirred by the slightest breeze, clung to our sweat-soaked bodies and found its way into our lungs every time we breathed. At the time we were convinced no work could be worse than this. Still, no one attempted to escape because we now all believed in an early release. Rumor had it that all inmates would be released as soon as a group of immigrants from the North arrived to take over the land. It sounded temptingly logical as part of the current government policy to consolidate the defenses of the southern border; besides, we had now been "reeducated" for more than three years—the official maximum period for minor offenders according to a government newspaper article we read at Xuan Loc. The more these rumors were repeated, the more genuine they sounded, and they were useful in helping to defuse frustration and anger. We were all on alert, observing the *bodoi* for any indication that the camp was about to be dismantled.

All of a sudden I was called to the command center, together with others who had been involved in laying a telephone cable connecting the Bu Gia Map camp to its regimental headquarters. Told to help the *bodoi* collect cable, we assumed a new link was to be laid somewhere. At regimental headquarters we boarded a truck and proceeded back in the direction of our old camp. Reaching a junction, we saw a deep trench running across a road that led to the border, and huge piles of earth were seen everywhere.

"Why all this?" I asked a *bodoi*. "As if we were preparing for war?"

He answered importantly, "This area is now considered 'front line'; all these are precautions against invasion by the enemy."

Not a soul was in sight. We sped past our former camp, heading toward what previously had been regimental headquarters. In sharp contrast to the busy barracks it once was, we saw ony a few sloppily dressed *bodoi* moving about staring at us. We were told to remove the lengths of cable that we ourselves had laid. Those posts that we had so proudly erected were now easily toppled, thanks to the termites eating away at them. We made our way over the land we had cultivated on the hillsides; the sweet potato fields we had planted just before leaving were bursting with exuberant plants. We dived at them, hastily digging up huge roots. To our bitter disappointment, this God-given extra food supply turned out to be rubbish. It had all been ravaged from within by insects, and we understood why the potatoes had not been harvested by the local *bodoi*.

Removing the cable led us back to our old campsite, now deserted and depressingly run down. Wild plants grew inside the huts, and the bamboo floors had buckled, even though the earthen foundations had been carefully beaten. In the granary, the bins were half-filled with rice, and rat droppings were everywhere on the floor mixed with grain. Spilled grain was ankle deep near the doorway. We helped ourselves to the rice, carefully concealing it in our lunch bags. Who could have thought that the result of our sweat and blood was now being so wantonly wasted here? Or had it been abandoned as a result of some fighting nearby?[3] Behind the huts were our outdoor kitchens and plots of garden. After these months of inattention our vegetables had become bushes, some reaching shoulder high. There was enough here for all the inmates in our camp. We rushed in to pick vegetables and red peppers.

Breathless from carrying our harvest and the heavy reels of cable to the main road, we rested, having sent one of our younger companions back to the old headquarters to fetch the truck. From our vantage point on a hill, we commanded a panoramic view of the surrounding fields of cassava, some plants as high as three meters. We were tempted by the thought of the big roots underneath, but one man told us that two-year-old roots like these would be as big as logs and unsuitable for consumption unless they were processed to remove harmful elements in them.

"If you are right," I said in amazement, "then all these vast tracts of manioc crop are wasted. Was all that work we did in vain?"

"That's right! What else can they do with these roots? Didn't you meet those farmers from Dac O near Bu Gia Map? They wanted to sell their crop, but they could find no buyer nearby because manioc is now grown everywhere. They couldn't afford to go to the cities, and there was no means of shipment."

"Those farmers might be right," I said, "but it would be illogical for these Northern communists to waste so much valuable food. We all know they used to suffer privation; therefore, they should know better than to waste resources."

My friend laughed. "That's not the way it goes at all! You're right to say that they used to live in destitution but completely wrong if you think they know how to conserve resources. Can you give me any example of it. In my opinion, they are irresponsibly squandering our country's resources! They obviously are not concerned about all this scandalous waste as no one bothers to do anything to stop it."

"But they seem to be living the ascetic lives of monks. How can they waste

---

[3]We were aware of border skirmishes with the Khmer Rouge.

when there's nothing there to waste? All they have are two meals of rice and dried fish a day."

"Pooh! How can you be so blind! I agree that they don't have enough to eat or to wear, but they are squandering *billions*, not just *millions* of dong! Take the specialists—technicians, doctors—who are in reeducation camps. Imagine how much investment our people had put into them! What a waste, not using them! It took at least seven years to train a doctor, four or five for an engineer, a university lecturer and other specialists . . . not to say of the money it cost."

"Well, yes, but it's part of the government policy not to use employees of the former regime; in other words, these people are not needed."

"Are you *sure* they are not needed? Do you think they have enough specialists to meet the needs of our country? Our people? Haven't you heard of the many cases where seriously ill patients are treated only with herbs? Don't you know that the *bodoi* themselves have to ask us for medicines? Do you remember at Xuan Loc camp we saw the *bodoi* dismantling electric generators to get the copper wires to weave baskets for their wives back home? Expensive imported generators? What about cutting up brand new tires to make sandals? And right here we had to burn down vast tropical forests to make way for temporary crops. As soon as the soil was exhausted, we moved on to destroy more forests. Do you know that it used to be our soldiers' duty to discourage the Montagnards from using this primitive slash-and-burn technique? And now we're doing it ourselves; it's systematic and large-scale destruction! All these fields will become wasteland, especially the cassava fields because the soil is very quickly exhausted. Think of that granary we have just been to! All that rice we grew, harvested, processed. What will become of it now? It's left there for wild animals while we don't have enough to eat! If you ever bothered to sit down and think, you would see that they are very poor and very wasteful at the same time. The trouble is, the people who suffer as a result of all this are the ordinary citizens."

The truck came back, and we managed, with enormous difficulty, to load all the heavy cable in a hurry and then get the vegetables we had picked on top. Looking back at the deserted camp receding in the distance and the abandoned fields all around us, I felt a terrible sadness as my friend's words began to take hold of my belief.

The installation of a telephone link between our camp and the new regimental headquarters occupied us for the next several days. Then came orders to build more houses at the headquarters, and once again we ventured deep into the jungle to find the good timber required. Instead of a mixture of clay and ash, the new foundations were to be built of beaten earth, covered by cement mixed with earth. The cement bags still bore the words "Gift to the People of Vietnam" and came from various countries. The results of this new technique looked quite nice at first, but it turned out to be a flop because the cement mixture did not hold up well.

All kinds of work progressed at a snail's pace as the weather preceding the rainy season got hotter and hotter, and more and more inmates were laid up with illnesses.

Anyway, the clearing of the forests was near completion. We suspected now that our food supply would soon run out because the *bodoi* were bustling about discussing ways to bring in supplies. The shortage of food seemed to match earlier rumors about inmates soon to be discharged, but common sense prevailed as no "immigrants" were in sight to take over when the time seemed right. To make matters worse, those "progressive elements" like Bui Quoc Khanh, an inmate doctor named Cung, and a former pilot named Bay, who were our foremen, did not hesitate pushing other inmates to the limits of their endurance to get quicker results or higher work quotas. They even openly reported us to the camp authorities. However, we kept the anger and frustration to ourselves to avoid reprisals. Some, who could not contain their feelings, mocked them. "Look! It's about time for us to kill our former friends to help our own cause!" Nothing happened to these men although the *bodoi* learned of their talk. The atmosphere of shifting hopes and anxieties was maintained as it fit in with the command's aim of preventing escapes.

The much-awaited news finally came. One morning as we were about to set out for work, orders came for us to stay put and have our luggage ready until further notice. My heart beat faster with expectation. We jumped at the slightest approaching footsteps. Those who had been informed in advance now excitedly went about giving away items they no longer needed.

Tran Minh Chau came to say good-bye to me and to give me a jar of preserved ginger, a valuable delicacy as it could be kept for quite some time in addition to its medicinal effect on coughs and stomachache. This act of friendship got me worried, though, as it could be confirmation of my fear that I would not be among the lucky ones.

"Can it be that all my wife's efforts and money went down the drain," I thought. Looking around, I seemed to read similar thoughts on many other faces. Chau, a former lieutenant, stood the best chance of being released this time as he had a relative who was a high-ranking official in the communist government.

There was much talk. Thé was calmly moving about asking the hopeful ones for this and that, as if content with his fate. We were made to wait on in this agonized state until noon when we were ordered to assemble in the main yard. Our belongings were to be left where they were.

As it was nearly impossible to hold a working meeting in the bare yard under the relentless sun, we were escorted back to our quarters and then to a field with many tall trees and plenty of shade. Everyone was there except for those who were seriously ill. We began the "class" with a song, dispiritedly rendered in spite of the many "encouragements" from the guards. Thinh did not even bother to order a repeat. With his permanent grin and his slow, deliberate movements, he fished a piece of paper out of a leather briefcase, cleared his throat, and waited for the noise to die down. His fake seriousness clearly amused the study monitors and the guards. They chuckled at first and then burst into laughter as the inmates waited expectantly, staring at Thinh. There was loud swearing from the audience.

Finally, Thinh spoke. "I've received orders from my superiors to hold this class to study the Revolution's lenient policy."

There were immediate protests, "We've already had enough propaganda!"

"Bloody hell! The more they see us suffer the more they enjoy it!"

"For God's sake! We've heard that before! We have had enough of this!"

The guards and study monitors shouted back, "Be quiet!"

"Shut up! You insolent lot!"

"You there! What have you just said? Say it again!"

Thinh just smiled on. "Our superiors have always stressed a fundamental principle that every problem must be approached in a well-planned, well-organized manner. Therefore, according to our lenient policy your release will take place in a well-planned, orderly manner.

"As everyone knows, the government cannot let you go all at once, so groups of you will be gradually released over a fixed period. If you think that the number released this time is large, you'll have every reason to believe that subsequent numbers will be even larger. Therefore, don't panic when you see your friends go first. As far as I am concerned, you have all made progress, so there's no reason why you should not be able eventually to reunite with your families. However, it's impossible to let all of you go at the same time as this will adversely affect the economy in many ways. So the Party and the State have decided that . . . "

We knew that this lengthy preface was only meant to calm down the inmates in preparation for disclosure of the names on the list of released prisoners.

Thinh's voice was heard clearly in the uneasy silence. "The list of those to be released should have been announced this morning, but was delayed due to last-minute changes. Even now we are still waiting for additional names to be dispatched from higher command. In the meantime, you are dismissed to continue with your normal work. Come back here tomorrow. Keep up your spirits! Don't forget, this is only the first batch, there will be more to come! Remember what I first said when we moved here, that your stay would not be long. Now, let's sing a song before you go."

That night there were celebrations by those who knew they were on the lucky list, but overall the air was heavy with depression, frustration, and anger. Some of the cool-headed ones went briskly about the business of asking those who were leaving to relay their whereabouts to their families.

Early the next morning we assembled in the main yard in front of the command center; we were told to bring all our luggage, "Not leaving behind even a needle or a length of thread," in the guards' words. The cooks got so excited that they made a mess of the manioc roots for breakfast.

Unlike on previous occasions, the guards now formed a line dividing the yard into two areas. We stood in one. Thinh read out the names of those who would soon be free. There was absolute silence as everyone strained to catch the names. Those who were called moved to the other area. Having read about thirty names, Thinh stopped for a moment, then said, "Reading all this has made me short of breath. However, there's plenty more to come."

As he read on, applause began in the inmate ranks; we had not witnessed so many releases before. When he had read over fifty names, Thinh paused to acknowledge the applause. Then he read on to the end, a total of eighty-seven names.

Thinh stopped smiling and looked down at us from the porch where he stood; the applause suddenly came to an end. Sober now, the inmates realized that although the number released was unprecedented this time, it was woefully small for a camp of over a thousand men. Thinh just stood there awkwardly and finally said, "I hope that the next group will be much larger than this. The remainder of you follow the study monitors back to your quarters now to rearrange the accommodations. Dismissed."

We made our way back in gloom while the fortunate ones waved cheerfully from their corner. There was angry swearing in our ranks all the way back. The study monitors ordered us to evacuate the huts nearest the jungle and occupy the spaces left vacant by the departing men. We were then instructed to keep watch on ourselves. Two inmates were to stand guard at each end of the rows of buildings, to be relieved every two hours. As we rearranged our quarters, we heard the excited voices of the newly freed men saying their good-byes to friends. "Good luck!" "Take care of yourselves!" their voices grew fainter as the procession moved away in the direction of the regiment's headquarters.

As the initial disappointment died away, I was able to adjust myself to the reality. Others clearly did not fare so well; the pain still showed on their faces, and they sullenly threw down their cases, heading for their beds without saying a word. Thé's new place was still next to mine. We tried to make a list of those released; some of them were those who had registered for reeducation on the same day with me so long ago, and there were others who were close to us: former army dentist Pham Van Tuong, former lecturer Ha The Ruyet, former naval officer Trieu Minh Chau. To our great joy and relief, those callous turncoats like Bui Quoc Khanh, former doctor Cung, former pilot Bay, and a few others who had tormented us and reported on us in their earnest search for a quick release were now gone forever. The strain of being constantly on our guard was now greatly reduced. However, it hurt to think that our former comrades-in-arms had so eagerly stabbed us in the back in order to gain early release for themselves.

From that day on security was tightened, aimed at thwarting escapes. As soon as dusk fell, the study monitors came to our quarters to oversee the security arrangements after the compulsory roll call. Details as trivial as how to go about relieving oneself at night were carefully explained. No sooner had the gongs been heard signaling bedtime than the guards rushed to their positions around the compound; hordes of them deliberately made their way past our huts showing off their guns, and they shouted at us to extinguish fires and go to bed. The pair of inmates on watch at the ends of each row of huts had to keep a fire going that lit the small space between the rows. An inmate wishing to have a pee would have to ask the guards for permission to go out and report to them again on the way back inside.

The number of guards escorting us to work each day also increased from two to four for each group. Opportunities to gather food on our way to and from work-sites now came to an end as the guards insisted on "disciplined journeys to work." The atmosphere became unbearably tense as we were constantly reminded of our imprisonment in addition to the daily hardships. The initial euphoria caused by the release of eighty-seven inmates and nurtured by Thinh's promise that "your stay here will be short" had now faded. Once again we felt we had been cheated. How easily manipulated we were as our spirits rose or fell on the strength of a promise, some small act, or even rumor.

Our main job now consisted of reclaiming the neglected fields left behind by the Montagnards. The exhausted soil could hardly support the wild plants, and it was baked hard by the burning sun. A hard strike with a hoe would go only a few centimeters deep, but hoeing was the only way to remove the dried clumps and roots of rice plants, maize, or just weeds. The number falling ill increased steadily. I went about my work like a zombie; somehow I knew it would be years before I was released.

One night, a few weeks after the big release, a freak squall struck at night. It blew the roofs off some huts that had been poorly secured in anticipation of our "early release." It was all cloudy and windy the next day, heralding the start of the rainy season, and I was included in the group charged with rethatching the roofs of the command center. The rains actually arrived a week later, accompanied by howling winds that battered our bamboo shelters and helped drive the pouring rain through the leaky huts. We protected ourselves and our belongings with sheets of tarpaulin, sharing them with friends who had no means of protection. Everyone cowered beneath the rainproof sheets.

All field work was suspended now so we could gather timber to build new, more sturdy buildings. We now had an incentive to work fast, for the sooner new huts were completed, the less risk we ran of sickness through exposure to the rain and cold. The whole camp became a busy construction site. Tree trunks were turned into beams and rafters, bamboo was split and woven into wattles for walls and roofs.

A new site was chosen for the camp on top of a hill that was separated from the dense jungle by a stream winding around its foot. We had a hell of a time carrying the heavy logs to the hilltop, but the rest of the work was routine as by now we had become quite experienced. It took us nearly a month to complete the new buildings.

When we were about to move to the new site, we were awakened early one morning by a *bodoi* who ordered us to declare all the money in our possession because the government had decreed a currency exchange and would issue all new banknotes. All signs of sleep vanished as soon as money was mentioned since it was a matter of life and death to us, especially when we were sick and in need of scarce drugs. Excited discussion erupted as the *bodoi* went about making their announcement.

Worrisome thoughts churned in my head. We had been repeatedly reminded that all cash should be entrusted to the camp authority for safekeeping, although they knew full well that almost all of us kept some money hidden somewhere. That this always had been tolerated could have been due to the *bodoi*'s relaxed attitude or to some more specific reason. Now by declaring my own funds, I would indirectly admit the violation of one of the rules. Besides, who could guarantee that I would be able to recover all my money once it was changed? I had about 700 dong, a relatively large sum as far as the *bodoi* were concerned. I had carefully saved it for use in case I needed medicines or had the chance to buy food but also because I would certainly need it if I made a successful escape. Tidying up my bed, I went about uncovering my money "caches" that had so far survived many searches. An idea flashed in my head as I was washing my face.

I went to see Thé and handed him 300 dong. "Please do me a favor," I pleaded. "Can you take this money and change it for me as if it were yours? I'm afraid I may run into trouble if I declare too large a sum."

"Of course," Thé smiled knowingly. "There's no problem. With this money-changing order, we can find out who of us in this camp are 'millionaires' and who are not. Imagine all those complaints about lack of money!" He was really enjoying this. "However, we are outwitted this time by Uncle[4] and the Party! Ha ha!"

Our group leader came to make a list of those wishing to declare. When my turn came, I entered my particulars and got a good long look at the list. Almost

---

[4]Uncle is Uncle Ho Chi Minh.

every inmate had money to declare, although the average sum was several dozen dong; only a handful possessed more than 200 dong each. I registered 270 dong although I had nearly 400 on me. Thé declared exactly 300 dong. When I finished, I hurried out to see a friend to ask him to dispose of my remaining 100 plus dong.

We idled about until past nine o'clock when a *bodoi* came to tell us that we were being granted a rest for the whole day as all the guards were mobilized to process the cash declarations. We were than required to hand in our money in person, forming two long queues in front of two desks. Shouts of abuse were heard now and then.

"Bloody hell! What a fortune you have been hoarding!"

"Look at this! And you claiming you have made progress!"

"Ah . . . That's why you haven't been allowed to go home!"

We could only smile back stupidly.

All inmates except the "blacksmiths" had the day off. We attended to our long-neglected clothes and talked over the morning's events. I learned that the richest of all the inmates was assistant cook Tran Ngoc Diep, who had nearly 2,000 dong even though he had asked others to help him dispose of some of it. This came as no surprise to us as we knew he had previously been a bank manager.

Another story from the day, which the inmates found very interesting, concerned the *bodoi*'s quartermaster. It was told to me by Thé, who, in turn, had learned it from Hung, his *bodoi* friend. The quartermaster was on a shopping trip to Saigon at the time of the currency roundup, and his comrades had forced open his trunk to get at his money and exchange it for him. To their amazement, his "savings" turned out to be no less than 3,000 dong plus a gold watch, a coveted item among the cash-strapped *bodoi* who received a mere six dong a month as wages.

The collected currency was carried away, leaving us restless and anxious. But after days of worry and all our pessimistic predictions, we were called to the command center one evening and given back all our money. The *bodoi* quartermaster was not so fortunate; his 3,000 dong were confiscated, and he was reprimanded and transferred. According to other *bodoi,* this was because he could not prove any legitimate means by which he had obtained this gargantuan sum.

Later on, Thinh smugly boasted, "Do you know that our orders were to change no more than fifty dong for each inmate, that anything above this had to be justified. Some of you brought out several hundred dong! So we divided the total amount by the total number of inhabitants of this camp, including the *bodoi,* to arrive at an average of less than fifty dong for each of us. Therefore, thanks to our resourcefulness, we were able to change all your money without any trouble!"

We had to admit that when it came to outsmarting government cadres, Thinh was quite competent.

From that day on, the *bodoi* invariably greeted us with the same remark, "What kind of inmates are you who always have plenty of money to spend?" But they took full advantage of their knowledge by offering to buy things for us whenever they had a chance to go to the village of Ming Hung or, better still, Saigon. For this service, they charged considerable fees.

More and more young vendors were seen hanging around our camp, although they were officially prohibited. They came in small groups, mostly teenage girls. They bribed the guards with fruits, rice cakes, sweets, or cigarettes, and then they would openly sell their wares to us—mostly sugar, meat, even the rice that was becoming more and more scarce even for them.

It came as a surprise to us at first that even the aloof study monitors joined in this racket. Officially, each of us was allotted several dong a month by the State to buy food to supplement our rice. But this money was arbitrarily used by the cooks to buy vegetables grown by the study monitors. What was left was taken away from us under a formula that determined a certain amount of vegetables grown by the inmates to be equal to the "state benefit." This was deducted on the grounds that "the inmates don't need it as they can grow the food themselves," and it was then set aside "for a government fund." As a result, most of our vegetables now came from the jungle again.

The bountiful tropical jungle provided another source of income for the *bodoi*, one that also was quite popular with the inmates: deer for venison. The *bodoi* ventured deep into the jungle to hunt the well-fed deer and then sold the delicious venison at cutthroat prices. Only the richest of us could afford a piece of it as most of us held on to our previous savings for emergencies. We supplemented our meager diet with the more plentiful wild pigs and foxes, and the *bodoi* hunted smaller game for themselves. We all craved meat.

Everyday a team of inmates was selected and charged with running errands for the *bodoi*. If wakened in the early hours of the morning by distant gunfire, they would know that they had better be ready for a long trip to some spot in the jungle to retrieve the game, usually a big deer. The *bodoi* themselves avoided the arduous job of carrying the heavy carcasses over difficult terrain for long distances. The best part of the trek, of course, was the end of it when the game was cut up and distributed; the inmates always got some pieces of meat and a few bones.

As the rain started in earnest, we began the sowing of rice seeds. The familiar sight again: Teams of three moving in straight lines, two men digging holes with hoes while the third deposited seeds into them and then covered them up using his feet to push and tamp the soil. The weather changed abruptly and we became more subject to colds. At times, I had above normal temperatures for a whole week, but I chose to go out to work as it would have been impossible for me to get up once I lay down—the fever tended to turn nasty if a person was laid up. Besides, outdoor work trips gave us the chance to buy food. I worked while my body was damp with sweat from fever one minute and shivering with cold the next.

At this time the food supply also dropped. It became harder and harder to buy rice and other staples from outside as there was scarcity everywhere. As a supplementary source of energy we resorted to a kind of sweet made from manioc roots, sugar, and water. Our rations were reduced to the point where we did not have the strength to do a reasonable amount of work. A *bodoi* doctor was sent in to ensure that only those who really were ill were spared labor; even so, their number was staggering. Successful escapes also were staged. The escapees often vanished during breaks or when work parties made their way through the jungle. It was almost impossible to find any trace of them once they had covered any distance. Despite heightened security, not a single week passed without somebody missing. Like most of us, I was often tempted to make my move as conditions got worse. But I knew I would not have the stamina to make it hundreds of kilometers through jungle to a population center.

Suddenly, orders came for carpenters and others who had some building experience to quickly put up additional accommodations for inmates. This came as a complete surprise because we felt our present quarters were not so cramped as to require this urgent erection of more buildings. What's more, the new site was a clearing right in the middle of a stand of bamboo about two hundred meters from our present quarters. There seemed to be no logic to this choice as it would require extra *bodoi* to guard the compound. We concluded that the new buildings would be used to detain those suspected of planning to escape. The spot was surrounded by an impenetrable wall of bamboo thickets. Some of us had once attempted crossing one of these thickets to gather young bamboo shoots but were defeated by the thick, thorny, intertwining branches. Our only way of making an opening was to burn a section of the bamboo, and we had a hell of a time containing the fire.

While we were putting up the building frames, I was struck by a bad accident. Each frame consisted of four heavy posts about four meters high and equally heavy rafters, each more than five meters long. We raised the posts gradually, using wedges, until they stood upright, a technique we had successfully employed before. This time I was on the team at the lifting end. As we tried to lift the post high enough to insert the next wedge, our pitiful strength failed, and the heavy trunk came crashing down. I caught the blow, felt a searing pain in my back as if the spine had snapped, then blacked out.

When I came round, I was on a bed in the clinic with a searing pain in my back; every time I moved, it stabbed like a thousand knives. Inmate doctor Tran

Ngoc Khue was in charge, and he told me that some of my vertebrae had been compressed. His only available remedy was application of heated grains of salt to the affected part and the advice to lie as still as I could so the damaged vertebrae could heal by themselves.

It was torment to have to lie still day and night with this searing pain. I had to relieve myself lying on my back, and bowel movements were not only painful but terribly awkward. I was sure I would be crippled for life. Dark thoughts churned in my head as for five days I lay flat on my back, weak, despondent, and nearly sleepless. I was turned over for the salt treatments, also a painful process. I had to content myself with this crude remedy as the only acupuncture practitioner—who was reputed to have performed miracles—had escaped from the camp.

After about ten days the pain abated, and I was no longer in despair. I could move my limbs about without much pain, although I took care not to strain my back.

The whole camp was nearly paralyzed with sickness, although only about a dozen of the most seriously ill were in the "clinic." Among them were the dying musician Khuyen and the formerly robust Sanh. Although we lay next to each other, there was little conversation.

One day Tuong, a former pilot who was allowed to work as a cook because of his asthma, came to the clinic to tell us that new buildings were being put up to house visitors. We were overjoyed, for this meant medicine might be brought to us. For my part, I was now able to roll myself about without pain. Shortly after this, we began to get permission to write to our families to inform them of our whereabouts, and not long after that, the first visitors turned up. But they brought very bad news. Some visitors to other camps had been robbed and even killed on the way. People now had to protect themselves by traveling in large groups.

Among the first visitors were the wives of Khuyen and Sanh. Khuyen's wife brought in the right drugs for her husband as she had been well informed, but Sanh's wife had not and she had to return to Saigon immediately after discovering her husband's condition. A few days later it was my turn to write to my wife, but I declined, fearing for her safety if she made the trip at this time. Instead, I managed to send her a letter, via a visitor, stating clearly my condition and advising her against coming to see me. A week later an old lady turned up to see her son who was seriously ill; later she came to see me and handed me a bag full of tonic medicines and money. I asked her how she had met my wife.

"It's now quite easy for a person to ask visitors to carry a message, to send in a letter, or to bring some gifts to relatives in the camps," replied the woman. "People are quite willing to help each other as they are now all in the same boat! All your wife had to do was go to a bus station, ask the drivers which bus goes to which camp and then approach the passengers. That's how we met."

Having got the proper drugs, Khuyen made a miraculous recovery. But by the time Sanh's wife came back with his medicine, he had already begun passing blood, and he died that night with his wife beside him. The widow moaned and cried in misery, "I've tried my best to raise money to buy medicines for you. Now you've passed away before you even have a chance to take them. Why did it happen to you? Why, my God?"

Her heartbreaking cries gave me goosebumps. What a sorrowful sight! This went on for a while until a *bodoi* arrived. "Mrs. Sanh," he said, "we are really sorry that your husband died in spite of all our efforts to save him."

"What kind of efforts are you talking about?" retorted Mrs. Sanh angrily. "My husband has been ill for months without proper medication, and now you talk about your 'efforts to save him'! Why didn't you let him tell me earlier? I could have brought him medicine! What kind of 'lenient policy' is this? Why are you all so wicked?"

Not knowing how to answer, the embarrassed *bodoi* hurried off. Mrs. Sanh went on crying, calling her dead husband's name and cursing the *bodoi*. It was not long before we saw Study Monitor Chuong and a couple of *bodoi* hurrying toward the woman. She was sitting flat on the ground next to the body of her husband, which lay on a bamboo wattle. In the fluttering light of an oil lamp, the group of living people looked as pale as the corpse on the floor.

Chuong said in irritation, "Mrs. Sanh, we regret that your husband died while undergoing reeducation! We really understand your grief. However, you should be careful with your remarks about the government; remember that this is a reeducation camp. Don't forget that Mr. Sanh's brother is still here with us."

By now, we noticed that Sanh's elder brother, Ha Phuoc Loc, was already there, obviously summoned by Chuong. He stepped forward and said to his sister-in-law in that down-to-earth way of a peasant, "Shut up! That's enough! What's the point of crying when he's already dead? When he's dead, he don't need to worry no more! What the hell have you been cursing about? Do you want to harm me as well? Let them bury him!"

Chuong then ordered, "You there! And you there as well! Give us a hand to carry Sanh to the meeting house for cleaning and changing of clothes before the burial."

The group moved away like a procession, in heavy silence.

We lay still in our sickbeds, angry for the loss of a friend. Finally, one man broke the heavy silence, "Sanh used to be so fit. Who could have thought that he would die so soon. On the other hand, a weak fellow like me lasts so long."

Another voice from the corner cut in, "He died because he ate some poisonous root! He himself told me that day when we moved here that he had stomach pains after eating some unknown root. He was unwell ever since then."

The conversation turned to the promiscuous eating habits of some inmates. Then we heard the sounds of hammers banging away and a voice saying, "Good, that's quick! The coffin is now ready!" After a while heavy footsteps were heard approaching and then somebody said clearly, "Lift it onto your shoulder . . . slow down . . . careful! You'll stumble!"

Then Sanh's wife was heard, "Oh, my husband! I can't stand it! I hoped I would be here in time to look after you. Who could have thought . . ."

Sanh's brother pleaded, "Now, stop it! You can cry if you want, but don't keep nagging like this!"

Their voices grew fainter and fainter as they moved off.

Dr. Khue came to see me the next day. "You are now on the mend," he said, "and you can go back to your place to convalesce. It's not that I want to throw you out; it's the *bodoi*'s orders. They want five of you out today to make room for others who are very sick and whose relatives are due to visit them soon."

"I can see that! I don't want to stay here any longer anyway; it's depressing in here! I'll be glad to be back with friends over there."

Khue fetched some hands to carry me back on a stretcher. On the way one of them remarked, "You are not as heavy as Sanh; I helped carry him yesterday."

Another wondered, "Why are dead people always heavier than live ones?"

All my dark thoughts gradually died away as I spent more time with healthier people. It took me another month to be able to get up on my own, but I was still weak and in need of help to go to the latrine. Thé proved to be an unselfish friend, and he cared for me like a close relative, from cooking for me to helping me to relieve myself.

As we got further into the rainy season, the skies seemed to open without warning. The inmates toiling in the open were not allowed to take shelter in the jungle for fear of escape; besides, they themselves did not want to shelter under the trees that were teeming with jungle leeches.

As soon as I was up on my feet, the study monitors gave me the job of putting up bamboo wattles for "other new buildings for inmates." Friends told me those buildings were now near completion in a glade about two hundred meters from camp. This compound was to be called "subcamp C" to distinguish it from the one surrounded by the thick wall of bamboo that was called "subcamp B."

My friends advised me against doing any work. "You're still not strong enough; you should continue to rest; otherwise your spine may snap again!"

I argued that light work would help get my back in shape. Finally, we agreed that others would put up the wattles and I would fasten them onto the frames.

One day while at work, I heard the rumble of engines nearing the camp. Later, Thé told me that a convoy brought in a group of men. "I guess they have just been arrested," he said. "They were beaten and shouted at by the guards as they were taken to subcamp B." From then on, the study monitors made it a habit of coming to our quarters every evening to call the roll and remind us to keep away from the newcomers.

One morning Chuong came to see me and said, "Mr. Vu, you have been selected to instruct the newcomers on how to organize themselves for the new life. You will have to show them how to attend to details like tidying up their sleeping berths, putting away their belongings, writing appropriate slogans to put up at their sleeping places, keeping watch, how to report to the guards when relieving themselves at night, in short, you will show them how to observe the rules and regulations of this camp. Now you go with these *bodoi* to subcamp B. Remember, don't socialize with them!"

Although surprised at these orders, I just said, "Yes," and followed the four submachine-gun-toting guards to the new camp. As we entered, I saw men hanging around everywhere, some standing, some sitting on the ground, all looking indifferently at us. A guard shouted, "Where's your group leader? Assemble yourselves!"

Someone answered back defiantly, "All right! We'll assemble, there's no need to shout!"

The *bodoi* flushed with anger. Another barked, "Hurry! We don't have all day! Assemble!"

They then raised their guns and strode forward threateningly as if they were about to hit someone. As they made their way inside the big building, they shouted, "Roll up your mosquito nets! You're not allowed to hang them during daytime!" "You there, hurry on! Move out to assemble yourselves!"

The new inmates deliberately dragged out their actions. Their group leader, an amicable-looking fellow, nervously went about assembling his men, then reported, "We are ready now."

A *bodoi* introduced me. "This inmate has been appointed to help you organize yourselves for the new life here. He will also inform you of the rules and regulations. If you have any question just ask him."

He then turned to me, "It's your turn now. Step forward."

I knew I was still too weak to shout like the *bodoi,* so I said, "I am still convalescing, and I don't have the strength to talk to them like this. Let me talk to their team leaders first, and they can relay the instructions. Besides, in this way I can show them how to arrange their baggage while talking to them."

"All right! It's up to you to teach them as many of the rules as possible."

We were then dismissed. I stepped to the entrance of the building followed by the group leader and the eager crowd. The *bodoi* looked on from outside.

I said, "Let me talk to the group leader and team leaders."

An inmate retorted, "What the hell are 'team leaders'? We only have an elected group leader."

Seeing that I was surrounded, the *bodoi* shouted, "Move back! How can you do anything in all this noise?"

I pleaded in a low voice, "Please follow their orders; if they think the situation is getting out of control, they won't let us do anything. If you scatter about, it will help us watch them and we can talk more privately."

"Did you hear that?" said the group leader. "Why are you still crowding up like this? Leave me alone to get information from this guy!"

The majority scattered out, although the younger fellows still lingered as if waiting to ask me something. I stepped forward and said aloud, "First, I will show you how to put away your belongings and tidy up your sleeping berths."

I stepped up to the raised bamboo floor, saying in a low voice, "We have to pretend that we are actually carrying out their orders by talking and doing some work at the same time."

The new inmates hurriedly went about tidying up their places. The *bodoi* looked on and began to relax. I quickly asked, "Where do you come from? I've heard that you have just been arrested."

"We come from all walks of life," replied the group leader. "Some have been arrested recently, some were transferred from other camps, some were arrested as members of the resistance movement. But the majority are noncommissioned officers of the previous government's army. Are you officers? What rank are you?"

A young man put in, "When we got here, your commander boasted that you guys were 'progressive elements' who had received an award for outstanding performance. Is that true? What kind of officers are you? How can you be so subservient?"

I was taken aback by this sudden insult. But it roused in me the shame that lay at the back of my mind, and the contemptuous remark kept ringing in my ears.

The group leader defended me. "You cheeky boy, get lost! Why didn't you ask him something useful? Leave him alone, will you?"

"I must admit there is an element of subservience in us," I sighed. "The majority of us hold the rank of lieutenant. From the day we first registered, we have been enduring all hardships and humiliation in the hope that we would soon be released."

"Pooh! Has any one of you been released? You will certainly be released when you are about to die! Don't be so naïve!"

"Shut up! Didn't I tell you to go away? Why are you so ridiculous? He used to be an officer unlike you, you worthless idiot! This young man was arrested after a fight with a local *bodoi*."

I just smiled. "They have cleverly tricked us into believing that all of us would eventually be released! Since we came to this camp, eighty-seven inmates have been released, leaving a little more than a thousand now. About a dozen have escaped in the last several weeks."

"Did they really make it?" they cut me short in surprise. "Were there any captures? What direction did they head for?"

Realizing I had touched the right chord, I said deliberately, "Now that I have set up one place as an example, it's your turn. When you have finished, I will answer your questions."

Now it was the cheeky boy who responded enthusiastically. "Friends, come on! Let's tidy up!"

The guards looked at all this activity with contentment. They sat on the ground, chatting away. I walked back and forth, helping the men speed up the process, and it was not long before the pieces of baggage were neatly stowed beside "beds," gangways were cleared, and the whole place looked quite tidy. I then asked them all to gather on one side of the huge room, and I proceeded to recite the rules and regulations. They also asked questions, and we were able to intersperse our talk with murmured exchanges such as, "When you were moved here, did you notice anything unusual on the way?"

"No, we didn't see anything as our trucks were completely covered with tarpaulin."

"Well, unlike many other camps, our camp is situated near the village of Minh Hung. Some village children used to come here to sell their wares. I've heard that the successful escapees usually made their moves while at work in the jungle where they would hide and wait for nightfall. They would then head for far-off villages to try to avoid detection. However, there have been fewer escapes in the last few days because security has been increased."

I told them about the situation in the main camp, the geography of the area, and I tried to pass on some survival tips. From these men I learned of the hatred that the general public held for the new regime. There was open criticism of the government, and there were many outbreaks of revolt that appeared unrelated and spontaneous in spite of extensive deployment of troops and police. In the vast area surrounding the city of Bien Hoa, in which there were settlements of Roman Catholics who emigrated from the North in 1954, the number of *bodoi* and policemen assassinated and beaten was so high that they no longer patroled in small detachments. In some particularly hostile settlements, the *bodoi* withdrew to their barracks as soon as darkness fell.

A few weeks later we heard that the inmates of subcamp B were staging a hunger strike to protest the severe regime of hard labor and insufficient food. While I was busily mending bamboo wattles on partitions at the command center, Thinh angrily came in and barked out orders for all his *bodoi* to assemble immediately. Facing his troops, he ordered, "Comrades, each of you get some lengths of rope to tie those reactionaries. It's about time we showed them how to observe discipline!"

They all set out for subcamp B, and after a while I saw them coming back escorting a group of about fifty inmates whose arms were tied behind their backs. They were pushed forward and forced to kneel down in the sun-baked yard in front of the command center. Some resisted being forced into that humiliating position only to be severely beaten. The *bodoi* expertly hit them with the butts of their guns, trying to force them down. There was a loud chorus of protests.

"What have I done to deserve this?"

"Go on, beat me! Beat me to death if you can!"

The *bodoi* went on beating them relentlessly without saying a word. The battered and now subdued prisoners prostrate on the ground were then raised up and forced to kneel down in rows. Thinh dismissed his *bodoi*. "Two of you will stay here to keep an eye on them; the rest can go back to your quarters. I am going to phone the regimental commander for instructions. You have to be firm with these reactionaries."

Thinh looked annoyed when he saw me and another inmate standing nearby mending the bamboo partitions, and he said, as though trying to defend his action, "These guys were so insolent to us! When I visited their camp, they didn't bother to get up to pay attention. When I asked them who gave them permission to lie down in their mosquito nets during the day, they answered back rudely, 'We lie down because we are sick and hungry.' These reactionaries come from the Roman Catholic settlements in Ho Nai, Bien Hoa. You can go now. Have your lunch break."

As we went out, the tied-up, kneeling men out there in the burning sun looked up, contempt in their eyes. I felt my face flush, and we hurried past them with our heads down. Never had I felt such shame before. Although beaten and forced to kneel, they looked so brave! This was the first time that I witnessed this kind of incident, where the *bodoi* beat prisoners, not out of anger but because they were ordered to do it.

In the afternoon, when we got back to the command center to resume work, the "reactionaries" had gone. We were told they had been brought to regimental headquarters. We never heard of them again. I once had the opportunity to go past their camp. Some saw me and shook their heads. One young fellow openly laughed at me and jeered, "You have feet of clay!"

Since that fateful day, many of us became introspective and moody. We thought more about what we had been doing. We had submitted to all our hardship and suffering in the hope that this would bring about early release, which now seemed out of our grasp. In contrast, the new inmates had always been rebellious, as if they knew their fates were sealed. But what really made them stand apart from us was the fact that most of them had been arrested because they had had the guts to rebel.

Their presence in this camp also carried with it an ominous implication. Why had these "ultra-reactionaries" been brought here to stay with us? Was this a confirmation that we, former officers of the previous regime, were also considered "ultra-reactionaries"?

Our worries were temporarily interrupted by the arrival of a convoy bringing in a group of some three hundred prisoners wearing odd-looking clothing. It was made of unusual material, normally used to make sandbags for military fortifications. The men were escorted to subcamp C. We later learned that they had been officers with the rank of major in the former army and that these middle-aged people only looked so old because of their gray hair and their unusual clothes. They were living evidence of the kind of treatment the new rulers meted out to their former enemies, and their appearance made our hearts sink.

All hands were now mobilized to help sow more rice seeds before the rainy season came to an end. The fields that had been planted earlier were now all green with flourishing seedlings.

One night, when the sowing was completed, we were all awakened by the ear-shattering noise of loudhailers directed at us. Startled, thinking there was some emergency, we got up, but the voices ordered us to lie still and await the *bodoi*. They came right up to our beds, pointing their electric torches at those whose names were on lists they carried. Those inmates were made to gather their belongings immediately, then were escorted out to the brightly lit yard full of armed *bodoi*. We just lay there, helplessly listening to the names of friends being called out, watching them being led away, one after another. The full number, once assembled, was then marched away into the darkness, their footsteps fading.

It was not until dawn that we were able to find out who had been snatched away: a former teacher of the famous Chu Van An school; Le Dinh Dieu, a former official of the Ministry of Communications; and former security agents, military policemen, and persons who had worked in the propaganda apparatus of the former regime—altogether, about forty men. When the morning roll was called and assignments were given out, the study monitors remarked, "You should be glad that you were not among those taken away earlier!"

What was happening now began to confuse me. On the one hand, if we were regarded as being of the same ilk as the new inmates, we would be "ultra-reactionaries"; on the other, compared with those taken away that night we, the remaining men in this camp, were "progressive elements."

Visitors kept turning up regularly. I managed to keep in touch with my wife and was able to receive some food from her. The most frequent visitor was Chiêu's wife; she managed to come at least several times a month. When she was prevented by the regulations, she would ask someone to bring her husband supplies on her behalf. She acted as my courier, helping bring in things for me many times. My wife kept repeating in her letters that "you will soon be free," but what I mainly wanted to know was how my loved ones were coping with the harsh realities of life. As for hopeful news concerning my fate, maybe she had been cheated in her efforts to secure my release or she was deliberately cooking up news to boost my morale, I thought.

It rained more and more. In some places bushy rice plants grew as high as thirty centimeters. But many of their leaves turned yellowish, an indication of insect infestation.

At the end of August preparations were made to celebrate the declaration in 1945 of the establishment of the Democratic Republic of Vietnam on September 2. The festivities lasted two days. A thousand plus inmates were given two pigs and additional rice, and we were given the green light to entertain ourselves as we wished in the evening. Together with the former singer from the Da Nang Broadcasting Authority, we sang melodies from the good old days. Among us sat many *bodoi*, who clearly enjoyed the sentimental songs. We were allowed to stay up late, and with the festive mood of the guards and the rest of the *bodoi*, some inmates of subcamp B managed to sneak in. They were surprised at the *bodoi*'s easygoing attitude toward inmates in the main camp. They told us it was normal for the *bodoi* and policemen at camps in Bien Hoa, Long Thanh, and Thu Duc to beat up the inmates and insult them at the slightest provocation. The atmosphere at those camps was quite tense, they said, because the inmates there were not as obedient as we were.

One of them then asked, "Why are you so obedient?"

"Our only wish is to be home with our families and to contribute to the rebuilding of our country," someone replied. "The war is now over. Every Vietnamese has a desire to rebuild his war-torn country and to enjoy peace. We all want to finish our reeducation as soon as possible so that we can be back with our families. We are tired of fighting and killing each other."

"Good Lord!" exclaimed a man from subcamp B, shaking his head. "I never thought you could have been so brainwashed! Do you think they will leave you alone once you have been released? Even if you are out, who can guarantee that you will be left alone to go about your business? Do you think we are so dumb that we would have thrown away a good life in exchange for imprisonment here by rebelling? No! They wouldn't leave us, and they won't leave you alone. They tried their best to make our lives miserable. They discriminated not only against us but also our wives, our chidren, our parents, our brothers and sisters. Those who were involved with the former regime are now being shunned like lepers! Once their files have been marked 'elements of the former regime,' it becomes impossible for them to find a job, to enroll their chidren in higher schools, to move elsewhere, or even to sell their own houses. At first we tried to endure, hoping for the best. Now we are left with no choice but to revolt! Many have been arrested. In some places they did allow our children to enroll in higher schools, but most of them failed in the examinations."

Someone else picked up the theme. "As far as we are concerned, life outside is not much different from that in this camp! There were policemen everywhere. We were forced to adopt their ways of life. Some people had to move to jungle areas to build New Economic Zones, which we think are essentially reeducation camps. They give us no future! That's why we rebelled and why we will keep on rebelling as long as we are alive! Especially in this camp of ours where we've been kept on a starvation diet and have to do hard labor for long stretches at a time. We're better off dead than with this lot. You are only deceiving yourselves believing obedience will bring about your release. You'll find out the truth. Our only choice is to fight back."

Seeing that the talk was getting into dangerous territory, some hurriedly slipped away, and someone else said aloud, "We are supposed to entertain ourselves tonight, so let's sing some more songs. Try to make the best of our time as this is our last night of celebration."

There was loud applause. "Go on! Let's sing 'Intimate Feelings,' 'Farewell,' and 'Waning Night at Ben Ngu.'"

The men from subcamp B stood up then and left in haste as if annoyed at our festive mood, although there was nothing offensive in those previously popular songs. The artificial joy lasted for a while; then the crowd dispersed.

Back under my mosquito net, I listened to the distant sounds of music intermingled with the general din of celebration. It was not long before I saw Thé coming back.

"There you are!" he said. "I wondered where you were. I've had enough of all this entertainment. All those sentimental songs only made me remember the good old days when I used to slip away to Saigon to enjoy myself whenever my wallet was full. I used to go to nightclubs to listen to music. Now, hearing these songs again, all I feel is sadness."

All this depressing groaning was getting me down, so I interruped, "Did you listen to those fellows from subcamp B talking about life outside?"

Thé looked surprised, "Did they manage to get here? Security over there is quite tight; maybe the guards took it easy today. What did they talk about?"

"They told us about the discrimination suffered by families of those who used to work for the former government, about the unbearable life, about revolts here and there."

"I thought I might hear something different! We've heard stories like that from the visitors many times before. Yes, we are cornered with our backs to the wall. It's bad enough here in this camp, but it won't be any better once we get out! It drives me mad to think of that. Sooner or later, we shall have to do something; we can't just sit here waiting for some miracle to happen!"

"What else can we do?"

"I must do something instead of waiting! People like you must have thought about our predicament; perhaps you could come up with something. One moment of freedom is worth a thousand days in prison! What do you think? Can you tell me? Or are you afraid that I'll sell you out?"

"No, I'm not! Well, it's true. I have spent a lot of time thinking, but I don't know what to do. I haven't seen any way out. Those chaps at subcamp B have come up with a simple philosophy. Their only alternative to living a life condemned to be nonpersons is to revolt, no matter what happens, even death. This viewpoint is simplistic, but quite correct in our case as we really have become nonpersons in the eyes of the communist government. What's the point of putting up with insults, hard labor, beatings, or even outright executions when it doesn't do us any good?"

"That's enough! It's no good thinking like this," Thé said. "By now I'm tired of thinking. It nearly drove me mad once! I used to ask myself, 'What's the point of living like this?' My only regret is that I wasn't killed in the many battles that I fought. Or maybe I'm destined to die in prison. But why should millions of people have the same destiny? And why should they endure everything in silence?"

Outdoor labor now consisted of two activities: weeding the rice fields and preparing the land for the forthcoming sweet potato crop. One day, while hoeing the ground preparing potato beds, I was called to the command center to do repairs. Rainwater had blown into the *bodoi*'s huge meeting hall through the windows, and we were told to cover them with shutters made of bamboo wattle. That done, we then mounted at the front of the hall two huge "blackboards" that we made from wooden planks. No sooner was this work completed than another inmate and I were instructed to build a bamboo "triumphal arch" in front of the hall. This puzzled us as the important anniversaries for which an archway might have been built were now over. Asking our young guard what the authorities had in mind, I got a vague answer that a meeting of Party members in the area was forthcoming. As we cut some bamboo, it began to rain, so we ran back to the hall while the guards headed for the command center in the opposite direction. We saw someone in the distance carrying a bulky pack and heading for the command center. As he came nearer, we were able to make out a rain-soaked *bodoi* carrying a bicycle, all wrapped up, reminding us of a wounded and bandaged person. As he came closer, we recognized none other than Commander Thinh.

"Ah, I see!" said my teammate knowingly. "He must be back from Saigon, having assembled his bicycle. Were you with those carrying the *bodoi*'s luggage when we moved to this site?"

"No, I wasn't. I was among those doing the cooking."

"Well, then you didn't have the fun of witnessing the sight of Thinh's bed being accidentally dropped and the scattering of bicycle parts all over the place. It took several of us to retrieve them. There were enough gears, pedals, spokes, chains, ballbearings, etc., to assemble several bicycles! God knows how much Thinh has collected! He must have been to Saigon to exchange or sell the parts for the frame, wheels, and handlebars. Do you know where those parts come from? They are bribes from the visitors! Do you know why people like Quach Dong always got light work assignments? Ask his relatives. I've heard that his Chinese relatives even gave Thinh's family a house in Cholon. No wonder he has been released."

"I don't see any point in bribing Thinh. He alone had no power to let Dong out."

"You're right. Buying off Thinh and his study monitors would only ensure safety here. But if they could afford to give Thinh a house, then surely they could buy off his superiors as well, at a steeper price, of course. If you ever take a close look at the study monitors' beds, you will find that they all have hidden compartments to hold bicycle parts. Those are their favorites."

Having changed clothes and put on a raincoat. Thinh came to see us. He smiled and told us he had been to Saigon, and he gave us each a Vam Co cigarette. "Taking advantage of a government trip to Saigon, I managed to assemble that bicycle," Thinh said with pride. "I had to do it now because the price of bicycles has been doubling since the beginning of this year. Those bloody merchants are greedy! It took me a hell of a long time to find the right foreign frame."

We just smiled and feigned admiration at his cleverness.

Thinh then took a long look around the hall. "Bloody hell!" he exclaimed. "I've told those stupid study monitors to have it done urgently, and now they forgot it!" We looked at each other.

"We were only told to put up these shutters; they're all in place. The arch will be finished within the day. What else is there to be done?"

"What about the altar?"

"Altar?" We looked at each other in amazement. "There was no mention of an altar."

"Shit! As soon as you're finished with that arch, put up the altar immediately, understand? Hold on, I must fetch some more hands to speed it up. By the way, all *bodoi* will have to study tomorrow; therefore, you two will have to come to the kitchen to give a hand, just in case. There won't be much to do, however. Now, get on with your work! Just bring the bamboo in as it's still raining outside."

As soon as the rain stopped, we ran out to put up the arch, which did not take long. Then we were taken to an open space near our quarters to build the altar. The choice of its location puzzled me almost as much as the altar itself.

The next day as we got to the command center, we found out that our job was to run errands for the *bodoi* who would soon attend an important meeting. We just sat there in the open-sided kitchen while the *bodoi* cooks busily went about cooking rice, soup, and vegetables. They were all neatly dressed in uniforms, complemented by red badges on their collars.

Suddenly one of them pointed and said, "There he comes!"

A *bodoi* was approaching the gateway on a bicycle. As he drew near, there were loud greetings, "Hello, Commander! How are you?"

The commander cheerfully waved back. Apart from its rider, the bicycle was laden with rolls of red and white cloth on the handlebars and on the rear seat. There also was a carefully wrapped bundle hanging beside the saddlebag.

A cook jokingly told us, "He's our sorcerer."

We looked at him, "Why did you call him a sorcerer? There're no such things as sacrifices or making offerings to gods in our socialist society."

"There are still such activities—the socialist way. The altar is there. The offerings are Party flags, national flags, slogans, pictures of Uncle Ho. Only joss sticks and food are missing! Ha! ha! No, that's only a joke. Don't tell anyone, will you? Otherwise I will be reprimanded."

The newly arrived *bodoi* leaned his bicycle against the wall of the command center. Thinh rushed out to meet him, eagerly helping unfasten the various items. The carefully wrapped bundle turned out to contain a framed picture of Ho Chi Minh, which was then entrusted to political cadre Tu. The cook said drily, "Only political cadres have the privilege of handling pictures of Uncle Ho."

The walls of the meeting hall were decorated with flags and slogans except for the one with the two huge blackboards. We watched as a group of *bodoi* carried the newly arrived items into the hall in single file; in the lead was the newcomer, next came Tu who clung to the precious picture of Ho Chi Minh, and he was followed by Commander Thinh, who had two flags in his hands, one the hammer and sickle flag of the Soviet Union and the other the red flag with the gold star of communist Vietnam. The study monitors carried slogans painted on large sheets of cloth. They all wore an air of importance. They carried the banners to the triumphal arch and hung them up, one over the other. The top one read "Long live the Party!" and the other, "We proudly await the award for having achieved an outstanding rice harvest." So that was it! In addition to the meeting, there was going to be a ceremony to accept the coveted award for that harvest!

Two cooks hurried off in the direction of the stream. After a while, we saw them coming back proudly showing off several plucked and cleaned chickens. Obviously this was a big occasion for them.

The cutting up of the chickens and discussion about what dishes to prepare went on in earnest. There was to be chicken soup, boiled chicken, chicken with ginger . . .

Suddenly we were aware of the presence of Study Monitor Chuong, who asked curtly, "What are these two doing in here?"

"They have been assigned here by comrade Thinh," replied a cook, "though they haven't yet received any instruction."

Chuong went back to the command center but soon returned to bark at us, "Fetch some brooms to sweep the floor of the hall. Once you have finished, take your lunch break and then come back for further orders."

The hall was now fully decorated, ready for the great occasion. At its front, facing the audience, were hung the flags of the Soviet Union and Vietnam and between them the picture of Ho Chi Minh. On the blackboard on the right was a list of the names of Party members headed by Le Van Tu and Nguyen Van Thinh, followed by the names of the study monitors. The blackboard to the left bore a "List of Members of the Communist Youth League"; this list was quite long and was followed by another list of those still trying to become members. The latter names were crammed into the remaining space, which indicated the low status of their owners.

We finished cleaning the floor of the meeting hall and reported to Chuong, who told us to take our break. "Don't forget to come back early! When you get back, just wait in the kitchen."

Back in our quarters, we were surrounded by inmates whose health spared them work in the fields. They all were eager for news. We told them about the forthcoming meeting of Party members and the award ceremony, and one man remarked, "We may receive some meat to celebrate these very important occasions." We had a quick lunch of boiled manioc roots and a long rest. Finally we walked slowly back to the command center.

"I only fear that when we get there, they will still be having their meal," said my partner, "and we would be looking on . . . it's ridiculous."

"Ridiculous? It's humiliating for us to look on while they are having a feast!"

"Walk as slowly as possible. If they are still feasting, maybe we can slip away."

Fortunately, lunch was over when we arrived. We headed for the kitchen, and immediately a *bodoi* called out, "There you are! Come here." Stripped to the waist, he was spreading ashes upon the red-hot embers to keep them alive. "Take this bag of washing powder. There are some dirty bowls and dishes by the stream. Wash them up and bring them back here for me," he said.

On the way to the stream my partner groaned, "I tried to avoid the humiliation of watching them feast only to have the humiliation of washing their dishes."

"F . . . them! Even my wife didn't ask me to do the washing up, and now we have to do it for them. What an insult!"

My friend ran to the stream ahead of me. He called back, "We're lucky! There are only a few dishes and bowls here. Leave them to me!"

"No, we have to share everything, happiness or humiliation."

It was standard practice for each of the *bodoi* to keep a pair of chopsticks and a bowl as private possessions. They always washed these themselves so they could use the same bowl for drinking tea after each meal. This crockery here apparently was the property of the State.

My friend said, "I wouldn't accept these crude pieces even if they were given to me! They must have been made in the North; ugly crockery like this would never sell here."

"They defeated us partly because they used ugly, simple utensils like this bloody crockery! Remember, people in the North were used to only the bare necessities of life so their communist government could pour all its resources into the war effort. This would not be possible in a democratic country like ours used to be. Just do some simple arithmetic. It didn't cost much to feed a *bodoi*; therefore, they could afford to send lots of them here during the war."

It took us only a few minutes to finish the job. When we got back to the kitchen the *bodoi* cook said, "When the water in this pot boils, put some tea in it and bring it to the command center; put it next to the entrance. Don't forget to extinguish the fire."

A military voice was heard bellowing, "Hurry, assemble!"

We watched from the kitchen doorway. When all the *bodoi* had assembled in the hall, somebody barked, "Attention!" and they all stood up facing the flags and sang their national anthem. A *bodoi* stepped forward to read from some list, but we were too far away to hear properly. There was loud applause and slogans were shouted now and then as the *bodoi* read on. The "commander" who had arrived earlier that morning then addressed the assembly. As the long speech dragged on, the *bodoi* in the back rows yawned, talked to each other, or cracked jokes. Some just stared out the window at the distant jungle.

It seemed an eternity before two *bodoi* cooks emerged. They headed for the kitchen, taking off their shirts as they walked. One picked up a long knife from the wall and said, "You two, follow me." We headed for the pigsty.

Four pigs were inside, two big ones of about sixty kilograms each and two smaller ones weighing about ten kilos each. They rushed forward, eager for their meal. "We've got to kill the biggest for the feast today," said one *bodoi*. "The second biggest will be for the inmates tomorrow. The two remaining ones are also big enough to be slaughtered for meat. They eat too much rice and refuse to touch anything else. If I force them to give up rice, they will certainly lose weight quickly. My only choice is to get rid of the whole lot now, but it won't sit well with the logistics fellows, who insist that these two pigs be kept until the New Year. But it costs more to feed them than they're worth."

His comrade smiled, "There are many ways to talk them into killing these two."

"Try it if you think you can persuade them. I tried once before only to be told that I still had a bourgeois tendency to want fancy foods."

"That's ridiculous! Why can't you explain to them that it is too costly to feed pigs on rice when even humans don't have enough of it."

"I did explain to them, but they wouldn't accept it. If you think you can, try it."

"I won't have to do any talking! I've got a little trick that will do the job."

"Ah, you want to beat them to death, don't you? That won't work, I tell you! The bruises will show when you shave off the hair."

"I won't have to resort to that crude method. I've got a nice little trick that won't leave any telltale signs. Do you want me to try it?"

"I do! Quite agreed! You two keep your mouths shut, will you? You can only have your shares if the whole lot is slaughtered at once."

"Of course we will. Let's see your little trick," we said.

The *bodoi* fetched a length of bamboo about two feet long. Using the big knife, he split one end of the stick, leaving the knife stuck there. Then he told me to follow him. We got to a heap of logs that had been lying there for some time, and taking a few steps back, he ordered, "Push back this log for me!"

We rolled it back, revealing nothing special. I thought he was looking for poisonous mushrooms. As we rolled back the third log, the *bodoi* nimbly rushed to a spot and pointed the bamboo stick down at a black scorpion as big as a thumb. He twisted the knife to enlarge the gap at the split end of the stick, put the scorpion between the split ends, and pulled out the knife, clamping the scorpion tight. He ran back to the pigsty and planted the stick firmly in the ground. The big insect struggled violently but was held fast by the bamboo. The cook went back to the kitchen and returned with rice for the pigs.

The animals happily rushed forward, pushing each other to get at their meal. As they greedily dug their snouts into the rice, the *bodoi* pulled up the deadly stick, went to the pigs, and placed the scorpion's tail at the ear of one of the smaller pigs. The poisonous sting plunged deep into the poor animal's flesh. It squealed shrilly in pain but kept on eating. Before long, the pig slumped down, groaning. The second small pig met the same fate. The sight of them groaning in great pain was unbearable. The two cooks then jumped into the pigsty and tackled the bigger animal, expertly trussing up its hind legs first, then pinning its head down and tying up the front legs. We passed a bamboo pole through the tied legs and carried the pig to the stream for cleaning. We were told to stay away while it was being slaughtered.

When we came back to the kitchen, the pig's carcass was lying on the floor, having been soaked in boiling water that had now accumulated in a pool nearby. We were told to carry the carcass to the stream to help shave and disembowel it. This was the first time I had to do this kind of work. The *bodoi* kept a close watch, directing us how to go about the job. It was relatively easy to cut up the carcass, but quite tricky to prepare the entrails and various organs as they had to be properly cleaned and salted. It took us the whole afternoon to finish the job. When we brought the cut-up meat back to the kitchen, we were each given a piece of intestine.

My friend asked the cook, "Could I have some rice to cook the intestines with? These would be best cooked with rice to make a porridge."

The cook hesitated, then seeing that there was still plenty of rice left in the pot, he scooped up a bowlful for the man, who hurriedly took off his shirt and used it to wrap up the rice. Seeing me standing off a bit, the cook asked, "You there, don't you want some rice too?" I also took off my shirt to hold the rice as I had no bag or bowl.

That night we had our first rice porridge with intestines. However, it tasted awful without the necessary spices, and we were very disappointed.

The next day we were ordered to assemble in the yard in front of the command center. By now I realized why the altar had been erected in the open: We all were going to gather before it. The detainees were assembled in three separate groups; we were in the middle between subcamps A and B. We were told to stand up facing the flag and keep quiet. When all was ready, a study monitor turned to the "commander" who had arrived the previous day and said "Permission to report, Commander. Assembling of all inmates completed."

The "commander" stepped forward, heading for the altar. "Tell them to sit down."

The study monitor shouted, "All inmates, sit down."

We sat on our sandals or just squatted. Thinh, smartly dressed in a crisp uniform and wearing red badges on his collar, stepped forward. He produced a text, cleared his throat, and started reading. He praised us as progressive elements who were so conscientious that "they stayed up late at night to plan work for tomorrow," so dedicated that "they kept on working in spite of their illnesses," so dedicated that "they put forward brilliant ideas for increasing productivity."

All this took us by surprise; we did not expect this rapid change of heart from Thinh. At one point, he lost his voice from having read so loud. Even the visiting commander could not hold back his chuckles, although he quickly covered this up by applauding. The spectacle was so amusing to the inmates that many of them could not help bursting into laughter, then loud applause. Determined not to be less enthusiastic than the inmates in showing appreciation for Thinh, the *bodoi* provided even louder applause. It went on for a while until Thinh realized that we were making fun of the whole affair. He sternly barked, "Stop! That's quite enough."

He went on to praise our exceptional performance in achieving the highest yield of rice in the whole province, leading to today's award. Then he urged us to shout slogans glorifying the Party. The less than enthusiastic response from the bored inmates infuriated the *bodoi*, who shouted "Louder, louder!"

At the end of the ceremony, a study monitor handed the visiting "commander" a small embroidered flag, and he in turn passed it to Thinh, who placed it on the altar next to the picture of Ho Chi Minh.

The "commander" then urged us to keep on striving for more outstanding achievements to ensure our early release, adding, "Many of those who have been released early, as a result of our government's lenient policy are now showing their gratitude by exposing enemy agents planted by the American imperialists and by moving to the New Economic Zones to till the land to make our country rich. I know that quite a few of you will soon be released."

Unlike earlier times, the now-experienced inmates refused to applaud at the mention of imminent release. The only good news so far was the announcement that we would be spared labor in the afternoon to celebrate the award and the Party meeting. I was then "mobilized" to help with the preparation of lunch for the *bodoi*. As predicted by that resourceful cook, all four pigs were slaughtered. As I was shaving the carcass of the big one, the cook told me that his boss thought the two smaller pigs were sick "because they missed their bigger companions," and he roared with laughter.

As the pig had to feed more than a thousand inmates, we ended up having only a tiny morsel each. Still, the distribution was done by drawing lots again, and no one complained about his share. Some inmates collected individual shares and converted them into a "big prize" to be won by drawing lots again, this way making it more worthwhile to cook the pork. Each of us also received a bowl of rice and some dried bamboo shoots that we ourselves had gathered at Bu Gia Map. We had a nice dinner that day, partly because of the extra food received and partly because of food brought in by our visitors or bought from the young vendors.

Early one morning a few days after the celebration of our award, we were rolling up our mosquito nets and were about to go out to the latrines when four *bodoi* strode in and ordered, "Go back to your places, and don't put your feet on the floor!"

They approached us and started reading our name tags stuck on the walls above our beds, comparing them to a list one of them carried. I was first on the list. A *bodoi* pointed at me, "You there, hand me your bags."

Although stunned, my first thought was that they were searching for hidden cash. He briskly went through my bags, then left. I was the only person searched in our house. There were surprised looks all around, and Thé whispered, "That's strange! Why did they search only you?"

As soon as the *bodoi* were out of sight, we rushed out to check with others. About twelve inmates had been searched like me. I was sure that some mole had reported on me, although I could not think what I had done wrong. Back from work that evening, we learned from the inmate cooks that all inmates of subcamp B had been thoroughly searched during the day.

"The *bodoi* not only went through their luggage," said one man, "but also their beds and around their huts; they even searched the surrounding bamboo forest." But we heard nothing more.

The next day I worked hard—I was back in the fields again—and after the evening meal I went out to the latrines. As I was urinating, I suddenly felt dizzy and cried out for help. Others nearby rushed toward me and helped me get inside to my bed. Some said I was struck by a "harmful wind." Thé was going through his bags for an ointment, a popular and readily available treatment for chills, fainting spells, and other ailments.

Suddenly Thé exclaimed, "My God! Where's all this blood coming from? Are you injured?"

Although half-conscious, I could hear him clearly. I touched my body and felt it was wet. My friends gathered around me trying to find the source of the blood. Then inmate doctor Tran Ngoc Khue arrived. He quickly discovered that I was passing blood, not water. He told me to try to urinate into a jar, and as I stood to try to do so, I felt so dizzy that I could not stand up any more.

"Stop! Take it easy." Khue ordered. "This is really fresh blood. You must be hemorrhaging."

I felt better after lying down for a while, and Khue asked me what I had done during the day—what I had eaten, whether I had fallen, stumbled, whether I had been beaten. The answer to all these questions was no, so Khue just advised me to lie still and said, "I can't tell why you are bleeding; I don't have the equipment to examine you. And I don't have any of the right drugs here, so my only treatment is pressing a bottle of cold water on your back, against the kidneys, and then wait to see what happens. If you want to urinate, just lie down and ask somebody to hold a tin for you, just as you did when you hurt your back. If you need me, ask somebody to fetch me. I'll be sleeping in the clinic."

The men hung around for a while, then Thé lowered my mosquito net for me, and everyone went off to bed.

I woke up early the next morning feeling an urge to urinate. I asked Thé to hold the tin; the dizziness seemed to be gone. Dr. Khue examined the fresh specimen and said there was still some blood in my urine, "but it's not as much as in last night's specimen, which was really bad," he added.

I was spared work that day. At noon Thé came back from the forge. He whispered, "Do you know why you were searched the other day? Do you know why they concentrated their efforts at subcamp B, what they were looking for? That little flag on the altar, the one given to the *bodoi* as an award, has been stolen! That's why there was such a frantic search. You were among the many suspects! Hung also told me that someone even dared smear Uncle Ho's picture with excrement!"

I could not help laughing at this, although I was frightened by Thé's disclosure. "Why should they suspect me?" I asked. "I'm not the reckless type."

"Hung told me that the *bodoi* really had those guys at subcamp B in mind. But the guards said that they had seen some shadows moving from our quarters to the command center; in other words, someone must have passed the altar. The *bodoi* all claimed that none of them went to our quarters that night and that none of them had any inmate come to them for any reason. Therefore, they suspected some of us, including you."

Later I got up to go to the latrine. As I passed the clinic, Dr. Khue ran out to ask, "Where are you going? To the latrines? Why not use the patients' latrines; they are not as smelly."

The main purpose of separate latrines for the patients was to help contain contagious diseases, and they were located on a spot not far from the clinic. I took a good look at them since I had never been allowed to use them before. These latrines were actually individual booths separated by bamboo wattles and were situated on top of a long pit. There was a heap of ash next to them used to cover up the excrement right after the user had finished. As expected, the place was relatively clean. As I was about to sit down, a bright red color down the hole caught my eye. I jumped and rushed out, instinctively thinking it was some kind of poisonous snake. I went back for a closer look and my heart skipped a beat. Down there in the pit was the missing flag that had prompted all the searches!

My first thought was to run away immediately to avoid any possible risk of "being caught red-handed throwing down the flag." However, I thought better of it as this might amount to an acknowledgment of the crime on my part. I scooped up some ash and threw it down the pit, trying to cover the flag. After a few attempts, the damned thing was still clearly visible; it had somehow clung to the wall of the pit midway down. It was too far for me to reach, so I threw more and more ash on the flag, but it was still partly visible. I finally sat down to do what I had come there for. Dr. Khue then appeared, asking why it took me so long, whether I was constipated.

I changed the subject. "Thank you very much for treating me. What a simple and yet effective remedy. I feel much better now."

"It's a sham treatment," Khue laughed. "It should have been ice instead of water. Besides it wasn't enough. It was just an emergency treatment. Your condition may have been prompted by strain at work, kidney stones, or something else. I just can't tell exactly as I don't have the facilities or X-ray equipment to find out. Although your symptoms are clearing up on their own, I still don't understand it. That's why I was waiting for you, to ask about the condition of your stools; you were gone so long. Then I forgot because I was so busy looking after other patients."

The more he talked, the more worried I became. I must find a way to stop him wondering about this. What would happen to me if the flag is found?

Finally I decided to confide in him. "Do you know why I stayed so long at the latrines? I'll tell you the truth because I trust you are a conscientious man, not one of those disgusting informers."

I told him the whole story, from the moment Thé disclosed the loss of that flag—even the part about Ho Chi Minh's picture being smeared with excrement—to the moment I saw the flag down in the hole and tried to cover it up with ash. The more Khue heard, the paler he became. At last he said hesitantly, "Do you know that I was also searched this morning? Even the clinic was searched. You know they hate me very much, partly because I am so popular with the inmates. I can't help that because I am a doctor, I have to treat patients. However, the main reason is that I was once reported by Bui Quoc Khanh as intending to escape. Even when we moved to Bu Gia Map, the bastard didn't stop reporting on me! Therefore, out of the many doctors registered, I am now the only one left here. And every time the inmates are suspected of something, they automatically think of me first. What can I do? Forget about this! Don't ever mention it to anyone else. Let time take its course."

He then hurried off, apparently forgetting to tell me how to look after myself.

After a few more days of rest, I asked for some light work. I was included in the group weeding the fields nearest to the camp. One day my team was told to go to a field "where the rice crop is not very healthy," in the words of the study monitor. As we approached it, we saw swarms of brown insects clustering on the rice plants, bending them down with their weight. Our team leader, a former agricultural specialist, told us, "These are brown beetles. Many fields outside are being ravaged by them."

"Why are they here? We are so far from the infested fields!"

"Well, they used to be contained in the forests in small numbers because their food supply was scarce. As rice fields are planted nearer and nearer to the jungle, we provide a more accessible food supply, and the beetles multiply fast. I was told by my relatives when they last visited me that there were outbreaks of brown beetle plague in nearby areas as a result of careless destruction of forests plus the mindless cultivation of food crops near the jungle without any use of insecticides. Burning down a forest and then growing a rice crop on the land without using insecticides is like laying down a red carpet for the damned insects into the rice fields."

We were amazed. I asked why the authorities had not taken any precautions in the first place.

"Maybe someone knew about this but didn't dare to make it known," the team leader replied, "for fear of reprimands or even denunciation as a reactionary. The Party and the Revolution always have been known to be infallible!"

As I had felt weaker since the day I urinated blood, I asked for permission to have my family visit and bring me some medicine. The permission was granted since my wife had not visited since we moved here.

A few days after I wrote to my wife, a *bodoi* was stopped on the way to Minh Hung and robbed of his brand new bicycle that had been given to him by relatives in Saigon. A bicycle was a prized possession for a *bodoi*, and he made a great fuss at the camp, having run all the way back after the robbery. Luckily for him, a truck was about to depart for Saigon, and it was immediately requisitioned by a group of *bodoi*, armed to the teeth, who set out to catch the thieves.

The local people knew very well where robberies were most likely to take place, and with their help it did not take the *bodoi* long to catch up with the fleeing culprits. They turned out to be none other than those "progressive" Voluntary Youths from Thai Binh in the North. The incident reinforced our worries that these young men might have been responsible for earlier robberies involving our visitors.

Ten days later, I came back from work and was told that my wife had arrived. I was granted two hours visiting time. After making sure that I was neatly dressed, the guard allowed me out. There she was in the visitors' room together with several other women. She could not help crying at the sight of me, and I could not hold back a steady flow of questions about her and our daughter, who stayed at home this time. My wife and the other women had come in a large group with two hired escorts. They had stayed overnight in Phuoc Binh and then taken a local bus to Minh Hung. From there they had walked for miles to our camp, and my wife's feet were swollen and sore.

When she finally got over her initial emotion, my wife gave me news of our family. My brother was worse off than before. He had a hard time feeding his large family, and they had made several aborted attempts to escape the country by boat. Fortunately, they had never been caught; the plans had fallen through for other reasons. As for her efforts to get back my freedom, she insisted she had contacted the right persons, claimed by my brother and others to be influential. She kept on saying that I would soon be free. Faced with her optimism, I held back the bad news that I was among those "blacklisted"; this was evident from the two hours of visiting time I was given compared to a whole day for others.

My wife confirmed everything I had learned from others about life outside, with one exception. "It seems to me everyone is planning escape from the country nowadays!" she said. "Some have made it to other countries, some never heard from again. But they keep fleeing in spite of captures. Some families have been detained for months; as soon as they are released, they try to escape again! Some have been captured several times. It seems unstoppable."

As darkness fell, a study monitor came and ordered those of us with two hours visiting time to go back to our quarters. I took the two large bundles that my wife had brought for me, said good-bye to her, and hurried off. Looking around, I did not see anyone else leaving. I had to stop several times on the way back to catch my breath; even these bundles proved too much for my weak body. At the entrance to my barracks, I was stopped and the bundles searched before I was allowed to go in. Fortunately, the search was not very thorough.

I got up early the next morning, having slept little. It made me angry to think of all those female visitors staying together in a cramped room just to protect themselves from molesting *bodoi*. I ran to the visitors' quarters without asking permission as the study monitors were still asleep. When I got there, my wife's companions were about to leave in a bus waiting nearby. I asked her to leave with them for her own safety.

At first I had thought of telling her of my plans for her to manage her own life, separating herself from my fate. But I did not do it. Whether I would have done so had I been given more visiting time, I do not know.

Now as they called out to each other, preparing to leave, I hurriedly told her, "Take care. Look after our little daughter. Don't hesitate if an opportunity comes along! I can take care of myself."

She held my hand tightly. "Don't do anything foolish! I am sure we can manage to get you out soon. There's no need to try to escape."

"Come on!" the other women called out as they boarded the bus. "You'll see him again next month, right?" I helped her get on the bus and then ran back toward our quarters as I could not bear the sad parting.

The meeting with my wife only made me more acutely aware of my helplessness. My morale sank as the days passed. In the packs she brought were about five kilos of assorted drugs, vitamin tablets, tonics, and food. As usual, the perishable items were handed out to friends. Thanks to a daily intake of additional nourishment and vitamins, I gradually got stronger. But my mental state did not fare any better; I became more and more worried as instinct told me that what was about to happen to me would not be good.

As if things were not bad enough, I began having some sort of fever. One night shortly after my wife left, I slept only fitfully, and as dawn neared, I felt someone shaking me and I heard my name. Then the beam of an elecric torch pointed directly at my face and a voice ordered, "Mr. Tran Tri Vu, get up and carry your baggage to the command center right away!"

"Now, this is it!" I said to myself. My throat was dry. The order—when it came—was without warning. I tried to stay cool, but I could not stop trembling. Thé and some others also got up. I hurriedly rolled up my mosquito net and went about collecting various items.

Thé pleaded with the *bodoi*. "This man is ill now. Please let me help him so that you won't have to wait so long."

"All right. Hurry up! Leave all bulky items behind. Our orders clearly say that each inmate may carry only one piece of luggage."

Thé whispered to me, "Put on all your clothes. Only carry medicine and food."

"No, I want to leave behind all the food so that I can carry more clothes. What if they move me to the North?"

"I think you'd better carry all the food you can with you and put on as many warm clothes as possible. You'll need the food more than the clothes on your journey."

"Shut up! You have only five more minutes to pack!" the *bodoi* shouted. "If you drag on, you will have to leave empty-handed."

I hurriedly searched for my sandals. As I followed the *bodoi* to the doorway, voices called after me, "Good-bye!" "All the best!" "Take care!" "Good luck!"

I felt a lump in my throat. It was sad having to part from those who had been sharing hardship and suffering with me up to now.

I regained my self-control and briskly followed the *bodoi* to the command center. There in the meeting hall about ten worried inmates stood beside their bags.

Thinh barked, "How many more are there to come?"

"About twenty," a *bodoi* answered.

It took them a while to assemble the designated number. When dawn broke, Thinh ordered us out to the main yard. Then he said, "According to our superiors' orders, you are going to be transferred to another camp. First we are going to examine your bags to make sure they do not contain prohibited items of metal and glass. Now, hand them over."

By now, I noted that the majority of us had at least two bags each. As the search progressed, Thé rushed toward me from nowhere and handed me a bag full of instant noodles.

Thinh shouted angrily, "Thé! Who gave you permission to come here?"

"Commander, I am willing to accept all responsibility for this action. But I have to help Mr. Vu; he's ill! These noodles belong to him, but he left them behind by mistake."

"All right! Leave them here! Get back to your quarters right away; you will have to start work soon. There will be plenty of food for these people at their new camp."

Thé hesitated, looking sadly at me. "All the best. Probably we shall never meet again."

I just shook his hand without saying a word. Then we parted. He had become my best friend, this peasant boy from Central Vietnam.

Suddenly, there was a shout. "I've already told you! All metal articles are prohibited!"

A middle-aged inmate pleaded. "Please let me keep it. This is my rice bowl."

Thinh snatched the aluminum bowl, raised it up, and threw it away. The inmate ran to pick it up. Thinh ran after him, caught up with him, and angrily raised his hand to hit him, but the man ducked. Thinh then snatched the bowl from him, threw it down, and quickly crushed it with his heel.

"Oh, my God!" cried the man.

I knew that the bowl was his cherished souvenir, one that he had meticulously beaten into the shape of a bowl from a piece of aluminum that he had found at Xuan Loc.

The other inmates consoled him. "Forget it! We've left behind more valuable belongings than this bowl! Why are you being so ridiculous?"

The gray-haired man just stood there crying. The cup, it was clear to all, had far greater meaning than its value would suggest. The atmosphere turned very tense.

Thinh angrily raised his voice. "Don't ask me why you are being transferred! I am sure you all know why! Just ask yourselves and think of what you have been doing so far. Before you leave, someone from Logistics will settle pending matters with you."

A *bodoi* then stepped forward. "Some of you have entrusted some cash to us," he said. "Now I am going to hand it over to the escort, who will in turn hand it over to the authority at your new camp. Now, we in this camp no longer have anything to do with you. Do you have anything to ask?"

Faced with sullen silence, he hastened to conclude, "Well, in that case, sign here."

We set out in the direction of regimental headquarters, escorted by a group of armed *bodoi*. Looking back, we saw a large crowd of inmates on the hillside staring at us, some waving. We walked silently on, without looking at them again or even waving back.

Five trucks were waiting when we got to the headquarters. Some were filled with men, probably inmates transferred from other camps. We were made to board in some prearranged order. Then the trucks were covered with tarpaulin; in each one the inmates were accompanied by two guards sitting at the back facing us.

We worried about our fate, but momentarily we were more annoyed by the tarpaulin that prevented us from looking out. Beyond any doubt, bad things were awaiting us, for we knew this transfer was a punishment.

Chapter 7

Camp Six: Ham Tan

It was still raining hard when our truck, rocking from side to side, came slowly to a stop. A neon light filtering in meant that the *bodoi* planned a rest stop in an inhabited area. The two *bodoi* sitting at the rear of the truck took their time raising the tarpaulin. As they jumped down from the vehicle, a voice outside said, "Detainees are requested to remain seated in the trucks. Is that understood?"

Sitting near the rear of the vehicle, I was able to raise a corner of the tarpaulin slightly to risk a furtive look outside. I saw a camp surrounded by a barbed-wire fence, behind which was another fence made of small logs about two meters high. The perimeter was brightly lighted by neon lights. Suddenly there was the sound of people splashing through the water. A *bodoi*, wrapped in a plastic sheet, made his way toward us followed by five men clad in dark gray *ba ba*.[1] He gave us his instructions.

"Everyone, listen carefully. Hand your belongings down to these *trat tu vien*,[2] who will bring them into the camp for you. Then get down and follow them. You must absolutely obey the *trat tu vien*. Is that clear?"

The rain-soaked *trat tu vien* silently took our bags and carried them through a fairly large gate. We climbed down and followed them into the camp, noting that it contained houses as large as the barracks we had built at Bu Gia Map and Bu Loi camps, but taller and with secure doors made of wattle. We were brought to a meeting hall. In a low voice, I asked the *trat tu vien* ahead of me, "Could you tell me where I can relieve myself?"

The man stopped short, stared sternly at me, then loudly retorted, "Who gave you permission to talk to me? Have you asked the cadre? Cadre, this man tried to talk to me without permission."

I was astounded. This person who I had assumed was a pathetic prisoner like me, who had to walk rain-soaked on bare feet, who took orders from the *bodoi* like a servant, turned out to be an arrogant inmate, who did not hesitate to report on us. This signaled a completely different way of life ahead.

The cadre said loudly, "I repeat for the *last* time. In this camp every inmate

---

[1] A suit of pajamalike trousers and jacket worn by both sexes in the South.

[2] Detainees appointed by the *bodoi* to maintain discipline; equivalent to trustees.

must get permission to do anything. No one can do anything without permission, including talking or asking questions of each other. Is that clear?"

"Quite clear!"

When we all got inside the hall, the *trat tu vien* positioned themselves around as if guarding us. A *bodoi* in a yellowish uniform said, "You new inmates, collect your luggage and form a line on the left. The *trat tu vien* will show you your sleeping platforms for the night. You will be assigned to a group tomorrow. Remember that discipline must be adhered to. All infractions of rules will be dealt with severely. Is that clear?"

"Quite clear!"

Looking around, I saw stunned disbelief on the faces of the "new inmates"; our eyes told each other that life here would be unbearable!

A *trat tu vien* stepped up and said, "Follow me; bring your luggage."

The rain was abating as we were led to a large room half-filled with people about to sleep with their mosquito nets already hung up. As in the previous camp, there were sleeping platforms along either side of the aisle. But here an upper deck of bunks had been added, making the room more crowded. It could accommodate about two hundred inmates. The occupants sat quietly inside their mosquito nets staring curiously at us. I was assigned a place on a lower platform at the end of the room. The bed assignments completed, the *trat tu vien* introduced a man standing next to him.

"This is Ngu, your room leader, the only person here you can talk to. Ngu, show these newcomers where to relieve themselves! They are here only temporarily. They will be assigned to groups tomorrow."

The *trat tu vien* walked out the only door of the room, closed it, and bolted it from outside. In the bright light of an electric bulb, we saw a big blackboard near the door. Across the top, written in big clear letters were the words, "Rules of Thu Duc Detention Center." The rest of the board was covered with the "rules the prisoners should comply with." So, we definitely were in a prison! But Thu Duc prison? I wondered if we were near Saigon. I indicated the blackboard to the man next to me; he nodded his head as if to say, "We are now true prisoners in a real prison!"

A loud voice was heard. "My name is Ngu. I welcome you on behalf of all of us in this room. I would like to emphasize that the toilet in the next room must be kept absolutely hygienic! Those who foul it must clean it. It's the duty of those sleeping near the toilet to keep an eye on those using it. Any unsanitary condition must be reported to the authorities right away to find out who fouled it. Decency requires you to ensure that those who sleep near the toilet do not suffer."

Having put my belongings away at the head of my bunk, I climbed down to go to the toilet, joining a queue of the new inmates. I thought how even something so ordinary as carrying out bodily functions had been deliberately raised to a ridiculous level of importance. Standing near the end of the queue, I looked inside the room, searching for a familiar face among those silently observing us from under their mosquito nets. So far they had offered no greeting. I whispered to the man in front of me, "These guys sure know how to follow the rules."

He turned to me. "What a horrible place!" he said.

Suddenly someone spoke from under a mosquito net. "You are talking to each other while waiting to pee!"

We were startled as if caught red-handed in a serious crime. From the mosquito net a head emerged, followed by a hand that gave us a mock salute. A young face broke into a broad smile. "Only joking," he said. "Go on talking."

Not knowing what to reply, we kept our mouths shut. Fresh from the initial shock of being reported on by the *trat tu vien*, I was not going to take chances with someone I knew nothing about.

The toilet was unlike anything I had seen before. The urinal was a concrete trough with drainage holes at the bottom, and the stool—of primitive Western design—was a wooden container with a precariously small seat.

Having prepared my bunk, I was about to open my bag to get some noodles when the door opened and a *trat tu vien* walked in, followed by two inmates carrying a steaming basketful of something covered by a sheet of plastic. The *trat tu vien* called out, "This is dinner for the newly arrived inmates. Come get it, starting with those near the doorway."

Tins and bowls of all sizes were proffered by the eager inmates. We each got a bowl of cooked grain called *bobo* (sorghum), which I had never seen before, and a tinful of boiled water. I devoured the *bobo* in a few minutes and then softened the dried noodles in the hot water and ate them. In spite of the mood this place put me in, I felt somewhat consoled by a full stomach.

The brightly lit room seemed unusually quiet for a place occupied by some two hundred people. The aroma of good coffee wafted in from somewhere. I sat on my bunk looking around. On the opposite side of the room silent figures were gathered inside a mosquito net, apparently eating something together. They proceeded without saying a word. Several other groups were doing the same. Suddenly, they all quietly went to their sleeping places and laid down as if on cue. I followed suit. Footsteps were heard outside, lightly at first, then very clearly. I lay quietly until sleep came.

I awoke feeling better, my fever gone. Crowing cocks greeting the sunrise were heard from outside. The other occupants of the room were already up, holding tins and toothbrushes, waiting to be let out. One of them asked me with a friendly smile, "Where did you come from? Why did you arrive so late?"

One of the newcomers responded, "Are we allowed to communicate with you? Didn't you make fun of us newcomers?"

"It doesn't do any harm to joke once in a while, does it?" the other fellow replied with a smile. "So long as we keep quiet in front of the *trat tu vien*. In this camp they are as powerful as our fathers. The cadres are our grandfathers! Just pay careful attention to them and you'll be safe."

Then the conversation stopped short, as did the talking among the other inmates. The morning atmosphere was heavy with the unnatural silence. At the sound of a gong outside, the old inmates put their feet on the floor in unison. We new ones looked on in amazement. Then came the clicking sound of padlocks and the door was opened. Early morning sunlight flooded in. The electric lights went out, one by one, leaving the room in near darkness in contrast to the bright doorway. We gave way to the "old inmates" as they filed out. Outside, everyone quickly formed into lines and squatted on the ground awaiting morning roll call. Chatter suddenly stopped as the men saw the approaching figures, a cadre in yellowish uniform and a *trat tu vien*. The cadre took a position facing us, counted us, then consulted a notebook several times before asking the room leader in puzzlement, "Why are there so many people?"

"Sir, some were brought in from another camp last night."

The cadre instructed us to form into two groups of old and newly arrived inmates. He then recounted us and entered the numbers in his notebook. At long last he barked, "Now exercise!"

The room leader stood aside and started the exercises, shouting, "One, two, three, four. One, two, three, four."

The cadre looked on critically for a while, then headed for another group. When he was out of sight, the room leader shouted, "Everybody!" To which the "old" inmates joyfully replied, "Strong!"

Then they all raced off in the same direction. Curious, I followed and found them scrambling to get the best place in line for the toilet! Two inmates brought out the wooden container full of excrement. The stench was unbearable. Moments later an empty container was brought in.

After my turn at the toilet, I ran back to the room just in time to get my breakfast of boiled grain and hot water. A *trat tu vien* then came to assemble us in the main yard, and as we were led to it we discovered that to the right of the main entrance to our compound was an area for female prisoners. Women were filing out of the camp, followed by a couple of female cadres wearing the same yellowish uniforms.

The camp was generally laid out in rows of bungalows parallel to each other, the whole place surrounded by white sand lending an air of cleanliness. Each bungalow was enclosed by a fence made of small tree trunks topped with three strands of barbed wire. The compound reminded me of a giant chessboard. Footpaths were bounded by barbed wire, forming an intricate mazelike pattern. I later learned that this elaborate construction was to prevent occupants from communicating between buildings.

We were now led in groups of fifty into the meeting hall where we registered and got paper and pens to again record our personal histories. We were sent back outside, and I sat by the fence writing; it was very hot in the sun. An inmate sweeping the yard drifted toward me. When he was quite close, he said in a low voice, "You are going to be thoroughly searched. If you have any cash, hide it now."

He then hurried off. Quickly I fished out my banknotes, cast a furtive look around, saw no one watching, and stuck the precious bundle into a hollow bamboo stem that was part of the fence. I was confident that this open spot would never be suspected as a hiding place. I tried to warn others of an imminent search, but it was too late, for it was now our group's turn to submit the personal histories.

We were ordered to get our luggage and form into lines with each man's bags placed neatly to his right. When the formation was satisfactory to the *trat tu vien*, he went off and returned in a moment with a cadre of apparently high rank.

"Attention!" he barked. "Cadre, all inmates now assembled."

The cadre wore a neat, starched uniform, a rarity among the *bodoi*. His complexion was unusually dark for a Vietnamese. He stepped forward and said, "Welcome to this camp. From now on you are under the jurisdiction of the police."

Now I realized that the unusual yellowish uniform was that of the police, not the army. The cadre began to explain that the police way of doing things was "always to maintain discipline and to follow instructions unquestioningly, not in the easygoing way of some military." He ended his lecture, saying, "As you may have noticed, the buildings here are spacious and weatherproof to protect your health. The infirmary provides all sorts of medicine. Here, there is no torture room, no beatings of inmates. The *trat tu vien* will assign you to your groups, but first your luggage must be searched. Items you are not permitted to keep must be entrusted to the camp authority, particularly gold rings, watches, and so on. These will be returned to you when you are discharged. Is that clear? When the search and registration of money is completed, you will continue writing your personal accounts."

From our experience in other camps, we were puzzled by this procedure of search first, then registering of goods. The *trat tu vien* perfunctorily went through our bags. At the declaration of possessions, no attempt was made to force us to list everything in detail.

Our fears were allayed by this apparent relaxation, and we felt quite relieved as we were taken to our new barracks. But once there, the *trat tu vien* and policemen swooped down for a second and entirely different type of search. They proved to be experts at their task as they checked the hems of clothes and the steel bands on metal suitcases. They turned up banknotes, gold rings, watches, razor blades, papers, letters. Everything was packed into a bundle and handed to the chief cadre. We got no receipts.

An anxious inmate asked what would become of his property, and the cadre replied calmly, "You were told to declare everything. These items do not exist since they do not appear in your declarations, do they? They are now confiscated!"

We restrained our protests, realizing we had been cleverly tricked. My team went to its assigned room. Most of its occupants, including the room leader, were outside working. Those in the room were the sick; they lay on their bunks staring at us. We were simply told to await further instructions from the room leader when he returned and to continue writing our histories. We did not talk to the others in the room, and they continued to regard us with distrust. The click of the door lock reminded us of our imprisonment; we were now in the pit of existence, treated as dangerous criminals.

The gong rang, announcing the noon meal, and the room's remaining inmates returned. They greeted us silently with nods and forced smiles. No one showed any curiosity or tried to ask us anything. We put it down to the iron discipline of the prison. Soon the sullen silence was broken by a shout from outside, "House No. 5, send somebody to get the lunch."

Four inmates were sent by the room leader, and in a short time they returned, stopping outside the door. Two carried a bucket of boiled water on a bamboo pole, one a steaming basin of cooked grain on his head, and the fourth a smaller basin of rice soup for the sick. We were told to move outdoors and put our food containers in straight rows on the ground to make it easier for the room leader and his aides to distribute the food. When completed, the room leader asked, "Do you have any question about the distribution?"

When no one answered, he shouted, "All right! Take your share. Don't rush, or you will kick dust and sand into other people's food."

As we squatted in the yard and ate, the gong sounded three times. Inmates hurriedly headed back to the room, taking their food with them. The room leader explained that it was the signal for a mandatory siesta. All inmates were to stay indoors and keep quiet. Later, the gong rang again, and inmates hurried to the central courtyard. Excused were the sick and we newcomers, who were locked in to continue writing our accounts. At five o'clock a *trat tu vien* came to collect the personal histories. As he was leaving, he said, "I'm leaving the door open since the rest will soon be back from work. However, no one is to go out until the gong sounds. Understand?"

No one bothered to reply. About twenty minutes later the others came back dripping wet. I guessed that they had taken a bath in a nearby stream and that their worksite was near the camp.

Four inmates went to the kitchen to bring back the dinner of boiled grain and water. Two less lucky ones exchanged the excrement container for an empty one. I noticed that inmates were allowed to stay outdoors longer than during the lunch break. They stood around for half an hour before the gong sounded. I picked out a quiet corner and sat down. About a meter from me sat a gloomy looking man. He forced a smile, then shook his head sadly without saying a word. There was a buzz of conversation in the background as if this were the only time the inmates could vent their feelings. I tried to strike up a conversation with the fellow but could not think how to start. I thought of asking him his name but decided that was too personal. I ventured, "What did you do before?"

He immediately gave me a hard look. His face went red. "What the hell did I do?" he retorted. "If only I had done something worthwhile to deserve this! I didn't do anything. I wish I'd killed some commies so I wouldn't regret ending up here! All I did was earn a living. I did nothing important enough to deserve four years in this prison!"

He spoke louder and louder as though arguing with me. I kept my mouth shut for fear of attracting attention. When the gong sounded three times I started back to the bungalow, but seeing the "old" inmates forming into lines in the yard, I followed suit. Our flock of emaciated prisoners gloomily squatted on the ground awaiting the arrival of the police for the final roll call. As our bungalow was situated at the end of the row, we waited quite a while before a policeman arrived and counted us, using his eyes.

He said, "New inmates in Group 5 will start work tomorrow. The group leader will assign each to a team and to his position in the group formation. Now, back to your bungalow!"

We slowly filed in, row by row. The door was slammed shut and locked. Those near me quietly went about preparing their "beds." I did not begin a conversation since no one had spoken to me. Once they had completed their bed preparations, they went over to their pals and were soon chatting openly, unconcerned about the possible presence of a mole. The room was dimly lit by a single fluorescent light in the center. I lay on my "bed" thinking. The sweet music of a guitar was coming from a nearby building. Suddenly, it was interrupted by a woman's loud scream. We all went quiet.

"Kill me if you can! Do you feel superior by beating a woman? Go on, beat me to death! You're only a lackey of that God-damn bunch! You scoundrel! Oh God!"

The air in the room suddenly became heavy because of the painful cries. The two fellows next to me came back to their beds. One stared at me and remarked, "You're going to bed early, aren't you?"

This was the opening I had been waiting for! I quickly replied, "No, I am not ready for sleep. How can I sleep with all that screaming and crying!"

"That must be a female prisoner being beaten up by that bastard Ba on orders from the female cadres!"

They told me about this prison. One said, "Did Mai Lien tell you when you registered that this camp is called Z30-D? Z30 indicates a prison in Binh Tuy Province; D means it's in the Ham Tan area. There are four prison camps—A, B, C, and D—in this area, all under the jurisdiction of the police. It seems to me this is the main detention area since new buidings are being put up, all in concrete. On the way to work, you will see the building site of the headquarters of the whole Z30 network. A huge complex is being built by a big Saigon contractor. Several hundred bricklayers are working on the project."

"By the way," I interrupted, "you mentioned someone called Mai Lien. Who's he? I only noticed a dark-skinned cadre who addressed us when we first registered."

That's Comrade Vong! We guess he has some Cambodian blood, so we call him Mai Lien![3] He's the political commissar here. Did he boast that he has been to the Soviet Union? Did he say that there was no torture in this prison?"

I realized that inmates of this camp seemed more inquisitive than those I had known in camps under the military administration.

"Is Vong the one who always formally receives new inmates?" I asked.

"Yes, he is."

"Did he lie about the torture? If not, why are there beatings and screaming like I've just heard?"

"Well, not really! It's true that the police themselves don't beat you up here but only because they don't want to get their hands dirty! The work is usually given to that bastard Ba, a common criminal convicted of manslaughter. With the 'prestige' of being a *trat tu vien*, he is so energetic and loyal to the police that he beats up any inmate on orders. The screams we've heard must have been from a female prisoner being beaten up by Ba in the meeting hall. When he punishes a male prisoner, he comes straight to the offender's room, calls him out, forces the poor man to account for his faults, then throws a hail of punches—all in front of the laughing policemen. He stops only when the poor fellow collapses. The police use Ba's service when someone annoys them. Inmates who commit serious offenses are sent to the 'disciplinary cell' where one leg is shackled to the wall. I've never seen anyone let out in less than one month! The sculptor who made the famous 'The Mourner' statue at the Military Cemetery has been in the disciplinary cell for five months, for making fun of the Revolution. Those let out are usually skeletons, with not enough strength left to work."

He told of other acts of cruelty by the police and concluded, "They deliberately pick monsters for *trat tu vien*, mostly common criminals serving long sentences, but some were policemen in the former regime. Most have been

---

[3]A play on words. Because of his dark skin, Vong was believed to be a *miên lai* (Cambodian half-breed). This was inverted, and *miên lai* became *Mai Liên*, which is poetic (lit., wild cherry and lotus).

indoctrinated with 'class struggle' attitudes and jump at every opportunity to get even with us 'intellectuals.' "

"Police of all regimes always tend to oppress the ordinary citizen," remarked another fellow who had until then remained silent. "These communist police consider this a once-in-a-lifetime opportunity to revenge themselves on their enemies.

"By the way," he said, "what's your name? Which camp are you from? My name is Tâm. I used to be at Blood Stream camp near Bien Hoa. I've been here for about a month."

I told him my name and that I was from Bu Loi camp in Song Be Province. I told him that life there under the military administration was not as restrictive as here where we were locked up most of the time. Tâm said the most horrible conditions he had experienced were in a Saigon prison. It was a former hotel in Lang Cha Ca district, once used by the Americans. Twenty-five inmates had been crammed into a single room. Since there was not enough floor space, detainees had to take turns lying down, and they got only a few hours sleep a day. All doors and windows were kept shut. It was so hot and stuffy that everyone was soaked with sweat, and the tiled floor was literally a pool of it. Everyone used a piece of clothing to wipe himself off, but soon the cloth was soaked as well. Several thousand people were kept in that place.

Here, in a well-ventilated room with a thatched roof, Tam felt he was fortunate!

Soon they fell asleep, but I stayed deep in thought. Sleep did not come easily in the lighted room. Suddenly I saw a swarm of tiny insects climbing up my mosquito net. I started to swipe at them but then saw they were on the outside of the net. However, it was not long before some managed to get in. I picked one up, crushing it with my fingernail, its fat belly burst and out came evil-smelling blood. It was a bedbug. Soon they were all over. It took quite a while to get rid of them, and then my whole body itched so that I could hardly sleep.

The next morning I told my neighbors about the bugs, but they just laughed. One pulled up his shirt to show me his torso covered with red spots. "These are bite marks from bedbugs. In this place we don't get enough to eat to feed these blood-sucking insects!"

I suddenly felt terribly itchy. I pulled off my shirt and there were the same sort of red spots all over me. Carefully inspecting my shirt, I found the culprits in the seams, their bellies filled with my blood. Having suffered in our jungle camps from mosquitoes and leeches, I was hoping my torment by insects had ended. But the words of a philosophical prisoner rang in my ears, "A prison would not be what it's meant to be without bedbugs!"

Police organization of inmates for work was different from what I had experienced with the *bodoi*. After a monotonous breakfast of cereal and boiled water, inmates assembled in the central courtyard at the sounding of the gong. On average, there were about two hundred inmates available for work from each barracks. The seriously ill were spared labor. Inmates were then divided into two groups, half from each side of the barracks. In practice, each group had exactly the same number of workers depending on how many were available that day.

Assignments were made by a team of clerks headed by Ba, who was, I learned, a communist soldier who had defected to the nationalist side. He cheerfully briefed group leaders on the details of the work to be done. The latter then led their members away, each stopping at the checkpoint at the main entrance to give the sentries the name of his group, the number of inmates, and so on. Only then was the group put under the supervision of a study monitor, assisted by armed escorts whose number varied depending on the location of the worksite. Usually, two policemen armed with AK submachine guns made up the escort if the work was near the prison perimeter and four if the site was farther out, near the forest. I was told by "old hands" that work was usually confined to a specific area to prevent escapes.

For a study monitor, an escape meant a delay in joining the Party. This also applied to police of junior rank. The road to promotion and privilege invariably started with membership in the Youth League and then the coveted Party membership. However, there were shortcuts for children of high-ranking Party members. I also learned from the "old" inmates that the police, unlike most *bodoi*, exploited the poor inmates and their families. I was to witness this often during my time here.

My group was charged with preparing the land for sweet potatoes. Quotas were less stringent than at Bu Loi, and the pace of work not as urgent. There was no one like Commander Thinh here to push us to achieve exceptional yields so he could get an award.

We were allowed a fifteen-minute break one hour after starting. Food was quickly prepared and as quickly consumed. We then worked for another two hours before a longer break during which the hitherto tired inmates suddenly turned energetic as they prepared extra food, their source of energy for the day. The place bustled with activity. Then came more work, which progressed at a snail's pace as everyone was tired from working hours in the burning tropical sun with only partially filled stomachs. We rushed to assemble for the walk home at the first sound of the gong. On the way back we were allowed to stop briefly at a stream for a quick bath or to wash our clothes, all under the watchful eyes of the study monitors and guards and with each group confined to its own stretch of the stream. The river was swollen by heavy rains and was as wide as ten meters in some places. My new friends advised me to take only a quick dip, then wash my clothes. Returning to camp, we stopped at the entrance where the study monitors reported to the sentries, who counted us and then signed us in. Only then were the study monitors and the escort guards allowed to take their own lunch break.

We had a quick meal of the familiar cereal and then rested. Few napped as it only made them more tired. In the afternoon we suffered the scorching sun at its worst. Ham Tan was a coastal area. The earth was a mixture of soil and white sand, which relentlessly reflected the heat of the sun. Our bodies quickly became dehydrated and I dived into the stream at the earliest opportunity.

One night, after immersing myself in cold water too long while my body was still hot and dehydrated, my fever returned. The group leader agreed to summon a medic and, since the doors were locked, he called out to the occupants of the next barracks, asking them to relay a message to those in the barracks beyond. Thus, the call was relayed from house to house until it reached the infirmary.

The door opened after about half an hour to admit a policeman, a *trat tu vien*, and the inmate doctor, Pham Van Hat. He was an old man of about sixty, whom I later learned had been a senator in the Republic of Vietnam and the president of the South Vietnamese Red Cross. He was now in charge of the infirmary.

After diagnosing my illness, Dr. Hat gave me some tablets from a carton. The *trat tu vien* just stood there keeping an eye on us. When the door once again slammed shut, inmate chatting resumed.

I was excused from work the next day. I was weak from hunger as I had eaten only thin rice soup. Tâm came to see me during the lunch break.

"How could you surrender to this Ham Tan climate so easily?" he teased. "I think it's because you stayed too long in the water yesterday. Next time just wet your face even though you are hot. The air, the water, and the soil here are more unhealthy than in a jungle."

When the inmates returned in the evening, a study monitor came to see me and demanded, "What did Tâm say to you during the break?"

I hesitated, and the group leader interrupted: "Cadre, this man does not know Tâm since he has been here only two days."

The study monitor ordered a *trat tu vien* to take Tâm's belongings away as they left. We were again locked in after evening roll call. I asked the fellow sitting next to me, "Do you know where Tâm is? Why were his belongings taken away?"

"Didn't you hear the gun shots?" he replied. "That signaled an escape! I knew someone was missing when the count was made at the stream. It turned out to be Tâm, who was assigned to return the hoes to the storehouse. Obviously he took advantage of the fact that no guard was watching him and slipped away. I don't know how he managed it! The bathing took only ten minutes, counting and checking another fifteen. By the time the alarm was sounded, Tâm had been gone a half hour. The police then rushed to the highway to try to intercept him, and even now they are combing the whole area for him. I wonder if he made it! Usually two out of three escapees are recaptured. You are fortunate you knew Tâm for only two days; otherwise, you would be summoned to the command center 'to help the police in their investigation' and would be asked questions like 'why didn't you inform the authorities when you saw signs of Tâm preparing to escape?' "

"What will happen to Tâm's other neighbor?"

"Although he hasn't been here long, they certainly will transfer him to another group."

Next morning we remained in camp while other groups were escorted to work. Once everyone else was out of sight, the police and *trat tu vien* went through our luggage, and we were moved to different barracks. I was transferred to barracks 3 located near the central courtyard—and nearer the police and *trat tu vien* than before!

I now was assigned to the carpentry team because of my previous work experience. The work was similar to what I had done at the other camps, although we did not have to get lumber from the jungle but had it supplied by a contractor. Forests in this area consisted mainly of shrubs.

We were assigned to build houses along the national highway. Traffic could clearly be seen when we were thatching the roofs. Our escort guards relaxed under trees some distance away, confident since there were plenty of sentry boxes around. But we were free to talk, and I learned many things from my work mates who confirmed that all of us were here for a fairly long stay. Some had been sentenced to five to ten years by kangaroo courts. The majority had been transferred from other reeducation camps. A tiny minority were young men recently arrested for defiance of the communist regime. One man disclosed that a few days earlier a group had been brought in consisting of an engineer named Truong of the famous Phu Tho Institute of Technology who, together with about twenty of his students, had been arrested for allegedly plotting a revolt.

I had a pleasant surprise at the stream one day when I was reunited with friends who had been with me at Xuan Loc camp. I first caught sight of Thach, the award-winning body-builder, who still stood out from the rest of the emaciated group in the stream, although he was much thinner. Seeing my hesitancy, a work mate said that since the moles had yet to learn all the newcomers' names, I should go ahead and greet my friends. Thach said that after my group moved to Bu Gia Map, the remainder at Xuan Loc were transferred to a camp at Long Giao, the inmates there having been sent to another camp. In effect, all inmates were rotated from camp to camp continuously—hence no camp was abandoned as previously assumed. This unusual policy of the communist government must have been very costly due to the large number of vehicles required to move people around over long distances.

A few weeks later I experienced the psychological sadism of the police. Usually we were allowed to stay in camp on Sunday and were free to gather in an enclosed area near the toilets to cook food brought in by visitors. Those for whom visitors were due eagerly awaited them, but first we had to see whether or not the police were going to indulge in their usual tactics.

"It depends on the whim of the police," explained an old hand, when I first asked what it was all about. "Every Sunday morning everyone anxiously looks to headquarters for signs of the assembly of police or *trat tu vien*. A meeting of the former signals a search of our rooms and luggage, followed by transfers of inmates to other groups and a general rearrangement of accommodations. This is done primarily to discourage inmates from hiding cash in their rooms. An assembly of *trat tu vien,* on the other hand, only means reshuffles for a few groups. Every time searches are carried out, someone is bound to lose something—usually money, letters, textbooks, crucifixes, combs, chess pieces, etc. However, when only one *trat tu vien* heads for the cooking area, keys in hand, everyone is over the moon; it means we really will have a free Sunday."

"Natural worriers suffer most on Sundays as anyone may be searched anytime on a tip from an informer," interrupted another inmate. "Once started, a search lasts for hours until something is found. Even if nothing worthwhile is found, the 'earmarked' man is certain to be transferred to a special group with plenty of moles or whose group leader is a wicked mole himself, ready to hurt his members to gain a favor, such as extended visiting time with his wife. In these groups discipline is strictly maintained, usually enforced by a vicious study monitor. These groups are normally housed just off the central courtyard near the command center."

I was also told by one inmate that some men have the misfortune of a sudden transfer to a "disciplinary cell" without explanation. The victim later is forced to confess some crime, usually dreamed up by a mole. "This happens to some prisoners simply because a crazy study monitor does not like their looks," the man said. He added, "They try their best to crush prisoners' spirit so the poor men dare not look them in the eyes! One study monitor is known to hate inmates who wear glasses. He regards them as self-proclaimed intellectuals."

As we were talking, a man carrying a bunch of keys passed by, and everyone rushed to get his food, pot, and fuel ready. It took only a few minutes to line up facing the gate, the only opening in the fence surrounding our barracks. The same eager scene went on at other barracks. Each man knew he would have to be quick to grab a space in the crowded cooking area shared by over a thousand inmates.

After opening the gate to the cooking area, the *trat tu vien* went to each barracks to let the inmates out onto the footpath.Every time a door was flung open, the men rushed out, fighting each other to get ahead. The ferocity was no less intense than in the morning when we were queuing up for the toilet. I was one of the fastest in the morning race for the toilet, but I ended up nearly last in the cooking line. I had no need to hurry as I had nothing left to cook.

Onlookers like me were quite numerous in the cooking area. Some were out of touch with their relatives. Others had families who were too hard-pressed to make regular visits. We gathered in a separate corner enviously watching our fellow prisoners cook their food. Compared to the restrictions in this prison, my situation at Bu Gia Map and Bu Loi had been quite tolerable. The more I thought of those times, the more sorrow I felt.

A week after joining Group 3, I and some others were suddenly searched and transferred to Group 22, one of the groups housed around the perimeter of the camp. I took great care not to talk unnecessarily to my new barracks mates. I did not know them, and I believed I was under surveillance, a fact confirmed by several transfers in less than a month. Our group leader was Dao Trong Ky, a former diplomat at a South Vietnamese embassy and later an official in the Ministry of Communications. He had been a protégé of Hoang Duc Nha (nephew and close aide of former President Nguyen Van Thieu). Ky was jovial, and members of his group seemed reasonable. They flocked around me when I had settled down in my new spot, asking me about life in other camps. In the ensuing talk I realized that labor here was not as severe as in reeducation camps in the jungle highlands. This was primarily due to the poor health of inmates who had been exhausted by hard labor in other camps. So we were not actually much better off here as far as work was concerned. In addition, our minds were constantly tormented by the many brutal aspects of prison life.

Most of my new group mates held discussions almost every night about American policies in Vietnam and Americans in general, since they had been closely involved with the Americans. More often than not these discussions were acrimonious. One evening as the younger inmates were gathered around a fellow with a guitar, a middle-aged man approached and startled me with a question I remember well, "Would you like to join in our discussion of erroneous American policies in Vietnam?"

I stared at him and his friends, trying to ascertain whether this was an informer trap. All I saw were sincere looks, but I dallied, "I think before we criticize someone else, we should first criticize ourselves."

"That we've already done," replied the man, "many times. We always concluded that our downfall was due to wrong policies of the Americans."

Another fellow impatiently put in, "That's right. To reduce boredom we've come up with this game of analyzing the policies that resulted in our humiliating imprisonment here. We've spent many nights talking about our mistakes and wrongdoings; we always come to the conclusion that the collapse of South Vietnam was due as much to the Americans as to the Soviets and Chinese! It was they who made us fight their way, their wasteful ineffective way."

Seeing that they were on the edge of a taboo subject, I interrupted, "Are you not afraid of moles?"

"Our mole is that fellow playing the guitar and singing 'golden songs,' the kind banned by the authorities," replied a gray-haired inmate with a melancholy look. "We have discussions every evening. No one bothers to report on us. Even that informer disregards the rules sometimes. Our bodies may be imprisoned but not our minds. Don't worry about taking part in our discussions. At the least, we must find out why we have ended up in this wretched prison. The majority of us here were involved with the Americans and therefore can see their many mistakes, such as their economic aid which often led to unjust distribution of wealth. As a result, some lived in luxury in the city while the peasants suffered the effects of war. Corruption, prostitution, and other vices were stimulated by artificial prosperity brought about by the infusion of dollars. Their initial mistakes were killing President Ngo Dinh Diem, who had originally been supported by them, and their clumsy choice of a Diem successor. Those corrupt and incompetent military men installed by the Americans actually contributed to the downfall of South Vietnam. The mindless installation of useless leaders was as futile as changing the roof of a house while a storm is raging. The conduct of the war was poorly executed. Our combat consisted mostly of uncoordinated defensive efforts. The American advisers were ignorant of communist 'people's wars' which can last a century. Having expected quick victory through the use of masses of soldiers armed with sophisticated weapons, they began to lose their will to fight after easy victory failed to materialize. We Vietnamese were like a reluctant audience watching a play in which something goes wrong, and the actors and actresses flee, leaving the poor audience to shoulder the blame!"

"Was there no way to avoid American intervention?" I asked in bewilderment. "I mean, there was talk of nonalignment."

"No, that wouldn't have been possible. Since the communists received plenty of modern weapons from the Soviet Union, we had to turn to someone equally powerful for modern weapons and diplomatic support. If they shot at us with their Soviet-made AK-47 submachine guns, we should be able to shoot back with M-16s. It was a shame that those who fought for freedom couldn't find decent allies. They ended up in humiliating defeat, abandoned by their so-called allies."

The attentive audience joined in as if to give vent to long-repressed bitter feelings. They criticized Americans' disregard for the local population's feelings and sovereignty of the nation by delegating formulation of strategy to such organizations as the CIA, which only trusted people who could speak English or shared the CIA employees' carefree way of life, shunning public-spirited and truly patriotic Vietnamese as anachronisms. That was why those shallow CIA men, because of their shortsightedness, failed to see the long-term value of a just cause!

I remember well what one young fellow said at that moment. "Now that we know why we were defeated, I wonder if there is any way to fight communism without relying on the Americans. If there is one, why hasn't anyone tried it? I hate to be called an American mercenary—I was fighting for freedom."

"F . . . them!" swore another. "That's right! We suffered the hardships simply to live in freedom, and some call us mercenaries!"

The gray-haired inmate shook his head, "In today's world, it's impossible to find a country not under American or Soviet influence. We could not be nonaligned to dispense with the Americans or the Russians. The fact is the political influence of the two superpowers is all pervasive and irresistible. There is no such thing as true nonalignment. Those proclaiming to be neutral court the Soviets and the Americans in order to survive. As for our country, from the beginning Ho Chi Minh and his comrades wholeheartedly adopted Soviet communism in the struggle against the French colonists. The term 'the non-aligned Republic of South Vietnam' as used by the communists initially after their takeover of the South, was only designed to make their brutal annexation of the South more palatable to the rest of the world. All said it was inevitable for us to rely on the Americans even though in the end they couldn't help us ward off communism."

Until now I had never heard anyone dare, quite so openly, to analyze our defeat or criticize the communists. The more I listened, the wider my eyes were opened. I had spent time pondering the debacle of South Vietnam, despairing over the humiliating haste with which South Vietnam defenses had collapsed, but I had not gone into the causes of our downfall.

The discussion was cut short by the gong signaling bedtime. The guitar music and singing abruptly stopped, and everyone went back to his place to prepare for bed. My neighbor, who had been in the discussion, asked me, "Do you also have difficulty sleeping?"

"I used to get to sleep very easily," I replied. "However, I have the habit of staying awake all night if my mind is troubled." Questions were churning in my head now after the discussion!

"I have the same problem," he smiled. "I've been troubled by something I can't make sense of. Let me tell you my story. I was stationed at Phu Bai airport outside Hue when the North Vietnamese army attacked. I didn't witness any big fighting, but the situation was painted pessimistically by the intelligence people. Even when the American consulate was closed, the war situation wasn't as hopeless as rumored by a panicky public. When the communists overran Quang Tri, I thought fighting would become even more fierce than during Tet 1968. Then all of a sudden, our defenses crumbled. Do you know why? It wasn't because of heavy communist pressure. This part of the country had seen fiercer fighting before. As we were getting ready for the big assault, my commander was flown out. We were a headless snake. I soon learned that the same type of 'evacuation' had taken place everywhere. Then the whole defense crumbled before the communists intensified their offensive. We all believed the Americans had made a deal with the communists behind our backs and thus had abandoned our country. Do you believe that hypothesis? You know that guy with protruding eyes who sat in front of you at the discussion? He's Son Ngoc Duc, nephew of Son Ngoc Thanh, a leader of the Khmer Krom movement.[4] Duc is certain the Americans changed their strategy and actually paved the way for the takeover of South Vietnam by the communists. The proof is the evacuation of our commanders from tactical outposts, he says. The more he has reasoned this way, the more confused I have become, even though some of his explanation is nonsense. Do you think what he says is true?"

"Well, I've had enough discussion," I said, trying to put an end to his questioning. "We will get no sleep if we go on like this. In my opinion, what Duc says sounds like something out of a Chinese novel like the *Three Kingdoms*. I am certain the Americans didn't want us to lose the war. The fact is there are many political parties in the United States, and in their elections candidates vie with one another and court voters by making promises they later have to keep. They abandoned us because their leaders lacked the will to fight for noble ideals, not because of some strategy. Let me give you an example of their vacillation. One day their advisers exhort us to fight the communists to our last drop of blood. The next day they pull out, criticizing our leaders for being corrupt and depraved. They forget that corruption was encouraged by their easy dollars. Having made us dependent on their weapons, they cut off military aid at a critical point in the war while the communists were still getting generous aid from both China and the Soviet Union. Our defeat should not have come as a surprise to anyone. I used to discuss this with friends in previous camps. When we came to this point, inevitably they came to the conclusion that I found so painfully true: 'We need no enemies as long as we have Americans as allies.' On the whole, the Americans caused us the greater damage. Moscow and Hanoi were not strong enough to lick us; Washington brought about our shameful downfall. Now, let's stop. The more we continue, the more outraged I feel!"

"Why are you afraid of facing the truth?" my neighbor said. "Our bodies are imprisoned, but our minds are free! When I stay up thinking alone, I feel free. Why not see this as the only pleasure in this wretched place? I prefer spending the whole night in thought so that I get up tired and unable to do much work for the communists, not sleep like a log only to end up working like hell for them. However, as you don't want a long conversation, I will stop now. Good night."

---

[4]Khmer Krom (lit., lowland Khmer), term designating ethnic Khmer whose ancestors came from Mekong Delta in what was then Cambodia, many of whom remained after the area was absorbed by the Vietnamese in about the mid-eighteenth century. During the Vietnam War, some members of this traditional cultural group were formed into anticommunist guerrilla units, operating in Cambodia on their own and in the Mekong Delta of Vietnam as paramilitary units sponsored by the South Vietnamese government.

I was annoyed by his mocking, contemptuous tone. I lay still, my eyes open, thinking hard. Why did the Americans give up while they still had means to help us defend ourselves? I posed the question and tried to answer it. Hundreds of reasons to justify my condemnation of the Americans flooded my mind.

I woke up with a terrible headache, surprised to find other participants of the night's mind-boggling discussion relaxed and cheerful. Later I realized that they had got used to both the stringent life of prison and to the discussions held almost nightly in the room. They started a day in this repressive place composed, their minds free. This truly earned my respect—this strength of will under the most difficult conditions.

When I praised my neighbor for this, he replied, "The more they restrict us physically, the more fiercely we have to fight mentally! Even if we die in this hole, it will be knowing we found out why we lost the war, why we ended up here. We should be proud of discovering the true causes of our defeat. It would be a shame to die still ignorant."

His stubborn optimism caught me by surprise. After all, life here is not so terrible, I thought.

I was fortunate to be transferred to Group 22 where there was this atmosphere of openness. The group leader was not an informer, and he had even managed to win favor from some of the police and *trat tu vien*. The informer, whom we all knew, was quite easygoing as if reluctant to play his role, indispensable as it was in a prison full of political prisoners. There were no common criminals in our group. It was trusted by the authorites and was assigned the delicate task of harvesting and drying the green bean crop.

To prevent theft, our escorts, study monitors, and police made us strip to the waist after shelling the beans or drying them on large, flat bamboo mats. I felt relieved because the work was light.

That night, as I lay awake, the aroma of beans being cooked wafted to us although the doors and windows were shut. My neighbor disclosed that some beans had found their way back into the room despite all the police efforts. I wondered how this was possible. It did not take long to cook the beans since they were fresh and soft. They were cooked in condensed milk tins placed on a makeshift stove made from larger tins. One night shortly afterward as we prepared for bed, the door suddenly burst open and in came prison supervisors, some police, and a bunch of *trat tu vien* including the monsters Ba and Thach. A policeman barked, "Everybody sit still. Don't move!"

We were all caught off guard. Ba and Thach strode to the corner near the toilet where two inmates were caught cooking beans. We were ordered into the yard, where we formed into lines and squatted on the damp earth facing the menacing guns of the guards. The *trat tu vien* began searching our room. Group leader Ky and some others were called in a little while later. From outside we heard grunting and swearing. Then the *trat tu vien* emerged carrying bags of confiscated items. At long last we were locked in again, and everyone rushed about trying to assess his losses. It turned out that the only things confiscated were the green beans hidden around in sleeping berths.

The next morning we were taken to a separate location instead of being escorted to the worksite. Female prisoners were assembling nearby. Some knowledgeable inmates said we would be subjected to "disciplinary measures."

When the formation was assembled, a policeman stepped forward and read an "Order for Disciplinary Actions." Everyone got quiet to catch the names of the offenders and their "crimes." The main "culprit" turned out to be Dao Trong Ky, the Group 22 leader, who was charged with the theft of six kilograms of beans. The rest of his group were revealed to have stolen some eleven kilograms of beans. The policeman then announced Ky's sentence—two months in a "disciplinary cell." As he finished, two *trat tu vien* rushed forward and took Ky to the infamous cell not far away. He was not seen for the next two months.

I kept wondering how Ky and the others had managed to steal that many beans under such close police surveillance. Each of us wore only shorts while at work to prevent us from removing the pods. I could not hold back my laughter when eventually I learned their technique. Ky and the others wore old army boots to the worksite, then took them off after a few hours as though their feet were uncomfortable. When an opportunity came, they furtively filled the boots ankle-deep with the beans. At the end of the day, each tied up his boots, slung them over his shoulder, and carried them right past the guards. On average, each had stolen 300 to 500 grams of green beans a day. This had gone on for some time until they grew careless and forgot to watch for the *trat tu vien* who patrolled around the barracks at night.

After our group leader was sentenced to solitary confinement, we were assigned the punishing job of cleaning the newly built toilets used by the police. These were lavatories with underground receptacles connected to waste disposal pipes that went by the picturesque name of *ho xi* (lit., "shit-hole"). The police in charge instructed us, "Two of you are responsible for the cleaning of one toilet. You will have to remove everything that blocks the pipe. When it is cleared, wash out the toilet, then wash the whole place clean. Finally, put on a new layer of paint as important visitors will be here soon to inspect the camp."

We were shocked when we opened the door. Before us was a revolting huge heap of stinking excrement on the floor and on jack-tree leaves strewn all around. There was no sign that toilet paper had been used. The walls were smeared, and fingerprints were clear in the filth on the painted walls. Knowing we would never be able to do this sickening job with our bare hands, I asked the policeman in charge if we could borrow a spade and a wheelbarrow from the storehouse to shovel out the waste. He waved to the two AK-toting guards and ordered, "One of you take them to the storehouse and tell comrade Sau they need tools to clean up the toilets."

We were taken to Sau, an old cadre of captain's rank well known for his bad temper. He spoke with the peculiar accent of a Quang Nam Province native, which was barely understandable, and in a drawling voice like a drunkard's.

He growled, "What can these useless inmates do? They will only make a mess. Let me fetch Vinh, who can show them how to do the job. Why do they need spades to clean up a toilet anyway?" He led us to the inmates' latrine area and called out, "Vinh, come out! I want you to do something for me!" We waited while someone went to fetch him, and soon he came running from the direction of the main entrance.

"Take these chaps to our toilets and show them how to do the cleanup!" ordered the cadre. "Take these wheelbarrows and spades with you, and show them how to clear the choked pipes, and make sure they wash the whole place clean and put on a new layer of paint. When they are finished, lock up the toilets! I won't let anyone go in unless they know how to use them!"

"That's all right!" Vinh said with a smile. "With me as their leader, everything will be fine!"

Vinh was a jovial chap, but no one liked him because of his manner. "Who would have imagined," he said, "that a downtrodden coolie like me would one day lead a bunch of intellectuals to clean up toilets for the commies." He kept laughing as if enjoying our suffering. We walked on in sullen silence. Vinh was alongside me and my friend when we finally got to the site. Looking at the revolting mess, he spat in disgust and mocked, "Aren't you afraid of excrement?"

"Who isn't?" I shook my head. "Especially when it has been here for some time. We can only hope for some advice from you, the expert!"

The guards just looked on in disgust from a distance. "That's all right!" said Vinh, seeing our friendliness. "As you seem to be reasonable, I am willing to help you, but I'll let you have a go at removing the crap to learn what life is all about. All you have to do is fetch some water, plenty of it!"

Vinh then made the teams scoop up the excrement and remove the leaves that blocked the pipes with their bare hands, while my teammate and I went to get water from the pump near the police kitchen. Vinh then plunged his hands into the choked drainpipe full of foul-smelling excrement and pulled out the jack-tree leaves, swearing all the time.

"F . . . the Viet Cong! Do you know they don't know how to use this kind of toilet. They wipe their asses with leaves in the jungles and can't seem to drop the habit! That's why the toilets got choked after only a few weeks of use. Some of them go to the forest near the stream to relieve themselves!"

We could not help laughing while pouring water through the pipes. I whispered to my teammate, "This guy is so kind. We should compensate him with something, shouldn't we?"

The man nodded his head and pointed to his pocket. We had finished early thanks to Vinh. My teammate handed him a cigarette, which had been carefully wrapped in plastic. Vinh smilingly accepted it and tucked it behind his ear. He pointed at me, "Is this guy a newcomer? I've never seen him before."

"My name is Vu. I've been here for only a fortnight."

"It's a shame you were transferred to Group 22 just as the good group leader went to the disciplinary cell. Your new leader is Driver Dien. I heard about his appointment this morning from Sau, who ordered Dien to be tough toward you 'self-proclaimed intellectuals.' "

We were all well behaved that evening, having heard about our new leader. Everyone quietly settled in his place as soon as we were locked in. Dien wandered about trying to strike up a conversation but he received only curt answers from reluctant mates, who volunteered nothing.

Members of Group 22 were again searched on Sunday, and I was then transferred to Group 7. Fortunately, I was given permission to write to my wife and asked her to pay me a visit.

My new group was quite heterogeneous. Few were political prisoners, and the majority had been arrested recently. My "neighbor" was a young man of about twenty. He introduced himself as Sang and said that he had been charged with an "offense against public morals," although he did not explain what that meant exactly. My other "neighbor" was Pham Nam Long, brother of lawyer Pham Nam Sach, a well-known member of the opposition to President Thieu. (Sach had been in Chi Hoa prison until the final days of Thieu's government and had had the good fortune to escape abroad just before the fall of South Vietnam).

It was normal to hear swearing by younger members of the group all day long. And there were fights. I was later told that there were several moles in the group. The *trat tu vien* occasionally carried out searches and never failed to come up with something—banned literature, English textbooks, or even firewood, which inmates were prohibited from having.

One night, a few days after I was moved, most of us were asleep, some loudly snoring, when suddenly the lights went out. The silence of the night was pierced by shrill cries for help.

"Cadres, please help me. They are killing me! Oh, my God! Oh . . . Oh . . . they are hitting me! *Trat tu vien*, cadres, help!"

This went on for about ten minutes. Then all was quiet. I lay still, not knowing what had happened. About twenty minutes later, a crowd of *trat tu vien* and police arrived. The yard outside lit up brightly. Suddenly the door was flung open and flashlight beams were pointed at us. Someone asked, "Where's the group leader? Why are the lights out? Who called for help?"

"They hit me," someone groaned. "They hit me, all of them together, cadre!"

"What's all this? What? . . . Who threw the waste bucket here?"

I realized then that the new group leader and some informers had been beaten up and their places fouled by excrement.

We were ordered into the yard. The stench was unbearable inside the room. I was lucky to be far from the foul stuff. Under the bright yard lights, the new group leader's face appeared bruised and his clothes soaked and filthy. He stood to one side. A *trat tu vien* sniffed our hands, trying to identify the culprits, but no one was found. Another hour was spent waiting for the room to be cleaned up. Only then was the poor group leader allowed to wash himself. I stayed awake most of the night.

We were all searched the next morning, and the young inmates suspected of the night's incident were transferred to other groups. Even my neighbor Sang was among them, although I was certain he was innocent since he had been near me while the beating took place.

When I asked about Sang's crime of "offense against public morals," Long laughed and said, "Sang was simply a naughty schoolboy. His family turned him over to the police after he arranged for his friends to have a look at his sister taking a shower. He was accused of having 'sabotaged' traditional familial morality. However, some idiot took the word 'sabotage' literally and sent him to this prison with real saboteurs! He's been here for two years. His family is trying to appeal for his release, but nothing has happened so far."

There were many such stories. One fellow, chatting with his pedicab driver, said too much and ended up being turned over to the police by the driver. He was charged with "vilifying the Revolution." Vinh, leader of the cleaning detail, had been arrested for some vague reason. He told me that previously he had been an undertaker's helper. When the *bodoi* overran the South, he volunteered to help track down employees of the former government. Initially he was rewarded by the police, but later he was arrested for "having made enemies due to handling of money," as he put it. Even now, he said, he did not know what the exact charge was.

After a month with Group 7, I was told that my wife had arrived. It was Sunday morning, and there were no searches or transfers of inmates. Having put on my best clothes, I sat in the yard waiting and soon realized that a sad incident was playing itself out in front of my eyes, the cruel work of the police and that monster *trat tu vien* named Thach. As I squatted on the ground watching, Thach meticulously searched an inmate who was waiting to see his wife; he carefully fingered the man's clothes, particularly the hems for hidden objects. Finally, holding an old jute sack to the sun, he slowly plucked out a tiny piece of paper hidden in a fold. He calmly declared, "Cadre, this inmate has a letter hidden in the jute sack."

His face expressionless, the policeman in charge said, "Confiscate the letter. Note his name. Tell Ba to fetch the keys to the disciplinary cell and then take this man there."

He then turned to the poor inmate. "Your visit is suspended because you have committed a breach of camp discipline! You've only yourself to blame! Disciplinary action will be taken against you!"

The poor man's face turned white. His body shook as if he was about to collapse. As I sat some distance away, I could not catch his pleading. The policeman just shook his head. Two *trat tu vien*, Thach and Ba, regarded by many as evil genii, came for him. One held the door of the cell while the other pushed the victim in.

We onlookers were trembling as if we had been victims of the same treatment. It seemed an eternity before my name was called. I was searched by Thach, the same meticulous procedure repeated. At last I was cleared. My wife was holding my daughter and standing with the other visitors near the entrance to the visitors' room. She waved to me. I was led to a long table flanked by two long benches shared by two other inmates. We were told to sit all on one side. A cadre then called out, "Visitors, come in."

My wife, my daughter, and the others entered and were told to sit on the opposite bench facing us. The cadre stood at one end of the long table. My family and I were lucky to be at the other end. I spoke aloud, asking my wife about her health, and that of our daughter, to show the guard that we were not engaged in any tricks. An old man and his inmate son who were seated near the policeman, refused to say anything in his presence. The policeman exploded, "Say something! Or is it because I am here? Go on, you two. You've got only fifteen minutes."

At that moment, my daughter crawled across the table and reached for my hand. The policeman rushed at us shouting, "Who gave you permission to hold your daughter? No one can do that sort of thing without permission! Understand? Do you think you're free to do whatever you like here?"

My wife hurriedly pulled the little girl back and held her in her lap. She was near tears. A deep anger seethed inside me. My poor little girl's frightened glance darted at the menacing policeman, and then she tried to hide herself in her mother's lap. Everyone in the room stared at us in silence. Embarrassed, the policeman pretended to consult his watch, finally saying, "Ten more minutes to go. If you have anything to say, say it now."

My wife said aloud so that everyone could hear her, "We are all fit and well at home. Your 'uncle' sends his regards and asks that you visit him when you are released."

"Let's talk about something else!" I said and shook my head. "I am fed up with him. How is my brother's family doing? Do you get any letters from your parents?"

"Why don't you trust Uncle?" said my wife as if annoyed. "He's kind to you! He cares about you. I have given him our house and I'm staying with brother Hai's family. Everything is positive!"

I was stunned. I knew what it meant. How could she be so foolish as to hand over our house to a total stranger in the faint hope he would somehow rescue me from prison?

"How could you be so stupid?" I cried out in exasperation. "How could you be so foolish at your age? This 'illness' is so serious, no one can cure it. You're only wasting money!"

"You're too pessimistic!" retorted my wife. "The illness will be cured. I know another 'good doctor.' They are all good. It's not a question of being cheated. Don't worry, everything will be just fine! All you have to do is take care of yourself. I'll see to it that everything at home is fine."

The guard ordered loudly, "Time's up! Visitors, go next door to get your gifts and bring them back here. Don't forget other visitors are waiting outside. Inmates remain where you are."

My wife left our frightened daughter in the yard while she went to the room next door to collect her bag. She returned and emptied bundles of various sizes on the table. Other visitors did likewise.

"Inmates pick up your gifts and go back to camp. Visitors leave now to make room for those in the queue!" ordered the policeman.

"Take care. Don't waste time worrying," said my wife in tears, "I'll take care of everything at home. All signs are positive."

I put the packages back in the sack and hurriedly made for the exit as the watchful policeman was about to move toward me. As the *trat tu vien* was hurrying others out, I turned at the exit to wave to my loved ones. My wife, my daughter in her arms, was urging the little girl to wave good-bye.

I felt depressed by so brief a reunion. I walked the sandy footpath like a robot, my heart sinking with every step. We were stopped at the camp entrance. A *trat tu vien* ordered, "Get your bundles ready for the search!"

We were led to a large room with six tables. The sole occupant was an old cadre with long hair falling over one eye. He stood watching us without uttering a word.

"Put all your bundles on the tables," ordered the *trat tu vien*.

I laid out a package of dried salted meat, a sack of salt, fried sesame, and sugar, three bags of powdered milk, several bundles of dried bread, about twenty packs of instant noodles, and a package of still-warm rice.

The old cadre now moved forward, pausing at a table, saying, "This and that are not allowed. Nor this."

A *trat tu vien* behind him picked up each "unacceptable item" and dropped it into a sack. The inmates silently collected what was left and stepped back. When he came to my table, the cadre pointed at the packs of instant noodles and dried bread. "What a heap," he exclaimed. "You can't keep all this! Let's inspect the bags of powdered milk."

The big package of dried bread and five packs of noodles disappeared into the *trat tu vien*'s sack. Then he got an aluminum basin and a pair of chopsticks and emptied the powdered milk into the basin, meticulously stirring it with the chopsticks looking for hidden objects. Finding nothing, he moved on to the next table.

At the checkpoint, the sentries took down our names and waved us through. The *trat tu vien* headed back to the visitors' room.

"What did they take from you?" asked the fellow walking beside me. "I've lost a bag of dried ground meat and several packs of noodles!"

When I told him I had lost some dried bread and five packs of instant noodles, he was surprised at my luck in losing so little.

Once back near our barracks, we were surrounded by our eager roommates hanging around the yard. They asked, "How many packs of noodles did you lose?"

"How do you know it was noodles?" I said in surprise.

"The cadre in charge of the search today was Hai 'Noodle.' You automatically lose noodles to him!"

My impulse was to ask them why this daylight robbery was tolerated. However, I thought better of it in case a mole was around. I recalled searches by *bodoi* at previous camps in which gifts were openly examined in front of both visitors and inmates and the questionable items returned to the visitors instead of being stolen behind their backs. I later learned that the present practice was philosophically accepted as typical of police behavior.

I spent the rest of the day fretting over what I had learned from my wife. How could it be that my wife had turned over our house to a cadre from the North in the faint hope that one day he would lobby for my release?

As far as I was concerned, my luck had gone down ever since my wife first announced she was trying to buy back my freedom. My first bit of bad luck was when I was transferred to the Phuoc Long camps from Xuan Loc. Then came accidents and denials of leave in the camps. Now, I had ended up in prison. There had been no sign of success for my wife's efforts. I had lost my house to some vague promise from a communist cadre. I wished I had known and been able to write to my wife to dissuade her from the foolish scheme. I kept asking myself how they could have made such a stupid move!

After the visit my diet improved. Our basic ration was the grain called *bobo*, which I found nearly indigestible although it was better than the mildewed manioc that I ate at Bu Loi. *Bobo* was a cereal that I had never seen prior to the communist takeover. Some said that it was an imported grain used to feed horses. *Bobo* grains were as large as a green bean and when cooked had an aroma similar to that of corn. It was even tasty. However, once consumed, it could not be digested. One felt an urge to move his bowels half an hour after eating the stuff. If this was delayed, terrible stomachaches developed until the damned grain eventually found its way out. Even out, the thick outer skin of the grain remained. "Only horses can eat them," explained an inmate doctor. At first, I was one of the most frequent visitors to the toilets before we were locked in at night. Then the only available means of waste disposal was a bucket in the room, which was often filled to the brim the next morning. However, no one could afford not to eat *bobo* as it was our only staple.

I gradually learned from experienced friends how to eat the grain. It first had to be ground, then mixed with water; then the skins would surface and could be removed. At this point the mixture could be boiled into a kind of porridge. This method was time-consuming, but the alternative was to eat the *bobo* little by little over a period of time, meaning it always had to be carried around, which was a nuisance. One also had to slowly chew the kernal into a fine paste, a method suitable only for those with enormous patience. On the whole, most of us practiced this art of survival poorly, and the toilets were always jammed.

I remained an early riser, although I had mastered the art of eating *bobo* and had supplemented it with the food brought by my wife. Toilets were the most deserted and cleanest early in the morning and less visited by swarms of flies. Late risers were assaulted by revolting insects that flew into their faces, finding their way into noses or mouths. They were not only irritating but dangerous as disease carriers.

My typical day in this prison consisted of meticulous planning to keep disease at bay. Once up, my first chore was to race to the toilet, then rush to the best place to brush my teeth and wash my face. Then came the competition for cereal and boiled water for breakfast and the task of preparing something edible to carry with me during the day. While at work in the forest, I stayed alert to gather leaves and roots. On the way home, I would take a quick bath in the stream, wash my clothes, and fetch some clean water for the next morning. I was watchful all the time for pieces of paper or bits of wood to be used as fuel. At night I spent hours catching bedbugs. Carefully, I tucked in my mosquito net so the bugs would have a hard time getting to their "food supply." Even so, I always awoke with several dozen bite marks. The careless did not fare well, their neglected bites developing into sores. Most inmates suffered from scabies, all sorts of stomach trouble, and hemorrhoids—all due to poor diet, lack of medicine, their own carelessness, or simply loss of the will to live.

Many people became tight-lipped after some time in this prison. I knew an old man who refused to say anything apart from yes and no. His name was Mo, a professor of dentistry, who had been in various detention centers. Since he never conversed with anyone and was even stingy with his yes's and no's, everyone assumed he was crazy. For my part, I thought he was quite normal. Sensing he was interested in me as a new face, I once tried to strike up a conversation, only to receive shakes of his head for answers. But he smiled all the while and his eyes seemed to say a lot.

Having told him my life story, to which he had listened attentively, I teased, "Now that I have told you my story, it's your turn to tell me yours. It's unfair if you don't and arrogant to remain silent."

His face brightened but he did not speak.

"You should say something, or I will take you to court, even before Uncle Ton."[5] I pressed on. "How clever, to listen to my story pretending to be dumb. It's unjust!"

His face redened, and he bit his lip. His shoulders shook as if he were having difficulty holding back laughter. But he refused to utter a word.

After that, every time he saw me, his face brightened and his eyes seemed to speak. We became friends although he never said a word to me.

The longer I stayed in Ham Tan prison, the more hopeless seemed my chances of being released. How foolish my initial optimism had been. I did, however, have many opportunities of meeting knowledgeable people in this heterogeneous place, men whose ideas helped clarify the many questions that troubled me. And, I heard many interesting tales, one of which concerned a rumor about the ghost of an inmate. The morning I was transferred to the group with the bad reputation, the group leader showed me my place, and said, "Take your luggage to the spot next to Mr. Ty. It's quiet in that corner!"

Ty had been seriously ill for some time. I could not see him clearly because he was laid up all day inside his mosquito net. I was told he had been to the infirmary many times, but his intestinal ailment did not improve. Though I was his neighbor, he did not talk to me or ask anything of me. All I heard were deep sighs. When I came back after lunch and during the evening, I would try to catch a look at him, but he did not emerge from his net. This went on for several days. One night I was awakened by him kicking me. I sat up. He was motionless, but his leg was still pressed into my side. I thought he had rolled over to relieve bedsores. After a while I gently pushed his leg aside. It was as stiff as a log. Seeing that he refused to move, I said, "Mr. Ty, move your leg. Please. I can't sleep like this."

There was no reply. I shook his leg. It was stiff. Suddenly I realized he was dead.

I called out in fright, "This man may be dead. His limbs are stiff!"

Others sleeping nearby immediately woke up. "Is he dead? . . . Call a doctor!" . . . "Call the group leader."

A crowd gathered around me. "Let's call the medic," suggested the group leader.

"No. At this time of the night, they will only dump him outside the meeting

---

[5]Ton Duc Thang, president of Vietnam.

hall and won't bury him until tomorrow. His body would be eaten by the rats. No, we can't let that happen."

"We can't sleep beside a corpse either. It's too horrible!"

"What's so horrible?" retorted someone. "Let's ask the newcomer if he can stand sleeping beside a corpse. In my opinion, we should leave it here until tomorrow."

"Leave it," I said. "I don't mind sleeping beside a corpse."

One man went over and pushed the body into a normal sleeping position. He muttered, "Mr. Ty, you have finally escaped. If you care about us, please leave us alone. We'll build you a nice coffin tomorrow."

He rolled up the mosquito net and wrapped Ty's body in a blanket. The crowd lingered for a while, then dispersed. I could not sleep lying next to the corpse. My body shivered with fear. At the same time, I felt such pity for him, having met an unjust death, never again to see his loved ones.

I remained in a semiconscious state until the sound of cocks crowing came from the distance. I climbed down and headed for the toilet. Some inmates were up, sitting inside their nets saying their prayers in a low voice. Having tidied up my place, I sat pressing my back against a bundle of clothes.

"Now we can inform the authority of the death!" said someone.

Another inmate went to the window and shouted to the occupants of the next house, "Tell the infirmary there is a death in House 10."

The message was relayed house to house. Suddenly there was a shout, "Shut up! Can't you wait for a few minutes? The gates will soon be opened. There's no need to report this way."

"That's Mr. Sau," remarked someone. "Now we can relax."

Everyone else in the room was now up and tidying up his space. Our mood was different because of the death, and we sat waiting for the door to open. An hour passed before the gong signaled the beginning of a new day. A few minutes later, the door opened and in came a policeman and several *trat tu vien.*

"Where's the dead man?" demanded the policeman. "When did he die? Does anyone know what he died of?"

The group leader rushed forward and pointed to the corpse. "Cadre, the dead man is Ty. We found out about his death at dawn although we don't know exactly when he died. Mr. Vu here discovered the death when he tried to push aside the dead man's leg, which had touched him."

Sau arrived. The old cadre calmly stared at the corpse, then ordered, "There's no need to call the medic! *Trat tu vien,* take the corpse to the meeting hall and put it where bodies are kept before burial. Fetch Vinh and tell him to change the dead man's clothes and prepare a coffin."

The two *trat tu vien* rewrapped the corpse with a blanket and carried it away. The job was done briskly and expertly as though they did it often. Another *trat tu vien* was instructed to collect the dead man's belongings and bring them to "the office."

That evening I was summoned to the command center to report on the death. I was taken to an office and shown a document, in which Dr. Hat stated that Ty had died of an intestinal ailment and that there was nothing suspicious about his death. I was then required to date and sign the document and include at the bottom of the statement, "My name is Tran Tri Vu, Ty's neighbor. Mr. Ty died while sleeping."

The death was quickly forgotten. But three days later, on the way home after a hard day's work, I was stopped by Vinh.

"Mr. Vu, I've got to ask you about something!" he said in a demanding tone.

His urgent tone caught me by surprise. We walked in silence to a deserted spot. Vinh then said, "Answer me just one question: What did you tell the cadres about Ty's death?"

I was puzzled by the unexpected question and replied, "He died a few days after I was transferred to this group. I know nothing about him. No one asked me anything about his death! I've never talked to a cadre. Why do you ask?"

"It's nothing." He shook his head, worry showing on his face. "I just wanted to know out of curiosity. Well, er . . . a cadre accused me of theft. He said that he had been told by Ty's ghost that I had stolen twenty dong hidden in Ty's shirt."

I burst out laughing. "I thought it was something important. This is rubbish," I said. "How could you believe such a story? It was only a cadre trying to trick you!"

Vinh hurried off without bothering to reply. I was then surrounded by my roommates asking what we were talking about. I told them the whole story. Everyone laughed.

One told me, "That guy is a troublemaker. Don't associate with him!"

The next evening back from work, some inmates who had been sick and stayed indoors told me that Ty's wife had arrived and was tearfully demanding to see her husband's grave.

"She said she had learned of his death from his ghost," one said in amazement. "Also she said that the ghost had complained of being robbed of twenty dong by Vinh who took the money from his clothing prior to the burial."

The story of the persistent ghost spread until one day a *trat tu vien* acting on orders, searched Vinh's bags during his absence and came up with a twenty-dong banknote.

When I met Vinh again some time later, he said with a smile, "Ty has some ghost! Even dead he can complain to the authorities and his wife."

"What happened with the twenty dong?" I asked.

"I had to admit the theft." Vinh grimaced. "I thought the money was no use to a dead man, so I took it. It's been confiscated."

"Were you punished?"

"There's no point. If they punish me, they must make a report and declare the money. They could not keep it for themselves. That's why they left me alone."

Vinh then told me he had been unable to put the corpse into the coffin because the body was too long.

"I prayed, 'Please don't be so stiff, or I will have to be heavy-handed and break your skeleton, and the corpse immediately relaxed and fell easily into the coffin with a thud," Vinh claimed.

I laughed at this typical undertaker story, but Vinh became serious. "Don't laugh. Everything I said is true. As soon as the theft became known, I prayed before burning joss sticks that Ty would forgive me. He scares the shit out of me. Even an experienced undertaker like me is frightened by him!"

During my early stay in this prison, I did not make any real friends although I met many notable people. Among the inmates were former members of the communist-led National Liberation Front of South Vietnam, some of whom had left the Front a long time ago. Most famous of these was Mai Van So, brother of Mai Van Bo, the Front representative at the Paris Peace Talks. These people deliberately kept their distance from the rest of us.

During one transfer to a new group, I was assigned to a place next to an old Front member named Nam. The former communist, about sixty, was very reserved although he did not show hostility toward me when I took my place next to him. I tried to maintain a silence as I knew he did not like talking. He would mutter a few words when silence was unavoidable, such as when we were cleaning our sleeping places or catching bedbugs together.

A week passed, and I had not asked him a single question. Perhaps this was why he became more friendly. Each evening as the others gathered for talk, I remained sitting in my place thinking. Nam would lie near me, also deep in thought, eyes fixed on the ceiling.

One evening, he suddenly asked, "Why don't you join the others? They are having a good time, you know!"

"They seem to be talking about nothing important. Why don't *you* join them?"

"They don't like me. They make fun of me for having been a member of the Front!"

"How long were you in the Front?" I asked, hoping to prolong the conversation.

"Well, quite long! It began in my underground days against the colonist French in 1945, 1946 . . ."

"That was a long time ago. Why have you ended up here?"

"They thought I had committed an offense. My stay here is only temporary, however. People like me are usually kept elsewhere."

Knowing that I had to seize the opportunity if I was to get to know this man, I confided, "I would like to ask you a question if you don't mind. I must ask someone. My head now is full of disturbing questions. I wonder what will become of me, what should I be doing now. When I find even people like you imprisoned, I am really lost. Let me ask you a frank question: Do you regret having been in the Front?"

"Since you ask, I will give you a frank answer. I have no regret whatsoever."

I was taken aback by this unexpected answer.

"That's a clever answer! I've heard of communists so loyal to the Party that they show no hatred toward former comrades who want to imprison them, even kill them."

"That's rubbish! By saying 'I have no regret,' I meant I had no regret for what I have done. As for being imprisoned, who the hell wouldn't be angry over this sort of treatment? However, if one commits an offense, he should show remorse."

"Are you saying that you have *not* committed an offense? Why did you say you have done something wrong?"

"I didn't say I committed a crime. I said they thought I had committed an offense. The two are completely different."

Realizing that each utterance by this man was carefully weighed, I paused for thought, then went on.

"Well, if you are innocent and here only because they think you are guilty, how can you prove your innocence? And why should an early follower with your seniority be treated like this?"

Old Nam shook his head sadly and with a smile said, "You are so ignorant of the communists. In your years of imprisonment, have they ever given you a chance to prove your innocence? Have they ever tortured you for a confession?"

"No, and I wonder why. They only made us write our biographies, which I suspect they never bothered to read. Does the Party detain people without trial?"

"I hope you're not angry with me for my frankness. Your type is so naïve. You have not learned much from your years in prison. Your weakness is lack of reasoning power, lack of mental training."

"It has been nearly three years and a half since I registered on June 25, 1975. During this time I have not learned much, I admit. I've been hoping against hope for early release. I don't know why it has been delayed for so long, when it's likely to take place, or what I should do for a living once released. What I hear from the outside confuses me and fills me with hopelessness. I am so confused I don't know what to expect. I won't even be angry with you if you call me stupid."

"Sometimes I want to explain things to your friends, but they won't listen. They clearly hate me, swear at me, say to me, as you just did, 'You are a communist yourself, and even though imprisoned by your former comrades you still defend them and try to spread propaganda on their behalf.' "

"I only want to learn from you," I said. "May I ask what is the point of detaining us like this? In my opinion this action only invites hatred from us and alienates the public, at least the public in the South."

"Your reasoning is not objective. It's based on personal feelings. Don't you know that every communist move must be based on well-defined doctrine and must be referred to and compared with similar responses in the Soviet Union? The reeducation camps in this country are based on a similar system that has existed in the Soviet Union, East European countries, and China. Therefore, the reeducation camp was inevitable in Vietnam, especially in the South where building a socialist state is just beginning. Do you know why the first act of the new government was to detain all members of the previous government, no matter how good or how highly specialized they were?"

"I am puzzled by your question. They explained that we had to undergo reeducation to become 'New Socialist Men,' suitable for a better and brand-new society."

Old Nam uttered a sarcastic laugh and retorted, "Have you met a 'New Socialist Man' in the last few years?"

The thought seized me, but it was one that had been lurking in the back of my mind. Since the day Saigon was overrun by hordes of *bodoi*, I had been bombarded with political lessons glorifying the virtues of the "New Socialist Man," his consuming ideals, his work ethic, his integrity, his lack of selfishness, his spirit of sacrifice, his willpower, the purity of his soul, and so on. However, I had never met a *bodoi* or cadre possessing those virtues. What was described was worthy of sainthood, but what they did was evidence of selfishness and insatiable greed. It was they who profited from charging cutthroat fees, who forced us to remove corrugated iron sheets so they could sell them, who made us make suitcases and wooden trunks for their use, who forced us to gather timber, firewood, and bamboo, which they sold for profit. Rank-and-file *bodoi* scrambled to supplement their meager earnings, using their limited opportunities, while higher-ranking cadres openly took much more rake-off.

I offered Nam these observations. I said we inmates had been astonished by the theft of timber by the Voluntary Youth from Thai Binh, then shocked by their acts of murder and looting, that it was they who had robbed a *bodoi* of his bicycle and watch.

"How can the generation that has grown up under socialism in the North behave in this terrible way?" I asked Nam.

"It's rather late for you to be asking this question," he sighed.

"Why are they keeping us in jail so long?" I persisted.

"In the first place, detaining you is a necessity. Positions in the government and other institutions must be made available to the 'revolutionaries' so the process of building a socialist society can be carried on throughout the country, the South included. How could a new communist state be possible with key posts occupied by managers, engineers, doctors, and administrators who know their jobs well, who are more competent, and have better qualifications than the revolutionaries? Lenin preached that a newly formed socialist state could be run by those who had mastered only the three Rs. Employees of the former regime must be removed and detained to make room for the revolutionaries."

As I listened, my puzzlement and confusion gradually diminished. A few well-defined examples plus logical reasoning helped me see the truth, once and for all. Once the old positions were filled by the newcomers, there would be no more obstacles in their way. The newcomers would learn from deposed experts, who eventually would no longer be needed.

"Now that a new government exists and key posts are controlled by the new state, why are we still in detention? And are there really enough trained people to fill our former jobs? It's obvious the country needs more specialists—doctors, engineers, technicians, teachers."

Old Nam waved his hand to dismiss my protest. "You are subjective and quite ignorant of the communists. Who will employ you? Haven't you heard the words 'vigilance of the revolutionaries'? It means that they will never trust their former opponents. Your chidren have already been excluded from a normal existence in society. That's what Marxism-Leninism is all about."

"Good Lord! Does this mean we will all be exterminated?"

"Nonsense. The Revolution will not kill you all. But it will see to it that you and your families will have less responsibility, less influence in society. Your 'dimension' will be severely restricted."

"My God! What will become of my dimension then, narrow as it already is? What you've told me scares me to death. Get to the point. Don't beat about the bush like this. Do they intend to keep us in jail like this until we all die? Don't be offended by my frankness. You communists love to be progressive and scientific, but I think you're old-fashioned and unbearably outmoded! Let me give you some examples. While inspecting the drying of manioc roots, the commander of Bu Loi camp picked up a thin slice of the root that was unusually dry and declared, 'This has only reached 72 percent of the norm.' I nearly exploded. Here in this camp the political commissar once declared, 'The residue from the burning of coal is used in the paving of roads in the North. Once the Japanese offered to buy it to use in the manufacture of 117 different items. Naturally the request was turned down. Our government intends to maintain economic independence at all costs.' Now you talk about the dimension of prisoners and the new regime's restrictions. Obviously, you're still infected by the communist disease—unscientific reasoning!"

Old Nam remained silent, allowing me to vent my indignation. Then he calmly replied, "It's true that I *had* that kind of 'disease,' and to show you the essence of the communists' policies concerning your fate, I deliberately adopted their way of thinking again. That's why you object to my 'unscientific reasoning.' A true communist has a limited vocabulary regardless of whether he is a lowly cadre or Prime Minister Pham Van Dong. The Revolution doesn't want its followers to use too many words since this might extend the scope of their thinking. The communists want to ensure that everyone speaks and behaves exactly as the revolutionaries do. I am used to their way of thinking, and don't mind if you call it a disease."

"Then what do you mean by saying our dimension will be severely restricted? Do you mean we will be detained here forever or that we will be put under house arrest in a New Economic Zone when we are released?"

"Ah, at last you have come to the point. According to communism, each person has a political dimension, a cultural dimension, an economic dimension, and a social dimension. Members of the former regime will be deprived of all but their economic dimension, which will be limited to the duty of producing goods. Those supervising inmates in reeducation camps have been briefed on this policy. So have I, and perhaps I can shed some light on this and warn you to keep your eyes open. Lower-ranking cadres have not received a careful briefing. They tend to emphasize the lenient policies of the State, the Revolution, and the Party in answer to all questions. You eventually will be released so you can participate in production. You will be left alone as long as you accept your restricted role. Of course, they won't say publicly that you are denied political, cultural, and social rights, but they will certainly make sure that you do not engage in those activities. Actual implementation of policies will depend on location and on regional authorities."

The more I listened to him, the more Machiavellian the government's policy sounded. At first, I hoped old Nam was only bragging about his knowledge, but gradually I became convinced that what he said was true.

"When do you think I shall be released?" I pressed on. "What should I do for a living once released? Tell me what you think. It doesn't matter whether you're right or wrong so long as I have some insight into the future."

The gong abruptly sounded, signaling bedtime. Everyone quietly went back to his place. Old Nam shook my hand and said in a low voice, "I have explained everything. The rest is up to you. Le Duan wrote a book called *Under the Glorious Banner of the Party, Move Forward to Achieve More Victories*. It has been published and distributed to all Party members, but lower-ranking members only receive an abridged version. You see, even Party members have limited access to information. Therefore, it's not surprising the government has told you so little about your future. We have talked enough. Let's not talk tomorrow since someone will report us. I only fear for you. My fate has already been sealed."

I persisted. "From what you've told me, should I adopt a wait-and-see attitude? I mean, I shouldn't expect trial or early release . . ."

"Since they have detained so many people, there can be no trials. They need some resolution from the Politburo to decide your future. I was told by a visitor that they have decided to purge Christians from the Party without further inquiry. What can you expect? It's become a general procedure; trials take place only in exceptional cases. Let's get to sleep! The communists have a logic of their own that outsiders like you can't understand."

I lay there, troubling thoughts churning in my head. Why is it that inhuman practices invented in Lenin's time are still present today? Why is an old political theory still revered as if it were an irrefutable physical law that must be imposed on the rest of the human race? It's unbelievable!"

Old Nam would not talk to me for several days. The mutual silence was once again maintained, which was unbearable for me as I knew there was still much to learn from this old revolutionary. I realized that to learn more about communism, I had to make friends with people who had been living long in the communist ranks, a prospect that had been unthinkable not so long ago. No sooner had I arrived at this conclusion than I was transferred to another group.

I was lucky to be reunited with old friends in the new group. However, all I found in them was despair. They spent their free time collecting news, which often turned out to be rumor. Most of these reports originated in casual talk and took on substance as they passed from mouth to mouth. Typical was the report that the Americans were having talks with Hanoi on resettlement of political prisoners in America. Another was that the communists were being criticized by the rest of the world for their treatment of employees of the former regimes. The first rumor was probably based on the fact that some lucky prisoners had managed to get to the United States after bribing their way out of prison. The second rumor was probably a statement on the BBC by some international figure about political prisoners in Vietnam. For three years, not a day passed that I did not hear some hopeful report. It seemed that most inmates could carry on with their wretched lives only by deceiving themselves with false hopes. It was beyond our belief that the communists were to be influenced by world opinion.

The only genuine news we got concerned food shortages and all sorts of outside difficulties. Most inmates who had had visitors every month now had to content themselves with quarterly visits or even fewer. More often, they got letters promising visits when their families had saved enough money. It was obvious that our people outside were having a hard time. The prison authority eventually adoped an every-other-month policy as monthly visits were no longer practical. This resulted in additional privation, as even those fortunate enough to have visitors every two months could not stretch their supplementary food supply over the period. Obtaining additional food on site became everyone's objective.

The most popular way to do this was catching rats, which were numerous in the area. The most common trap consisted of a noose fastened to a flexible branch, one end of which was firmly planted in the ground near a fence, and the other end with the noose held down by a catch. The contraption was set in such a way that the poor animal's head went into the noose, which would spring the catch. The bent rod would then assume its normal straight position, and the more the animal struggled, the tighter the noose became. Every evening a crowd of prisoners gathered near the fence to set traps. Locked in, they gathered by the windows to watch the rewards of their efforts. Soon the night was pierced by joyful cries, "It's caught!" "That's my trap!" "Your trap failed!" This cheap entertainment lasted until the compulsory bedtime. The only sufferers were the poor rodents dying a slow and painful death. Their bodies had long become stiff when the doors were opened the next morning. Each successful trapper would quickly and expertly chop off the rat's head, then skin, disembowel, and clean it. Then he would take it to the worksite to be cooked during the break.

Such breaches of camp discipline were ignored by the authorities as they knew we would not survive without the rats. The police themselves suffered from the nationwide food shortages and they raided nearby cornfields. One day my group was preparing land for sweet potatoes when a policeman ordered me to fetch a large empty pail. I followed him to a cornfield with stalks bearing relatively large ears. The policeman expertly found his way among the stalks; other inmates were already there stealing corn. As we were busily gathering the ears, the policeman suddenly said in a low voice, "Get down. Somebody is passing by."

Women's voices were heard. Once they were out of earshot, the policeman slowly stood up, looked carefully about and said, "Stay where you are. I'll go out first. When you hear my signal, come out—with your corn of course."

Nobody replied. The policeman hurried off. It was not long before we heard, "Come out."

Once we were away, the policeman laughed, "This corn belongs to the province committee. The field was planted by some government employees under a food-growing campaign. Now, the crop is ready for harvest, but no one has turned up to claim it. We have every reason to help ourselves. We can't let the corn get old. Besides, those government workers don't need it. They grew it only because they had to."

I filled three large barrels with the young, juicy cobs and cooked them. One barrel was divided among the four policemen and the rest given to us.

One time I saw a policeman shoot a dog that had strayed into camp. He then made us boil water and shave off the dog's hair, after which he butchered it. The police took the meat with them to a watchtower to be cooked later on.

I was assigned one day to the team charged with tidying up the supply warehouse. It was a newly built brick building with padlocked doors. Inside, we found wheat flour spilled all over the floor, and we used spades to remove the flour mixed with rat droppings. We then unloaded a truckful of sacks of flour that had arrived from Saigon. Each sack was labeled "Blé Tendre" in big letters with "Don de la France" in smaller letters. This "gift from France to the people of Vietnam" was to be used by the police. The flour would be made into dumplings, which were usually steamed. It was apparent that the food shortage had become critical if even the police had to supplement their rice diet with flour. The prisoners' main staple remained *bobo*.

These trips to the warehouse permitted one inmate to collect enough flour to contribute to a Christmas dinner. But this plan was spoiled by an unforgettable argument.

Among the inmates was a priest named Quang (there was also a Catholic nun among the female inmates in the adjacent compound). It was Father Quang who reminded us of the coming of Christmas, and one morning word was passed among Catholics that confession would be heard before Mass. Both, of course, would take place clandestinely. Father Quang stood by the fence near the toilets as if in line, and the other Catholic inmates stood about nearby. With his "congregation" gathered, Father Quang said in a low voice, "Now everyone, make the sign of the cross and pray for atonement for your sins. Then I will perform the rite of absolution."

Everyone hurriedly said his prayer. Father Quang repeated his in Latin. Then he declared, "I wish you a happy Christmas blessed by God!"

He then hurried off. Some of the men trailed after him, deeply moved by the ritual, however brief. The inmate who had been hoarding wheat flour had made a Christmas cake; in place of yeast he had used bicarbonate of soda, donated by those who regularly used it for stomachache. During the break, we set fire to a pile of wood, let it die down to a heap of embers, and buried the dough, contained in two clamped aluminum pots, in the red-hot embers. We took care to stir the embers every now and then while ensuring that the thin aluminum did not burn through. The cake was removed from this makeshift oven after half an hour, and it was a success. The brownish-yellow cake gave off a nice aroma that made our mouths water. The baker insisted that we wait until Christmas Eve to eat it since Christmas was after all the occasion for which the cake had been baked.

His piousness invited chuckles, and some swearing from his hungry friends. A guard was attracted to the noisy scene.

"How did you manage to make such a well-risen cake!" he asked admiringly.

On Christmas Eve, when everyone was inside his mosquito net, the owner of the cake summoned his fellow Catholics and close friends, and we gathered in his bunk under his mosquito net. We said our prayers in low voices, and then the cake was divided into tiny pieces and distributed. It was aromatic and tasty, although not sweet, of course, due to the scarcity of sugar. As we were eating, a voice from nearby mocked, "Are you so content in this place that you celebrate Christmas? Is Christ's birth such a happy event?"

The joyous mood ended abruptly. We were stunned by the hostility. An elderly participant among us said, "We are sorry to disturb you. Please excuse us, but we must celebrate the incarnation of God, who descended from heaven to redeem us from our sins!"

"Why are you so happy?" retorted the voice. "How can you be cheerful when you know that this is the birthday of a baby who is to be crucified later on!"

The remark was so venomous that we almost choked on the cake in our mouths. We looked at each other in bewilderment, wondering who was speaking. The same elderly Catholic meekly said, "We are joyful for the descent of God to earth to teach the human race to love each other. If you can't get to sleep, please join us and have some cake."

There was no reply. We returned to our celebrating, but in silence. The mocking voice resumed. "Although God has been telling us to love each other for 2,000 years, nobody's bothered to listen to Him! If we did, there wouldn't be revolutions based on the use of force. You are celebrating our suffering, which is outrageous. The sad fact is that Jesus died in vain. So why are you celebrating?"

We were irritated, but also disturbed by his logic. There were mischievous chuckles as if the rest of our roommates were enjoying our embarrassing inability to answer him. Our elderly friend was about to reply, but we unanimously cut him short. "Let him talk. We will only make a row out of a trifle if we keep answering."

We finished our cake and returned to our places in silence. I lay awake deep in thought. As he could not sleep either, my neighbor broke the silence.

"That fellow who has just caused you trouble is Hao. He's quite sarcastic and always has a sullen look on his face as if about to start an argument. You can't win with him; he seems to have a bagful of spiteful arguments, and he has a real grudge against society. I was amused by his remarks on your celebration, but I also found his reasoning logical. God has failed to teach us to love each other. His revolution, based on human kindness, never materialized. We are now victims of a revolution based on the use of force. After all, we've only got ourselves to blame. When some human beings want to build a paradise on earth by using force, other human beings are bound to suffer as a result."

Every Christmas since, I have remembered that occasion in prison. It fills me with sadness.

Chapter 8

Camp Six: Ham Tan (cont.)

The year 1978 ended in an atmosphere of hardship, despair, and hopelessness. Our situation became tense suddenly with the appearance of a leaflet denouncing communist rule. Word went around that the leaflet was on coarse paper, the kind used for cement sacks; it bore the words: "Down with the inhuman communist regime that oppresses the common people!" At first, we thought the leaflet would only be a nuisance for the authorities, as it only appeared in the toilet and was intended to provoke the police into reprimanding the *trat tu vien* and informers for their lack of vigilance.

Therefore, we were surprised by the explosive reaction of the police. They immediately went into action to try to catch the culprit and prevent more leaflets from appearing. Group leaders were to inform the authorities who was likely to have access to that kind of paper; *trat tu vien* searched for paper of all kinds including notepaper. It turned out that almost everyone kept the coarse paper from cement bags that were always available at the construction site. These strong bags were popular because the paper could be used as a sleeping mat, to wrap food, or as toilet paper. Now, of course, it was taboo. As if mocking the police for their failure, a second leaflet appeared, also in the toilet. Unable to find the culprit, the authorities decided to punish all of us by denying small "luxuries" such as the freedom to cook our own food on Sundays, by closing all ventilation openings during lunch break, and by curtailing the evening outdoor relaxation period. A *trat tu vien* was now permanently posted in the toilet area. My already restrictive life as a prisoner became more unbearable as the clamp tightened. However, more damnable leaflets appeared, now at the worksite and then on the fence.

The angry police told the study monitors to warn us that "ultrareactionaries" among us would be ferreted out and transferred to "hard-labor camps." What we thought of as psychological moves eventually turned out to be real!

As Tet approached, the more risky became the distribution of antiregime leaflets. We feared that our holiday observance might be suspended by a vengeful prison authority. Then, one week before the New Year, we were briefed on the situation in Cambodia.

One morning, we were instructed to get ready for a political lesson rather than going to work as usual. Political lessons in this prison usually meant gathering in the central courtyard under a burning sun to listen to a cadre read a boring text and then returning to our quarters for a compulsory discussion. Everyone was gloomy after a political lesson had been announced.

Once assembled around a platform with a loudspeaker, a cadre approached. He was none other than the camp's political commissar, Comrade Vong, alias Mai Lien. Vong smiled, cleared his throat, and said, "I am sure you have all heard the good news about our beloved country. I know that you are all quick at gathering news."

He caught us by surprise. To the puzzled inmates Vong explained, "The reactionary regime of Pol Pot in Kampuchea has been hostile to us for some time. It has raided our territory on the western border . . ."

So, the lesson was about the war between Hanoi and communist Kampuchea! The authorities must have realized we would be puzzled by a war with our former friends, so they arranged this briefing, I thought.

Vong proceeded furiously to denounce the Pol Pot regime as bloodthirsty, one that had detained millions of people in hard-labor camps.

At this point loud applause erupted in the ranks of inmates, which took Vong by surprise. Every time the political commissar shouted earnestly into the loudspeaker to denounce the Pol Pot gang, he was greeted by boisterous applause and laughter. When Vong shouted, "Down with the reactionary Pol Pot gang that has been torturing the Kampuchean people" and "The blood-thirsty Pol Pot gang is a lackey of the expansionist imperialists!" he got loud and prolonged applause. When he bellowed, "Down with Pol Pot and his cronies who have been holding millions of people in hard-labor concentration camps!" the applause erupted into a roar, interspersed with shouts of "That's correct! Quite right!" The more earnestly Vong condemned, the noisier was the reaction. I had never witnessed such black humor. Who could have imagined that a dedicated communist cadre would one day proclaim his Party's policies to the cheers of inmates in a concentration camp. All those crimes denounced by the political commissar were identical to those committed by the Hanoi regime against Vietnamese political prisoners like us.

At last, Vong smugly concluded, "Therefore, the Party, the State, and our people, being obliged to fulfill our 'international duty' to the Kampuchean people, have sent our soldiers to Kampuchea to liberate its people from the bloodthirsty regime of Pol Pot. At this moment, our invincible army, marching beside the brotherly Kampuchean people, is annihilating the last remnants of the murderous Pol Pot army. We have completed the Great Revolution initiated by Chairman Ho!"

Now, the audience went silent. Hanoi's powerful army had marched into Kampuchea!

Vong then declared, "This New Year thus will be another victorious New Year, a good start for our people. To celebrate victory, this camp will certainly enjoy a well-prepared New Year."

Though promised a celebration, the inmates were not as happy as expected. There were whispers, "So Kampuchea has been swallowed!"

During the afternoon, Vong and his study monitors took turns supervising the compulsory discussions on that day's briefing. Vong justified the invasion of Kampuchea: "We had to move into Kampuchea or the Chinese would have done so. How could a thinly populated 'granary' like Kampuchea defend itself against China? Once the Chinese took over, it would be impossible to kick them out. Among Uncle Ho's will is a pledge to protect Kampuchea, you know! The Party is planning to bring in manpower to help the Kampucheans exploit their rich soil to the fullest. Our international duty is a burden. We also have to take care of Laos."

At the end of the day, each group had to draw up a report on the discussion and submit it to the study monitor in charge. Once the discussion ended, my group leader set about to note questions from individual teams. He stopped at my team and asked, "Does this team have any queries?"

One fellow raised his hand. "I have several questions that can only be answered by a high-ranking cadre. Prepare to note them down. They are . . ."

The group leader stared and sighed. "Come off it, Hao," he said. "Have mercy on me. Don't mess up this discussion. Please don't make my life miserable."

It was the same fellow who had mocked us at Christmas, I thought.

Hao said, "I have always behaved myself during discussions, haven't I? Am I a troublemaker? If you won't take down my questions, I am afraid I'll have to see the study monitor and pose the questions to him."

"All right! What are your bloody questions?"

"No! You take them down!"

"Tell me first!"

Hao's teammates urged, "Tell him first. He can take it down later."

Hao spoke, emphasizing each word. "I have two questions. The first is, What political doctrine created Pol Pot and his cronies? The second is, Was it the CIA that taught the Pol Pot gang to be so bloodthirsty?"

We burst into laughter and applauded. The frightened group leader hurriedly put an end to our chorus. "Stop this bloody noise. I'll be crucified if it attracts the *trat tu vien.* Come off it, Hao! If you have a grudge against me, hit me, but don't ask that sort of question. I wouldn't dare write it down in the report even if my grandfather rose from the dead and told me to do it. Don't you want to be reunited with your family?"

"I don't have a family any more. My wife is remarried to a cadre, her boss. I don't even know to whom she has given my children. I've no need to get out."

"Well, I won't trouble you any more. You scare me every time you speak."

After that, I paid special attention to this sorrowful character.

When Tet came, some calves and pigs were slaughtered, and we were promised rice. However, I was unlucky and came down with a fever. The standard treatment was quinine, which often did not work. The right treatment could be arranged if one had connections. I was introduced to a *bodoi* medic named Hung, who was addressed as "Doctor." Almost any kind of medicine was available if one made a deal with him. I asked a friend to act as go-between and bring gifts to Hung. Not long after, this diminutive though resourceful medic came and gave me an injection in the arm. He then said, "Don't eat rice today. I guarantee you will be better tomorrow when I give you another injection."

Thus I missed the Tet rice. At noon, we got glutinous rice cooked with green beans as a New Year's Day treat. It turned out to be inedible because it contained grains of sand. We later found out that the rice had been husked in a concrete mortar, which flaked off cement chips. Using a concrete mortar instead of a granite one as usual was the idea of some government technician!

Rumor had it that the female prisoners in the adjacent compound were to be transferred because their presence caused inconvenience for everyone. A few prisoners had managed to get to know some of the women and disclosed to me that the highest ranking prisoner was the former commandant of the White Swallows unit, which had been run by the South Vietnamese intelligence agency. Female prisoners went out to work in two groups. Their main job was cultivating green beans and sweet potatoes. When they met us on their way back from harvesting sweet potatoes, they would drop some for us to pick up. Some had made friends with the men and even managed to send them potatoes or letters. It was known that romance had blossomed even in these circumstances. There was a young fellow in my group called Trac who had joined the South Vietnamese police to avoid the army. He was arrested by the *bodoi* while undergoing an officer's training course. When he learned of the imminent departure of the women, he was despondent, for his girlfriend was among the inmates. Out of curiosity, I asked him how he had managed to exchange letters and develop a romance in spite of all the restrictions and surveillance.

Trac calmly replied, "Romance will exist wherever there are men and women!"

I thought he was only joking, but his face was serious.

Each evening, Trac played his guitar and sang the same sad song, "Autumn leaves flutter in the wind . . . she's far away from me . . ."

One day while we were weeding along the road connecting the camp to National Highway No. 1, a convoy of five Molotova trucks left camp heading toward us. They carried the female prisoners and their belongings. The women sadly waved at us as they passed. Trac was standing near the road. A voice called out, "Trac, good-bye dearest!" Once the convoy was out of sight, the guarding policeman barked, "Come on, get back to work. What has their departure got to do with you?"

Trac went pale. He was close to tears. He sighed, "That's it. We may never meet again."

Someone said cruelly, "Mothers of four or five children have the courage to leave their famiies, to say nothing of a girlfriend one has yet to hold hands with." It was none other than the sarcastic Hao!

With the women gone, the entire camp became depressed and quiet. My eyes turned to the empty, soulless women's barracks to the right of the entrance as we went home at the end of the day.

After dinner I went out to breathe the cool fresh air. Hao was sitting in a corner facing the sky as if daydreaming. I ventured, "Why are you sitting here alone? You look sad!"

"I am not sad!"

"Though living this kind of life?" I said in surprise.

"What can we do? We're defeated soldiers, you know!"

"Despite your detention, this hard labor?"

"Well, what do you expect from communists?"

"Even as you deny it, the sadness shows on your face." I tried to provoke him into speaking more.

"I am disgusted with my face, the face of a defeated soldier who has never been to the front! The face of one who lost a war without taking part in one."

"I'm sorry. I was only teasing you with silly questions," I said quickly seeing his mounting irritation.

"You may be joking, but I am not. I am serious."

I changed the subject. "Your remarks on Christmas Eve provoked much thought. Are you a Catholic?"

"No, I am not. My parents are Buddhists though not very devout. They visited the pagoda now and then and made offerings to Buddha and to the gods every full moon. I know nothing of Buddhism. I know a little bit of Catholicism as I went to a Catholic school when I was young. I don't believe in Jesus, but I was sympathetic to his cause. I often regret that His revolution—He who had a humble beginning and inspired resistance by the poor, the oppressed—somehow was superseded by other revolutions based on the use of force. The poor and oppressed remain poor and oppressed though they are now labeled 'Masters.' Tell me, can you make anything of 'the Party leads, the State governs and the People own'? How in hell can they be called 'owners' if they have absolutely no say in the running of the factories, mines, farms, offices, and other enterprises? By the way, are you a Catholic?"

My throat became dry. I said, "I am a Catholic, but I don't think I can answer your questions about Jesus and His revolution. You're a deep thinker, you know."

"I am puzzled by almost everything because I haven't much education. If I were a Catholic, I would try to find out why the revolution initiated by Jesus hasn't been carried out but was replaced by a communist revolution. I think revolutions based on human kindness are better than revolutions based on use of force! What do you think?"

"In my opinion this thought of yours is shared not only by the rest of us in this prison but also by all the Vietnamese people though they wouldn't dare speak."

"I think some day someone will have to speak out. When we reach a deadlock, we will rethink the issue, don't you think? Otherwise, all that these so-called revolutions mean is replacing one form of oppression for another. I wonder which regime—czarist or Leninist—has put more people into concentration camps."

The talk was cut short by the gong signaling the end of this relaxation period, when all inmates had to be locked in.

An atmosphere of fear and anger hovered over the camp the following day. A search began for those suspected of distributing anticommunist leaflets. Police came to each barracks and called out certain inmates, who were then escorted away, taking their belongings with them. I was among them, as were many I knew.

We were taken to a clearing outside the camp, searched, and our clothing, mosquito nets, and other belongings examined. The police busily scribbled in their notebooks. Then, we were divided into two groups. I was put in the smaller of the two. So, disaster has struck once again, I thought bitterly. We were escorted back to the camp. My group was led to the center of the compound while the other was taken to the barracks with the corrugated tin roof that had housed the women prisoners. (We later learned that the women had been moved to the central prison for women offenders in Long Thanh.)

Members of my group were escorted to different brracks to fill in vacancies left by departed inmates. A *trat tu vien* told me, "You're lucky. Those in the corrugated tin roof barracks will be isolated—no communication with other inmates, no visits, no outdoor work."

The terror lasted the whole day. Talking among ourselves, we figured out that the isolated building held among others, former body-builder Thach; old Nghiem, formerly Government Representative to Central Vietnam; Professor Phan Thanh Truong of the Phu Tho Institute of Technology; Son Hong Duc; Father Quang; old Huong Hoi (father of General Hieu), and many others whose names I have forgotten.

The next morning we went to work as usual. At the lunch break we learned that more inmates had been sent to the isolated buiding. We lived in fear that the "purge" had not yet ended. The terror was made worse by the study monitors' threat that more punishment was awaiting those already in isolation.

So we were both cheered and worried by the continuing appearance of anticommunist leaflets. The innocence of the isolated men was established, but now the rest of the inmates had to shoulder the blame. I lived in fear day and night, as if all eyes were on me.

We were searched again on Sunday morning, after which I was transferred to a new group of mostly old men. We were given only light work. I later learned my assignment to this lucky group was on account of my poor health record, a record that existed simply because I had been treated by "Dr. Hung" in return for my bribes.

While I was queuing for a place at the cooking fire, a commotion broke out because of the discovery of someone reportedly caught with a leaflet on him. He was one of the cooks who was housed in a building near us. He was being manhandled by police trying to take him to the command center. I was puzzled that it turned out to be a cook, the most trusted and privileged of inmates with access to a plentiful supply of food.

I was told by an old inmate who had been staying at "home" most of the time that the culprit was Pham Viet Thanh, son of South Vietnamese historian Pham Van Son. His father was also a colonel in the Ministry of Defense of the former regime.

The events leading to Thanh's "discovery" were later related to me by one of my old group mates. According to him, Thanh was framed. He was well known for his command of English. The *trat tu vien* used him as a tutor. They even gave him books. Earlier on the fateful day, Thanh was tutoring a *trat tu vien* when a policeman and two *trat tu vien*, Thach and Ba, swooped in to search Thanh. They produced a book that he acknowledged was his property. In examining the book they "came across" a leaflet of the type that was being distributed. After being interrogated all afternoon at the command center, Thanh was sent to the "disciplinary cell." His fellow cooks were certain he was not a reckless person. Further, they insisted, it would have been impossible for Thanh to carry out this sort of activity since he was always in the company of someone or was too busy.

The old man's detailed knowledge of the case amazed me as few were able to obtain that much information. He had been a member of the National Liberation Front, and the story of Thanh came out only after we had gotten to know each other and I had introduced myself as a friend of his fellow Front member, old Nam. The old communist's real name was Huu, but he was generally known as Chin (lit., nine). The South Vietnamese communists tended to address one another by aliases, often using ordinal numbers, which was a common practice among Southerners.

I approached old Chin one day, saying, "I've always wanted to learn more about communism and the communists. I wonder if you could enlighten me with your knowledge?"

The old man laughed and stared at me as if weighing my true intentions. "I'll try if you really want to learn," he finally said. "However, I can't offer you any useful information as my memory is fading—if that is what you want."

So he thought I might be an informer! "I am not after any particular information; I just want to kill time by trying to find out from former communists why they had such faith in their eventual victory that they could endure hardships for so long."

Old Chin hurriedly corrected me. "I've never been a communist myself. I didn't join the Party, but I fought alongside the communists. They didn't want me to join either, as we came from different backgrounds."

"Did you believe your side would eventually win?"

"Once we joined, we were expected to have great faith in the communist cause and eventual victory. However, some of us gave up as time went on and left, like old So over there. He left a long time ago and joined the Nationalists."

"I have heard so much propaganda, it's hard for me to believe what they say. Can you honestly tell me what is it that made you believe in victory?"

Old Chin paused for thought, then replied: "It will take time to explain this; it's a complicated thing. My belief was based on two main grounds. The first was entirely theoretical—Marxist-Leninist determinism. I believe you are now familiar with it. The second was drawn from the practical experience of those involved in people's warfare, that is, revolutionary warfare. Theoretically, as you must have heard, the downfall of capitalism can be brought about by intensifying the 'three powerful currents of revolution.' Although profound, the logic in this theory is somewhat farfetched. Our faith in final victory was not based on a belief that we had more manpower or sophisticated weapons, but on our belief that the enemy, or more precisely the Americans, would provide us with the means to defeat them. On the one hand, we had a strong and solid rear, namely, the North. For various reasons, the Americans did not seem to intend to occupy North Vietnam. On the other hand, as the Ameicans poured enormous amounts of manpower and equipment into Vietnam only to be stalemated, their conduct of the war vacillated and became wasteful, heavily hampered by politics and public opinion. The longer the war dragged on, the more uncomfortable the Americans were. The fundamental mistake made by the Americans in their military thinking was to plan the war in terms of manpower and weaponry, while leaving strategy to be decided by politics. The Revolution then was able to play an active role in persuading the world that the Americans were waging a war of aggression while we were fighting for national liberation, in other words, a just cause."

I interrupted in irritation. "We in the South were also fighting for a just cause—freedom—and the Americans were only supporting us."

Old Mr. Chin cut me short. "Cool down! We won't get anywhere if we don't keep our heads. I didn't say I was right and you were wrong, as the present regime often does. I know that many of you believed in the righteousness of your cause and made the sacrifice of your lives in the fight against the Revolution, which you called a communist one. But your cause could not be sustained. Why? Because of the Americans! The United States is a nation with a tendency to intervene in other countries' affairs as if it were the policeman of the world. Its politicians have no guiding principle. More correctly, the only principle they respect is what is called 'pragmatism.' So when they decided to intervene—to support you, as you put it—they also wanted to make decisions on your behalf. When we proposed private talks between us and the Americans, they gladly agreed without even consulting you. That was why they, by their own mistake, lost their cause—if they had any. It was a fundamental mistake in the eyes of the world. Kissinger was hailed as a genius for having succeeded in bringing about those talks, but that was a myth. If the Revolution was fighting it was only with the hope that negotiations and diplomatic recognition would follow."

Unable to stand Chin's conceit, I retorted, "From what you say, your side has always been right."

"No, I didn't say that. But the fact that you are here proves you made mistakes, doesn't it? I too must have made serious mistakes to end up in this place. Have the patience to hear me out. Let me show you why the Americans were beaten or, to put it another way, why you were beaten. You may not agree with me; what I say is just my own opinion."

"Based on what you say, it seems you never felt any doubt about the outcome, did you?"

"Of course we did, sometimes! There were times when we thought we would soon be brought to our knees. Fortunately, the Americans came to our rescue. As the war dragged on, they showed increasing embarrassment. As for us, a war of attrition was something we could sustain. Sometimes when we were drained of strength and resources, we had to make believe outwardly that we were in top form. The worst was when we were harassed by B-52s. I would say that throughout the war there were three dark moments when our morale was at its lowest ebb: when B-52s began their massive bombings, when the combined American and South Vietnamese forces launched the major offensive that thrust deep into Kampuchea, and when Hanoi was inundated with bombs from B-52s. But for reasons unknown, after these three peak offensives the American war efforts quickly waned. When the flow of troops and materiel to the South was interrupted by heavy bombing, we were ordered to step up our activities to show that we hadn't suffered a bit. And the trick worked; the bombings and similar forms of attack abated; probably they were thought not to have had much effect.

"Had their offensive against Kampuchea lasted a few more months, the whole revolutionary strength in the South would have suffered a serious shortage of supplies. However, the Americans, in their conventional way of thinking, wrongly assumed that their enemy must have been crushed following every major attack carried out by modern weaponry. In reality, the revolutionaries in the South never engaged the totality of their forces in any phase of the war, knowing they just needed the strength to prolong it. Therefore, after each military operation carried out by the Americans, they had to devote themselves to an all-out effort to maintain the tempo of the war. We had to stage attacks even though we could ill-afford to do so.

"In 1968, no sooner had General Westmoreland declared that the Viet Cong were no longer in a position to mount large-scale attacks than the order was given to launch a general offensive on every town and city in the South. Although our losses were massive—nearly all our reserves—we succeeded in staging a diplomatic coup that forced the Americans to come to the Paris peace talks. The result of the talks was clearly in favor of the Revolution, and, what's more, it was obtained at a time when the whole of North Vietnam went through hell because of constant air attacks by B-52s. Had the bombing lasted a few more weeks, we would have had to settle for much less favorable terms, if only to help lessen the military pressure and play for time. I'll tell you this in all sincerity; whenever the Americans are directly involved in a war, they are impatient for a rapid solution. If one can prolong a war, they will be shaken. The American GI has not been trained to sustain a prolonged war. The Americans were ignorant of the nature of various kinds of war; our war was a revolutionary or people's war that could last up to a century. They didn't get anywhere in Vietnam because they didn't have that patience."

Annoyed by old Chin's one-sided rhetoric, I retorted, "You can only say so because your side happens to have won the war. What about the Korean War where you communists were pushed back by the Americans and the war ended in their favor?"

"I am not defending the communists as I am now their victim. In Korea, the Americans had a just cause. Besides, the Chinese 'army of volunteers' could not stay there indefinitely like an occupation army, and the North Koreans had made a mess of their attempt to liberate South Korea in the first place. When the cease-fire was finally declared, the two Koreas remained divided by the same 38th parallel as before. So the war ended in a draw. The Americans were clearly not victors because they failed to take over North Korea."

Seeing my unconvinced look, the old man said, "You asked me why I believed in our final victory, and I told you what I and my comrades have discussed almost daily and the conclusions we have drawn from our studies. You have the right to reject my views. In short, the communists won not because they were stronger but because the Americans made so many fundamental mistakes.

Although beaten, the Americans remain as strong militarily as ever. Their military capability would be best used in conventional types of operation, say, blitzkriegs. They would need enormous amounts of patience and perseverance if they were to win a people's war."

"It seems to me we have done enough talking today. I'll have more questions to ask you next time." I tried to put an end to this troubling talk.

Old Chin smiled. "You will need to come to me more often if you really want to learn about communism and the communists. Remember, nothing is absolute in this world. But the communists' reasoning and behavior seem to suggest the opposite; they are therefore bound to have fundamental weaknesses. I'll tell you about this later on."

The regime of work in this group was fairly light as most members were either old or convalescing from some ailment. The oldest among us was Vu Huy Chan, a man of over eighty who I was told was a contemporary of the famous nationalist, Nguyen Thai Hoc, who was executed by the French colonialists.

Old Chan also was said to be one of the founders of the Nationalist Party. He was looked after by his inmate son, who cooked porridge or vegetable soup for him every day as all his teeth were gone. Too weak to do any kind of work, he was allowed to stay at home, and every now and then he would get up from his bed and shuffle across the room as if exercising. But his mind was sharp. Every time I talked with him, I had to phrase my questions so he could mostly answer with a yes or no, as even talking put a strain on his fragile body and made him cough.

One day, telling him of my talk with old Chin, I asked, "Do you think there's any substance in what he says?"

"I think there is. But there are other considerations. It would be good if you could learn from other people as well."

"May I invite old Chin and old So to have a chat with you some day? It seems to me you don't want to talk to one another because you all are too proud."

Old Chan just shook his head and smiled. However, he finally said, "That's a good idea."

Now there began for me what proved to be an exhilarating experience. These knowledgeable old revolutionaries so far had been living in their respective "ivory towers," oblivious of reality as they pursued their private thoughts about the past. They accepted my request for them to get together. Only Mai Van So remained cautious with his remarks most of the time. Old Chin often joked, "Mr. So still has high hopes of being forgiven by the Revolution."

These former communists had sharp minds whenever it came to discussing politics, and old Chan, the nationalist, did not prove any less keen. When I was first told that he was a contemporary of Nguyen Thai Hoc, I was skeptical that Chan was of that calibre. Why had his name not been mentioned before?

When I put it to him, the old revolutionary replied, "My obscurity is that of nationalists in general. We failed to establish ourselves as a united and disciplined force. What we lacked was solidarity and discipline. That's why we were pushed into obscurity."

Both So and Chin agreed that an effective and viable political organization had to consist of dedicated activists free from family obligations and that its methods had to be efficient, its activities serving the needs of the common people. The nationalist parties lacked all of these. Therefore, many patriots who wanted independence and freedom for their country had no choice but to fight alongside the communists, only to end up staying with them.

On the virtues and weaknesses of the communists, they pointed to the crisis of faith the Vietnamese communists were now facing.

"You don't have to go anywhere to find out about this; just listen to different cadres and you will see how confused they are," said one. "I am sure that you have had their explanations about the continuing detention of employees of the former regime. Each low-ranking cadre comes up with his own reason, trying to defend his government. Some might say that you have not made progress in your reeducation; another that your release would adversely affect the security situation outside as the country was facing possible attacks from China; still others might say that the government had yet to find enough accommodations for you and your families to welcome you back. People at the top, like Pham Van Dong, at one time declared that all political prisoners had been released; at another they admitted that 'about 50 percent' were still detained, mostly 'ultrareactionaries' who showed no repentance for their crimes. Actually, the enormous number still in detention are specialists, technicians, or junior civil servants who were barely involved in politics in the former regime. All these confusing and conflicting explanations are excuses rather than reasons and reflect a crisis of faith among the communists."

His remarks confirmed what I had been noticing during the last few years, although the cadre explanations had been seen by us as efforts to delude us rather than indications of a crisis of faith.

"A typical cadre is also facing an economic crisis that forces him to forego his ideals," another said. "He certainly wants a bicycle, a refrigerator, a TV, or a radio cassette recorder, or even a house in spite of his small salary. If an investigation were conducted on every cadre, from the lowest ranking to the highest, illegal sources of income surely would be unearthed. One of the fundamental strengths of the Party—the integrity of its members—is now a thing of the past. To you integrity may not mean much, but for a communist once he lets it die away, he isn't going to be worth a penny. He can't regain it once he has tasted easy-to-come-by luxuries; how can you make him throw away what he has obtained, legally or illegally? What they have inherited from the carefree South is so poisonous!"

For evidence of this loss of integrity, we had only to look to our own camp. Training of police cadets was being organized by the prison's police force. As soon as the new buildings were commissioned, a group of about 300 cadets were moved in. They were mere teenagers, their complexions fresh and their bodies well fed. Some could not help being shy when they had to deal with us; they reminded me of students from wealthy families. We later learned that these young men were children of high-ranking Party members whose entry into the prestigious police force had been arranged by their parents, mainly to save them from being conscripted into the army as the war with Cambodia raged on.

After a few weeks of compulsory military training the young cadets received instruction in police techniques. To enable them to practice what they had learned, the inmates were made available as "suspects," and every Sunday we were assembled in the central courtyard for them to practice their skill at conducting searches. When examining our clothes, they knew how to look for hidden objects in hems or seams and they even knew to pry open steel frames of rucksacks to look for hidden money or letters. Any cash they found they immediately pocketed, knowing we would not protest for fear of making our breach of camp discipline known to the authorities.

After every such practice session, the cadets' instructors would smilingly ask them what they had collected. The future policemen would eagerly display nail clippers, English texts, printed or handwritten "golden songs," poems written by inmates, etc. None of them showed any money stolen from the poor prisoners.

Usually if searched by senior policemen or study monitors, we would lose five-dong notes or more. Smaller amounts were ignored, but the cadets would not overlook anything, even rusty nail clippers. We always ended up losing something after this "on-the-job training" by the young cadets.

One Sunday evening, having heard my account of that blatant looting, one of my roommates said, "I wonder how much suffering the public will have to bear once these guys become actual policemen."

"Don't worry," said old Chin. "The public will certainly be better off with this kind of police—the very products of the Revolution. Stop to think how would the public fare if all government cadres strictly adhered to the rules? The ordinary citizens can bypass government restrictions only if cadres take their bribes and turn a blind eye to their activities! A nephew of mine who was a soldier for the former regime once applied for permission to visit me. His request was immediately turned down until he bribed the cadre involved. A policeman who takes bribes is a 'friend of the people.' How can people in the South get on without bribery?"

A former communist sighed. "We were strong in the old days because we were willing to sacrifice for a common cause. Nowadays everyone keeps everything to himself. The Revolution grew during the war but may die during peacetime!"

This talk led to the subject of the communists' bad economic management. Most obvious was their inability to satisfy the basic needs of the people due to rigid central planning and control of all aspects of the economy. Even the leader of all communist countries—the USSR—was known to suffer all sorts of shortages.

"One day while on an official visit to the Soviet Union," said one of the former communists, "I had a headache and asked the interpreter to request some medicine. As we were guests of the Soviet government, I got the right thing without any difficulty. But the interpreter took advantage of the opportunity and asked me to request some cough medicine as well. He said he would be unable to buy it due to the acute shortage of drugs as well as food.

"Our leaders praise State enterprises as 'the good housewives of our society,' yet even the Soviet 'resourceful housewives' fail to feed the people. They are obviously much less capable than the 'capitalist housewives.' In my opinion, the people in socialist countries are condemned to economic hardship by the conservatism and obstinacy of their governments."

One day we were guessing at the number of political prisoners still in detention. One of my roommates produced an old newspaper, the *Tin Sang* (*Morning News*) whose editor was former Assemblyman Ngo Cong Duc. The daily was rumored to be more popular than those run by the Party.[1] Hints of the number of political prisoners as well as conditions in detention centers were cleverly dropped in an otherwise dull and propagandistic article. It featured a subdistrict police officer's letter answering a complaint from a theatrical troupe: "Why is it that a man convicted of a serious offense is allowed to go back to live in the same place where he had recently committed the offense?" According to the letter, the Thanh Minh–Thanh Nga troupe had been losing money from the sale of counterfeit tickets. One day the culprit was caught by members of the company in the act of selling these tickets and was handed over to the local police. He was swiftly convicted, but a few days later he was seen walking around free in his neighborhood. The police officer's letter answered the complaint this way,

> Having been convicted, the defendant was first held overnight in the local police station. The local policemen then requested the district police to take him, but they said their prison was filled up. However, they would see to it that the prisoner would be held in a reeducation camp under their jurisdiction somewhere in Hau Giang Province. Again the authorities there refused to take him as all their facilities were filled up. The defendant was thus returned to the jurisdiction of his

[1]In reality, it was also controlled by the Party, although its editorial staff included some of its former writers. The paper was closed down permanently in 1983 by government decision.

neighborhood police to be placed under some sort of house arrest. Therefore, there was no such thing as the release of a convict a few days after his arrest.

One of our old men spoke. "The facts speak for themselves. There are so many prisoners that all police prisons are full even though they are supplemented by a network of 'reeducation camps' under the jurisdiction of individual district authorities. Even these additional 'prisons' have no more room for criminal offenders unless they are involved in politics.

"Saigon has eleven districts, and each of these has its own network of reeducation camps. So, how many political prisoners do you think are currently detained by the authorities in Ho Chi Minh City?"

Everyone suddenly became animated, trying to suggest a number. I said, "Not long ago, when I was still on the carpentry team, we were instructed to go and load up some timber supplied by a contractor, which turned out to be no other than the whole Thuan Hai Party committee. When we arrived, we came across a group of prisoners who introduced themselves as inmates of a reeducation camp run by the local authority. So *Tin Sang* has done us a service by confirming the existence of two parallel networks of reeducation camps, one run by the central government such as this one and the other by local authorities."

Someone added, "The centrally controlled network is further divided into two jurisdictions, one run by the police and the other by the army."

As we were congratulating ourselves on our analysis and conclusions, old Chin remarked, "You have seen only the outward aspect, not the heart of the problem. The main reason why so many political prisoners have been kept for so long is that they provide a cheap source of labor for the government. This cruel form of exploitation is even worse than that adopted by the czars in Russia!"

Another elderly man said, "There used to be three detention centers in the Thu Duc area, one for delinquent juveniles, one for prostitutes, and another for male offenders. These three, in addition to four former army barracks, are now being used by the present government to hold political prisoners. Apart from these seven, how many more prisons are there in Thu Duc alone? Considering that there are eleven districts in Ho Chi Minh City whose population is about a hundred times that of Thu Duc's, the number of prisons, large and small, must be enormous!"

One talk we had on factors responsible for a flagging economy in a communist country focused on the leadership's obsession with fixed production quotas and schedules and its attempts to get workers to compete with one another for higher production figures at the expense of quality. One participant remarked that once an economic policy failed, it would take time to put it right because leaders in a communist country would refuse to admit they were capable of making mistakes.

He went on, "In a capitalist economy where competition is normal if not essential, firms that produce goods of poor quality or at unaffordable prices would certainly lose customers, and if they don't solve their problems, they would certainly go bankrupt. However, all these incentives for efficiency and sound management are not taken seriously in the nationalized economy of a communist country where costly mistakes are cushioned by subsidies and poor goods continue to be produced for years. In the North most nationalized enterprises run at a loss and are kept alive by subsidies. Most goods are of poor quality, for example, bicycle tires that don't fit in the rims because they vary in size. How can this be possible in a competitive market?"

Everyone agreed that the best communist government would act as a watchdog to see to it that all enterprises, State-owned or collectivized, would respect the law and turn out reasonable goods for the public. We concluded that the ordinary citizen of a communist country was the one who suffered most; he or she got low wages and had to stand in long queues to buy shoddy goods grudgingly dealt out as if they were favors.

An old inmate added that although the government placed a heavy emphasis on the "eduation" of government employees, bribe-taking and theft of public property were still commonplace due to the starvation wages of the employees, who, out of necessity, had to dispense with honesty.

"I bet nowhere else in the world does an ordinary employee receive so little for his work," he said. "So, we shouldn't be surprised at so much theft, bribery, and inefficiency. Inefficiency and corruption lead to a deteriorating economy, which results in higher inflation and more shortages, hence more theft and bribery and inefficiency; thus the vicious circle starts afresh."

Another interesting view on the causes of poor economic management was that the tactical measures used effectively during the war were still being used, even though they were not applicable to the present situation. One person pointed out that many important managers were former army officers who had run their respective units with flexibility and independence. They tried to do the same now and came into conflict with the rigidly planned policies of the central government with disastrous results. Amateurs at economic managment, these men were too proud to admit mistakes and would try to cover up by submitting exaggerated reports. And, the speaker went on, inaccurate statistics were usually tolerated by superiors because big numbers made good propaganda. Another concurred.

"The leadership is imprisoning itself in an economic fallacy created by grandiose statistics and blown-up reports. Real prosperity is nowhere in sight as long as these fundamental mistakes are tolerated."

"Well," I said skeptically, "if you can see those mistakes of theirs, why can't the communists themselves?"

"Of course they can, especially the younger generation of specialists trained in Eastern Europe. Unfortunately, their suggestions fall on deaf ears. The old guard in the Party argues that the younger ones 'do not have a firm grasp for the Party's objectives because they were not with the Party throughout the two wars of resistance.' Some of my friends who have been to the North openly complain about the conservatism of old leaders such as Do Muoi,[2] the minister of economic planning, who would oppose any change, beneficial or not! Fundamental changes that are the key to a better economic performance, the younger experts believe, will not come about until the old leaders pass away. Such is the current inertia in socialist countries that mistakes often take generations to overcome."

While I was allowed to stay in the group of old folks, reshuffles were taking place in other teams as the authorities stepped up their screening process. Not a week passed without someone being sent to the isolation building where the diet could barely sustain life. Usually those who were regularly praised for their achievements at work received a ration of fifteen kilos of rice or rice equivalent (either *bobo* or sweet potatoes) a month. The average inmate worker got thirteen kilos, and those who could not do much work got 10.5 kilos. Logistics decided on the kind of basic food to issue to us, and study monitors decided on the amount each inmate got. Rations issued to inmates held in isolation were much less. They also were prohibited from cooking their own food and were not allowed to work outdoors or to receive visitors. Not surprisingly, the result was a marked increase in the number of sick, as disclosed by the cook responsible for feeding them. He also noted an increase in the number of requests for rice gruel, which was getting thinner and thinner every day. Our sympathy for these men was made more poignant by the confiscation of their homemade guitars.

In spite of heightened vigilance by the *trat tu vien* and the policemen, anticommunist leaflets were still appearing. This made the tense atmosphere even more unbearable. During the outdoor relaxation periods in the evenings, we no longer gathered together to talk, but waited until we were locked in our rooms to form into groups of all sizes for casual conversation or serious discussion. Watchers were posted at the windows to look for prowling *trat tu vien* who hoped to catch us in some forbidden act. The safest place was under someone's mosquito net, which effectively blocked visibility. I usually joined the old folks, and I was always welcome, probably because I was the only one who seemed to want to listen to them. The knowledgeable old Mr. Chin was my favorite, and I often came to him for information and advice. I sensed that I finally was gaining his confidence.

One night, as we discussed the causes that led to the pitiable defeat of the Republic of Vietnam, Chin undertook to analyze the errors of "Mỹ, Thiêu."[3]

---

[2] He is now the prime minister.

[3] The Americans and the Thieu government; typical Viet Cong parlance.

He had concluded that, owing to its well-orchestrated propaganda campaign, the revolutionary side had enjoyed the full support of public opinion, especially of intellectuals in the West. I said that as far as I could see, the intellectuals were not very active; only the French Communist Party gave wholehearted support to the Vietnamese communists, in fact, they openly displayed the National Liberation flag during soccer matches."

Chin smiled and explained, "When I say 'intellectuals,' I mean intellectuals in general. In fact, the words 'Western intellectuals' meant 'leftists' to us. Among the most prominent were Bertrand Russell and Jean-Paul Sartre. They were profound thinkers, straightforward and fearless in their opinions, but whenever they spoke, it was only for the sake of speaking. Western intellectuals were—and are—affected by a chronic disease that consists of too much speech but no deeds or only half-hearted deeds. The majority of them are not intellectuals in the true sense of the word because they never dig deep enough into their thinking. They borrow leftist ideas to fill up their writings, as a sort of fashionable ornament, but few know how to explore the possibilities in their ideas. Without the backing of communist propaganda agents, they would have been unable to achieve anything at all.

"In the case of Vietnam, as you rightly said, if there had been no intervention by the communists worldwide, there would have been no such vigorous and far-reaching antiwar campaign. During the bloody repression by the Soviet Union against the national revolutions in Hungary and Czechoslovakia, Russell and Sartre also voiced their strong opposition to the Soviets' brutality, but to no avail; this was because they were not backed by communist activists. Generally speaking, those intellectuals have no organization of their own, no regimented followers; their masses lack the knowledge to convert ideas into deeds. They are not true intellectuals; they're only people who try to keep up with the mood of the day. Among this lot, Russell and Sartre are exceptional cases. Some intellectuals join the communist ranks out of frustration. You people have the habit of 'putting everybody in the same bag.' But for us, there exists a clear distinction between those who fight for national revolution on the one hand and the communists on the other."

At this, I raised a question, which had once been a subject of discussion among my friends.

"Your words, sir, remind me of the story that Ho Chi Minh had first asked the Americans for assistance; only when he did not obtain complete satisfaction did he side with the Soviets. The story is supported by the fact that during the fight against the Japanese invaders, the Americans helped Ho's troops by dropping arms and ammunition."

With his usual knowing smile, Chin replied, "Those who believe in that story are ignoramuses. Old Ho was an international communist agent. Ho Chi Minh had worked for international communism for scores of years before being assigned to the Indochinese theater of operation. In 1920, he took part in the creation of the PCF [French Communist Party]. The Americans did not give him their full support because his activities were well known to them. In his various activities, even in his thinking, Ho always showed complete obedience to the obligations of international communism. In his writings and books, Ho, like the other agents trained in the Soviet Union, always kept to a position consistent with that of an international cadre. That is why you have never seen a book entitled *Ho Chi Minh's Thoughts.* Mao Tse Tung was the only one who dared to write books to disseminate his own ideas and thoughts. Ho Chi Minh was a faithful agent of international communism just like Le Duan is at present.[4] Do you know that Lenin was really a tricky and greedy fellow? After the success of the 1917 Revolution, not only did Lenin not liberate the satellites of the former czarist regime; he also designed a formula aimed at retaining all the former Russian colonies under the guise of a worldwide proletarian revolution. Eastern University in the Soviet Union specializes in the training of international communist cadres selected from among various peoples and races in the world; and it is their task to incite those peoples and races to rise up and demand independence or autonomy. But as for the former czarist colonies, they still have to remain as members of a block of Soviet republics, under the leadership of Moscow."

This was the first time I had come across information of this kind.

"Then according to your revelations," I said, "the Soviet Union planned for worldwide interference long ago?"

"Perfectly right!" replied Chin. "Therefore, if your goal is national revolution, independence, or autonomy you're supposed to have known which door to try."

"Yet I still think that before you try a door, you have to weigh the consequences, do you not?"

"You don't need to resort to hints or allusions. I have already admitted that the fact we are here today is living proof of our mistakes. I am too old to need to deny that I have committed grave errors. Of course, a person should repent his mistakes. The fact that I am here, in a way, is a self-imposed penalty."

Seeing that he appeared to be both sad and angry when conceding that he had erred, I cut Chin short.

"Let's forget about it. My intention is not to criticize you. Before, we might have confronted each other and tried to kill each other, but now that we share the same fate, I only want to listen to your stories. We've heard about the Vietnam sell out by the Americans many times over, but the reason for your being in prison, you have yet to tell us. Mr. Chin, did you ever have a presentiment that one day you and your comrades would be driven into a corner like this?"

Old Chin remained silent for a long time. I waited without knowing whether he would speak. Finally, he decided to relate a series of anecdotes; slowly they

---

[4]Party general secretary until his death in 1986.

emerged, some of them with unexpected impact. He said that once or twice there had been signs that the communists in Hanoi did not really want to help build up the strength of the Revolution in the South, and although the Southern revolutionaries were aware of Hanoi's insincerity, they faced innumerable difficulties and had to accept Hanoi's attitude. According to Chin, the precise moment when he and his comrades realized they had been betrayed by Hanoi was immediately after the complete occupation of South Vietnam by the Northern armies. He and many of his comrades were then still occupied with minor tasks in the North. All were impatient for a transfer to the South so they could start the buildup of that dream of theirs called the Nonaligned Republic of South Vietnam. But the leaders of the North, under the pretext that their scant means of transport were still needed to bring supplies to the army in the South, told them to bide their time. His voice rising in anger, old Chin continued.

"You can imagine how impatient we were to return to the South! Especially when we had not been able to get in touch with our 'brothers' who were there in order to find out what they had done, were doing, and what they were planning to do. Meantime, we received a secret report, the substance of which was as follows: 'Delegations from the socialist countries coming to Hanoi to participate in the Great Victory celebration had expressed the wish to meet with representatives of the Liberation Front of South Vietnam, but they were told there was nobody from the Front left in the North; all had already gone to the South.' That meant that Hanoi considered us a nonentity!

"One day we were invited to join a reception party to welcome comrade Corvallen, chairman of the Chilean Communist Party, on his visit to Vietnam. On arrival at the appointed place, we found that we were not supposed to go to the airport but were to attend a 'working session' between the Chilean delegation and representatives of the Lao Dong Party.[5] When Corvallen spoke, we saw very clearly the real intent behind the invitation to attend the meeting. In the course of his talk, the Chilean Party chairman demonstrated that President Allende had been deposed then killed by his capitalist opponents in collusion with reactionary elements and the American imperialists due to his inability to grasp the opportunity when it arose to side with the socialist bloc. The cause of the downfall of the Chilean revolutionary regime was President Allende's irresoluton and delay in deciding which position to take. At the close of the session, we were advised by the Vietnamese Party leaders that the comrades should learn from the experience of the Chilean Revolution because it was 'a torch that lights the way for us.' The visit of the Corvallen delegation was given full coverage in the papers. The reason for all the fuss became clear to us only later when we realized that the Chilean delegation may have offered advice that was very much in line with the thinking of the Lao Dong leaders.

"Weeks later, in the face of our insistence, the Hanoi government finally

---

[5]Vietnamese Labor Party or Workers Party, predecessor of the Communist Party of Vietnam (CPV).

agreed to make arrangements for us to return to the South. In Saigon, we met our comrades and were informed that everything had gone wrong. Our armed forces had been disarmed and thinly scattered to the point where contact with units, considered components of an organized force, was no longer possible; their leaders had been transferred to serve as low-echelon cadres in the People's government machinery. Many comrades who voiced strong opposition to these circumstances were arrested. Lawyer Trinh Dinh Thao had had a harsh exchange of words with the represenatative from Hanoi, and he demanded to meet with Le Duan and Pham Van Dong but was turned down. Some of us who were in contact with the Chinese diplomatic delegation were informed that China had strongly protested against the betrayal of the South Vietnamese Revolution by Hanoi."

At this point, Chin paused for a long while. Moved by his sadness, I was about to leave him to his thoughts when he resumed his account.

"You know, those days and nights when news of the forceful advance of our armies into Hue, then Da Nang, and finally into Saigon reached us, we in Hanoi were too excited to sleep. We sat up all night to listen to news broadcasts and discuss the situation. A bulletin originating from the Party gave us the greatest hope; it said, 'South Vietnam would be granted complete autonomy for a five-year period to prepare for the ultimate reunification of the country.' The news was received with joy by my comrades who enthusiastically suggested that plans for building a strong and prosperous South Vietnam should be discussed right away. It took only a few days for our joy to turn around. So quickly, so blatantly."

Feeling no need to raise any further question at the time, I decided to return to my place, my heart heavy with pity for the old man even though I still thought that he and people like him were partly to blame for having helped bring about the miseries of our present situation.

A few days later, walking along with Chan, I related the stories old Chin had told. He kept shaking his head. I asked him why he made a gesture of denial, and he said, "Just bear with me for the moment and I'll tell you. We're all victims of the situation; that's what we are."

On a Sunday morning a short time later, after the *trat tu vien* had opened the gate leading to the area reserved for inmates to cook their meals on holidays, the barracks was deserted. I was about to start up a conversation with Chin when Chan happened to pass by. He stopped, and very slowly sat down between us. Chin asked him in surprise, "The old gentleman is not averse to sitting near me today?"

Chan smiled; he spoke with great difficulty. "Mr. Vu here told me that you too had been betrayed by Hanoi," he said. "I've given much thought to that ever since."

The reply was forthright. "Frankly, we never thought that we would one day end up like this."

After an exchange of banalities, Chan asked, "My dear sir, you must now concede that our young men in the South were right when they fought against your kind of revolution, mustn't you? And that freedom is invaluable and worth fighting for, even at the cost of one's own life?"

"I entirely agree," said Chin in a loud voice. "However, you must have known that the so-called leaders of the South, from Diem and Nhu to Thieu and Ky, were not able to bring independence and sovereignty to the people of the South. You must have felt sorrow and pain in your heart when the Southern society became one where prostitution, depravity, and drug addiction prevailed. There's no reason why you should remain unmoved in the face of the sufferings of the people because of the war."

Chan nodded in agreement; he remained silent for a long moment as if to recover his breath, then continued in a low voice that sounded complaining.

"I do not intend to engage in a debate with you. Our sons on both sides have done much killing already. There's no point in arguing further. What I would like to say is that we have now acquired the painful experience that is the lot of weak, small nations. We, as well as our sons, wish for our country to be independent, free, peaceful, and happy. But we have been goaded by two opposing sides into using weapons provided by this side or the other to mutually kill each other, and that in the name of the same ideal and objective. You, dear sir, must agree with me on that point, I think?"

Chin hesitated for a time before replying. "Well, I should think that when you fight for independence and liberty, you ought to choose the right way."

"Then, which is the right way? The way you have chosen or ours? Tell me! Which way has not turned this country into a battlefield? Which has not pushed our people into internecine seas of blood? I've never said that the way we chose was decidedly the right way, nor have I ever said that the way you and your comrades chose was entirely wrong. But considering the price we have paid in human lives and suffering only to end up at this juncture, you must surely admit that great mistakes have been made. That, I don't think we can deny. I am not accusing you of having contributed to bringing this about. We have simply been victims of a juggernaut intent on crushing to death small countries desirous of achieving independence, freedom, peace, and happiness. Meanwhile, the countries that supplied us with weapons were trying their best not to harm each other!"

His tirade was interrupted by a fit of coughing. When it ended, he tried to stand up, breathing laboriously. I hurriedly helped him get to his feet and guided him toward the sunny courtyard. The discussion between the two veteran freedom fighters was a revelation to me. Never before had I seen the truth in such a clear light. All my pent-up feelings of shame and sorrow, worry and doubt now appeared to have been rearranged in an orderly manner. We had indeed been placed under the influence of an implacable law devised by the big powers. For the first time in my life, I was able to find for myself an explanation as to why people who claimed to be "revolutionaries" had been encouraged and given help to plunge with great enthusiasm into the war, and why we had been affected in the same manner, though to different degrees, and why a great many of us had decided to enter the war as a countermeasure against the revolutionaries. The two sides claimed to be fighting in the name of the same ideal, to serve the country and people.

When Chan had gone, I remained alone with Chin. He said sadly, "The old gentleman showed profound thought. Indeed, if we stood up for the cause advocated by one side only, we could kill each other to the last man. Nevertheless, the communists always stand up for their cause; that's why they hurl themselves so enthusiastically into the fight!"

I suddenly recalled something, so I said, "Mr. Chan was right, you know. The Soviets and the Americans have installed a 'red' telephone line linking Moscow and Washington directly to communicate with each other to prevent misunderstanding or unintentional conflict. Meanwhile, the two big bosses put forward every reason to induce their protégés to 'exterminate without pity' the 'Americans' lackeys' or the 'Russians' henchmen.' Now, I'd like to ask you a question, and I expect from you a frank answer: If the United States is the godfather of the exploiting capitalists and the personification of all the blackest evils in the world, then why has the USSR not undertaken to annihilate it directly instead of inciting revolutionaries in the remotest corners of the world to shoulder the task of 'exterminating American imperialism and its servants'?"

Chin shook his head; he remained silent for a long time before launching into an explanation that sounded like an acknowledgment of guilt.

"I should say that you don't know what happens in the communist world. For people on the side of the Revolution, especially among the ranks of Communist Party members, the rule is always to defend your superiors. From the lowest to the highest ranking cadres, everyone believes that his superiors cannot be fallible. For that reason, the thought never occurs to them to challenge their superiors' actions or the reasons they use to justify their actions. They see the USSR as being on the offensive against American imperialism everywhere, all the time. At every echelon of the Party hierarchy, members and cadres repeat again and again the trite argument that the answer to the problem, 'Who's the victor, who's the vanquished,' is inevitably 'Capitalism is in the throes of death.' One can say that the further down in the hierarchy you are, the more vulnerable you are to the argument."

Unable to contain myself, I retorted, "How could one believe so blindly in such reasoning? Theory is one thing but reality is another, must not reality be stronger than empty words?"

"The communists see reality in a different light," replied Chin. "And they do make out a good case for their point of view. Let me elaborate."

He proceeded to explain that day after day the ordinary citizen in the communist world was allowed to listen to news of the outside world only when it was about strikes and demonstrations against capitalists. Commentaries consisted of excerpts from communist or procommunist newspapers and magazines. Therefore, the public was able to hear and see only what the propaganda services arranged for them to hear and see. The communists never did anything without aiming to achieve a political end. As for justifications for their actions, these were always relevant and very clear.

"I don't think that outsiders could ever understand that relevance and clarity," he added thoughtfully. Chin then spoke emphatically.

"The communists firmly believe that their side will inevitably defeat the capitalist side. They say the lessons of history show that a revolutionary war always ends in victory. It should begin with the ideological preparation needed to foment an uprising. Once the uprising has taken place, the countryside should be caused to 'go rotten'; to achieve this, an atmosphere of insecurity should be created by such means as terrorism, assassination, and destruction of crops and property to the point where country folks are forced to abandon their land to seek refuge in the towns. The deterioration of the situation in the countryside marks the beginning of the encirclement of towns and cities. Because the surrounding countryside has gone rotten, the towns and cities will be plagued by unemployment and hunger. The crisis brought about by the situation becomes more and more serious as time passes. Social problems such as injustice, robbery and theft, prostitution, and so on, become more acute, leading to a deterioration in public security. This is the propitious moment for the Revolution to rise up and seize power. The Vietnam War was entirely waged according to this strategy. Can you see that?

"From that point, the communists undertake to expand their local strategy into a global strategy by using small, underdeveloped countries to encircle industrially developed capitalist countries; by fomenting uprisings and sabotaging production, the industrialized countries can no longer exploit the small countries, indeed, because of the uprisings, insecurity, and production stoppages, the small countries cease to be markets for the goods produced by the industrialized capitalist countries. The latter, having lost both their sources of raw materials and their markets, will have to compete with one another for the few such sources and markets left; their constant bickerings will eventually turn into open conflict. Their industries, without raw materials and markets, will give rise to unemployment and social disturbances, in other words, to the very circumstances that incline people to listen to the call to revolution. A seizure of power will then follow as the inevitable outcome. In the face of such an argument, with news that has been carefully screened and blown out of all proportion, and amid signs of economic crisis, it's no wonder that low-echelon cadres and Party members firmly believe in the 'capitalism is in the throes of death' axiom. Naturally, high-ranking members of the Party have a better understanding of things than their subordinates. In any case, the Soviets are still strenuously pressing on with their undeclared war against the capitalists by 'using Third World countries to encircle capitalist countries.'

"It seems that the West has not yet assessed this danger at its true value. In small countries, revolutionary organizations are being continuously assisted by the Soviet Union to engage in activities aimed at causing deterioration in the society and creating more and more crises wherever and whenever possible. The Arab bloc was caught in a snare when it created the oil crisis. The oil-producing countries undoubtedly reap great benefits from the sale of oil and because of that their interests are closely linked with those of the capitalist countries. When fighting capitalism, they are in fact harming themselves. They hoard masses of American dollars and other Western currencies, only to see those currencies finally diminish in value. The oil crisis brought about by the Arab countries particularly contributed to the Americans' decision to 'drop' Thieu and Ky in South Vietnam."

Listening to Chin, I wanted at times to question some of his assertions, but thought better of it. I listened on in the belief that the more he disclosed of what he had learned from the Revolution, the better. And the more I heard, the more aware I was of the perversity of the Soviets. Finally, he concluded his analysis.

"Indeed, as old Mr. Chan has rightly remarked, for a small nation it's extremely difficult to get away from the influence of the Soviet revolution. Marxism-Leninism is the strategy, the weapon to achieve world domination. The quarries that cannot escape from the claws of that doctrine are inevitably the small nations. Karl Marx had to leave Prussia and seek refuge in England in order to be free to found his doctrine. Lenin had the ability to put it into practice and thus create the Soviet state whose aim has been to rule over other nations. Such is the irony of history, so painful, so bitter."

I hastened to ask, "Then you recognize that you and your comrades were mere instruments used to realize the ends of that doctrine, do you not?"

"I myself regard that as a mistake on my part," he said. "But do you know this? The avowed commmunist does not admit that he is the means to an end; he justifies his action by declaring his duty as a member of the international proletariat, even taking pride in performing this duty. Frankly speaking, until now the revolutionary organizations of small countries have been making sacrifices on behalf of the international proletariat only to benefit the Soviet Union. Owing to that, the USSR is now able to play the role of a big power."

Perhaps, if I had had the patience to stay on longer and listen to Chin, there would have been plenty to talk about. But sensing a headache, I stood up.

"My head aches from listening to this discourse on communism and the communists," I said. "I find that the communists are full of contradictions. When we first began our political studies, we were given lectures about 'the right to collective ownership of the working people' and 'identifying patriotism with the love of socialism.' Because of our impatience for an early release, we tried to digest these ideas without raising any queries. But the longer we associate with them and the more we learn about communism and the communists, the more convinced we are of the false nature of their logic. Both Marx and Lenin had to flee their countries in search of freedom of speech and action. But now, in the name of Marxism-Leninism, the communists are setting up regimes where no freedom is allowed! Can you see any sense to that? They say they are fighting in the name of the working class, but now in socialist countries, the workers are the most heavily exploited. Does that makes sense at all? They talk about collective ownership, but what exactly do the workers own? I think that the true aim of socialism is to collect all capital and means of production into the hands of the State. With its power and its police as a means of repression, the State is free to stifle the voice of the workers and prevent them from expressing their wishes. In fact, socialism is a form of state capitalism that is above par in regard to exploitation of the working class. Anyway, I know that you can justify anything just like the communists who explain away everything but cannot bring about the necessary conditions for the people to live in freedom and happiness. The closer your association with them and the longer their control over you, the less confidence you have in them. So, what's the point of discussing it any further?"

Chin stood up without saying a word. We separated, each of us lost in his own thoughts. In me at least there lurked a feeling of utter despair.

Although our situation in the prison had reached a complete deadlock, we still nurtured vague hopes of release based on rumors and information supplied by our relatives when they visited. My wife continued to affirm that someone would intercede for me. But the promise of "an early release" had been made again and again for four full years now. Adding to the general gloom was the continued tension that pervaded the whole camp over the effort to locate the culprit who had produced and circulated the leaflets criticizing the regime.

Suddenly on a Sunday morning, the atmosphere changed. The policemen all seemed to be occupied with something somewhere else. There were no study monitors making their usual rounds, no searches, no reshuffling of sleeping places or team assignments. When the gate to the cooking area reserved for inmates was opened, the men hurried along with their pots and pans, kindling wood and food, all looking extraordinarily happy. One of my friends, seeing that I still sat with some elderly inmates looking idly around, asked in surprise, "I say, Vu, are you short of things to cook?"

"I don't feel like cooking today," I replied.

"Come on! Cook something! The whole camp is celebrating today. If you have something extra, prepare a good dish to celebrate the occasion."

Surprised by his enthusiasm, I got to my feet and, on the pretext that I had to relieve myself, made my way to the area where my friends were busy cooking. A number of them winked at me as if I too were aware of the secret that had brought about this festive air in the camp. I approached one of them.

"Why is everyone so happy today?" I asked.

"You're joking! Don't play the innocent and act as though you didn't know."

Annoyed, I took an oath. "I swear that if I know what it's all about and pretend not to, I'll be . . ."

"Good heavens! Don't you really know? 'They' are finished! But, is it true, you don't know?"

"But what *is* it?" I asked in surprise and impatience. "I have been with the elderly group and no one there was aware of anything unusual."

"My goodness! You're really good for nothing! Red China's armies have launched an attack upon the North. Today, the whole lot of 'them' appear very gloomy, as though someone in the family had died. This morning a *trat tu vien*, who had been furtively listening to a policeman's radio, disclosed that Chinese troops have crossed the border in a huge attack against the northern provinces. Hanoi radio is calling upon the entire population to prepare for war against the Chinese invaders. The *trat tu vien* also said that just last night he had heard the news of Pham Van Dong's visit to Kampuchea to celebrate the victory over the Khmer Rouge, and by early this morning, the war with China had already begun. A head-on collision with that giant of a communist country can only lead to a complete breakdown. That news has made the rounds of the camp, and everyone is so pleased with it, except you!"[6]

I hurried back to my group and came across Chin, who was returning from the camp kitchen, a tin of hot water in his hand.

"Ah, you've been to the kitchen, haven't you?" I asked. "Have you heard the news?"

Chin was all smiles. "Yes, I have," he said. "Heavy fighting in the North. This must be China's reaction to what happened in Kampuchea. The Vietnamese people once more have the opportunity to die for socialism. What's fun this time is that 'socialism' is fighting against 'socialism'!"

"Do you think this is going to bring a change in our situation?" I asked.

Chin hesitated. "I really don't know. Maybe, maybe not. Let's wait and see. I still have with me a copy of *Tap Chi Cong San* (Communist Review), fairly recent—end of 1978, I think—in which there is an article dealing with 'the duty to protect our border.' It may have some relationship to the present fighting. Anyway, I think you had better go and cook something, we have to share everybody's joy, don't you think?"

I brought my utensils to the cooking area to join the others. They were speaking to one another in low voices. From time to time, laughter burst out.

---

[6]The Vietnamese invaded Kampuchea and overthrew Pol Pot in December 1978; the Chinese incursion over the border began in January 1979 and lasted three weeks.

Every optimistic hypothesis possible was advanced. It was estimated that approximately two hours were needed for a rumor to make the rounds of the camp, which showed, among other things, that the stricter the surveillance, the quicker a rumor spread.

But as time passed, nothing more happened. During a study session held in the camp courtyard, we were informed that the "Peking expansionists" had failed in their attempt; they had been unable to advance on Hanoi as they had been checked everywhere. Despite all their efforts, they had only succeeded in penetrating a few dozen kilometers beyond the border. A few weeks later, there was news that Hanoi had begun to claim victory. Visitors said that China had proclaimed their objective in launching the attack was to "give Hanoi a lesson," that the attack was limited in duration and scope. And at last, the inmates realized there was no hope that Peking would bring down Hanoi. Their fate was to stay on in the camp with no clear perspective on release. They now scoffed at China and called it a "paper tiger."

I told Chin about the low opinion the men had of China, and one night he asked me to join him for a talk. I went to his bunk and got under his mosquito net with him. He wanted me to read the article he had mentioned earlier from the December 1978 issue of *Tap Chi Cong San;* it was written by a General Song Hao, as I recall. Chin had underlined various sentences he thought were important, but to me there was nothing special in the article. Mainly it called upon the *bodoi* of all echelons to prepare for the defense of the nation's border, but Chin saw more significance in it. First, he said, the article showed that Hanoi seemed to anticipate an attack across the frontier, and, second, the proposed strategy was clearly different from that adopted during the war against the "American imperialists." In the latter case, the strategy was, "If the enemy is too strong, we shall avoid direct combat, wait for our chance, and counterattack when the odds are in our favor." But now, the general wrote, "The duty to protect our border consists in preventing the enemy from breaking through the defensive line of our soldiers."

"The article," Chin said, "shows that Hanoi's leaders made careful preparations in anticipation of this eventuality. Nevertheless, Chinese troops were still able to force their way across the border. In light of this, the Chinese breakthrough was clearly a Hanoi defeat."

He concluded by saying that in the past Peking had conducted military operations that were limited in time and space—in the border war against India and in the Korean War—so it was possible that they also meant to limit their attack on Vietnam. Chin seemed to favor Peking.

"Well! You're certainly an ardent Peking supporter, aren't you?" I said.

"Not at all! My remark was based on past experience. But to be honest, I have to say that Peking supported the revolutionaries of South Vietnam. The attack by China against 'our side' did not bring any change in our situation except to provide the low-ranking cadres with more reasons to say, 'You cannot go home yet. It would be a serious mistake to let you go as our people outside have yet to deal with internal enemies and external foes.' "

A few days later, without warning, "Doc" Hung's belongings were searched, and he was found to be in possession of a number of necklaces, wristwatches, and rings that he had gotten as bribes from inmates for his drugs. It seems that he and some of us whom he had treated had been reported on by *trat tu vien*. The result was that I was transferred to another group and no longer had the privilege of doing only light work. Old Mr. Chan finally was moved to the prison infirmary. From time to time, as I passed by, he waved his hand weakly to greet me. Looking at him, all skin and bone with his thin white hair and unsteady walk, I felt great pity for him. Someone, half in jest, wondered "if he can survive until full moon this month." But although hanging onto life by a thread, he managed to live on in this prison.

After the search of Hung's belongings, it was the turn of the *trat tu vien* who had been given the task of calling out inmates to meet their relatives on visiting days. They were searched, bribes were discovered, and the offenders joined Hung in the disciplinary cell.

Time dragged by. We used to look forward to the official holidays to see if there would be any releases, but at Ham Tan prison nothing happened, even on such important days as Ho Chi Minh's birthday. One day, at the close of a study session—organized for form's sake now, because "they" knew full well that we no longer had any faith in the Revolution and the lessons would fall on deaf ears—the prison's political cadre disclosed an item probably intended as a warning.

"Inmate Tam, who excaped from this prison some months ago, has been apprehended by the People and handed over to the police. So you see, he could not make it and no one can. The 'People's net' is so dense that there's no possibility for anyone to slip through."

A few days later Tam was brought back to the prison, and to our surprise, instead of being shut up in the disciplinary cell, was assigned to my group as there were still many vacant sleeping places in our barracks. That first night he got under my mosquito net to start up a conversation, for he recognized me as one of his former "neighbors." I was somewhat fearful of having this reported by informers, but Tam was unconcerned and smiling as if nothing unusual had happened since he saw me last. Looking much thinner than before, he said that before he was handed over to the prison camp police, he had been held at Chi Hoa penitentiary in Saigon.

"I felt miserable having to stay in a concrete jail," he said. "It was hot and dirty; I sweat heavily all the time but was not permitted to have a bath. Now that I am back here, I feel much more the coolness of a thatched house." He was as cheerful as if he had just returned from a trip to some far-off place.

"Haven't you had enough of being caught trying to escape? If you feel you're 'happier' here than at Chi Hoa, then try to see to it that . . ." Tam cut me short.

"I failed this time, but I intend to try again. And, mind you, I won't fail next time. I was caught because I was impatient. If I had waited a few more hours, I would have made my escape across the border."

I asked how he had been caught and whether he had been beaten. Tam then related in detail the story of his escape. On that day, after returning his group's hoes to the storeroom at the end of the work shift, he pretended he had to bathe and wash his dirty clothes. He jumped into the stream, swollen by the recent rains, and taking advantage of the strong current, he ducked under the water and let himself be carried along. To a policeman standing watch on the bank, it would seem that he was being swept along by the current because he was no swimmer. When he emerged for breath, he noticed that no one was paying any attention to him. Ducking under the water a number of times as he moved with the stream, he found himself well outside the area of police surveillance. He got up on the bank and ran fast in the direction of the forest without stopping for rest. It was a fairly long time before he heard a gun fired three times.

He chose a shaded spot with plenty of leafy trees and brush where he stayed until midnight. He then moved out to try to get his bearings and find the way to the highway. He walked without stopping until he came to a field of maize where he picked and ate some corn. He then walked along the field toward the prison until he changed direction and went through the forest to National Highway No. 1. He crossed it and hid in the forest on the other side. When morning came, a number of people appeared and began to cut wood nearby. He showed himself and approached a group of kindly looking elderly people, confessing that he had escaped from prison and asking for their help. An old man showed him a secure hiding place for the day and an old lady went home to fetch some clothes and food for him. Thus, the initial stage of his escape was easy.

He decided to follow the national highway at first, traveling by night and resting during the day. When he came to an inhabited area, he would find someone to ask for help. In this way, he eventually got as far as Nha Trang on the South Central Coast. There, some local folks introduced him to the driver of a bus running between Ninh Hoa and Ban Me Thuot, and thanks to their help, he got to the Central Highlands without a hitch. When he told a Montagnard family about his intention to cross the frontier in order to make his way to Thailand, they showed him the way to the Kampuchean border. It took him one month and eighteen days to get near that border. The day he prepared to cross it, a Montagnard guided him part of the way, then advised him to wait until nightfall before attempting to go farther. If he could not make it, the man said, he could come back to them, and they would show him another route. At this, Tam said he realized he had reached the critical point, and he told himself to use good sense.

"But you can imagine how difficult it would be for me to turn back when I was so near the border!

"There was a new moon that night. I walked until my back was bathed in sweat, and then I spotted frontier posts in the distance. I hid in spots along the edge of the forest and looked for some place where the crossing would be safe. At long last, I reached a stretch of land that seemed secure enough. There were a few scattered houses, and when I drew near, dogs began to bark. I beat a hasty retreat and went farther on. But there were houses everywhere, and as soon as I got near them, barking rang out, louder than ever, and I would fall back again. In the end, as dawn was approaching, I took the risk of walking quickly towards some houses with the intention of running across a cassava field lying between the buildings and the border. Of course the dogs barked furiously, and suddenly a shot rang out. Voices with a Northern accent called out to each other, "There's someone on this side, comrades!"

Tam went on, more slowly. "There was still enough time then for me to escape by turning back. But I was too impatient to let the opportunity slip away, so I ran straight ahead. Then dogs were set loose and behind me torches flamed in the darkness. Suddenly, a voice nearby shouted, 'There's someone here, no doubt! There he is, over there!' I heard the dogs approaching and a gun fired. Someone shouted, 'Stop, if you don't want to die!'

"In front of me other men with flashlights appeared running toward me, and I had to stop. I raised my hands and they rushed forward and began to punch and kick at me. 'Where are the others?' they demanded."

When Tam told them he had escaped alone, they did not believe him. They tied him and led him to the guard post. Only then did he see *bodoi* in uniform; all the men armed with rifles, torches, and flashlights who had surrounded him were in civilian clothes, some of them naked to the waist. Tam was held at the post while the men resumed their search of the surrounding area. They threatened to torture him if he did not reveal the whereabouts of his "accomplices." Afraid they would make good on their threat, he declared immediately that he had escaped alone from Ham Tan prison. Upon hearing this, the *bodoi* looked at each other in astonishment.

"Did you walk all the way from Ham Tan? What bravado! You're a lousy braggart, you know! You must have accomplices somewhere."

Only after the search failed to turn up anyone and after Tam had repeatedly explained how he had gotten this far, did they believe his story. He was later taken to Ban Me Thuot, then to Saigon.

"In Saigon, I was interrogated several times about my accomplices. I declared that as I had been posted in the Highlands in the old army, I knew my way around and did not need anyone to help me. After I submitted several written confessions, the investigation ended. While I was in Chi Hoa jail, I constantly regretted my actions at the border. If I had been calm and patient enough to turn back, then waited for a rainy day to make the crossing, I'm sure I would have succeeded. I failed because I chose a night when the air was clear and still so the dogs could easily pick up both sound and scent.

"Besides, I was so stupid! I should have realized from the way they built their houses strung out along the road that the people living in them were in fact border guards. They live like ordinary farmers, cultivating the land; the houses are sixty to seventy meters apart from each other, and they keep a large number of dogs, apparently shut up in cages placed in open spaces between the houses. The way they organize the watch is very thorough. I had walked such a long way without coming across an uninhabited spot that I took the risk of trying to get through. Next time I escape, I'll follow another route."

The following day, I was transferred to the carpentry team, so I heard no more about Tam's unlucky capture. Returning to the barracks during the lunch break a few days later, I found the camp in a turmoil due to the presence of some empty buses parked before the main gate. Moments after, although we were confined in our room, we were able to hear the noise of people being assembled in the courtyard and the sound of the buses being loaded. Only when two buses crammed with inmates drove through the gate, which we could see from our window, did we learn that some of our fellow prisoners were being moved to another place. They were escorted by two truckloads of policemen. We wondered who had been transferred and where. The next day we discovered that those who had been kept in the isolation area had been moved, including Thanh, who had been involved in the affair of the subversive leaflets. There was one exception though; a major of the former intelligence service, whose responsibility had been to make contact with members of the resistance to persuade them to defect, was kept behind and assigned to a team. The reason was that every month or two he was summoned to Saigon for a "working session" with cadres who were drawing up lists of members of the resistance who had clandestine dealings with the *nguy* administration.

I was also told that Nam and old Chin were among those transferred. We managed to learn from policemen who had been in the escort party that the group had been taken to "the labor camp at Tien Phuoc, a place north of Binh Dinh, situated far from inhabited areas and very difficult of access."

A few days later a general reshuffle took place in the camp, and shortly afterward a military convoy arrived, in the evening as usual, with a load of prisoners, who were handed over to the prison warders. The next day when the men returned with the morning distribution of grub, they said they had been told that the newcomers were from various camps, a number of them from Suoi Mau

(Blood Stream) in Bien Hoa Province and others from Phuoc Binh in Song Be. At the mention of Phuoc Binh, my heart leapt in anticipation of a reunion with former inmates of that camp. When we gathered in the courtyard to go to work, the newcomers were there, waiting to go through the formalities of admission to the prison. Cadre Vong was giving them the usual instructions, ending with his oft-repeated boast that "he had been invited to visit the USSR" and the platitude about "the residues from the burning of Hongay coal are capable of being converted into 117 items of goods."

As I was looking to see if there was anyone I knew, a voice called out, "Hey Vu!" immediately followed by the shout of a *trat tu vien*.

"You there! Who gave you permission to talk?"

I pitied the newcomers; they were ordered to stand in straight lines by the *trat tu vien*, who shouted a string of abuse at them. That evening, after the meal, I went to the fence on the pretext of collecting my clothes, which I had hung out to dry on the wire; on the other side several inmates also were collecting clothes. This, in fact, had become one of the common ways to make contact with those in other buildings.

I asked one of the men, "Could you do me a favor by asking if there's someone from Phuoc Binh camp among the new arrivals. Please say that I would like to meet him if that's possible."

In exchange, the fellow across the fence asked me to go and fetch a friend of his who happened to be a member of my group. When I came back out, there stood Chan Thinh, the former navy officer who had been with me from our first days at Trang Lon through to Bu Gia Map and Bu Loi, now transferred to this prison.

Seeing me, he asked sadly, "Vu, how are you?"

"How is it that you're also moved here?" I asked without answering his question.

"Perhaps I was suspected of making preparations for escape. At present, our friends at Bu Loi are getting rough treatment. That bastard, Commander Thinh, no longer bothers to hide his innate wickedness and brutality. Every time he gets angry, he throws insults at us, and sometimes, he flogs the men with his rattan rod. His *bodoi* take that as a green light to beat us with a vengeance. Dr. Khue and Thé, your friend, have escaped. Escapes happen every week although the surveillance now is very severe. I have been reported as intending to escape; that's why I was singled out and moved here. There's no hope when you enter this camp, is there? The way they shut you up, it's very much like a prison!"

I tried to comfort him. "Don't feel too bad. You'll get used to it. The policemen here are very greedy; if you have anything of value, try to hide it, especially money. Hide it outside the house, not inside. The *trat tu vien* are experts at searching for concealed goods. You'll see, labor here is not as hard as it was up there. Only surveillance is more strict. But you'll be allowed more visits, once every two months. So, don't lose courage."

"I'm afraid I can't help it. You know, after you and the others left, that bastard Thinh had us assembled to tell us in a menacing tone that your group had been sent to prison and 'once in there, it would be very difficult to get out.' He said that you and the other fellows were 'ultrareactionary elements.'"

I was alarmed by the last words but tried to reassure him as well as myself. "I've noticed that there are both categories here, inmates 'guilty' of both serious and minor offenses. The oldtimers say that there have been some releases from time to time, but I haven't seen anyone released since I came here. In any case, I'm surprised that you've been moved to this place. Didn't the merit you acquired for bringing back your ship count at all?"

"In their eyes there's no merit whatsoever. It's clear now that they only trick us into doing things for them. When I first reported for reeducation with a certificate of merit for having returned a ship to the Revolution, I thought that I would be released soon. Now, I suffer in my very bones from the effects of their treatment!"

While we were still talking, the gong sounded for roll call before we were shut in for the night. I hastened to say, "Try to keep up your spirits! Life here is bearable; it's not too bad, after all."

Lying in bed that night, I felt no desire to talk to anyone. Chan Thanh's words only added to my despair; if, as he said, they had categorized me as a reactionary at the last camp and handed me and the other "reactionaries" to the police for supervision, it meant that my personal records must have been stamped with the word "reactionary"!

A few days later I discovered that Chiem Van Tuong, a fellow inmate from the first Xuan Loc camp, had also been moved to this prison. He told me that after our departure for the "jungle," the rest of them were transferred to Long Giao camp. Later, he was moved to Suoi Mau in Bien Hoa where the inmates were a tough bunch; he said everyone openly opposed the *bodoi* without showing any fear, and "all of us thought we would stay indefinitely at the camp." Tuong also said that among the inmates were sixteen students who had been tried in court for "national restoration" activities and sentenced to five years minimum. He also reported a rumor that an international conference was to be convened to consider a proposal to condemn Hanoi for having detained a great number of people without charge or trial. The mention of "rumor" reminded me that Chiem Van Tuong had been known as the most skillful man at Xuan Loc when it came to tracking down news or rumors as well as forming connections with the *bodoi* to get them to buy goods for him. Tuong complained that his family had spent lots of money to have strings pulled for his release but without any result. "And now," he said, "I am transferred to this camp to be shut up like a prisoner, no more no less."

All during the dry months in early 1979, I helped work the land to enlarge the area the camp management planned to cultivate. We also had to cut *buong* trees, the leaves of which were used for roofing. This work was regarded as the hardest of all the labor here, but having worked harder in the Song Be jungle, I found this to be fairly well within my strength, unlike many of my teammates who quickly fell ill. Our carpentry team had to work the land since there was no more joinery work to be done now. We were in the fields constantly until the first rains heralding the monsoon season began to fall. The rain at Ham Tan had all the characteristics of rainfall in coastal areas. It started unexpectedly and came down in buckets. As the season got under way, the stream near the camp, shallow and clear a short while ago, turned into a torrential river. As soon as rain fell, the policemen guarding us immediately ordered us to assemble and return to the camp; we would run all the way to try to get shelter before we were wet through. In fact, these policemen were very lazy; they waited for the chance to take us back to camp so they could play games or stroll to the populated area of the town. If the sky was cloudy when we were about to leave for the fields, they took us to a place near the camp and waited there for the first spattering of rain to bring us back. The old cadres grumbled at this, asking, "There have only been a few drops of rain! Why did you bring them back so early?"

"If we wait until it pours down, they will take advantage of it to flee. Then who would take the responsibility for that?" retorted their young colleagues. The latter were actually sons or close relatives of high-ranking cadres and therefore had no respect for the older cadres who they said derisively "had been fighting until their hair turned gray without being able to make the grade of field officer."

At the beginning of the rainy season of 1979, there was the news, or rumor, that a plane flying from Hanoi to the South had exploded in the sky over Ham Tan; the story also had it that on board the plane were several VIPs. We learned of it after a group of young policemen passed our worksite walking in the direction of the jungle carrying spades. A few hours later, they came back, spitting as they walked as if they had been exposed to something extremely disgusting. One of them said loudly, "My God! Never in my life have I smelled such a horrifying stench!"

The next day, on the way to the fields, we recognized among our guards one of the policemen who had been in the group, and one of the inmates asked, "Cadre, where did you go yesterday with your spade, and what did you have to do that made you complain about a terrible stench? Why not have us do the job, instead?"

"Because we were afraid you'd escape," the young policeman replied candidly. "We had to go deep inside the forest to find some dead bodies and bury them. Some of the corpses were already swollen. It appeared that their plane had exploded, so bodies were scattered all around, far apart from each other. In this area, we found only three; they were so disfigured that it was impossible to recognize them. We had to bury them right there."

We did not pay any more attention to the incident of the plane crash until one day about a week later when we were confined to our quarters due to rain earlier in the morning. We were not locked in and from the door and window of our barracks, looking beyond the fence to the rows of brick houses comprising the head office of the camp, we saw a convoy of shiny black American-made limousines pull up. An inmate claimed he recognized the car used by former President Thieu to make his tours of inspection. A number of military jeeps escorted the convoy, and the camp commander, Police Major Doan Mach, was running to and fro among the cars, which attested to the high rank of the passengers. A moment after, we saw everyone leave their cars and, together with their escort and the camp officials, walk in the direction of the spot where the bodies of the crash victims had been found. A number of our young policemen accompanied them, handkerchiefs over their mouths and noses and spades on their shoulders.

Later, we asked the young policemen what had happened and were told that "a delegation from Central Government came to examine the remains of the plane crash victims." Orders had come from "the top" to look for the corpse of a VIP, they said; one even identified Vice-Premier Le Thanh Nghi among the delegation and said he had talked to him in person. But when the corpses were exhumed, they were in such a state of decomposition that none of the high-ranking personalities present dared to come near, the policemen said, and they were ordered to rebury the bodies.

Later on, an inmate was told by visitors that one of their relatives had died when a plane carrying technicians had exploded in midair north of Saigon. Then, a few months later came news of the death of State Council Vice Chairman Nguyen Luong Bang, and it was rumored that he had been on the ill-fated plane.

"If the victims were mere technicians, why did a delegation from Central Government bother to come to the spot to search for their remains?" we asked. Such questions and the lack of reliable information to provide answers gave us food for discussion. One of the men even assumed as a hypothesis that "'they' were jockeying for position to the point of trying to eliminate each other."

As the season moved forward, it rained more regularly—for a certain period each day—and the carpentry team was ordered back to the task of building houses for the camp. Even so, there were times when rain kept us inside for a morning and sometimes for a whole day. At such times, we sat around talking. I related what my elderly friends—Mr. Nam and Mr. Chin among others—had told me, and a number of others also told what former members of the National Liberation Front (NLF) had revealed to them. We discussed and analyzed various problems, and it was then that we realized we had never seriously studied or given much thought to political problems. An inmate produced a book entitled *Engels' Youth,* originally written in German and translated into Vietnamese, and suggested we use it as a topic for discussion. Someone else asked for comments on another book, *Marx's Days of Youth.* Many of us remarked that the Communist Party organizational system exactly duplicated the organization of the Christian church. Obviously, Marx, Engels, then Lenin each had contributed to the setting up of a new church. If in the old days, people had to study the Gospel taught by the Church, now they had to study Marxist ideology under the guidance of the Party. The Party was now the Church. In the past, Europeans had to worship God as the Supreme Being; now people were forced by the Party to accept the Supremacy of Socialism over any other form of political and social organization. In the past, the Church had the power of life and death over the whole population, and now the control of the Party over its "subjects" was even more severe.

We often discussed the war and the cause of our defeat. One inmate mentioned the views of a former high-ranking cadre of the NLF who maintained that the Republic of Vietnam was defeated because its leaders did not know how to organize the life of the people during wartime, or, in revolutionary parlance, they did not know how to lead the entire population into participating in the war effort. On Hanoi's side, everyone's life was regulated by the demands of the war. People of all ages, from children to old men and women, and from all walks of life were regimented and had to take part in the war effort. Everything, from food to clothing, was controlled and rationed according to the needs of the war. Children, beginning at six or seven years of age, were given tasks to perform in the service of the war. That was what the communist government called "leading the whole nation into war." To achieve this objective, a firm and rigorous ruling machinery was required. Facing this "total war" machine of the North, the South had only a loose machinery at its disposal. The majority of its people stayed away from the war; only a minority actually took part. The noncommitted majority wielded more power and influence than the minority who had to do the fighting.

In addition to that, American economic aid introduced into the South a lifestyle devoted to the enjoyment of luxury, which rapidly brought about decadent habits and practices. The result was that the minority directly affected by the war became poorer and poorer; and the majority living in abundance sank deeper and deeper into decadence. When American troops joined the fighting, prostitution mushroomed; this was in fact unavoidable. It was not that the Vietnamese society had not the ethical and cultural standards to prevent the growth of that social evil, which was in fact a general phenomenon. Even Europe and countries boasting high moral traditions like Japan were not immune to the undermining effect of the American dollar, let alone a poor country like Vietnam. Basically, the determination of the two sides to endure the strains of the war was obviously in favor of the North, and as the war dragged on, prostitution became more and more pronounced. At the ultimate moment when that endurance had to be exercised to the utmost, the South suddenly collapsed, a collapse born of abandonment and despair. Hanoi took advantage of the situation and achieved victory without having to do much fighting. The war ended, not so much as the result of a fierce battle, but owing to the confusion of the South, which had given up hope.

At this point in the discussion, the men became silent; sadness showed in every face. I then told them what Chan had said to me.

"In the last analysis, the Vietnamese are simply victims caught in the struggle between the two superpowers contending for worldwide preeminence."

Some of the participants, formerly lawyers and judges, agreed with Chan. One of them said, "He was right. The world today has set up international organizations to deal with international problems just as the executive and judiciary bodies of a nation deal with domestic problems. But the difference is that in dealing with international problems, there's bound to be a lack of objectivity and fairness. And there is no code to effectively safeguard peace."

Thus the discussion went on day after day; sometimes so many people came that we had to disperse for fear of reprisals. One day, I asked a young inmate who had been closely following the conversation, "Let's see how you would you answer this basic question in all sincerity. Suppose we go back in time to the end of World War II; do you think we should follow Ho Chi Minh on the road to communism to recover our independence and freedom or do like the nationalists, that is, seek French and American support and fight the communists in the process?"

The inmates burst into laughter. Someone said, "That's a good idea! Let's hold a referendum to see who among us prisoners will follow Ho Chi Minh, who supports Bao Dai, or Ngo Dinh Diem, or Nguyen Van Thieu."

Everyone laughed; nevertheless, they all took the question seriously and thought before answering. One fellow asked, "Who wants to support Ho Chi Minh and become like those policemen out there after the great victory? Let him raise his hand! Come on! Raise your hand! This is only a game, why take so much time to reflect?"

We looked at each other, no one raised his hand. Another finally said, "Who follows Bao Dai?"

The laughter became louder. No hands went up.

"Who supports Ngo Dinh Diem?"

"Who supports Nguyen Van Thieu?"

The man who had put the questions grumbled. "That won't do! Do all of you want to abstain? You have to support somebody, right? Is it because you're afraid of being informed against? If you're so chicken hearted, why not vote for Ho Chi Minh?"

Many of us laughed and talked to each other. Suddenly, the youngest inmate in the group raised his hand. There was a sudden hush. The questioner said, "Now friend, whom do you support by raising your hand like that? It's too late; you will have to state whom you want to support."

"It doesn't matter who I support! But definitely not Ho Chi Minh! It's because I am allergic to being classified, categorized, as to which social class I belong to. If we could now go back in time, my only objective would be to fight communism to the last. I'd follow anybody. Our fault was that we were not determined to stamp out communism when it was still weak. I'd fight till my last breath. If I have to live in shackles, I'd rather choose death."

The whole group applauded, but the more cautious among us dissuaded the rest from expressing enthusiasm in such a noisy way.

Whether or not these gatherings to discuss politics, sometimes humorously, were the cause of the carpentry team being transferred to another house, we could not tell. In any case, due to the transfer, I was reunited with Ngu, the room leader who had been the first oldtimer I met the night I arrived at Ham Tan, now more than one year ago. Ngu had been a lieutenant in the former Military Police. He had a gentle nature and was liked by everybody, which was why he was appointed room leader. He had a pet golden hamster, a ratlike animal with a glossy yellow coat something like a squirrel's. Ngu looked after his pet very well. During the day, when he was out working, he kept it in a tin box; when he came back, he set it free and fed it with a few grains of corn, or a piece of manioc, or part of a banana some inmate had received from his family and given away. Sometimes, the hamster climbed onto the roof of the house to run about, but at Ngu's summons it immediately came back down. At other times, after frolicking to its heart's content, it would go into some shirt pocket to sleep. When it did not reappear, Ngu had to look into the pockets of all the many tattered shirts that hung here and there around the room. The creature slept like a log and didn't even stir when it was taken out of a pocket and put back into the tin box. Many an evening the whole room was awash with laughter as somebody chased after it in sport; after a moment, when it was nowhere to be seen, we knew it had got tired of the game and had gone into someone's pocket to sleep.

The carpentry team was housed in the same building as Ngu's team, which specialized in cultivating crops. All of a sudden, we were ordered to start building houses again to complete a new subcamp quickly. We had previously begun construction of some houses, but for some reason we had to leave them unfinished. We had put up the frames but had not covered them yet, so now they were rotted in places because of their long exposure to the sun and rain. We started by repairing the frames and then covered them with thatch. The work progressed smoothly. On the average, it took us about two weeks to put up the frame of a house, thatch it, wall it with bamboo wattle, and provide it with doors and windows.

We felt quite certain now that we would be detained for several more years before we would be released and moved to a New Economic Zone with our families. Some inmates told us that their wives and children had fled the country; some others said their wives had remarried.

My housemates seemed to have grown accustomed to this prison life and resigned to it; each evening, we gathered to sing and listen to guitar playing, the police having returned the guitars they had confiscated. The two fellows who usually played them and accompanied the singers were Trac (the young man whose girlfriend had been transferred to the women's prison at Long Thanh) and Ha Van Ngan, famous for his talent in composing music and conducting the singing of revolutionary songs—this had won the admiration of even the police and *bodoi* arts cadres. If there were informers among us, they did not report this kind of activity, so we were not disturbed as we sang and listened to sentimental songs and thought nostalgically of the old days. Since the carpentry team was in much demand to build more houses, we were no longer transferred as frequently as before. We spent this period of our lives in relative tranquility.

My wife regularly visited me every two months. Each time I saw my daughter, she appeared to have grown up a little more. In the course of our conversation, my wife spoke less and less of her bribery attempts to secure my release.

At the end of the year as the rainy season was drawing to an end, we were informed of an escape attempt involving many inmates; the police had fired on them, killing three and wounding ten. Afterward, a cadre named Loi was transferred from the back prison to ours. He was said to be very cruel. Each time he came to call the roll, he shouted at us in a ferocious manner, and we assumed he had been moved here to deal with the group of young, bullheaded prisoners accused of "national restoration" activities.

Our circumstances and state of mind may have varied, but we never stopped living in expectation of news, and the ever-present rumors flourished as always. On National Day, September 2, six prisoners were released. This gave rise to a rumor that a list had been drawn of inmates to be released on holidays to come. We paid special attention to this kind of rumor because visiting relatives were reporting that a conference was being held in Geneva to discuss Vietnam. Although the news was somewhat vague, we clung to the tenuous hope it raised in our minds. Most of us though agreed with one inmate who said pessimistically as we discussed the report, "The world decided to drop us long ago! Nobody pays any attention any more to what happens in this Vietnam of ours. At one time, it was rumored that the Americans were negotiating the ransom of reeducation inmates; at another, we heard that an international conference was held to find a solution to the problem of reeducation camps. Too many rumors, but we seemed not to get fed up with them."

When my wife came to visit, I carefully asked her about the various reports, but she could not answer any of my questions as she disliked and avoided anything to do with politics. From time to time, she gave me news of our friends and acquaintances—who had been released and who was still being held.

One evening after the meal, as we stood looking beyond the fence or walked back and forth as we used to do every evening while waiting for the gong to sound roll call, we saw a man, carrying his luggage and escorted by two policemen, walk out from the compound at the back of our own. I got a good look at him; he was thin and of a darkish complexion. As I sat down among the other men to wait for roll call, I suddenly realized who he was. Out of the corner of my eye, I saw the two policemen and the prisoner walk toward the prison office in the row of new, whitewashed houses. The *trat tu vien* locked us in for the night and I got up on an upper bunk as though to start a conversation with its occupant. From this corner under the window, I could see the gate through the bars made of bamboo joints. After a moment, I rather indistinctly saw the prisoner with his two guards get into a cream-colored limousine—a Peugeot 403—and drive slowly through the gate of the administrative area and off in the direction of the national highway, leaving behind a cloud of dust. After returning to my bed, I lay back, thinking about what I had seen and found that it tallied with the rumors we had heard. The departing prisoner was Le Quang Uyen, former governor of the National Bank of Vietnam whom I had met at the "military hospital" camp at Xuan Loc. For a simple change of camps, such an elegant means of transportation would never have been used. Rumor had it that at that very moment a conference was being held in Geneva to discuss the exodus of refugees from Vietnam by sea in small and fragile boats. We heard that Hanoi had promised to allow Vietnamese to leave the country officially and to release more reeducation camp prisoners. According to the information, Hanoi wanted to impress world opinion by releasing well-known individuals, among them the engineer Pham Minh Duong, former minister of Communications and Public Works; General (Dr.) Vu Ngoc Hoan, former chief of the ARVN Medical Corps; and perhaps the man I saw taken away in a limousine, Le Quang Uyen. At the approach of Christmas, all of these matters were widely discussed in the camp. I did not know who besides me had seen Le Quang Uyen taken away, but the news of "inmate Le Quang Uyen from the back prison" had quickly made the rounds.

The study monitor responsible for the carpentry team, whose name was Nam, was a very greedy cadre. Our team leader acquired his favor by flattery and bribes. Almost every day at noon, Nam took the team leader to a local family's home to eat lunch with him, and when they returned, they brought back some food they had purchased to sell to us. At the moment, the carpentry team was allowed to have its midday meals at the construction site to save time in the drive to complete the new subcamp. We had finished the houses for inmates and were now erecting buildings for the cadres and office personnel. Children in the vicinity, who were on the lookout for opportunities, knew that a team of inmates stayed outside of camp at noon, so they brought bananas, cigarettes, sugar, and sweets to sell. To do this, they bribed the policemen on guard duty at the road junction beyond the gate. More of them were coming in every day, and other work teams got us to buy things for them.

Several times, when our team was about to go out the main gate, we were ordered by the cadres to wait until the other teams had left, and when they had gone, the *trat tu vien* were instructed to search us very thoroughly. Many of us thus lost a lot of money in their searches, our own as well as that of other inmates who had given it to us. Monitor Nam was very angry at the treatment we received because he and our team leader could only go to buy items like meat, sugar, and powdered milk for us if we brought money when we left camp, to say nothing of his losing his chance to "eat out" for we inmates pooled our money to pay for his lunch. After many such unexpected searches, we came up with the idea of asking Nam to come to see us on the previous evening or early in the morning before we went to work to collect our money. From then on, we lost no more in the searches, but open animosity developed between the camp's cadres and the study monitors.

One day when we returned from work, we were suddenly stopped and searched. When our *go* cans were opened, most were found to be full of meat, sugar, or sweets. Some of the men had a whole bunch of bananas strapped to their bellies. The cadres responsible for internal regulation enforcement were very angry but could do nothing about it. I had my own way to conceal money and had never been caught, but the *trat tu vien* never failed to find my *go* can or cooking pot full of food. They looked at me as though they held a grudge. One Sunday, no one in the entire camp was searched except me. Cadre Loi, along with *trat tu vien* Ba, entered our room and ordered me to bring all my belongings out into the courtyard. The long search revealed nothing; my neighbors were then searched, but nothing was found. From then on, I had the impression that I was about to enter another dark period of my life similar to that at Bu Gia Map camp when I had been subject to every kind of mental torture. As I had to prepare for every eventuality, I was obliged to ask my friends to buy things for me to avoid the risk of being searched without warning. Cadre Nam himself asked me one day, "How come you have such bad records?"

I was very surprised at the remark; my answer was also a question. "I don't know. Maybe, at my former camp I was much informed against by a fellow who was not very fond of me. I don't know what was in the reports. You were able to read my records, weren't you? I would have thought that only high-ranking cadres would have the right to read the inmates' personal records."

Resenting this poke at his self-esteem, Nam shouted, "I can read records whenever I like. Your records contain such remarks as 'Has the intention to escape from the camp' and 'Reactionary.' That's why you were moved here."

I lay awake that night wondering how and why cadre Nam read my personal records. I was quite sure that ordinarily cadres were not curious enough to read the personal records of any particular inmate. What was more, after the new camp administration buildings had been completed, we were summoned to carry in locked filing cabinets (possibly brought from a Saigon office). Monitor Nam could not freely enter the office and rummage among the files for my personal records. Other cadres and certainly the office clerks usually regarded a study monitor as a sort of stupid prison warden, and I had observed myself that the monitors appeared to have had very little schooling. Therefore, the fact that my personal records had been taken out of the files and that cadre Nam had been given the opportunity to read them must hold some significance for me. From the moment I heard that my records had been picked out and examined, intuition told me that something untoward was going to happen to me.

I was on tenterhooks in the days that followed. Whenever a police cadre looked at me, I had the distinct impression that in his look was something showing he already knew what was in store for me and was keeping an eye on me. Many of my friends also felt that I was under surveillance. Meanwhile, our work became more urgent as we were told we had to finish construction of the third subcamp earlier than targeted in order to accommodate more prisoners who were to be transferred here. What with my worries and exhaustion, I fell sick, but I was not alone. The weather had changed—become unusually warm—and the number of inmates reporting sick in the house where my team was living suddenly increased. In addition, Ngu, the room leader, lost his pet hamster. He looked pitifully sad as if he had lost his own son. The other inmates did not care to gather and entertain themselves with music and songs now either.

As the year drew to an end, everyone felt the separation from family more deeply and could not help being unhappy. It was then that Ha Van Ngan was asked by a friend to improve on a piece of music the latter had recently composed to play at Christmas. Ngan played the music on his guitar. Listening to it, note after note as clear as crystal, our hearts broke to pieces! I asked Ngan what it was that sounded so sad. He said it was a piece of church music.

"Le Tan Loc has just composed it; he asked me to make a few changes and arrange it for guitars."

Loc was a former philosophy teacher. I knew him when he was still a student of philosophy at the teachers training college. He was then known as an atheist, and most of his teachers were Catholic priests. As he was an outstanding student, although very obstinate when it came to defending his atheist viewpoint, a French priest managed to obtain a scholarship for him to continue his studies in France. He was said to have passed with top grades two *certificats* each year, which was no mean feat. Back in Vietnam, he taught philosophy and was well liked by his students. Ngan told me that Loc decided by himself to convert to Catholicism after several years in reeducation camps. His present hobby was composing songs, and his piece that Ngan was now arranging was entitled "Rejoicing at the Tidings of God's Descent to Earth." The inmates, finding the story that led to this song interesting, asked Ngan to sing it. Plucking his guitar, he sang softly, and the whole room became silent. He had an excellent voice; the song was very moving, with a strangely plaintive note in the music. When he finished, everyone had tears in his eyes, but we had nothing but praise for the artist and the composer, and we asked him to sing the song again.

To be in prison at this time of the waning year with no prospect of release created a very subdued atmosphere; we had every reason to be sad and thoughtful. We completed the third subcamp on target, for which we were granted one day off. After that, we had to start hoeing the ground to prepare for rice planting. One day we stopped work as usual at noon, had a wash at the stream, and returned to the camp for the midday meal and rest. After getting my ration of *bobo*, I took it to the side of the house together with a *go* can of noodles I had cooked at the worksite. I was about to sit down to eat when cadre Loi came and called for the room leader to appear before him. Ngu hurriedly ran out of the house. He then led cadre Loi back toward me. Seeing him approach, my heart pounded, and there was suddenly a drumming in my ears, so I could not hear clearly.

"Vu, report to the cadre," said Ngu.

His voice sounded as if it came from afar, and when I answered, it sounded as if someone else were speaking.

"Yes, cadre! You want to see me?"

"You're Tran Tri Vu, right? What's your date of birth?"

Standing before the cadre, I tried to maintain my calm, but my whole body trembled as though I were having an attack of malaria. I made a great effort to concentrate, but I could not tell him what my birthdate was! Seeing the pitiful way I responded, Loi said, "After the meal, bring all your belongings with you to the gate. I'll wait for you there. I remind you that you have to bring all your clothes and other personal possessions without leaving anything behind, be it a needle or a bit of thread. Is that clear?"

"Yes, cadre."

Loi turned around and walked away. Ngu and many of my housemates surrounded me; no one asked me any questions. They looked at me with pity in their eyes. I sat down and tried to start eating, but I couldn't swallow a single morsel. My roommates, one holding the can of noodles, the other the bowl of *bobo*, stood around me. One of them tried to reassure me.

"Never mind! Eat your fill. We'll see you later."

I took the can of noodles, and tried to eat, but the food stuck in my throat.

Usually, instant noodles were much desired and made a nourishing dish, but today I felt I would throw up if I ate anything. I stood up and went to dump the *bobo* in a pail at the back of the house. Then I emptied the noodles in a friend's bowl and went into the house to fold up my clothing. While I was busy packing, *trat tu vien* Ba came in.

"Go and report to the cadre right away," he said. "You can come back for your things afterward. Go now! They want to finish with you before going out for lunch. They're waiting for you, you know."

I left my belongings lying in a heap on the bed and followed Ba. Seeing that I was overwrought, Ngu said encouragingly, "Keep calm! Even death is not to be feared, so why worry over trifles!"

I looked at Ngu with a smile, but I knew it was not at all natural. When I got to the gate, cadre Loi was standing in the guardhouse. A police cadre I had not seen before came forward.

"You're Tran Tri Vu, aren't you?" he said. "Have you registered any money for safekeeping with us?"

"Yes, I have."

"How much?"

"It's been a long time; I don't remember how much it was."

"Go back and bring me your receipt. Be quick about it. I'll be waiting for you here."

I ran back, but my heart was beating so furiously I had not the strength to move very fast. I could hardly breathe. The gong had sounded for everyone to get into the barracks and for the doors to be locked, but because our team was rated a "good" team, our door was left open. When I entered the room, my companions who were lying on their beds immediately sat up.

"How did it go?" one of them asked.

"They asked me to come back to find the receipt for the money I deposited."

"Did they, really?"

The room suddenly became noisy.

"You said 'receipt for money on deposit,' didn't you?"

"Yes."

"Then, that's it! That's it!"

A number of the men got down from their beds, ran toward me, and clapped me on the shoulder. They spoke without waiting for each other.

"If they give you back the money, it means your luck is with you now. That's true, old man!"

"Come on, buddy! Cheer up! You're released, it's as sure as eggs are eggs."

As I was fumbling for the receipt that had been issued to me by the camp management, the men surrounded me. Everyone was talking at once, as though in a marketplace. One of them said,

"Say, Vu. It's sure as hell you'll be released. Could you give me your *go* can?

I've made my choice and it's your can. You see, I've had to use this rusted tin for a long time already. Give the can to me, please!"

I looked for the receipt among my clothes. My body suddenly felt very warm and my face flushed. My heart was still beating hard, now it was for joy instead of the worry and fear of a moment ago. I found the receipt at last and ran quickly out of the house, pursued by requests for my personal objects and an exchange of clothing. At the gate, I gave the receipt to the cadre.

He said, "I am going to the finance section to get the money for you. Go get your belongings and have them inspected by the camp cadres; then go to the office. I'll be waiting for you there."

I turned around and went back, running and walking at the same time. My mind was back to normal. I told myself that the fellows could be right after all. If this were a transfer, they would not give back the money. Besides, the new cadre seemed to be fairly nice to me. When I arrived back at my barracks, the clothes I had left on my bunk to be packed had undergone a considerable change. Items that were in good condition had disappeared and were replaced by rags. My wife had provided me with an adequate supply of clothes, and I had not had to wear torn garments. Ngu, the room leader, was standing beside my bed, and he said apologetically, "I had to stay here to dissuade the men from exchanging any more clothes. And these guys are waiting to ask you something."

I looked around; one inmate was holding my *go* can, another my plastic bowl in which I ate *bobo* each day.

"We've never had visitors and don't have enough of what we need. Could you give me this can, please?"

"And this bowl to me, all right?"

"I'm not sure whether I shall be released or not," I replied.

"It's as sure as fate!"

"One thousand percent sure, believe me!"

Ngu smiled and said, "Well, it's up to you."

I gathered the rags and torn mosquito net and blanket—my own had also been replaced by these—and stuffed them into a big bag. Shouldering it, I made my way to the gate. Once more I felt assailed by doubts and worries: What if this was not a release after all? When I reached the gate, Loi and Ba were already there.

"Display all your belongings for inspection," cadre Loi ordered. Ba took the bag and poured its contents onto the ground. At the sight of the tattered clothes, he exclaimed, "Well, look at that! Only rags. Permission to report, cadre: the clothes, mosquito net, and blanket are all torn; there's not a single item in good condition."

Cadre Loi approached to have a look. He suddenly raised his head, a cruel look in his eyes.

"At this juncture, you're still obstinate! Take these back and bring your very own things out here. If you can't find them, don't come back out again. Understand?"

"Yes, I do."

I crammed everything into the bag and ran back to the house. The men again sat up, asking, "What happened?"

"Why do you have to come back?"

"Cadre Loi demanded that I produce my real clothing; otherwise I cannot leave," I replied.

Ngu ran forward and spoke firmly, "Those of you who have substituted your clothing for his, please give it back to him. Let him go in peace. Don't make him suffer because of this. Give everything back, will you?"

The men returned to me clothes, mosquito net, and blanket; naturally they were not mine, but they were in better condition than the rags they had given me before. Ngu refused to accept them.

"This won't do! There must at least be one set of clothes in good condition."

One of the chaps gave me one set that really was mine. Another reluctantly brought back my *go* can.

I said, "It seems to me that they want to confiscate only my clothes, mosquito net, and blanket. You can keep that can."

The fellow ran happily back to his place with the can in his hand. Another brought me a battered, blackened can, saying, "Take this one in case they ask you," he said. "You'll be spared another trip back. It has some holes in it."

I put my clothing in the bag and placed those items in good condition on top. Shouldering the bag again, I walked slowly toward the door. Only now did my friends' parting wishes register in my brain.

"Go in peace, mate!"

"No, the word 'go' is not enough. You should say 'return.' Happy return home, Vu!"

My housemates gathered around to shake my hand. Many had tears in their eyes. One of them took my hand, seeming to fumble for words.

"Vu, pray God you're released for good. If later you can escape from this country, try to find a way to tell the world how they detain people here. I was also writing articles for Chu Tu's daily, you know."[7]

I was surprised and a little apprehensive at this allusion to Chu Tu. So he knew I had been one of Chu Tu's associates, a detail of my past which I had not disclosed to anyone and thought was long since dead and buried. I didn't expect it to be revived by this fellow.

"What! You knew me too?" I said. "How come you didn't speak of this to me before?"

---

[7]Chu Tư was editor-in-chief of one of Saigon's leading daily newspapers.

"Never mind. Now, go in peace. Try to flee the country. Leave this bloody land of ours. You'll have to go abroad to be able to tell the world the truth. Do your best. I'm confident you'll succeed."

"You too. I believe you'll be released some day, sooner or later."

The man, still holding my hand, suddenly sobbed. "Look at me, hard! A sick man like me has no alternative but to wait here to die. And what's the good of going back. I'll only be a burden to my wife and children."

I could not hold back my tears. Ngu's voice was heard urging me to go. "Let him go! Cadre Loi's waiting for him."

I turned to wave good-bye to my companions. Everyone was looking at me, indefinable expressions on their faces. I ran to the gate with the bag of clothing on my shoulder. *Trat tu vien* Ba took the bag and dumped its contents on the ground, and cadre Loi stepped forward; with his foot, he pointed to various articles.

"As you're leaving the camp, you won't need this . . . and this, so leave them here."

Ba hastened to collect the items to be left behind, mostly working clothes in fairly good condition, and I stuffed into the bag what I was allowed to take with me.

Cadre Loi said, "Now, you can go to the office."

"Good-bye, cadre Anh[8] Ba."

Loi curled his lips and gave me an unfriendly look. Ba said, "Yes, off you go."

For the first time in years I had the impression of being a free man again; no policeman escorted me as I walked toward the gate of the camp. I passed the row of thatched houses and entered the area where the newly built brick houses stood. A policeman came out of the building that was the prison office. He stood on the verandah and said, "Come on up! Why such a long delay?"

I climbed the stairs and walked into the office.

"Sit down," the cadre said, pointing at a chair.

I put my bag of clothing on the floor, pulled the chair away from the table, and sat down. Immediately, I was struck by the sensation of sitting on a chair, a real chair. It seems ridiculous, but for a moment my mind was completely absorbed with how much more comfortable a genuine chair was than a tree trunk or a bench made of bamboo joints.

The cadre said, "Now, you have two things to do before you leave this camp."

I noticed that so far there had been no confirmation of my release.

"First, you will have to do this. The sooner you finish it, the better it will be for you."

---

[8]Elder brother.

He handed me a ballpoint pen and a sheet of paper bearing the mimeographed heading, "Report on the team situation." Looking at me, he said, "Now, you have to accomplish a feat, achieve some result by reporting everything you think is still wrong with your team, in the camp, or around you. As we all know, in every team, every barracks, at the worksites, and everywhere there are always people who have not yet achieved good reeducation, who do not yet support, or who even oppose the Revolution. Your duty is to denounce those people, expose their acts.

"I emphasize the point that you have to make a sincere declaration, that you have the obligation to make declarations. When you have finished, we'll give you the necessary papers that will give you permission to return to your family. The decision to return you to your family is a gesture of utmost clemency on the part of the Revolution. So you have to make your declaration in such a way as to prove yourself worthy of the clemency of the Revolution. I have to tell you that if you say you have nothing to declare, that means that you have not had a 'good' reeducation yet. And because of that, you will have to return to the camp to have time to think it over. You know full well that the Revolution has enough patience to wait until you prove yourself to be really sincere. Now, try to write down everything you know."

Having said that, the cadre returned to his chair behind the desk. Pen in hand, I sat there at a loss to know what to do. Who was I going to denounce? What to denounce? I had every reason in the world to think that if I did not make any denunciation, I would have to go back to that barracks that I thought I had escaped from, permanently. If I had to tell the truth, it would be that everyone in this camp—including myself—equally hates the Revolution. But to say that so-and-so was conspiring against the Revolution—in fact, there was no one.

The absolute majority of us wanted to return to our families to live a normal life. When accusing someone, you had to have proof; you could not make groundless denunciations. Besides, how could I inform on my companions, an act I loathed and had found to be utterly contemptible ever since I first encountered it in the camps?

On the other hand, if I could not think of something or somebody to denounce, I was sure that I would be kept imprisoned for days, weeks, or even months. Experience told me that the camp management was perfectly capable of keeping me on, as at Bu Loi camp when they kept eighty-seven inmates, due to be released, until the cadres were satisfied with the cultivation program at the camp. With the quantity of foodstuffs subtracted from thousands of rations and stockpiled by Logistics, they could feed me for several years on end.

I bit my pen, unable to come up with a single idea. Never before had I had to write something that I knew for sure I could not write! The gong sounded the signal to end siesta and begin the afternoon's work. I was desperate. I must write something, denounce somebody; but who? I had prided myself on being a fairly enterprising person, but now I found my mind was completely blank. I wanted to begin to write something down . . . I had to, somehow. Write something quickly so as to leave this place soon. Oh God! I was totally helpless! The cadre looked up at me, then returned to the book he was reading. I looked at the sheet of paper. I assumed informers wrote their reports on sheets of paper like this one; they were able to find something to write about every day. Then why wasn't I? Not knowing what to do, I bent my head and began to pray. I still believed I was blessed with a miraculous protection whenever I was in danger; it had been proved on many occasions.

A solution suddenly flashed through my mind. That was it! Why shouldn't I do that? Help me, oh God! I had been taught by the Revolution; I would be good for nothing if I didn't know how to do it. Why shouldn't I write a confession? Why shouldn't I denounce myself according to the very principle of criticism and self-criticism?

On second thought, I began to feel some apprehension. What if the cadre thought that "out of eccentricity" I undertook to denounce myself and thus used "a trick to mock the Revolution"? He had ordered me to denounce other people; would I show obstinacy by denouncing myself; would he be angry? I thought hard and came up with a better idea, one that would be clearly acceptable. Quite so! Did I know somebody reprehensible in my team? Of course! And I had tangible proof.

I bent over my paper and began to write. Seeing this, the cadre stood, looking pleased, and went to stand behind me to read what I had written.

"I the undersigned, Tran Tri Vu, executing the order given me to declare the wrongdoing in my team, sincerely confess to the Revolution that I participated in the acts I am going to relate and that my participation contributed to their realization. It all began from the day I was transferred to the carpentry team. From time to time, the study monitor ordered me to use the planks belonging to the camp to make chairs and boxes. Later, we were informed that the objects my teammates and I had made were sold to local people. Recently, we made a fairly big table, which we then had to carry to the roadside. A Lambro scooter came and took it away. I now repent of my participation in causing the loss of the socialist state property.

"Besides, my family has surreptitiously supplied me with some money that I entrusted to the monitor to buy such things as meat, sugar, milk, etc., for me. I am aware that by doing so, I have violated the camp regulations. Seeing that what I have done makes me unworthy of the favor granted me by the Revolution, I hereby sincerely and forthrightly criticize myself in the hope that the Revolution, always generous, will pardon me."

As soon as I had finished writing, the policeman shouted, "That's not good enough! What you've said is too vague. You must specify how many chairs and tables you have made, who sold them, what was the price . . . and so on, and so forth."

I was cheered by his demands. Apparently, this cadre agreed with my denunciation, at least in principle. In fact, what I had denounced was known to the whole camp, an open secret. I added, "I would like to specify that I have made four chairs and one table; Monitor Nam took them away and sold them. I have been told that he sold them for 140 dong. Cadre Nam 'rewarded' me with a pack of Vam Co cigarettes and some sweets."

The cadre took the paper and went through it while I waited anxiously. When he had finished, to prove he was versed in administrative procedures, he said, "This is not quite finished yet. You have to write down: 'Done at Thu Duc camp, Ham Tan—the words 'Ham Tan' should be put between brackets—on December 23, 1979."

With a joyful, "Yes, cadre!" I wrote down what he had indicated. Thanks be to God! He had helped me to write up the first—and I hoped the last— denunciation in my life. The police cadre slid the sheet of paper into a folder on his table, then said, "Now, there are some formalities to comply with before you're released. This is the money you have on deposit. Count it. Here are ten dong for your bus fare; in addition to that, you're given three dong per day for meals during the trip, and you're entitled to two days' travel, making it six dong for food expenses. The total for your travel therefore is sixteen dong. Count it carefully and sign here. You have to write, 'Received sixteen dong for travel expenses.' "

I counted the money, which consisted of crumpled one- and five-dong notes mixed together, to comply with the formalities, but I paid little attention to the amount. I wrote and signed the required receipt, taking care that every stroke be clearly legible lest the cadre blame me for "scribbling in the manner of the bourgeoisie." Only then did the cadre pull open his drawer and take out a single piece of paper, which he held out, saying, "This is a paper which represents a matter of life and death as far as you are concerned. Many, many people live in the hope of obtaining this kind of paper without being able to get it. Our last advice to you is this: When you're back home, make sure you abide by the law of the Revolution. Settle your personal affairs, then bring your family to a New Economic Zone and earn your livelihood by productive labor. Have a happy return home. Give our kind regards to your family."

Having finished his farewell speech, he stood up and gave the paper to me. Then he held out his hand in an awkward gesture, as though he were acting a part in a "renovated theater" play. I shook his hand, took the paper, and mumbled, "Thank you very much, cadre." I took a quick look at the paper; its heading read, "Order of Release." Skimming through the formal language, I came to the sentence, "Reason for Release: Reeducation satisfactorily completed"; beneath it a line bore the words, "Period of Probation: None." The cadre congratulated me.

"You're lucky not to have to be on probation after release. That means you can be granted back your rights of citizenship right away. Now go to the national highway to get a bus; it's getting late already."

I shouldered my bag, walked down the step, and then turned to look at this forbidding camp for the last time. A wave of emotion came over me, and I had the impression that thousands of inmates at that moment were standing inside the camp looking out at me with envy. I did not understand why I now was overwhelmed with sadness. Was it true that I had been released? It was so sudden, so unexpected!

I walked out the gate of the administrative area, and in the distance I caught sight of a few scattered groups of men hoeing the ground. I tried to make out which team it was—some of the men waved to me with their conical hats but they were too far away to recognize me. I waved back. All of a sudden, tears streamed from my eyes. I tried to hold them back, but in vain; I felt I was going to cry out loud.

How unfortunate it was for those who had to stay on! I looked in their direction, but the tears blurred my vision. I wiped them with my shirt sleeve, but they kept welling out. I struggled to regain my self-control by thinking of something cheerful. Surely my wife and child would be very happy to see me come home. It was certain that my release was due to my wife's efforts. No earlier than yesterday, I was racked by worries, terror even, when I thought about my personal records being stamped "reactionary." But today I was free despite that harmful rating.

Still I could not chase away the sad thoughts. Where did so many tears come from? I turned around for a final look at the camp; why did the sight of those thatched houses appear so sad? And what would become of my companions who had to stay? Lost in my thoughts, I suddenly came across a group of inmates who were weeding at the side of the road. The four policemen standing guard looked at me in surprise. The men stopped working and leaned on their hoes. From a grassy ditch below, a voice rose up, "Are you going home? Best wishes to you."

"Farewell . . . " I said. But I seemed to have lost my voice. I cleared my throat, then said loudly, "Best wishes to you too. Keep yourselves in good health."

I waved to them while tears fell more profusely than before. Someone said, "Why do you cry, you who are returning home? We who stay don't cry, as you can see."

They tried to smile, but their smiles were so pitiful. I walked away, their voices becoming less and less distinct in my ears. At the road junction, I turned and waved again, and they all waved back. Although we had been strangers, we had become like brothers bound by fate; now we had to part in circumstances that were far from cheerful. As I turned into one branch of the fork, they were lost from sight; I was alone on the dirt road.

I walked until I was bathed in sweat and at last reached the tarred surface of National Highway No. 1. To be able to walk on a smooth, macadamized road gave my feet a comfortable feeling. At an open stretch of the highway, I sat down on the right-hand side of the road to wait for a vehicle going in the direction of Saigon. Usually, when roofing buildings in the camp, I had seen much traffic on the highway, but now, waiting for some vehicle to come along, pick me up, and bring me home to my family, there was none. I waited and waited. Soon the sun began to lose its brilliance and the shadows of big trees lengthened on the surface of the road. Suddenly, I heard the sound of an approaching vehicle. It was going in the right direction, but it was a military truck. I signaled it to stop, but the *bodoi* just looked fixedly at me and drove on.

I thought I would have to find some hospitable house in the area where I could spend the night, then come back here in the morning to try to catch a ride toward Saigon. I began to walk. Then I heard the rumble of another vehicle behind me, and I saw a jeep that had been converted into a truck, crammed with passengers, driving toward me. Two people on the top of the truck were hanging on to sacks of goods strapped to its roof. I flagged it when it was still a short distance away, and the men on the roof waved their arms in a gesture of refusal. At the instant the "truck" passed by, I shouted, "I have just been released from a reeducation camp. Please let me come with you!" It did not slow, but I heard someone cry out, "Reeducation detainee . . . reeducation detainee!" The vehicle pulled to a stop. With my bag, I ran happily forward. The passengers— all women—were sitting among bags and sacks full of goods.

The driver grumbled, "There's no more room. If you women want him to sit somewhere, arrange a place for him. I give up."

A woman said, "Come on! He's a reeducation detainee just released from some camp in the jungle. Do we have the heart to leave him alone in the middle of the forest? Besides, it's already getting dark. Get up here and sit among us. You, lady, squeeze over, will you?"

I approached the car and said with a smile, "Please, let me hitch a ride to Saigon. I came out from the jungle a little after noon, but I haven't met with any bus or other vehicle yet."

The two women sitting beside the driver tried to make room for me, but as they were big and fat, they could only leave a narrow edge for me to sit on. Again, the driver objected.

"You'll be thrown out on the road in a little while. If there's an accident, you ladies must take responsibility for it."

"Get on up! I'll hold him if necessary. He can't be thrown out. If I hold on tight to somebody, it's hard for him to get away from me."

The passengers all burst into laughter. Fortunately, the woman was past middle age, so there was no impropriety. I got up into the cab of the truck, handed my bag to someone sitting in the back, and with my free hands groped for a support to cling to. As the heavily loaded vehicle drove forward at a moderate speed, one of the passengers said, "Try to stand the discomfort. I'll be getting off at Xuan Loc very shortly."

The car rumbled on. The passengers asked jokingly, "You've just been released, right? Tonight your wife will be very happy to see you back."

"How come you're the only one to be released? You must be very clever!"

"Happy and clever, indeed! After a short while, he'll be sent to a New Economic Zone. That's the same as being sent to prison!"

Worry and fear suddenly flooded back into my consciousness. I told myself that I'd have to report sick; I'd have to find some sort of illness that would permit me to stay in the city for a period of time. They'll have to believe that I am really sick.

I looked at my arms, all skin and bone, burned by the sun to a dark color similar to that of the Montagnards. Mentally, I braced myself to face up to the difficulties to come. I no longer paid attention to the noisy chatter of the passengers in the rear of the truck.

I made a rapid calculation. I had reported to the authorities on June 25, 1975; today was December 23, 1979. I had spent 1,632 days at various reeducation camps. To think I had believed the communiqué that said the period of reeducation would be seven days! For me, it was over, but for many of my friends, it would go on, perhaps for much longer. Was I being too optimistic to think they all would still be alive when the day of their release arrived at last?